FROM MY COLD, DEAD HANDS

FROM MY COLD,

DEAD HANDS

CHARLTON HESTON AND AMERICAN POLITICS

EMILIE RAYMOND

THE UNIVERSITY PRESS OF KENTUCKY

Publication of this volume was made possible in part by
a grant from the National Endowment for the Humanities.

Editorial and Sales Offices: The University Press of Kentucky
663 South Limestone Street, Lexington, Kentucky 40508-4008
www.kentuckypress.com

   10 09 08 07 06   5 4 3 2 1

Portions of chapters 3 and 6 appeared, in somewhat different form, in Emilie Raymond,
"The Agony and the Ecstasy," Journal of Policy History 17, no. 2 (2005): 217-39.

Library of Congress Cataloging-in-Publication Data

Raymond, Emilie, 1973-
  From my cold, dead hands : Charlton Heston and American politics / Emilie
Raymond.
    p. cm.
  Includes bibliographical references and index.
  ISBN-13: 978-0-8131-2408-7 (hardcover : alk. paper)
  ISBN-10: 0-8131-2408-5 (hardcover : alk. paper)
  1. Heston, Charlton—Political and social views. I. Title.
  PN2287.H47R39 2006
  791.4302'32092—dc22
  [B]

                          2006012092

This book is printed on acid-free recycled paper meeting
the requirements of the American National Standard
for Permanence in Paper for Printed Library Materials.

∞ ❀

Manufactured in the United States of America.

Member of the Association of
American University Presses

For my friends from Read Hall

CONTENTS

Illustrations follow page 190

ACKNOWLEDGMENTS

I WOULD LIKE TO THANK ESPECIALLY ALL THE PEOPLE WHO ASSISTED AND supported me as I worked on this book. My adviser, Robert Collins, pushed me to excel and did not lose faith in me. John Kyle Day tirelessly copyedited my chapters from their humble beginnings. Rich Traylor, my longtime office mate, offered his trusty thesaurus, emotional support, and practical advice. Patrick Steward helped me keep my sense of humor and my sanity. These colleagues are irreplaceable. I am also deeply appreciative of my dear friends—Kyle Moran, Abby Beetsma, and Gina Garcia—for their unceasing encouragement. My parents, Gary and Judi Raymond, fostered my interest in the historical profession and cannot be thanked enough. I am grateful to Leila Salisbury, my editor, and Adam Chromy, my agent, for bringing this manuscript to its book stage.

The research necessary for this manuscript could not have been completed without the assistance of several individuals and institutions. I am greatly indebted to the University of Missouri, specifically the History Department and the Graduate School, for financial support. I owe heartfelt thanks to several librarians and archivists who helped me locate gold mines of research material. Special gratitude goes out to Barbara Hall and the staff of the Margaret Herrick Library at the Academy of Motion Picture Arts and Sciences, Valerie Yaros of the Screen Actors Guild, Greg

Cumming and Ray Wilson of the Ronald Reagan Presidential Library, Allen Fisher and Barbara Biffle at the Lyndon Baines Johnson Presidential Library, Robert Holzweiss and Bonnie Burlbaw at the George H. W. Bush Presidential Library, and Joy Kiser of the National Endowment for the Arts Library.

Finally, I would like to express gratitude to Charlton Heston and his colleagues at the Mercury Group and the National Rifle Association for their invaluable cooperation. Heston graciously took the time to sit down and talk with me. Bill Powers and Jon Carter coordinated the logistics of that interview and provided me with valuable tidbits of information. Bill Powers also provided many of the wonderful pictures for this publication. Most especially, I want to thank Lisa Powers for making the interview a reality and negotiating my access to several helpful individuals in the National Rifle Association, especially Jim (Edward) Land and his staff.

I could never have completed this book without such a fine group of people providing valuable feedback, support, and assistance.

INTRODUCTION

CHARLTON HESTON, HOLLYWOOD'S MOST PROMINENT CONSERVATIVE, DID not register as a Republican until 1987. In fact, during the 1950s and 1960s, the actor also known as Moses used his celebrity status to promote causes and programs generally associated with the Democrats. For instance, he marched for civil rights in Oklahoma and Washington, DC, and participated in President Lyndon Johnson's Great Society efforts, particularly those programs related to the arts. Despite his association with these endeavors, Heston harbored sufficiently strong conservative inclinations to indicate that his relationship with liberalism was tenuous. Indeed, by the early 1970s, Heston grew disillusioned with the Democrats. He became uncomfortable with the liberal initiatives, like the Great Society, that he had once supported, lamenting the ballooning federal bureaucracy that accompanied them as well as their disappointing results. Furthermore, the leftward drift of the party alarmed him, as the Democrats came under the influence of political and cultural radicalism. The actor particularly rejected the neoisolationism of the Left as well as its insistence that America was a "sick" society.

When Heston switched his party allegiance to the Republicans, he acted independently, but he was not alone. Some of the most prominent individuals to abandon the Democratic ship were a group of intellectuals known as *neoconservatives,* or *neocons.* Led by Irving Kristol, the editor of the influential journal *Public Interest,* the neoconservatives consisted of academics and writers who, like Heston, had become disenchanted with liberalism—and for largely the same reasons. In fact, the neoconservatives expressed critiques and policy prescriptions that matched in spirit Heston's own lay judgments. They fostered suspicion of an active federal government, encouraged injecting religious values into the polity, and supported a strong stand for America in international affairs. The neoconservatives began to grow skeptical of liberalism when it no longer embodied those principles, and, by the late 1960s, that skepticism had grown to outright hostility. The Democratic nomination of the liberal dove George McGovern for president in 1972 represented the last straw for Kristol and Heston. Kristol believed that McGovern's nomination "signified that the Democratic Party was not hospitable to any degree of conservatism."[1] Heston more bluntly explained his disapproval, complaining that he was "sick to death of the doom-watchers and the naysayers" he believed McGovern represented.[2] Kristol, Heston, and their fellow neoconservatives would, henceforth, vote for Republican presidential candidates, especially applauding the GOP's newfound optimism and internationalism as well as its emphasis on economic growth and the bourgeois ethic. The post–Cold War world led some neoconservatives to focus on new foreign policy strategies—individuals like Donald Rumsfeld, for example, emphasized the dangers in the Middle East—while others, like Kristol and Heston, gave special attention to the domestic cultural arena, criticizing what they believed to be an increasingly relativistic and nihilistic American society.

Heston shared more than a political disposition with the better-known intellectual neoconservatives; he also shared a similar background. The intellectual neocons generally came from lower-middle-class or working-class families. Heston grew up first in Michigan and then in Illinois, where his stepfather worked in a steel plant. Kristol and many of the intellectual neocons were raised in immigrant households in Eastern cities. Furthermore, the neoconservatives were children of the Great Depression and appreciated the New Deal, even if they did not actually have to go on welfare. Finally, the neoconservatives served in World War II and believed that it was America's responsibility to stand tall in international affairs. Indeed, they largely supported America's crusade to fight communism both abroad and at home in the aftermath of World War II.

Despite his similarities to the neoconservative leaders, Heston differed in two significant ways. First, he was not an intellectual. The neoconservative high command was a tiny group that propagated its ideas in journals and in longer works of scholarship. Irving Kristol was reverently known as the godfather of the group. Other prominent editors included Norman Podhoretz of *Commentary* and Martin Peretz of the *New Republic*. Daniel Bell, Nathan Glazer, Gertrude Himmelfarb, and James Q. Wilson constituted the neocon scholarly wing. Their ideas influenced powerful political leaders like Jeanne Kirkpatrick, who would serve as a UN ambassador, and the New York senator Daniel Patrick Moynihan. These two made their mark by combining intellect and action. Although Heston received a degree from Northwestern University and boasted impressive political credentials, he certainly could not claim membership in this elite intellectual circle. Second, unlike most neoconservatives, Heston was not Jewish or Roman Catholic. Despite these differences in erudition and faith, Heston would evolve ideologically in much the same way as the neoconservatives.

Heston's political leanings paralleled those of Kristol and his associates, but neoconservatism has largely—indeed, exclusively—been understood as an intellectual phenomenon. Neoconservatism has been defined so narrowly for two reasons. The person who gave the neocons their name was himself an intellectual and primarily concerned with only his fellow scholars. Moreover, Heston and the intellectual neocons did not work together in a coordinated movement or share a working relationship. The fact that Heston and the intellectual neocons did not specifically work together but followed a similar political evolution only heightens the importance of their experiences. Despite the differences between them, that they grew similarly frustrated with the Democrats partially explains the success of the Republican Party, as the GOP appealed to widely different groups with its message.

Therefore, such a narrow definition of *neoconservatism* fails to capture the cultural trends that Heston represented. Neoconservatism should not be limited to a slice of the intelligentsia. It must be rediscovered as both an intellectual movement and a cultural impulse that animated Heston and others like him, everyday men and women who opposed liberalism from an emotional, or visceral, standpoint and who felt that the Democrats no longer championed their middle- and working-class values. Because of his celebrity status, Heston was not considered an "average American"; however, he remained consistently tied to bourgeois beliefs and was increasingly willing to defend those values in a public forum. An award-winning actor and international superstar, Heston should be recognized not only for his career in film but also for his significance in the realm of cultural politics, as the most prominent of the "visceral neoconservatives."

In fact, it was Heston's film career that actually fueled and legitimated his political activism. By the late 1950s, Heston was associated worldwide with the conservative morality of the prophet Moses and Judah Ben-Hur. By that time he had appeared in two of the most memorable scenes in film history, dramatically parting the Red Sea in *The Ten Commandments* (Cecil B. DeMille, 1956), and winning a spectacular chariot race in *Ben-Hur* (William Wyler, 1959). These films constructed a public image for the actor that embodied responsibility, individualism, and conservative masculinity, values that Heston himself embraced. He continued to accept roles exemplifying these qualities over the course of his film career, appearing in such movies as *Planet of the Apes* (Franklin J. Schaffner, 1968), *The Battle of Midway* (Jack Smight, 1976), and *Any Given Sunday* (Oliver Stone, 1999). In fact, he rejected scripts in which the characters did not personify, at least to some degree, the values with which he had come to be associated. Audiences worldwide could not separate Heston from his screen persona; almost fifty years later, he was still referred to as Moses. His public image lent authority to his political activism.

Heston's public activities in the 1950s, 1960s, and 1970s provide the avenue to understanding his neoconservatism. Despite the varied nature of his politics, his conservative inclinations would actually remain fairly constant throughout his political career. Kristol once said that in order to become a neoconservative: "All you had to do was stand in place."[3] Indeed, Heston remained devoted to his core values—moral individualism, equal opportunity, and anticommunism—throughout his public career. It was his political style, rather than his substance, that dramatically changed. Heston's early political activities were largely bipartisan and his leadership strikingly moderate. The increasingly ideological nature of both national parties, the rise of special interest groups, and his own political experiences led Heston to abandon his centrist approach to become a dogmatic, outspoken conservative activist.

Heston's political career can be divided into four stages. Initially, Heston repudiated celebrity activism, but he soon changed his mind and moved into the first stage of his public career, that of limited involvement. From 1955 to 1961, his activism was largely confined to national political campaigns. He supported Adlai Stevenson during the 1956 presidential contest and endorsed John F. Kennedy four years later, although he did not actually take to the hustings for either candidate. He also willingly lent his name to political events and causes in Hollywood. This engagement, despite its limitations, was important to Heston because he finally decided that, despite (and because of) his celebrity status, he needed, as he put it, to "stand up and be counted" on civic matters. Furthermore, he publicly identified with the Cold War liberal values of anticommunism and personal freedom.

Between 1961 and 1972, steady involvement in Washington and strong leadership in Hollywood characterized this, the second stage of Heston's public career. The actor continued to provide limited support to national political campaigns, including those of Lyndon Johnson in 1964, Hubert Humphrey in 1968, and Richard Nixon in 1972. Furthermore, he served in the Johnson and Nixon administrations as an appointee to the National Council on the Arts of the National Endowment for the Arts and as a cultural diplomat for the State Department. In Hollywood, Heston made forays into grassroots activism. He led the Arts Group at the March on Washington in 1963 to encourage the passage of a civil rights bill, teamed with several of Hollywood's "cowboy" stars in 1968 to bring publicity to LBJ's gun control measures, and aligned with other celebrities in support of the Vietnam War. Finally, he began a long affiliation with the governing body of the Screen Actors Guild. These national and local ventures allowed

Heston to make connections in Washington, lead a variety of public groups, and hone his negotiating skills. Although he associated with the Democratic Party during this period, he was not fiercely partisan. As president of the Guild, and in his activities with other organizations, he customarily sought to compromise with adversaries and to take a moderate course of action.

In 1972, Heston moved into a third stage of public activism, a period that lasted over two decades and was marked by a newly partisan and combative style. Even though his political beliefs remained largely unchanged, he worked almost solely with the Republican Party, and he began to see Democrats as a threat to American stability and superiority. Furthermore, he became more outspoken and was less prone to compromise than he had been in the past. Heston's close friendship with President Ronald Reagan deepened his partisanship, while his increasing involvement with special interest groups emboldened his newly dogmatic approach. As the Democratic Party adopted affirmative action and softened its anti-Communist agenda, Heston concluded that common ground had disappeared. His activities at the Screen Actors Guild between 1981 and 1992 especially reflected and furthered his newly assertive political personality. While the Guild leadership embraced the trend of "participatory democracy," Heston and his neoconservative allies believed that such an approach incited mob rule and the politicization of interest groups. Heston openly challenged the liberal leadership of the Guild and organized a caucus to force a change in policy, illustrating the frustration that a number of neoconservatives harbored against liberalism.

In 1995, Heston entered his fourth and final stage of activism: at the age of seventy-one, he became a dynamic political force in his own right. In order to campaign for his favorite conservative candidates, Heston established his own political action committee, ARENA PAC, to finance his travels. He also assumed office in the National Rifle Association (NRA), a time-consuming responsibility that demanded frequent campaign, lobbying, and publicity junkets. Finally, he delivered numerous speeches and authored several books, including *The Courage to Be Free*, critiquing the cultural changes that had taken place in American society since the 1960s.[4]

In true neoconservative fashion, he blamed the media and academe for imposing political correctness and multiculturalism on the citizenry and encouraged Americans to return to traditional moral virtues. Because of his celebrity status and high-profile position at the NRA, Heston became a leading and accessible spokesperson for neoconservatism.

Although Heston's public persona depended on an image of hardened masculinity, his wife, Lydia Heston, recently commented that the public would be surprised to learn how "nice and caring" her husband was. Heston shared much with the public but also fiercely protected his private life, letting few people penetrate his tough exterior. He was an independent loner. He was driven and stubborn and accused of egomania. He was also a tender romantic who married his first sweetheart and enjoyed a close relationship with both his children. He remained devoted to public service and maintained a combination of elegant dignity and toughness. He could be as comfortable reciting Shakespeare at a black-tie affair as hunting deer in the Michigan woods. He remained a gentleman throughout his long life and never dressed without his cuff links. He also maintained a sense of humor. A publicist recalled an amusing story from Heston's book tour for *The Actor's Life*.[5] "At a Seattle store," the publicist remembered, "a young woman told him, 'I didn't buy your book, but would you sign this?' She held out a book of The Fifty Worst Films opened to Heston's *Airport '75*. . . . [Heston] signed it, smiling. Within moments she was back. 'Would you add "Season's Greetings"?' He did."[6] Likewise, Heston twice guest-starred on television's *Saturday Night Live*, parodying his many films. Heston even made fun of his politics. In a small cameo in the comedy *Town & Country* (Peter Chelsom, 2001), he caricatured his prominent role in the NRA by playing a gun nut from Idaho. He took his career and politics seriously but was magnificently disposed to laugh at himself.

Even though Heston was most famous as an international movie star, his larger significance rests in his political evolution. He demonstrated how unchanging political ideas, in the volatile environment of postwar politics, often produced new political loyalties. In his own particular case, Heston helped propel a conservative resurgence, for his shifting allegiances mirrored those of many visceral neoconservatives. The Cold War consensus drew him, like many voters, into the Democratic fold, but he and other visceral neocons rebelled against the party as it veered leftward. As increasing numbers of Americans identified with conservatism in the 1970s, they ushered in the Reagan Revolution of the 1980s. Heston not only reflected American political trends but also shaped them. His celebrity activism, unlike that of many Hollywood liberals, promoted the traditional cultural values that he personified in his movies: responsibility, individualism, and conservative masculinity. By extending these principles into the political arena, he touched Americans in a way that went well beyond the silver screen. The ultimate message in Heston's political activities was that Americans actually could live the ideals that he embodied in his films. Heston's politics revived values that had come dangerously close to falling out of style in post-1960s America. This resuscitation was an important achievement because those principles—individual destiny, dignity through excellence, and responsibility to the community—constituted America's view of itself.

CHAPTER ONE

SUPERSTAR

CHARLTON HESTON WAS BORN ON OCTOBER 4, 1923, TO RUSS AND LILLA Carter. His first home was a small, white-framed structure on Michigan's Russel Lake. This, according to the actor, was "a fine place to be a boy in."[1] His simple surroundings did not lack comfort, for his family home enjoyed running water, central heating, and electricity. One of eleven pupils, three of whom were his cousins, he was educated in a one-room schoolhouse in the nearby town of St. Helen. Frequently on his own, the young Heston spent much of his time hiking the Michigan woods, hunting and fishing and using his imagination to develop solitary games. White-tailed deer, partridge, duck, rabbit, and other wild game roamed the surrounding forest, which was also blessed with ample streams for fishing. This vast expanse of nature gave Heston plenty of room to act out his creative imaginings. He often fancied himself as Kit Carson, rifle in hand, tramping throughout the woods to hunt for elk to feed starving settlers stranded in a blizzard in Donner Pass. Twenty-two miles separated Heston from the nearest movie theater, so to attend a show was a rare and "incredible event."[2]

Lilla Carter bore two more children, but Heston remained a loner because of the age difference that separated him from his siblings. His sister, Lilla, was born when Heston was six years old and his brother, Alan, when he was ten. His parents' divorce disrupted young Charlton's tranquil life, and he had to leave his beloved Michigan woods when Lilla briefly moved her children to Georgia to live with her sister. Eventually, she returned to Michigan and married a man by the name of Chester, or "Chet," Heston. Although Chet did not adopt Lilla's children, he cared for them as his own; Heston would see his natural father only one more time in the next ten years. This distance made it easy for Heston to take his stepfather's name. He later explained that, at the time, he was embarrassed and guilt ridden over his parent's divorce and, thus, "couldn't bear having a different name from my stepfather." Indeed, Heston's own daughter claims that the divorce "scarred him terribly," and the actor went so far as to say that his parents' divorce was more traumatic than his later service in World War II because he did not understand why it happened and blamed himself. Chet did his best to help Heston and his new family cope. Looking for financial opportunities in the midst of the Great Depression, he moved the family to Wilmette, Illinois, a suburb north of Chicago, where he found a job at the Bell and Gossett steel plant. Chet Heston's resourcefulness allowed the new family to survive the economic difficulties of the day without having to go on welfare. This is an achievement that his stepson found particularly striking. Heston later wrote about his stepfather: "I admire Chet Heston more for his desperate odyssey that summer than for anything else I know about him; he never quit."[3]

Heston attended New Trier High School in Wilmette, reputedly one of the best public schools in America. He was, however, unhappy in his new surroundings. Six feet, two inches tall by the age of sixteen, Heston described himself as having been a "skinny hick from the woods" when he first arrived in the affluent suburb of Chicago. His awkward physique, solitary upbringing, and extreme shyness did not lend to making new friends easily. Not knowing the basics of city living or socializing did not help matters. The single task of crossing the street in city traffic intimidated him. He also did not know how to drive a car or ride a bike, and he had no team sports background or dating experience. "On top of all this," he wrote, "I was a nerd before the word had even been invented—shy, skinny, short, pimply, and ill-dressed." A rapid growth spurt at age fifteen intensified his awkward image; his clothes barely accommodated his growing frame. By this time, Heston already possessed an independent streak by nature, and his new school accentuated this inclination. He attested: "Kids are the most conventional people in the world. It is more important than anything else for them to conform, and I was a kind of oddball. I was driven into being independent. I was very, very unhappy."[4]

Alienated from the social scene, Heston slowly acclimated to his new life through New Trier's extracurricular activities, including the football, tennis, rifle, and drama teams. During his junior and senior years, he focused more intently on drama and dropped his other clubs. Heston had discovered his love for acting and for the master playwright William Shakespeare. "What acting offered me was the chance to be many other people. In those days, I wasn't satisfied being me," he confessed. "You see, I always thought of myself as inadequate. Kids of divorced parents always feel that way—that, on some subconscious level, they're responsible. It comes from self-loathing. I suppose a lot of that has to do with my Scottish, Calvinistic background, instilled in me by my grandparents, that somehow you're responsible for what happens to you." Acting eventually proved to be his lifeblood, not just a way to cope with his guilt and shame. Trying to gain as much experience as possible, Heston also acted with local amateurs in the Winnetka Community Theater and made plans to attend Northwestern University. The school boasted one of the best theater departments in the country, but he could not afford the tuition. When he graduated from high school in 1941, the community theater offered to pay the $300 tuition, which assisted the aspiring actor greatly, although he still had to take various jobs, including a stint as an elevator operator, to support himself and to repay his benefactors.[5]

Heston's success did not inspire him to shed his shy demeanor. His confidence had grown onstage but not with people, and his solitary inclination still prevailed to the point that he did not even attend the senior dance held at his high school after graduation. "I can't imagine why I hadn't sorted out a solution to the Senior Ball. Like going to it for God's sake," he wrote in his autobiography. He made a brief appearance and then snuck out the side door to the shores of Lake Michigan. Not wanting to admit to his parents that he had skipped the dance, he filled the next three hours "wandering slowly south to Wilmette, feeling disgustingly sorry for myself."[6] As he matured physically and his confidence grew at college, Heston had no more of these types of painful experiences, but his loner instinct as well as a certain degree of shyness would remain permanent features of his adult personality.

Heston's experience at Northwestern established the framework for his future. His demanding acting teacher, Alvina Krause, did not coddle her students. As Heston remembered, Krause "wasn't interested in teaching self-esteem," and it was through her that Heston acquired the thick skin needed for the acting business. Another Northwestern student, David Bradley, persuaded Heston to star in his independent film *Peer Gynt* (1941). Although the film never surfaced beyond the borders of the local art scene, it gave Heston a taste of being in front of the camera. Most important, it was at college that Heston met the love of his life, Lydia Clarke. Immediately taken with the young law student, Heston secretly touched her chestnut hair when he sat behind her in theater practice class. Clarke's feelings were not, to say the least, mutual. She confided to one journalist that, when she first met Heston, "I thought he was arrogant and conceited, and supremely self-confident." Not until the two performed together in Harley Granville Barker's one-act play *The Madras House* (1910) did Heston convince the object of his crush to join him for coffee. "We had a very stimulating conversation and that was it," Clarke remembered. "I was insanely in love with him." Heston wooed Clarke with Shakespearean sonnets and also convinced her to drop law and study acting full-time. However, she did not fall completely under his spell. Having decided long before that she preferred a career to matrimony, she refused Heston's marriage proposals for a full two years.[7]

The entrance of the United States into World War II interrupted Heston's plans to finish school and Lydia's intention to remain single. Heston got his first taste of government service when he enlisted in the army air corps in 1943. During basic training and several months at various stateside air bases, Heston repeatedly begged Clarke to marry him, but she continued to refuse, insisting on at least finishing her studies first. Undaunted, Heston doggedly persisted. Finally, in a surprise telegram, Clarke relented, stating: "Have decided to accept your proposal. Love, Lydia."[8] Clarke joined

Heston in Greensboro, North Carolina, in March 1944 for a private wedding ceremony, but the new Mrs. Heston returned to Chicago shortly thereafter for school. The newlyweds reunited briefly in Detroit when Heston was stationed in the city. At this time, Heston also reunited with his father, Russ Carter, after fortuitously seeing his name in the Detroit phone book. At his bride's urging, Heston called his father, to learn that Carter had remarried and started a new family. (Heston has remained in contact with his father's new family ever since.) Shortly thereafter, the air corps shipped Heston to Alaska, where he served as a sergeant in the Eleventh Air Force. Heston, along with the vast majority of Americans, was relieved when President Harry S. Truman deployed the newly developed atomic bomb on Japan, thus obviating the need for a land invasion of the home islands and preventing the thousands of U.S. casualties that would, undoubtedly, have resulted.

At war's end, the newlyweds had big dreams of success. Amid postwar inflation, they moved from Chicago to New York City in order to expand their acting opportunities. They found an apartment in Hell's Kitchen on Manhattan's East Side, and, between the two of them, they managed to eke out a living, with Lydia initially being their sole means of support. Acting jobs were difficult to find. Both took modeling jobs. Heston drove an ambulance at one point and even posed for a series of art classes, wearing only a gray velour jockstrap that Lydia had sewn for him. Fortune called in 1947 when the Asheville Community Theater offered the couple a six-month position as the theater's codirectors. They enjoyed the tranquil setting and were proud of their productions. The theater, pleased with the Hestons' management, offered them a permanent arrangement at a higher salary. Although this offer was tempting, the couple decided to give Broadway one more go. The community theater did not satisfy Heston's needs as an actor. He loved theater, but the amateur players did not take their parts as seriously as he or his wife did. To the locals, the plays were a welcome distraction from their workaday lives. Heston needed a different environment. He explained: "I wanted the arena . . . sweat, sand, and blood, where it really counts. To take the test, and give your best . . . and then somehow be better." In August 1947, he and Lydia moved back to New York City, and

Heston bet his wife a new hat that he would find work within two months. Lydia won her prize faster than they expected. The very day they returned, Heston earned a position in the highly respected McClintic-Cornell Company on Broadway, and, soon thereafter, Lydia received several lucrative offers as well.[9]

Heston and Lydia both obtained substantial roles, in *Antony and Cleopatra* and Sidney Kingsley's *Detective Story,* respectively. Heston, however, owed his big break to the advent of live television. In 1947, only 2 percent of American households boasted a television set, with most televisions concentrated in New York City. This new and relatively primitive technology required shows to be broadcast live, and television producers had not yet developed substantial programming that would attract a regular audience. Stations unexpectedly found that audience with the 1947 World Series, featuring the New York Yankees and the Brooklyn Dodgers. This historic matchup propelled the status of television to that of the nation's fastest-growing entertainment medium. By 1956, 70 percent of American households owned a television set, and the two major networks, the Columbia Broadcasting System (CBS) and the National Broadcasting Company (NBC), competed to establish hit shows and maintain a loyal audience. Although the networks attracted millions of viewers, they could not draw big-name talent to star in their programs. As Heston remembered: "Most Hollywood actors considered television sort of tacky. Serious actors didn't do that kind of thing; nor directors, God knows."[10] NBC concentrated on variety shows starring Milton Berle and Ed Sullivan, while CBS pursued a more prestigious angle by converting its radio drama *Studio One* to the small screen. Live television proved fortuitous for a number of young actors, including Anne Bancroft, Jack Lemmon, Yul Brynner, and Walter Matthau, all of whom, under the direction of Worthington Miner, performed live Shakespearean drama. Because of his experience at McClintic-Cornell, *Studio One* considered Heston worthy, and Miner hired him as Cinna in *Julius Caesar,* which aired for the first time in the spring of 1949. Thereafter, Heston starred in a number of *Studio One* productions, including *The Taming of the Shrew* and *Macbeth.* It was in *Macbeth,* during which an Irish wolfhound played Macbeth's alter ego, that the legendary "starmaker" Hal Wallis first got a glimpse of Heston.

Hal Wallis had arrived in Hollywood in 1920 and quickly established himself as one of the film community's power brokers, maintaining a considerable degree of independence as a producer for Warner Brothers Studios, where he made between forty and sixty features a year. Contemptuous of the "perfumed melodramas" typical of other studios, Wallis made movies that were witty, modern, and tough, including *Dark Victory* (Edmund Goulding, 1939), *The Maltese Falcon* (John Huston, 1941), and *Casablanca* (Michael Curtiz, 1942). Despite these successes, Wallis chafed under the studio system, which maintained direct control over its employees. By the 1950s, he had moved to Paramount Pictures with a contract that allowed him more independence. His new studio gave Wallis and his partner, Joseph Hazen, profit participation, a producer's fee, and, most important, complete autonomy in film production. Freed from the old studio system, Wallis experimented with more modern approaches when signing talent. For example, he signed Kirk Douglas to a contract that required the actor to do one picture per year for five years but that also allowed him to accept other roles from other producers. "Those were the days when everyone was dying to be under contract because it was safe, it was guaranteed income," explained Douglas. "But to me it was like slavery." Indeed, each studio was its own entity, controlling production, distribution, and exhibition as well as its "players." While Heston conceded that studios did ensure that actors were well-fed and secure in their contracts, like Douglas he disliked the way the talent was loaned back and forth "like property" and the lack of freedom actors had in choosing their own roles.[11]

By the time Wallis discovered Heston, the producer had all but abandoned the standard contract of the traditional studio system. He signed actors to an agreement for a certain number of pictures, as customary, but, when actors were not working for him, Wallis was, as with Douglas, willing to allow them to undertake other projects, something the old studios forbade. Wallis's flexible contract was probably the only kind that the independent Heston would have accepted. Fortunately, Heston was just the type of actor for which Wallis had been scouting. Having already discovered Burt Lancaster and Douglas with his new agency, Wallis was on the prowl for more actors with their type of rough masculinity. As Wallis wrote in his memoirs: "Like Kirk and Burt, Chuck was exactly the type of he-man I was looking for. He was tall, rangy, bony. . . ." Furthermore, he could act. After viewing Heston on *Studio One,* Wallis called him in for an interview and hired him "on the spot." Genuinely impressed with Heston and aware that Warner had already offered him a contract, Wallis did not waste any time. Warner, indeed, had pursued Heston, but he was not interested in their antiquated way of doing business. He felt apprehensive about giving up his "modest reputation" on the stage and on television for the movies, especially since Hollywood producers had yet to allow their actors to appear on television. Now someone would. Knowing that the old studio system was dying a slow death, Wallis, Heston later recalled, "gave me what no one else had gotten up to that point: an independent contract with the right to do plays *and* television. It horrified the industry." Wallis signed Heston for five films and, having resolved the contract, also helped him tackle his next problem—his outdated attire. "Chuck arrived [for the interview] wearing a zoot suit. We took him out and bought him a wardrobe," he chuckled.[12]

Although he would, ultimately, find Hollywood distasteful, Heston had transformed from a "backward hick" into a sophisticated Shakespearean, suitably garbed for the glamorous Los Angeles scene. Already put off by the schmoozing bar scenes, on one of his first nights out in Hollywood he found that a passerby had tossed a lit cigarette into the backseat of his open convertible while he was inside a nightclub. This sort of experience left Heston feeling torn about establishing a residence in Los Angeles. Since Lydia was still acting on Broadway, the Hestons lived the first ten years of their marriage bicoastally, with apartments in New York and Los Angeles. Although they "hated" the long-distance separation and the constant traveling, Lydia recalled: "We never thought to change it; it was our life." Heston continued to accept roles in New York. Indeed, the Hestons were quite the successful acting duo. In 1950, *Theater World Magazine* named them the "most promising theater personalities of the year." This was the first time the magazine had chosen a married couple in the same year. Heston also continued to perform live television but had increasingly less time to do so because of his film roles.[13]

The so-called star system, established in the mid-1920s, was firmly in place by the time Heston arrived in Hollywood. Even as the studio system crumbled, Hollywood increasingly developed the "star circuit." The film analyst Steven Cohan considers stars to be those actors whose persona enters not only the films in which they play the lead but also different forms of public circulation, all this feeding into future performances. Items for public consumption included the pages of the gossip columns, such as Hedda Hopper's, and film magazines, such as *Photoplay*. Films of this era made the spectacularity of the actors the central dimension of their stardom, and Hollywood conscientiously sold the imagery of its stars both on the screen and as part of the film product.[14] This development, or "investment," resulted in photo spreads and publicity tours as well as more mundane television appearances, such as guest spots on game shows, essential aspects of Hollywood stardom.

The star system gave rise to what historians have termed the *culture of celebrity*, as Americans increasingly devoured celebrity gossip. The historian Charles L. Ponce de Leon argues that the culture of celebrity is closely related to the spread of the market economy and the rise of democratic and individualistic values associated with modernity. These developments steadily eroded the sense of authority previously associated with well-known figures. Americans increasingly wanted to learn about celebrities beyond their screen images, and the news media accommodated them by exposing, as much as possible, the "real selves" of actors.[15] Heston would not be immune to these pressures.

In 1950, Heston starred in William Dieterle's *Dark City*, a successful film that introduced him to the standard fourteen-city, twenty-three-day publicity tour. Publicity junkets never appealed to Heston, but he realized immediately that, even if he did not enjoy them, interviewing was "crucial to a film actor," as were other public appearances. Heston went on to star in a string of films throughout the early 1950s, some more successful than others, and acclimated himself to the publicity machine. "If you make your living as a star (I hate that word too), you have a responsibility to your public identity," he explained. He appeared on *Hollywood Guess Stars* and *What's My Line* in the mid-1950s, consented to numerous interviews with Hedda Hopper, and appeared in scores of photo spreads. He also started his own newsletter, in which he kept his fans up-to-date on his latest films and indulged them with personal anecdotes. However, Heston made it a point to pacify his fans without revealing too much of his private side. Furthermore, he refused to sacrifice certain aspects of his life, seen, for example, in his struggle with Paramount when the company told him that he needed to change his "elegant"-sounding name to something more common, like "Douglas" or "Kent." Heston countered that those names sounded as if they were out of a novel and refused, sneering that such a move "seems to me a Hollywood thing to do." Besides, he argued, even if moviegoers found his name more challenging to remember, few confused it with anyone else's. He would not, however, build a substantial public identity or become a strong force in the star system until 1956, when he portrayed Moses in Cecil B. DeMille's *The Ten Commandments*.[16]

Heston first worked for DeMille after he caught the director's eye while driving off the lot at Paramount one afternoon. Although DeMille and Heston had already met briefly in the studio's commissary, nothing had come of it. Heston then was preparing to return to New York, feeling "kick[ed] in the balls" after losing the lead part in the film version of *Detective Story* (William Wyler, 1951) to Kirk Douglas. As luck would have it, Heston made eye contact with the director and impulsively waved as he zoomed through the gates. As the story goes, when DeMille asked his secretary about Heston, she reminded him that he had seen *Dark City* but not liked it. Nevertheless, something about the actor struck the famous director. "Actually, I liked the way he *waved* just now," he told her. "We better get him in." DeMille immediately cast Heston in *The Greatest Show on Earth* (1952), a celebration of circus life costarring Jimmy Stewart, Cornel Wilde, and Betty Hutton. Heston played Brad Braden, the circus manager and the leading role. The picture made a record-setting $12 million that year and won an Oscar for best picture. The demanding DeMille was pleased with Heston's performance as "an effective, hard-driving boss of the circus." In fact, it was that role that brought Heston "the best compliment I've ever received on my work from a lady who wrote a letter to Mr. de Mille. She thought the picture had captured the feeling of the circus wonderfully, and that Hutton and Wilde, and particularly Jimmy Stewart, had been fine in their roles. 'I was also amazed at how well the circus manager fitted in with the real actors,' she said." Four years later, when DeMille tapped Heston for *The Ten Commandments,* it was just the quality role Heston needed after a string of disappointments, including *Arrowhead* (Charles Marquis Warren, 1953), *The Secret of the Incas* (Jerry Hopper, 1954), and *The Far Horizons* (Rudolph Maté, 1955). Heston admitted (referring to *The Naked Jungle* [Byron Haskin, 1954] and *Ruby Gentry* [King Vidor, 1952]): "In that whole period, until *The Ten Commandments,* I think I made two or three good films." Not very discriminating in his choice of scripts, Heston starred in only one other during those years, *Lucy Gallant* (Robert Parrish, 1955), that, he later conceded, you could watch "without bursting into laughter."[17]

DeMille had been a major player in Hollywood since first arriving in 1914 and had, by his fourth decade in the industry, firmly established a reputation as a creative, if not extravagant, director. He had directed numerous movies, many of which were silent, featuring handsome men, beautiful women, and as much sex as he could force past the censors. Heston said that DeMille "made seventy films in his life. As he is fond of saying, only one of them was a failure; a pic called *Four Frightened People* [1934]." The immense success of his films did not change the fact that DeMille chafed under the financial restrictions set by Paramount executives. Their consistently tight budgets forced him to reduce the quality of his productions. Although he struggled his entire life to achieve financial independence, he was never able to launch a successful independent company.[18] Ironically, the waning studio system and the advent of television provided him the opportunity to direct a film in the grand style to which he was so inclined.

The major motion picture studios announced in 1952 that, in order to compete with television, they would abandon their B-movie productions and concentrate on top-quality, big-budget films. This new strategy transformed the movie industry and allowed actors like Heston to achieve international stardom. Thereafter, the studios spent more money on each individual production while releasing fewer movies per year. Furthermore, the invention of the wide-screen "CinemaScope," first used by 20th Century Fox, allowed for a new kind of moviemaking with grander sets and more activity per frame. Paramount copied the concept of the wide-screen camera with its own "VistaVision," a camera process that allowed for a vertical perspective of the human body, as opposed to that of the horizontal allowed by CinemaScope. This major technological advance helped justify the big-budget approach. For its first production in this style, Paramount asked DeMille to remake his 1923 epic *The Ten Commandments*.

The decision to retell the biblical story of Moses made good financial sense. Audiences had reacted enthusiastically to DeMille's silent version and were sure to do so again with the impressive technological feats allowed by VistaVision. Furthermore, the story of the prophet Moses was enthralling and readily appealed to Christians and Jews alike, a large portion of the American public. After moving from Mesopotamia to Canaan, a group of shepherds and merchants known as the Israelites believed that they had found their home in Egypt. After six hundred years of peace, an Egyptian king enslaved the Jews, primarily because of their adherence to monotheism. An abandoned baby, known as Moses, was adopted into the royal family and, as a grown man, realized that he was of Jewish descent. With divine inspiration, Moses led his people out of Egypt and into the desert for ten years. There, God gave Moses a code of laws that came to be known as the Ten Commandments. The deity next helped the Israelites escape the Egyptian army by giving Moses the power to part the Red Sea. At last, the Israelites would return to Canaan and prosper.

When the Paramount executives asked DeMille to direct *The Ten Commandments,* they promised him an unlimited budget and allowed him to shoot the film largely on location in Egypt. Such an offer was what DeMille had dreamed of his entire career. He immediately went to work assembling his cast, selecting Heston as much for his looks and reputation as for his acting ability: "As I looked at these various paintings [assembled by his assistant] one face kept suggesting itself to me. That face was Heston's." DeMille then had a sketch drawn of Heston with a white beard and compared it to Michelangelo's statue of Moses—the Moses in the public mind. Heston's brief stint on New Trier's football team provided the final impetus for landing the role—his nose. Broken during an ill-fated game, Heston's perfectly imperfect nose added the biblical touch to matching his profile with Moses'. DeMille commented: "He looks like the Michelangelo statue . . . and [he] had the mental and spiritual qualities to play Moses— he has great honesty, respect for truth, spiritual integrity, and personal courage."[19] DeMille went on to recruit an all-star ensemble: Yul Brynner as the pharaoh Ramses; Anne Baxter as Queen Nefretiri; Edward G. Robinson as Dathan; and Vincent Price as Baka.

The attention accorded and the enormous success of *The Ten Commandments* can also be attributed to its scale of production and the unprecedented amount of publicity it received. Not only did DeMille use well-known stars, but he also hired an enormous cast in order to fill his large sets, on which he spared little cost. *Time* magazine estimated that the sixty-acre re-creation of the "treasure city" of Per Ramses probably constituted the biggest piece of construction work undertaken in Egypt since the building of the Suez Canal. Scenes such as Moses' parting of the Red Sea and the Exodus of the Israelites from Egypt shocked and pleased moviegoers with their enormity. In order to obtain a lot big enough to re-create the parting of the Red Sea, DeMille demolished the buildings between Paramount and RKO Studios, joined the territory, and built a two-hundred-thousand-cubic-foot swimming pool at the expense of $1 million. Special hydraulic equipment allowed the "sea" to part in two minutes flat. With equal aplomb, DeMille hired at least twelve thousand extras and rented fifteen thousand animals, including geese, sheep, camels, and donkeys, for the Exodus scene. Tallied at $13.3 million, *The Ten Commandments* was the most expensive film yet made. The grand epic took two years to prepare and shoot, during which time it received a montage of publicity before the film was even released, including multiple-page spreads in *Look* and *Life* magazines. This publicity further increased when DeMille suffered a near heart attack on the set, then kept working after only a few short hours of rest.[20]

Further aiding the success of this biblical epic was the so-called religion boom of the 1950s. As the Cold War heightened, many Americans turned to religion even more fervently than they had previously and equated democracy with Christianity. Congress placed "In God We Trust" on American coins, unprecedented numbers of Americans joined religious groups, and the Reverend Billy Graham launched a popular evangelical Christian revivalist movement that quickly swept the nation.[21] *The Ten Commandments* thrived in this religious environment and offered Americans a historical context from which to view the Cold War. At the beginning of the film, DeMille himself appeared onscreen and drew the parallel between the struggle for religious freedom in ancient times and the struggle for political freedom in the modern era. Few left the theater without understanding DeMille's obvious reference to the tyranny of communism in the Soviet Union versus the freedom of democracy in the United States. Indeed, *The Ten Commandments* premiered worldwide only a few weeks after the Soviets put down the Hungarian Revolution.

The Ten Commandments struck a resonant chord with the American public and, eventually, audiences around the world. The epic opened in the United States on November 8, 1956, and viewers flocked to the theaters to see it. By the end of its initial release, sales had totaled $83.6 million, and the blockbuster hurtled Heston to international stardom. By August 1959, after almost three full years of continual release, the movie had been seen by an estimated 98.5 million people. Steven Cohan writes: "The film's enormous popularity was unmatched even by the other big successful films of the period, . . . to the point where its continuous exhibition during the second half of the decade gave it the aura of a major cultural event in its own right, experienced by the entire nation and transcending the circumstances of ordinary moviegoing." Heston recognized the importance of the film almost immediately. In 1957 he wrote: "The film itself, and my role as Moses, will always remain one of the creative peaks of my career. I hope to play many fine parts in my life . . . but surely films can never offer me another part like Moses, not only in terms of its creative challenge to an actor . . . but also in the opportunity the part offered to attempt the portrayal of a man whose life had spiritual meaning to people of more varied faith than any other who ever lived." The excitement surrounding the movie was so huge that critics tended to view the epic with disdain, a judgment that has grown in acceptance as the 1950s has been characterized as a decade of Cold War hysteria and conformity. Although Heston admitted that DeMille was "terribly unfashionable and dismissed pejoratively as a corn merchant," he went on to argue: "I think he was much more than that."[22] Indeed, DeMille tapped into the religious fervor of a nation characterized by its wide variety of denominations and faiths.

The Ten Commandments allowed Heston to establish a public persona that emphasized an independence strongly influenced by morality and masculinity. Moses immediately illustrates his individualism and moral character during his ongoing struggle with his antagonist, Ramses. The two men are vying for the throne of Egypt and competitively attempting to build the city of Per Ramses in honor of the pharaoh. Moses demonstrates his moral brand of individualism when he halts construction to save a slave woman from being crushed to death. Ramses, on the other hand, treats his slaves with cruelty, an inhumanity not uncommon in ancient Egyptian society. When Moses returns as the hero in the triumphant building of Per Ramses, he successfully transcends his adopted culture and influences to become a self-made man of God's will. This individualism is expressed again when Moses leads the Israelites out of Egypt. He possesses an air of confidence, yet at the same time the constant insecurity of his followers causes him to doubt himself. Finally, Moses exerts his authority at Mount Sinai. DeMille's production notes reveal that he wanted an actor who could portray a leader who possessed "a mind in advance of its surroundings, in advance of its age," with no inclination for personal gain. Heston effectively conveyed Moses' internal struggles between royalty and heritage and, then, between the Israelites and God. His ability to chart his own righteous path built his public image as an independent and moral individual, going beyond the role of Moses and to the very character of Charlton Heston himself.[23]

The masculinity exuded by Moses became another permanent feature of Heston's newly prominent public persona. On the most basic level, masculinity is characterized as male-specific traits, especially virility, independence, competition, and aggression. Issues associated with these traits include skill, status, and hierarchy. Masculine characteristics stem from biological sources, but social forces also shape them.[24] Because of the varying degrees to which social forces can shape masculinity, a variety of masculine egos can emerge at any one time that differ from one another.

Because of *The Ten Commandments,* Heston became associated with the conservative and rugged masculinity of ancient times, a type of virility different than the one dominating America in the 1950s.

In fact, a number of cultural historians argue that American men experienced a "postwar masculinity crisis" that compromised the male image in the immediate aftermath of World War II. Rapid demobilization led many to worry openly about the breadwinning potential of returning veterans. Alfred Kinsey's famous study of male sexuality, published in 1948 and popularly known as the "Kinsey Report," stunned the nation when it revealed that more men experienced homosexual encounters than most Americans would have guessed. Finally, the large corporation appeared, because of its emphasis on consumption and, less overtly, conformity, to be in the process of relocating masculinity, moving it into what had previously been a "feminine" sphere. Men in general dealt differently with the masculinity crisis, and, during the 1950s, films portrayed this struggle for acceptable standards of masculinity in particular ways.[25]

The actor Cary Grant personified the most common expression of masculinity on film in the 1950s, his characters consistently overcoming the potential crisis of manhood. Grant often played an executive in the corporate world, someone who wore a suit to work and reveled in the consumer joys of financial success but who was no corporate stooge. Grant's characters were attractive, successful, charming, and tough enough to prevail in almost every situation. For example, in *North by Northwest* (Alfred Hitchcock, 1959), Grant's Roger Thornhill teeters on the edge of emasculation with his reticence for "expedient exaggeration" in the advertising business, his inability to commit to one woman, and his unwillingness to stand up to his domineering mother. The crisis of his manhood is resolved when he saves the Eva Marie Saint character's life, uncovers an international spy ring, and returns to his corporate job, only now with a new attitude. Cary Grant, the most popular movie star of the decade, restored the masculinity of the professional middle-class male and represented the culture's hegemonic masculinity. One historian labels this type of corporate character the *gray flannel suit* in honor of the novel *The Man in the Gray Flannel Suit,* written by Sloan Wilson in 1955. A number of other actors performed in similar roles, including Gregory Peck, who starred in Nunnally Johnson's 1956 movie version of the novel, and Jack Lemmon, who starred in *Three for the Show* (H. C. Potter, 1955).[26]

While Grant may have been a cultural fixture of the period, other actors offered alternative masculinities, images that relied extensively on muscles. Grant's characters used money and style to woo women, but those portrayed by other male stars focused on a muscular stature, a tough attitude, or an outsider status. Various actors offered such a renewed virility. These included Humphrey Bogart with his tough-guy persona, William Holden with his barrel chest, Marlon Brando and James Dean with their youthful rebellion, and Charlton Heston with his conservative, patriarchal authority of ancient times. Cultural trends beyond the movie screen indicated dissatisfaction with the gray flannel norm as well. The sociologist David Reisman critiqued this image when he argued that corporations drove men to embrace an "other-directed personality," one in which they behaved duplicitously, in manners directed by a "social radar" rather than by internal convictions, to succeed in the business world.[27] Another alternative to the gray flannel norm appeared when, in 1953, Hugh Hefner launched *Playboy*, which offered a sexualized, bachelor-driven image, but one that still emphasized consumption. And, in 1957, Jack Kerouac published *On the Road*, which detailed the Beats' dissatisfaction with the gray flannel lifestyle and the related focus on suburban values and consumption prevalent in the decade.

The Ten Commandments offered a conservative departure from the gray flannel version of masculinity. Heston's Moses represented a patriarchal, traditional version of masculine values that clearly was not enamored of corporate America and its many trappings—the other-directed personality, the playboy, or the consumer. Heston's six foot two, 210-pound frame counteracted the prototype personified by Cary Grant. DeMille used his star's muscular physique to the film's advantage and employed VistaVision to emphasize Heston's great height. This was, according to the film historian Steven Cohan, an important machination: "It was ultimately [Heston's] height more than anything else which forged his close identification with the epic genre that made him a star." The star's muscularity is especially apparent in the first half of the film when, as young Moses, Heston is

25

costumed so as to reveal his striking physique, a technique so transparent that *Time* magazine sneeringly dubbed the movie a "Sexodus." Furthermore, Heston sports "an authentic hair style of an Egyptian prince of that era" and has hair on both his head and his body. Heston's hairy chest as young Moses and his robed body and bushy beard as the older prophet differentiated him from Cary Grant and other modern male figures, who sported three-piece suits and clean-shaven faces.[28]

Heston's carriage and demeanor added to the physical strength and conservative aura of his character. The air of seriousness that enshrouded the actor conveyed a dignity and a set of ideals that did not even have to be put into words to be understood by an audience. When Heston spoke, his rich baritone voice further established his authority. He spoke in slow, carefully measured words, drawing out each syllable, or even breaking one syllable into two by lowering the second half of the word even further. His voice was so authoritative that DeMille recorded it and slowed it down to represent the voice of God when he spoke to Moses beside the burning bush. The determined set of Heston's jaw, the blazing emotion radiating from his eyes, and his powerful voice combined to form a physical package of strength, authority, and morality—quite different from the polished and charming demeanor of Grant.

Not a "Twentieth Century Man," Heston often compared his look to that of fellow actors. "I don't look like a modern man," he told one journalist. "My appearance qualifies me for historic characterizations, going back to the year one." Indeed, Heston's bony face, craggy features, and uncompromising persona harked back to another century. "All the good modern parts go to Jack Lemmon or Cary Grant," he once said. "When you see Jack Lemmon at the beginning of a picture, walking down the halls of a big office building, you immediately believe in him as the junior executive of a corporation and when people see me on horseback in chain mail, they seem to believe that I belong there." Not that Heston was complaining. He recognized his unique position as well as the connection between a star's public image and his private one, commenting knowingly: "Not every star can [play a historical role] convincingly. I do not mean that as a judgment of anyone's acting ability. But can you picture Cary Grant in a toga or Elvis Presley in a suit of armor? It would be a complete contradiction of the public images they have worked so hard to establish." Besides, Heston relished researching and playing historical roles, particularly when the characters were complicated and imposing figures. "I enjoy wearing costumes," he confessed, and he identified with what they represented: "I like portraying heroes of antiquity whose values were grander and more spectacular than those of today."[29]

In addition to his physical appearance, his acting style intensified his masculine image and contributed to the public's association of Heston with independence and self-determination. The film critic Bruce Crowther argued that Heston's particular strength as an actor lay in his ability to outwardly present inner emotional struggle and that he is far superior in largely solitary roles. Other critics and Hollywood insiders echoed this analysis. Pete Hamill concluded: "Heston is indisputably better when he is larger than life, leaving love affairs and social engagements to mere mortals."[30] However, some critics characterized Heston's acting as wooden and hollow since he could not consistently portray meaningful interpersonal relationships onscreen. Some argued he could play *only* imposing, larger-than-life figures. While Heston received critical acclaim for films like *Will Penny* (Tom Gries, 1968), in which he played an aging cowboy who discovers love, the public tended to prefer Heston in larger-than-life roles.

Heston was so credible as Moses that DeMille insisted that a spiritual quality actually enveloped the set of *The Ten Commandments.* Perhaps this happened because Heston and DeMille agreed that the actor needed to establish a persona of authority among the rest of the cast and not mingle with them between takes. Heston remembered that DeMille "cautioned me that while I wore the robes of Moses I must think of myself in that context. That I must never sit down on the set, never read a newspaper or drink a cup of coffee or talk on the telephone and indeed at all times I must try to stay within the context of the part." As DeMille remembered: "He would go off by himself for a half-hour, in costume, and walk up and down in solitary thought." Such a strategy had its desired effect. When Heston returned to the set "and walked through the crowd of Arab extra players, their eyes followed him and they murmured reverently, 'Moussa! Moussa!': to them, Moslems almost all, he was the Prophet Moses." A reverence for the divine appears, in DeMille's opinion, onscreen as well, especially in one of the film's most important scenes. After his encounter with God at the burning bush, Heston descended the mountain, barefoot, and, as De-Mille described it: "His face lifted and filled with the glory and the rapt awe of a man who had seen God." Heston maintained that he did not hear God on the mountain, but he says: "I do believe I found Moses there." Apparently, so did the rest of the crew.[31]

Heston's intensity came across the screen to audiences and established a moral public image with moviegoers. During the film's original run, the public surged to the theaters, and even forty-five years later the public mind still equated Heston with Moses. To this day, the movie is shown on television every Easter season. In April 2000, ABC showed its twentieth telecast of *The Ten Commandments,* and the biblical epic "proved to be a far bigger attraction" than its closest competitor. Much of this is because of Heston. The film critic Derek Elley argues that the 1923 version of *The Ten Commandments* is equal to the 1956 version technically but that the later film prevails because of the spiritual quality provided by Brynner and Heston. Even in Brynner's fine company, Elley maintains: "It is Heston's film— a remarkable transformation . . . into heroic terms."[32] Scores of critics agreed with Elley's estimation of Heston as hero at the film's release:

Moses, as played by Charlton Heston, is a handsome and haughty young prince who warrants considerable attention as a heroic man of the ancient world.

Charlton Heston gives Moses great physical nobility and spiritual strength.

With his majesty and nobility of face and bearing he might be a statue by Michelangelo come to life.

Charlton Heston as Moses is splendid, handsome, and princely (and human) in the scenes dealing with him as a young man, and majestic and terrible as his role demands it. He is the great Michelangelo conception of Moses, but rather as the inspiration for the sculptor might have been than as a derivation.[33]

Heston brought a set of special qualities to the role of Moses. This role changed his career from one of a successful actor to that of an international star. Heston became a household name forever equated with the prophet.

FINANCIAL DIFFICULTIES CONTINUED TO BESET the film industry, but Heston had little trouble winning roles. In fact, it was precisely because of the uneasy state of the industry in the 1950s that studios increasingly relied on the success of one or two expensive productions, and Metro-Goldwyn-Mayer was no exception. A number of changes forced the studios to evaluate their corporate strategies, particularly the advent of color television, after which their profits dropped considerably. By 1958, box office receipts sank for the first time since World War II, to a lowly $1.5 billion. Things were even worse at MGM, where a power struggle within the ranks threatened to bankrupt the company. In order to save the studio, the general manager, Joseph R. Vogel, risked its future on one huge gamble: the 1959 remake of its 1925 Fred Niblo–directed blockbuster *Ben-Hur*. Not only did the story promise a large-scale spectacle in the grand tradition of epic films, but it also carried a powerful element of human drama. In MGM's financially precarious situation, *Ben-Hur* was probably the least risky gamble that Vogel could have taken, especially when he recruited as director the highly respected William Wyler, who had worked with Heston on *The Big Country* the previous year. Already a best-selling 1880 novel by Lew Wallace, *Ben-Hur* became a stage production in 1899 and ran continuously in the United States for the next seventeen years. Meanwhile, in 1907 Sidney Olcott directed an unauthorized version of the tale that was only fifteen minutes in length. The popularity of this short film led MGM to invest $4 million in Niblo's project, a lavish production that prompted a "frenzied response." Now, at the end of the 1950s, MGM hoped to capitalize on *Ben-Hur*'s name recognition and on the popularity of the biblical epic genre and promised to go all out to do so.[34]

The film traces Judah Ben-Hur's struggle to accept Jesus and settle his love-hate relationship with his boyhood friend Messala (Stephen Boyd in Wyler's film), a friendship troubled by the two characters' ethnicities. Messala returns to their childhood home of Judea as the newly appointed tribune of the Roman province, with orders to crush the local Jewish rabble-rousers. Messala immediately reunites with Judah and finds his old friend a wealthy leader of the Jewish ruling class with his eye on the beautiful Esther (played by the Israeli actress Haya Harakeet). Messala pleads with Ben-Hur to reveal the names of the Jewish troublemakers and to persuade "his people" that defiance of Roman authority is futile. Ben-Hur refuses Messala's request, pronouncing: "I thought it was my friend who had returned. But I was wrong. It is a conqueror who has returned . . . an enemy." The two men swear vengeance.

Ben-Hur and Messala clash only a few days later, after which Messala condemns the Jew to slavery and sends his mother and sister to prison. It is on his way to the awaiting ship that Ben-Hur has his first, unknowing encounter with Jesus of Nazareth, the unrecognized healer giving a parched Ben-Hur water. After two years of rowing in the slave galleys of a Roman battleship, Ben-Hur's dismal fate changes when he saves Admiral Quentus Arrius from drowning. Arrius adopts Ben-Hur and awards him Roman citizenship, but Ben-Hur vows to find his mother and sister and carry out revenge against Messala. On his journey to Jerusalem, he has the opportunity to challenge his enemy in the story's highlight—the chariot race, a spectacle of grand proportions. Ben-Hur prevails, and Messala, who had ruthlessly attached knife-like extensions to his wheels, is brutally trampled and dies after several hours of suffering. At Messala's deathbed, Ben-Hur learns that his mother and sister have been condemned to the Valley of the Lepers.

Ben-Hur reunites with Esther and finally finds his mother and sister hidden from civilization, their condition hardening his hatred toward Messala despite his enemy's death. Esther has heard about a man named Jesus who has been preaching across the countryside and urging his listeners to "love their enemies," and she begs Ben-Hur to accompany her to one of his gatherings. Ben-Hur remains spiteful and loath to accept the newcomer's message, but, when he learns of the preacher's healing powers, he carries his mother and sister to him for his second encounter with the Savior. He is too late, it appears, because Jesus is being crucified, but, recognizing him as the man who once quenched his own thirst, Ben-Hur attempts to give Christ water as he carries his cross up the hill. After the crucifixion, the heavens pour down their rain and heal Ben-Hur's mother and sister of their disease. Ben-Hur, too, is healed, the hate in his heart extinguished.

Ben-Hur allowed Heston to reinforce his traditional conservative public image and to explore the various facets of masculinity even more thoroughly. The "ideal" male ego includes power, omnipotence, mastery, and control—all of which the Heston character gained in *Ben-Hur* after a series of tests. With these tests, Ben-Hur was forced by his antagonists to suffer in dramatic fashion, a struggle in which the audience identified with him; and, when he overcame them, the audience considered him physically and mentally superior and, thus, more masculine. "Within this structure," the film critics Steven Cohan and Ina Rae Hark point out, "suffering—torture in particular operates as both a set of narrative hurdles to be overcome, tests that the hero must survive, and as a set of aestheticized images to be lovingly dwelt on." With his fighting ability, self-confidence, and arrogance, Ben-Hur prevailed. Heston consequently added a more macho edge to his conservative masculine image than he was able to do as Moses.[35]

MGM spared no expense in bringing this mesmerizing story of nineteenth-century romanticism to life, shooting the film in Rome and promoting it to the public long before it was finally released. *Ben-Hur* set a number of film records, including being the biggest production in moviemaking history, being the biggest moneymaker as a first-run release, featuring the most expensive action sequence ever filmed, and winning more Academy Awards than any other single film. The public's interest in the movie centered on the source of the film's expensive production: the chariot race. Indeed, the arena in which the race was staged was at the time the single largest set built for a Hollywood picture. In his newsletter to his fans, Heston commented: "We became quite a tourist attraction . . . competing with the Colosseum and the Roman Forum for overseas visitors." Hollywood notables such as Kirk Douglas, Susan Hayward, Jack Palance, Harry Belafonte, and Audrey Hepburn frequented the set, and the arena became a regular stop for Roman sightseeing buses, which arrived hourly. The publicity would only grow—and exponentially at that, with $3 million of the $16 million budget going toward promotion, including a number of merchandising tie-ins such as cookies, draperies, wallpaper, carpet designs, tiles, babies' sunsuits, diaper suits, paintings, scooter-type chariots, gowns, costume jewelry, lipstick, perfume, paint-by-number sets, hats, bookends, umbrellas, raincoats, and even "Ben-His" and "Ben-

Hers" bath towels. In the end, MGM's gamble proved to be an enormous success. The demand created for the picture was so immense that it drove exhibitors to promise to remodel their theaters in order to get a booking. In its first year, over 16 million people saw the film in 286 theaters with over thirty-five thousand showings worldwide. Indeed, *Ben-Hur* won twelve Academy Awards, being the first biblical film to be "Oscarized" and Heston the first actor to receive the gold statue for a performance in a biblical film. By sheer numbers, *Ben-Hur* was the greatest picture ever to come to the screen.[36]

When Heston won the best-actor Oscar for his role as Judah Ben-Hur, he confirmed his public image as a self-made, masculine, moral savior. This was in part because of his dedicated preparation for the role. It had been difficult to assume Ben-Hur's persona, but Heston had desperately wanted the part and worked hard to live up to its challenges. He had been the first cast member to arrive on location in order to begin training for the chariot race with Hollywood's most renowned stuntman, Yakima Canutt. Wyler required that both Heston and Boyd learn the difficult task of driving a chariot, with four horses at the helm, and the director employed numerous close-ups so that the audience could feel the intensity of the race. As testament to their hard work, Heston and Boyd did all the driving in the chariot scene, except for two stunts. When Messala is dragged under his chariot and trampled to death by the racing horses, Boyd performed the initial part of this stunt with some steel coverings on his body, but the figure in the rest of the sequence was a dummy. The second partially rigged stunt, when Ben-Hur is tossed out of his chariot, was actually an accident, but the racing team used it to their advantage. The stunt coordinators used two different sequences with Canutt and Heston to show Ben-Hur flip in the air and land in between his galloping horses, climb back into the chariot, and win the race. Wyler proclaimed it one of the "greatest cinematic achievements" he had seen. Indeed, this scene has subsequently become legendary, considered by many among the best action scenes ever filmed. Furthermore, it showcased Heston's masculinity to its highest degree. While the chariot race is the ultimate example of physical strength, expert skill, and self-confidence, Heston also displays his physical prowess with other masculine activities. The movie required him to throw a javelin, use a broad sword, swim in the sea, ride camels and horses, and learn precision rowing.[37]

As with his work in *The Ten Commandments,* Heston's acting style was particularly appropriate for Judah Ben-Hur. Both epic stories focus on personal transformation. Although many, including Heston, characterized *Ben-Hur*'s plot as a struggle between two men, Ben-Hur as the good guy and Messala as the bad, the theme was more complicated than that. The overarching tension in the movie was Ben-Hur's own internal struggle between Christian love and un-Christian hate. Showing such internal conflict was Heston's strength as an actor. Indeed, for most of the movie, Ben-Hur is not a model of goodness and purity but, rather, someone in need of a good deal of self-improvement. In the opening sequence, when he receives Esther in his lavishly decorated home, he arrogantly looks her over with an air of superiority. Heston purposely played the scene in this manner, commenting in his journal on his attempt to "make [Ben-Hur] an untried, uncommitted man, thus allowing room for change, both in the galleys, and on Calvary."[38] While Ben-Hur has conscience enough not to help Messala capture the Jewish "troublemakers," he is not such a force of righteousness that he joins the anti-Roman forces. Instead, he is consumed by his search for personal revenge. Even after Messala's death, Ben-Hur is ravaged with bitterness and so disappoints Esther with his rage that she accuses him of replicating his enemy. "It was Judah Ben-Hur I loved. What has become of him? You seem to be now the very thing you set out to destroy: living evil for evil. Hatred is turning you to stone," she cries. "It's as though you had become Messala!"

The true representation of goodness in the movie was not Ben-Hur but his love interest, Esther. Although some, especially Heston, downplayed Esther's importance, treating her as an auxiliary character, her role was vital because she represented both the Judeo-Christian cause that ultimately Ben-Hur must embrace and a heterosexual relationship that proved his well-rounded masculinity. Although Heston somewhat accurately commented there is "no place for the love story here," he was wrong to downplay Esther's role in the story altogether. While the audience does not particularly care about the future of Ben-Hur and Esther as a couple, they do want Ben-Hur to pursue the moral course of action, and it is Esther who persuades him to do so. His relationship with Messala is certainly more interesting, but his relationship with Esther is more vital to the story line than Heston acknowledged. Not until the end of the movie, when Ben-Hur attempts to give Jesus water and embrace Christianity, does Heston's character truly represent goodness and moral authority. Until then, the script calls for Heston to let "deep, hopeless anger . . . smoulder in his eyes," to keep his face "hard" and "expressionless," and to speak "slowly, bitterly."[39] This is the sort of action at which Heston is particularly adept.

Again, as in *The Ten Commandments,* Heston was convincing because of his looming physical presence and unique acting style. As in the first film, he remains the central force in each scene—despite the excitement taking place around him or the crowds through which he walked—yet still succumbs to the larger narrative. Even the fastidious Wyler specifically complimented Heston on his abilities. Wyler paid for an open letter to Heston to appear in the trade papers, and it was later reprinted by the *Saturday Evening Post:*

Dear Chuck: It is an old story among actors that in a film like *Ben-Hur* individual performances are swallowed up by the enormous size of everything else. As you know, I am not given to easy compliments, but I feel that your portrayal of Judah Ben-Hur is an acting achievement of the highest order. . . . The fact that audiences everywhere become deeply and emotionally involved in the story of Ben-Hur proves that you have succeeded in bringing him to life. Much gratifying praise has been showered on the film for its handling of the figure of Christ. I wonder how many people realize that they saw Him only mirrored in your face and felt His presence through your emotions. . . . It was a demanding role both physically and emotionally, and you approached it with intelligence and humility.

Although this letter may have been something of a publicity stunt, Wyler's compliment highlighted the special qualities that Heston brought to his role. In turn, Heston repaid Wyler with his own tribute: he published in *Variety* an open contract to act in any movie at any time at any price for the director.[40]

Heston's voice, characterized by one critic as "bottled thunder," and his chiseled body further contributed to his success in the role. These physical attributes gave Ben-Hur dignity despite the hardships he suffered. Indeed, the protagonist of a typical Hollywood epic needs the perfect male body in order to carry out the often-amazing feats required of the hero. When Ben-Hur endures hardship, the exposure of Heston's unblemished body, either in the galleys or the arena, lends to the ongoing strength and masculinity of his character. Heston was scantily clad throughout much of *Ben-Hur*, and he himself commented that "my costume consists largely of a damp rag" in the galley slave sequences.[41] This partial nudity exaggerates the aura of masculinity surrounding the character. Heston's muscular physique made it entirely believable that Ben-Hur could survive the galleys for two years and subsequently become a champion chariot driver.

Heston, too, recognized the importance of his physique in his films. "Unfortunately I have to make my living partly through my body," he told the *Saturday Evening Post*. "When you are a young actor you're imbued with the high purpose of your art. You think, *they hire me for my talent; if that's not good enough, then they can hire somebody else*. Later you realize that your body is as much a part of what you do as your talent." Heston paid careful attention to his diet and exercised regularly, although not always enthusiastically. He enjoyed tennis and swimming but dreaded calisthenics, calling it "unutterably dreary, boring and unexciting and uninspiring." Heston continued this dedication to exercise throughout his career and deemed it acceptable because, after all, "no one wants a leading man with a pot belly." He and Lydia restricted their diets with Spartan rigor, and he certainly did not mind showing off his hard work. The lead photo for the *Post* article had Heston posed on his deck, feet up, hands behind his head, in a revealing bathing suit, thus establishing his place within Hollywood's beefcake parade. In fact, in a 1981 *This Is Your Life* special on Heston, the host told him: "We've checked on this—this is statistically accurate, that you have appeared sparsely clad in more movies than any other performer with the possible exception of Raquel Welch."[42]

Indeed, Heston's body was so readily on display in *Ben-Hur* that, much to his chagrin, he became something of a homosexual icon because of the role. The homosexual aura of the movie was significantly increased in the mid-1990s when the writer Gore Vidal publicly alleged that, when

Sam Zimbalist hired him to help improve the script, he had written homosexual undertones into the scene depicting the confrontation between Messala and Ben-Hur. Vidal had been hired along with Christopher Fry to elevate the dialogue, Wyler having been particularly displeased with the original scene in which Messala and Ben-Hur swear their vengeance. According to Vidal, he persuaded Zimbalist and Wyler "that the only way one could justify several hours of hatred between two lads—and all those horses—was to establish without saying so in words, an affair between them as boys; then, when reunited at picture's start, the Roman . . . wants to pick up where they left off and the Jew, Heston, spurns him." Vidal claims that Zimbalist, Wyler, and Boyd agreed to this interpretation, but Wyler refused to reveal the changes to Heston for fear that he would "fall apart." Some film analysts have accepted Vidal's version, while others have not. Heston denied Vidal's claims that the writer had fooled him, saying that Vidal "irritates the hell out of me" and that he was "out of his head" for making these assertions. Furthermore, the original writer, Carl Turnberg, Fry, Zimbalist, and Wyler had by this time all died, leaving no one able authoritatively to confirm or refute Vidal's claims. The intent to insert homosexual undertones cannot be proved, but neither can the masculinity, size, and strength of Heston be denied. Indeed, an article by Helen Van Slyke highlights Heston's emotional and physical appeal to both women and men: "It is formidable yet somehow strangely, majestically sexy. There is an inexplicable spiritual/physical attraction about this almost-too-perfect symbol of masculinity. A kind of involuntary magnetism that fascinates both sexes."[43]

Heston drew on both his physical and his acting strengths in his next epic, *El Cid* (Anthony Mann, 1961), the tale of the Spanish knight Rodrigo Diaz de Vivar, who, after suffering great hardship, eventually expels the Moors from Spain. Directly because of these films, millions of people have equated Heston with the moral authority and individualism that such epics celebrate. As Heston boldly told the *Saturday Evening Post:* "You can be sure that they'll be showing *Ben-Hur* somewhere for a long, long time to come. When you add that to *The Ten Commandments*—which passed the fifty-million-dollar admissions mark last January [1960]—before those two pictures have completed their merry-go-round, I'll have been seen by more people than any other actor in the history of the world." This statement was not just boastful swagger. Heston was recognized by millions and was able to strike awe not only into his fans but also into journalists, politicians, and even potentates. Heston's resonance in these epics is so dramatic that a journalist commented in 1978: "The standard Hollywood gag is that if God came to earth, most moviegoers wouldn't believe it unless he looked like Charlton Heston."[44]

HESTON WAS EVEN MORE CONVINCING in these epic roles because of his upstanding personal life. The credibility of both *The Ten Commandments* and *Ben-Hur* rested on a believable star in terms of a sense of morality. Heston's home life was amazingly free of scandal, and, therefore, his playing a biblical prophet—as opposed to someone like Kirk Douglas, whose sexual conquests were a matter of public knowledge—seemed credible. The actor's personal life and film career worked together to create his public image, and he seemed to revel in domestic bliss. The Hollywood press took note of his loving marriage even before the release of *The Ten Commandments*. *Photoplay* published "human interest" articles on the Hestons in 1953 and 1954, the titles of which underscored the romantic themes on which they played—"Charlton Loves Lydia" and "Their Marriage Is a Lifetime Honeymoon." The Hestons were famous for their preference to stay at home rather than make the rounds of the Hollywood party scene. No longer as antisocial as at the Senior Ball, Heston did recognize the need to acquaint himself with the industry's social scene and keep himself on the social radar. He did so but "was always uncomfortable with it," he admitted. "I still am. I don't like parties with hundreds of people: I tend to wander off and read the titles on the spines of books in the library, if there is a library. . . ." When on location, he did not care to engage in much of a nightlife, especially when he had to rise for an early call. This self-isolation did not lend to a particularly flattering reputation among the Hollywood partying crowd. According to one journalist: "Compared with Frank Sinatra and his friends, [Heston] is thought of pretty much as a cube. . . . Over the years, . . . [he] has acquired the reputation of being a rather pompous bonehead." Not that the Hestons had no social life. They would just rather socialize with a few close friends in a small setting. Jolly and Kathryn West, Walter and Mickey Seltzer, and William and Tallie Wyler were part of that circle.[45]

Lydia further contributed to the Hestons' domestic image when she consciously chose childrearing and put her husband's career over her own. Although she performed on Broadway and occasionally took small film roles in Los Angeles, such as in *Bad for Each Other* (Irving Rapper, 1953) with her husband, Lydia divulged to *Photoplay* that, although she wanted to "make it," she refused to sign a long-term contract for fear that she could not be with Heston at times of importance. Her career became more complicated after the birth of their son, Fraser (Fray for short), in 1955 and Heston's immense success, for Lydia did not want her work to interfere with either one. For Lydia, there seemed to be no question between a baby and a career. She told *Parents* magazine: "It's not that we put off having children so I could go on acting. It's just that we didn't have any and that's why I went on acting." The decision between her career and Heston's appeared almost as easy. A pivotal moment came in 1959 after Lydia had accepted a film offer but then hesitated on discovering that the location would prevent her from attending the royal premier of *Ben-Hur* in London. Heston recorded Lydia's exchange with her agent over the matter and her decision to commit herself to the domestic life: "'Look, honey,' her agent said, 'you've got to decide whether you want to act or go to Chuck's premiers.' 'All right then,' my girl replied, 'I'll go to Chuck's premieres.'" Heston also notes that this story is "unfashionable" but goes on to say: "I've always felt complimented by it."[46]

Because of Lydia's decision and Heston's financial success, the couple launched into their domestic bliss with style, publicizing their domesticity in features in *American Home* and *Look* magazines after the family moved into their dream home in Coldwater Canyon in 1960. High on a ridge, the Hestons' property comprises only three acres. However, in the spirit of Chuck's boyhood home, the acreage is surrounded on both sides by eight hundred acres of government-owned land, occupied by deer, hawks, raccoons, and other wildlife. A spectacular view includes Catalina Island to the west and Mount Jupiter, which is fifty miles east into the desert. These rustic surroundings shielded the Hestons from the growth of Beverly Hills. Inspired by the fountains of Rome, the Hestons created a cobbled court with a fountain and a pool along with several sundecks and patios and a tennis court. Inside, the house features a Jacuzzi, a gym, a library, and a screening room. Its tall ceilings can even accommodate the ten-foot top of the mature blue spruce imported from their property in Michigan every Christmas. Impressed with the Hestons' creation, *Look* lauded the "showplace" as "one of the finest examples of architecture in the U.S." The adoption of a baby girl, Holly, in 1962 completed the Heston family. Despite the grandeur of their new home, Lydia did not feel as comfortable in California as on the East Coast and "missed New York terribly." The Hestons decided to keep their apartment in New York, holding on to it for eighteen years.[47]

The closeness of the Heston family has been quite remarkable, considering that they lived among the excesses of Hollywood. Many Hollywood histories are plagued with sordid tales of peccadilloes and dysfunction. This was not the case for the Heston family. All appear to have missed each other greatly during their periodic absences, and Lydia and the children accompanied Heston on location as much as possible. Lydia and Fray relocated during the entire shootings of *Ben-Hur* in Rome and *El Cid* in Spain. When, in certain instances, they could not move for such a substantial period of time, they regularly visited for at least a few weeks or weekends. For instance, Lydia came to Rome for a week during the filming of *The Pigeon That Took Rome* (Melville Shavelson, 1962) and to Hawaii for part of the making of *Diamond Head* (Guy Green, 1963). Lydia and Fray even brought Drago, their German shepherd, to Spain when Heston made *55 Days at Peking* (Nicholas Ray, 1963). These visits facilitated closeness among the Heston family, in spite of their far-from-typical lifestyle. Once Fray started school, however, Heston made the note: "We're not quite as footloose a family as we were."[48]

Although they obviously missed each other during separations, the Hestons seemed capable of functioning fairly well under the circumstances. Heston often noted in his journal how happy he was and how blessed he felt because of his family, and he worked to maintain their close relationship. He and Lydia celebrated every anniversary together, no matter the circumstances or the travel required to do so. For example, on their eighteenth wedding anniversary in 1962, Lydia flew to Hawaii, where Heston was shooting *Diamond Head,* and the two celebrated with "champagne and pearls" and "satiated" themselves with "luxury."[49] Heston also strove to spend time with his children. He was able to attend most birthday celebrations and other family rituals like the opening day of hunting season, but he also made it a point to participate in more everyday parental responsibilities like driving his daughter to school or to ballet practice. He also regularly contributed to the children's Halloween costumes, working his connections with Hollywood wardrobe departments.

Despite the pain of long absences from his family, Heston never considered curtailing his work schedule. In fact, over time he became more and more involved in various acting projects as well as public service projects. By the mid-1960s, he seemed almost overcome by his activities. He had grown aware of his need for an active lifestyle early on in his career. He started shooting *Three Violent People* (Rudolph Maté, 1957) before finishing *The Ten Commandments* and set up his own production company, the Russel Lake Corporation, that year as well. He explained: "Actors . . . at any rate this one . . . get nervous about vacations, the hunger I have at the end of several months of sixty hour weeks to just do nothing at all lasts, I find, about two days." This workaholic mentality sometimes compromised the needs of his family, as Heston himself noticed. After Fraser had a tonsillectomy in 1960, Heston did not stay in California long enough to talk to his son after he woke up, nor was he able to help Lydia move into the new Coldwater Canyon house. Instead, he flew to New York and began rehearsals for Benn W. Levy's *The Tumbler,* a play with Laurence Olivier. He felt guilty and asked himself: "What am I doing, going off to do a play when my house and my son, not to mention my wife, need me here?" He contemplated: "I doubt if I can be both a family man and a dedicated artist." And his conclusion: "I'd rather be the former." His declaration of dedication to his family and his guilt notwithstanding, Heston did not change his plans or fly back to California. He explained in his autobiography: "But I had no choice. I had Olivier and a company waiting for me. I *had* to be there." Obviously, he did have a choice, but, in addition to his family, he also felt a responsibility to the project to which he had committed. Furthermore, it *was* Laurence Olivier, considered one of the world's most formidable actors. Heston made a serious effort to be the best family man he could, but he did so in a context in which his work and public involvement stole much of his time.[50]

To an outside observer, it does not appear that Heston's work was compromised in the least, but this judgment is relative. Heston maintained a rigorous view of his profession. "Acting, taken to the highest level, requires a fierce, total focus of your time and energy, at the cost of just about everything else," he argued. Although he admitted to compromising his family's needs at times, he also felt that he compromised his career—at least the quality of the films in which he chose to appear—for his family. He believed that he often fell "short of [the] draconian demand" that acting required. For example, when making *Pigeon,* he insisted that the interiors be shot in Hollywood, even though they would have been better and cheaper in Rome, so that he could return to his family. Perhaps Heston did allow his personal life to get in the way of complete dedication to each and every acting job, but his outlook is colored by the fact that he was critical, sometimes fanatically, of almost every film he made. He admitted: "I've almost never been content with what I've done in any film. My heart's desire would be to do them all over again (and not do a half-dozen of them at all)." This constant dissatisfaction with his work may have led him to feel as if he compromised his work more than he really did. Most often he gave his full attention to his work over his family. Nevertheless, his workaholic temperament was part of his personality, and the Heston family found a way to accommodate itself to his busy schedule.

Over time, Heston's lifestyle did take its toll on his family, however, most acutely on Lydia, when in the early 1970s she began to suffer from painful, frequent migraines. At least one writer blamed those migraines on Heston's demanding work schedule. There is little doubt that his absences played a role in her health problems. However, to charge Heston of being "egocentrically concerned with his own career" and imply his sole responsibility for the migraines is irresponsible.[51] Lydia herself blamed her feelings on California and the Hollywood social scene. She told one interviewer: "When I came out here, I began to disintegrate. I was deeply depressed by Hollywood and hated everyone, the atmosphere, the climate." Meanwhile, she had taken up a new artistic interest. When Heston made *The Greatest Show on Earth,* Lydia teamed up with the movie's public relations man and learned the basics of photography. Immediately taken with her new interest, Lydia turned out to be a natural, publishing and selling several of her photographs, and eventually launching a career in the field.

However, the demands of motherhood did not allow Lydia to become a professional photographer just yet, and her acting roles steadily declined. Hollywood became more and more of a depressing place for her. Not necessarily threatened by her husband's success, Lydia felt: "I was not doing anything. I didn't like being Mrs. Charlton Heston. I was Lydia Clarke." She continued: "The Hollywood scene is very bad for many women in this situation. It has to do with what the woman feels about her own self-confidence, but I do feel the Hollywood wife is the lowest rung on the social ladder. I felt entirely superfluous, even though I had the photography." Furthermore, a number of dramatic changes engulfed the family, and Heston's schedule became increasingly demanding. Between 1971 and 1973, the worst years of Lydia's migraines, her father died, Holly underwent adolescence, Fray left for college, and Heston made seven films while simultaneously working actively with the National Endowment for the Arts, the American Film Institute, and the Screen Actors Guild. In addition, Lydia continued to assist Heston with his career by hosting or attending parties and helping him with speeches. After *Julius Caesar* (Stuart Burge, 1970) and *The Hawaiians* (Tom Gries, 1970) nose-dived at the box office, Heston put considerable pressure on himself. Lydia, in turn, eased the pressure by doing as much as possible to support him. All this cut into her time to be a photographer, and, as she later remembered: "When I was not working and had the feeling that my work was getting away from me, the celebrity-wife pressures just seemed too much." Undoubtedly, these outside pressures and Heston's absences contributed to Lydia's migraines, but her own feelings of insecurity underlay her depression. She always believed that a woman should be "complete within herself" and was "disgusted" for allowing herself to be depressed. She then entered a hospital the following year. On her entrance, Heston wrote:

"This turned out to be one of the worst days of my life, I believed Lydia would leave me."[52]

Although Lydia's condition obviously concerned and distressed Heston, he never scaled back his work in terms of film, theater, or public service. His behavior may seem cruel in light of the pain Lydia suffered. However, the situation was something that Lydia had to handle herself. Heston may have been obtuse in his comprehension of Lydia's migraines, but he did not discourage her when she attempted to develop her burgeoning photography career. He encouraged her involvement in outside work—from acting jobs to photography—all of which were clearly contributing factors in overcoming her migraines. Lydia herself revealed what returned her to health: "The main element that has cured me is constant exercise, which I have just begun in the last couple of years." When Heston published his journal in 1978, he announced: "Miraculously, Lydia has not had migraines now for more than a year. Her photographic career burgeoning with jobs and exhibitions; she again is the girl she always was, beneath the pain." Indeed, by 1980, Lydia had shown her work in galleries in Taiwan, Chicago, and San Francisco. During their stay in Egypt when Heston was working on *The Awakening* (Mike Newell, 1980), Lydia shot photographs of the desert for a Los Angeles charity function to benefit the Retinitis Pigmentosa Foundation, one of the Heston's preferred philanthropies.[53]

After all the struggles with her identity, Lydia confided: "I am happy to say I feel very complete." But she also wished that she had not allowed "time in life for that kind of waste emotionally." Despite her regrets, Lydia's experience is not much different from what faced millions of women of her generation. Betty Friedan's *The Feminine Mystique* (1963) touched the emotions of millions of women like Lydia who felt that they were living in a "comfortable concentration camp" with no identity of their own and who had been blaming themselves for their feelings. Friedan's book convinced many that their unhappiness was a social problem, not just a personal problem, and urged women to seek personal development and work for social change. Although Lydia never became involved in the feminist movement, she did initiate individual action and take control of her life.

Not only did her migraines disappear, but the Hestons' marriage continued to be remarkably strong. In 2004, the couple celebrated their sixtieth
wedding anniversary. His aides note how much Heston dotes on his wife.[54]
The Heston family stood out in Hollywood for its longevity and closeness,
and this relationship contributed to the believability of the epic characters
he played.

Heston's personal religious beliefs also added credibility to his epic
characters. Heston was an Episcopalian and Lydia a Congregationalist.
The Heston family had attended church until, ironically, the release of *The
Ten Commandments*. After that, Heston felt that his presence at services
caused too much commotion and was distracting to the other worship-
pers. Thereafter, the Heston family rarely attended church. The actor actually displayed a rather earthy flair, and reporters sometimes noted their
surprise at Heston's penchant for cursing. Still, Heston remained a spiritual man, and he greatly respected religious traditions. He particularly enjoyed the historical aspects of the Christian faith. More recently, Heston
and Fraser collaborated on *Charlton Heston Presents the Bible* (Tony West-
man, 1997), a dramatic portrayal of various Bible stories, the project growing out of Heston's reverence for the intriguing scenarios presented in that
book.

Heston's upstanding personal life helped him win the role of Moses,
which became his signature character. Although he went on to do a variety of different roles—some great men, some average—all had heroic capabilities and the sense of authority and independence that he had
established as Moses and Ben-Hur. As Heston himself observed: "If one
carefully examines every one of my . . . films, a central theme runs through
the majority of them. . . . Almost all the characters I've played are men with
an individual sense of total dedication and responsibility which motivates
their triumphs." Heston enjoyed good timing with his start on live television and then with Hollywood's reaction to the new medium—the production of epic historical dramas in the late 1950s and the 1960s. Such fortune
struck again in the mid-1960s when Heston emerged, in a variety of films,
as Hollywood's modern-day action hero, a role that would become his standard through the 1970s. Even when Heston did not play larger-than-life

characters like Moses, Ben-Hur, and El Cid, he did play a number of different heroic types. Although the genres would vary—historical epics, science fiction, and westerns, to name a few—common themes of individualism and heroism ran throughout Heston's roles. By the 1980s, he had earned a position as one of Hollywood's "elder statesman," appearing in a number of cameo roles as a moral, authoritative figure.[55]

Superstardom such as Heston achieved with *The Ten Commandments* and *Ben-Hur* was the most visible aspect of the movie industry by the 1950s. Certain actors were becoming recognized worldwide, and their public images eclipsed the very films that made them famous. Fans eagerly gobbled up not only the stars' movies but aspects of their private lives as well. According to one historian, the obsession with celebrity made it increasingly possible for stars to "take on both a wider public life and to make a more profound emotional impact on the individual's inner life than had ever been possible."[56] After the birth of superstardom, actors increasingly felt comfortable turning their sights to politics.

By virtue of his screen persona, Heston embodied a type of politics even before he voiced his opinion on particular issues. As one journalist commented: "Charlton Heston is the epitome of the star who stands for moral certainties and patriotic beliefs that characterized Hollywood in its heyday." Likewise, another reporter explained that Heston is "able to impart . . . a heroic, broad-shouldered presence to movies and real-life issues." Heston's screen image represented a politics of large meanings that transcended particular issues, beyond the *conservative* or *liberal* label. The traits that he personified onscreen—masculinity, individuality, patriotism, responsibility, and morality—all translated easily to his life in public service.[57]

Sixteen of Heston's movies have been box office champions, and he starred in both blockbusters and cult hits, but one critic notes that, as an actor, he had a "questionable" personal following. Audiences appreciated his movies but did not necessarily attend just to see him. In fact, Heston's acting style—appropriate for epic presentations like *The Ten Commandments* and *Ben-Hur*—was often criticized for its "slowly paced, long, outdated melodramatic approach" and lack of spark.[58] Although Heston delivered critically acclaimed performances in such movies as *Will Penny* and in numerous stage productions, he shined in more solitary roles and was, thus, associated with epic films often panned by today's critics. Ironically, it was in the political arena that Heston acquired a truly devoted following.

After the release of *The Ten Commandments* in 1956, Heston capitalized on his screen image and established his credibility in the political realm. His conscientious work in the public arena over the second half of the twentieth century further contributed to his development into a powerful political persona. Heston first became involved in public affairs in the mid-1950s and rapidly turned into a genuine activist, working in a variety of different arenas, including the Screen Actors Guild, the Democratic Party, the National Endowment for the Arts, and, later, the Republican Party and the National Rifle Association. His hard work paid off. A poll conducted in 1996 revealed that Americans considered Heston to be one of the most believable spokespersons in the country.[59] Indeed, becoming a political activist was as much a part of Heston's public identity as playing Moses.

CHAPTER TWO

COLD WAR LIBERAL

In the early years of his film career, Heston believed that actors and politics should not mix, seemingly unconvinced that celebrities could make any legitimate contribution to the political debate. After he was cast as Moses, however, he changed his mind and felt that it was his duty as a citizen to "stand up and be counted" on public issues. In 1955, he began to make small forays into politics and by 1961 could be considered a genuine activist and leader. Over the course of the 1960s, he became involved in a number of activities, participating in the emerging civil rights movement and two Democratic administrations. Thereafter, he encouraged all Americans, including his fellow thespians, to exercise their full rights as citizens—that is, as long as they educated themselves fully on the issues before going on the record.

The 1960s signaled a new wave of celebrity activism in America; Heston assumed a leading role in this trend but differentiated himself from his more liberal colleagues. Indeed, Heston's conservative inclinations became quite clear. He admired John F. Kennedy primarily for his hawkish Cold War stance, and, although he believed strongly in equal rights for minorities, he remained suspicious of the coordinated group effort that characterized the campaigns for racial justice. Even though both the Democratic Party and the civil rights movement harbored noticeable radical elements, in the late 1950s and 1960s both coalitions were actually dominated by conservative leaders who proposed moderate policies acceptable to Heston. Heston acted on instinct, as opposed to partisan loyalty, in his conservative approach, and, as has been noted, often came to conclusions similar to those of intellectuals like Irving Kristol, Norman Podhoretz, and others who would, by 1968, be considered *neoconservatives.* In acting out his own conservative inclinations, Heston gave shape to their ideas and, subsequently, paved the way for *visceral neoconservatism.*

THE HOLLYWOOD-WASHINGTON CONNECTION was first established in the 1920s, changes in Hollywood itself allowing the partnership to blossom. The first development was Hollywood's elevation of its actors through the star system, a practice firmly in place by the 1920s. This celebrated attention to the stars challenged the long-standing supposition that actors were untrustworthy characters of ill repute. With the elevation of the actor's status, stars would subsequently be considered legitimate contributors to political campaigns. The second change in Hollywood was Louis B. Mayer's ascension as the production chief at MGM in 1924. Mayer felt that, even though the movie business was amassing more financial support than ever, New York City's financial district and the nation's capital still considered it a frivolous enterprise. Furthermore, as a Jew, Mayer did not enjoy complete access to America's social and financial institutions. He could not consistently accrue enough money to create the kind of movies he desired, so he turned to the national political scene in the hopes of improving his status as a movie executive and, in turn, raising more money for his film projects.[1]

The first to court national politicians systematically, Mayer campaigned for then presidential candidate Herbert Hoover in 1928, becoming involved in the California Republican Party. Mayer's efforts were rewarded when he and his wife were honored as President Hoover's first dinner guests in the White House. Mayer paved the way for "mogul politics" and led other film industry executives into the GOP. The moguls rushed to support the party in 1934 when the socialist author turned Democratic gubernatorial candidate Upton Sinclair challenged Governor Frank Merriam of California. Sinclair's call for higher state taxes prompted the moguls to pressure their actors, who were all under contract, to appear in radio programs and newsreels for Merriam's campaign.[2] This tactic backfired, however, when Sinclair lost the election and Merriam unexpectedly raised taxes anyway.

Still reeling from pay cuts that the studios had enacted during the banking crisis of 1933, writers and actors who had been corralled into the Merriam campaign retaliated, unleashing a grassroots leftist surge against the studio fathers. Thereafter, actors more willingly struck out on their own in political matters. Some artists even moved into the Communist Party, the opposite ideological extreme from the moguls' conservatism. Although the Communists never achieved numerical superiority in any of Hollywood's influential circles, the Party did dominate the liberal political scene. Party members actually controlled the leadership of the entertainment industry's largest political organization, the Motion Picture Democratic Committee. This takeover exemplified the Party's strategy of bringing together all leftist elements—from liberals to socialists to orthodox trade unionists—into a loose grouping known as the Popular Front. Writers and actors who were exasperated with the politically claustrophobic studio system found themselves especially attracted to the Front. When the California Democratic Party did not effectively regroup after Sinclair's loss, elements of the Front quickly moved to fill the void. The Popular Front successfully accelerated the film community's political engagement—recruiting figures who probably would have remained politically disconnected—and called public attention to the dangers of fascism.[3]

The Front worked throughout the war years and became a force in the Democratic Party, despite some fundamental differences between Communists and liberals. For example, the Front agreed on the goal of free political expression, but many liberals disapproved of the Communist hostility to capitalism and the Party's defense of Joseph Stalin, despite compelling rumors that he had ordered the widespread purge of Russian peasants. Furthermore, the formation of the House Un-American Activities Committee (HUAC) in the spring of 1938 prompted some wary Hollywood leftists to disassociate from the Front. The German-Soviet nonaggression pact, signed in August 1939, infuriated the remaining "fellow travelers," finally breaking the already precarious alliance between the Communist Party and Hollywood's liberals and greatly weakening the appeal of the Popular Front. The tension between liberals and Communists dissipated after Hitler's invasion of the Soviet Union, which made the Communist state once again an enemy of fascism. With the United States, Great Britain, and the Soviet Union allied against Hitler's Germany, liberals and Communists renewed the Popular Front strategy, operating under the auspices of the Hollywood Democratic Committee (HDC). The Democratic National Committee (DNC) enthusiastically recruited them to campaign for the incumbent president, Franklin D. Roosevelt, in 1944. Entertainers such as Douglas Fairbanks Jr., Humphrey Bogart, Henry Fonda, Groucho Marx, and Lucille Ball performed in radio broadcasts paid for by the DNC in the week before the election. In response, the screenwriter James McGuinness and a small band of conservatives in Hollywood formed the so-called Alliance, which included the future Screen Actors Guild (SAG) president Robert Montgomery, the gossip columnist Hedda Hopper, Mayer, and the director Cecil B. DeMille. The Roosevelt campaign, however, "became a maelstrom that engulfed Hollywood." Noteworthy stars such as Frank Sinatra and Orson Welles contributed sizable amounts of time and money to FDR's campaign. The DNC actually found it difficult to utilize all the celebrities who volunteered.[4]

The Popular Front effectively collapsed after Roosevelt's death in 1945, tainting celebrity activism in the process. The Communist Party's overt control of the HDC—which had joined with the Eastern-based Independent Citizens Committee of the Arts, Sciences, and Professions to form the Hollywood Independent Citizens Committee of the Arts, Sciences, and Professions (HICCASP)—drove away many moderates. For instance, the actor Ronald Reagan abandoned HICCASP, citing the "seamy side of liberalism" and especially the "ideological myopia" that prevented liberals from seeing Communists as they really were. The Popular Front had disintegrated by 1946 and splintered into a number of different groups. Even so, a new HUAC chair, Representative J. Parnell Thomas (R-NJ), was determined to hold hearings in 1947 to root out Communists in Hollywood. The committee found few remaining leftist sympathizers and uncovered none of the systematic subversion that it had alleged. However, the hearings intimidated liberal activists when a group of screenwriters and one director, famously known as the Hollywood Ten, refused to cooperate and were cited for contempt.[5] Furthermore, the publicity surrounding the hearings put the entire movie industry on the defensive.

Attempting to deflect accusations of being unpatriotic, studio executives responded by collectively blacklisting supposed Communist sympathizers, thus discouraging the political activism of the industry's stars. Likewise, SAG voted to require loyalty oaths from its members in order to insulate the organization from allegations of Communist sympathies as well as infiltration. Some stars, directors, and writers, such as William Wyler, Danny Kaye, Gene Kelly, Humphrey Bogart, and Lauren Bacall, formed the Committee for the First Amendment and traveled to Washington, DC, to defend the Hollywood Ten publicly. Having underestimated the resolve of Congress, the stars left the nation's capital defeated. Although SAG acted to protect its members in terms of jobs, the blacklist effectively stifled mass political organizing in Hollywood. Senator Joseph McCarthy (R-WI) further inhibited political activism after he rose to national power on his self-proclaimed campaign to destroy American communism. The actor Lauren Bacall recalled that, even "five years after the House Un-American Activities Committee investigations . . . with the McCarthy fear, Hollywood seemed terrorized." Thereafter, political activity in Hollywood was sporadic, often dependent on random celebrities who formed temporary groups in support of a particular cause or candidate.[6] Most celebrities reined in their political activity, contenting themselves with supporting presidential candidates every national election cycle, a relatively safe manner of participation.

The milieu of presidential electoral politics was actually better suited to most actors anyway. Celebrities looked for meaningful ways to get involved, yet they were also used to being stars, the centers of attention and the focus of publicity. While grassroots organizing required thankless effort, presidential campaign work involved high-profile appearances. Celebrities still donated their valuable time and personas, but national campaigns were more in line with what they craved. Lauren Bacall, the

Democratic presidential candidate Adlai Stevenson's leading Hollywood supporter, commented in her memoirs how the campaign experience allowed her to move beyond the life of a Hollywood leading lady: "My choices up to then had been Bogie [her husband, Humphrey Bogart] or work—now they had expanded to political life, to bettering the world and its people, or at least to advancing and being connected with a great man who was capable of doing something about it." Bacall traveled extensively for Stevenson, putting considerable time and effort into the campaign. Yet her work for the Democratic Party was hardly that of the typical volunteer campaigner. Her main role was to attract crowds. She was always in close proximity to Stevenson, in his motorcade, onstage, and even at his house anticipating the returns. "I got very pushy," she admitted. "No one who didn't have to be was allowed ahead of me in the motorcade!"[7] Indeed, politicians like Stevenson validated celebrities as vital members of their entourage, and celebrities soon became a crucial facet of the modern presidential campaign.

Heston chose to work for the Democrats during the height of his film career, but he never registered as a member of the Democratic Party. Like the intellectual neocons, Heston supported the Democrats less from party loyalty than from personal political inclinations, views that had matured by 1960 and that his own wife characterized as "very conservative." Heston's political disposition was strikingly similar to the ideas professed by the intellectual neocons at the time, despite the lack of an actual relationship between them. Both Heston and the intellectual neocons emphasized religious and racial tolerance and strong anticommunism as well as self-responsibility, independence, and equality of opportunity. The paths leading them to such conclusions differed, however. Heston's ideology evolved from his background; being a "hick from the woods," according to the actor, allowed him to form a tolerant personality and to develop the independent streak that rural living necessitated. The ideologies of the intellectual neocons derived, on the other hand, from their radical political backgrounds. Irving Kristol and his allies had been drawn to socialism in their youth. Kristol and Gertrude Himmelfarb met at the Trotsky Club of the City College of New York. Kristol considered his Trotskyism an "excellent education in communism" because he quickly realized the evils of the ideology. He and Himmelfarb left the group within a year and soon married.[8] By the 1950s, Heston and the rest of the neocons reached similar conclusions on a number of political matters, and, at that point, their conservative philosophies fit easily with the party for which they were voting.

Heston explained the development of his self-described "tolerant" personality in "Other Faces, Other Faiths," a speech that he composed while filming *The Ten Commandments*. He primarily addressed religious prejudice, but he alluded to racial discrimination as well, warning against "a dread disease . . . bigotry." Growing up in the Michigan woods, he explained, "inoculated" him because "men came in only one pattern . . . white Protestant." Thus, he learned to judge people for their actions, not their appearance, and maintained an innocence about difference. "White pines do not look down on yellow pines . . . the tamarack does not discriminate against the maple," he wrote. When he moved to Chicago: "The vaccination had apparently taken. There must have been many examples of prejudice around me, but the group and race labels that prompted them were never very clear to me. As far as I was concerned, . . . it never occurred to me to take into account where he worshipped, or how . . . or even whether!" Religious or racial difference meant little; strength of character represented the true distinction between men.[9]

As Jews, the intellectual neocons encouraged tolerance as well; as children of immigrant urban families, however, they tended to note the differences among ethnic and racial groups more than Heston did. They were very aware of the tensions among such groups and tended to view the liberal hope for a "color-blind" society as naive. In fact, Norman Podhoretz made it clear that he did not believe that integration could ever be fully achieved. Podhoretz provoked controversy with the article "My Negro Problem—and Ours," in which he described his own unpleasant childhood experience with integration. He told stories of how he had been persecuted by blacks, how he and his friends "had been repeatedly beaten up, robbed, and in general hated, terrorized, and humiliated."[10] Because of these unpleasant memories, Podhoretz had no illusions about the difficulties of integration, despite his support of the civil rights movement. He also had little sympathy for the calls for revolution or black nationalism articulated by Malcolm X and James Baldwin, individuals Heston also regarded with suspicion. Both Heston and the intellectual neocons would go on to call for a balance between integration and the retention of specific cultural values, without, as Podhoretz put it, trading one's past for present gain. Ralph Ellison particularly influenced Podhoretz in formulating this position, whereas Heston would be influenced by his contact with various elements of the civil rights movement.

Both Heston and the intellectual neocons also emphasized the importance of self-responsibility and independence in developing a healthy and resolute character, a necessity for both private and public life. Heston's allegiance to responsibility was obvious in his choice of movie roles. Moses, Ben-Hur, and El Cid all personified individual accountability. An advertisement for *El Cid* proclaimed, "We live today in an age that avoids personal responsibility," but praised the Spanish king for doing just the opposite. Heston frequently echoed the El Cid worldview, telling one journalist: "I think the most important thing a man must learn is to fulfill his responsibilities, and that he is responsible for whatever happens to him. He cannot blame others for what happens to him. That is the easy way out." Heston warned that those who ignore self-responsibility tend to slip into self-pity—"the least admired and the most common of all qualities." One Kristol disciple, Robert Bork, would share Heston's disgust, calling self-pity "arguably the most pervasive and powerful emotion known to man."[11]

Heston elaborated that the movie heroes he portrayed undertook responsibility not just for their own well-being but "for a wider and wider area around [them]." Heston's emphasis on being responsible for oneself as well as for the larger community illustrated the neoconservative belief in the interaction between the individual and the larger world. The intellectual neocons particularly stressed the need for "mediating structures," or, more common to the visceral neoconservative's vernacular, private voluntary organizations such as unions, churches, families, schools, and charitable associations. Mediating structures were felt to be important for three reasons. First, they instill the bourgeois values of tradition and responsibility. Second, they allow for a healthy balance between the individual and the community; they promote self-interest as well as the common good. Third, strong mediating structures guard against large government, the groups themselves fulfilling needs in a more localized and efficient manner than the state ever could. Neoconservatives believed that the political order could not survive without mediating structures and people willing to get involved in them.[12] Indeed, Kristol warned that, without mediating structures, a moral vacuum opened, driving restless Americans to find meaning in unexpected and dangerous places.

While the neoconservatives recognized the importance of connecting with the larger community, they also felt a strong pull toward independence. Heston instinctively resisted large-scale government action. Always a loner, he admitted that he "truly [felt] a very, very . . . deep yearning for an earlier time." He favored a "do-it-yourself" culture and worried that Americans were becoming "passive" as they rushed to the suburbs and engorged their lives with consumer products. Heston purchased land in his home state of Michigan because he felt that rural living required more initiative and effort. "I really feel a strong sense of identification with the woods, still," he explained, because of the "sense of . . . independence" to be gained there. In 1960, he worried that the trappings of the modern age stole the independence of even rural dwellers. "Even if you do live in the country, you can't be your own man there. . . . Your life is largely shaped by the increasing network of rules and regulations," he complained. "I'm not an anarchist, but I am afraid we are rapidly approaching a time when every breath we draw will be tagged and numbered . . . and assigned to us before birth." The intellectual neocons resisted the growth of government as well. They believed that large structures ran the risk not only of minimizing individuals but also of alienating them. Driving Americans into indifference ran counter to their goal of community involvement. Heston and the other neoconservatives valued a vibrant government but encouraged policies that allowed maximum independence.[13]

Heston found other trends of modern living oppressive as well. The pressure that Americans put on themselves to "keep up with the Jones's" could be just as suffocating as an overbearing government. In his newsletter, Heston complained about the homogenization of American life, "a world being crushed by conformity," and deplored that "every man's dearest wish seems increasingly to be as much like his neighbor as possible . . . to have everything that he has and like only what he likes." Heston did not disdain the middle class. He clearly favored the bourgeois values of capitalism, religion, and the nuclear family. Within that framework, however, he resisted outright conformity. Podhoretz experienced that same restlessness in 1960. "Bored with my own sensibly moderate liberal ideas, but with Marxism and all its variants closed off as an alternative," Podhoretz itched for a new agenda that would expose the problematic aspects of middleclass culture without relying on a reformist liberal agenda that increased federal power as a remedy.[14] In seeking such a balance, the neoconservatives would be forced to clarify their ideas about equality.

Heston believed deeply in the equality of man, but he also believed that individual talent and actions set people apart from one another. He favored a government that permitted the equality of opportunity but did not pursue the equality of outcome. To a man who worshipped independence, an equality of outcome was neither desirable nor possible. Heston believed that men were created equal but that, after certain rights were secured, it was up to each individual to determine his own destiny. As early as 1960, Heston made his opinions clear on this matter: "I think the founding fathers of the U.S.A. phrased it correctly: Happiness is something to pursue, not to possess. . . . You can't guarantee any man happiness." In his newsletter, Heston pointed out: "In our country, where we think of men as being created equal, there've been a few who started so, but soon grew greater than their fellows and taller than their times." The intellectual neocons showed similar reverence for the founding fathers and made comparable pronouncements about equality. Kristol pointed out that, when the founding fathers said that all men were created equal, they did not mean that everyone was the same. They knew that "inequalities in intelligence, talent, and abilities were there but not extreme enough to justify a society of hereditary privilege," and, therefore, they celebrated the differences in men as a source of excellence.[15]

The final, and perhaps strongest, aspect of the neoconservative view was anticommunism. Heston did not hesitate in revealing his strong anti-Communist stance. A man with such fervor for the qualities of self-reliance, independence, and equality of opportunity could not plausibly accept communism as a viable solution to the world's problems. Communism stressed equality of outcome and elevated the community over the individual. Heston viewed such a doctrine as anathema to his very being. His anticommunism hardened when he toured East Berlin in July 1961. As one of the last Americans to travel relatively freely there, Heston wrote in his journal that the Communist city was "far more memorable than anything else I've seen here [Europe]," adding that "the contrast to West Berlin was horrifying" in terms of economic prosperity and political expression. Only one month after his visit, in August 1961, the Soviets erected the Berlin Wall to halt the exodus of East Germans into West Berlin. Anticommunism remained a central tenet of Heston's political activism as a visceral neoconservative.

Anticommunism remained a cornerstone for the intellectual neocons as well. They considered communism to be the enemy of liberalism and the Soviet Union to be the greatest force of evil on the earth. For example, in 1953, Sidney Hook proclaimed: "It is now plain that the communist regimes of the world have turned out to be the greatest and cruelest heresy hunters in history, not merely in politics but in every branch of theory and practice." Furthermore, intellectual neocons believed that progressives or leftists who tolerated communism were outright fools. In 1954, Kristol warned: "It is a fact that Communism rules one-third of the human race, and may soon rule more; and that it is the most powerful existing institution which opposes such changes and reforms as liberalism proposes." He went on to ask: "Why, then, should not liberals, and liberals especially, fear and hate it?"[16] Throughout the 1950s and 1960s, the neoconservatives continued to warn their fellow liberals to remain vigilant against communism.

In fact, Kristol even went so far as to defend Joseph McCarthy, America's chief Communist hunter and also its most controversial. McCarthy's ascent to national prominence began on February 9, 1950, when he declared in a speech in Wheeling, West Virginia, to have a list of 250 people in the State Department known to be members of the American Commu-

nist Party. McCarthy rarely had the evidence to substantiate his accusations. Still, his claims resonated with the American public, and, in fact, the
senator was only exploiting an anti-Communist network, including HUAC
and the federal Loyalty Program instituted by President Harry Truman,
that was already in place. The discovery of several high-profile spies, including Alger Hiss, a former State Department official, and Klaus Fuchs, a
British physicist involved in America's nuclear program, seemed to legitimate the need for strong anti-Communist policies. However, some liberals, calling themselves anti-anti-Communists, defended Hiss and attacked
McCarthy. An incredulous Kristol derided them as "apologists." In fact, he
applauded the American public, with whom McCarthy enjoyed widespread support until 1954: "For there is one thing that the American people
know about Senator McCarthy: he, like them, is unequivocally anti-Communist. About which the spokesmen for American liberalism, they feel
they know no such thing. And with some justification."[17]

Despite his spirited defense of the Republican McCarthy, Kristol and
the neoconservatives generally voted for Democrats during the 1950s and
1960s and supported the party's brand of Cold War liberalism. The party's
philosophy had actually moved to the right during World War II and the
Cold War that rose in its aftermath when the Democratic leaders replaced
New Deal liberalism with a more conservative agenda. One area in which
this rightward shift immediately materialized was in economic policy. Rejecting the early New Dealers' restraint of big business, postwar Democrats patterned themselves after Franklin D. Roosevelt's post-1937 cabinet
and continued to encourage the cooperation among government, business,
and labor that World War II had necessitated. They adhered to the economic principles of the British economist John Maynard Keynes, first adopted by
FDR after the 1937 recession, as their formula for economic growth. Keynes
argued that governments should utilize fiscal policy, or taxing and spending,
to promote economic expansion, a notion that had proved its merits during
World War II. With factories running at full capacity, unemployment was
eradicated, and consumer spending skyrocketed. After the advent of the
Cold War in 1945 and 1946, the mechanism for prosperity remained, and
the government continued to pump money into the economy. The unprec-

edented economic affluence that characterized the postwar years not only made the United States the world's richest nation but also validated Keynesian policy in the eyes of most Americans.

The intellectual neocons accepted the compromise that the postwar Democrats struck between the anticapitalist business approach that had once characterized the party and the laissez-faire free market stance taken by the conservative Republicans. To be sure, Kristol and his allies were not impressed with the Republican Party's "simple economic policy." The neoconservatives accepted the Keynesian approach in the 1950s and 1960s, believing that a certain amount of government intervention in the economy was permissible, even desirable. They also considered pragmatically the relation between business and government. Kristol noted in 1960: "The economy is dominated by an interlocking directorate of Big Business which, while preaching competition and 'free enterprise,' manages things to suit its own convenience and sometimes the common good." Kristol more closely resembled the leading Democrats than most intellectuals in assessing the power of big business. "Unlike my friends on the Left," he noted lightly, "I have not been outraged by this state of affairs, since it always seemed more reasonable to me that something as important as Big Business should be managed by hard-faced professionals than by, say, the editors of *The New Left Review*."[18]

The neocons also applauded Democratic internationalism. Although liberal and conservative Democrats struggled over how best to handle the Soviet Union, the hard-liners prevailed in designing the Cold War policies that came to be known as *containment*. As early as 1946, President Truman had characterized the Soviet Union as an aggressive threat. In 1947, in pledging to give military support to the monarchy of Greece, he announced the Truman Doctrine, committing American support to any and all nation-states fighting Communist encroachment. The majority of Democrats supported Truman's stance, and liberal organizations quickly made their opposition to communism a prominent element of their platforms. For instance, Americans for Democratic Action advocated more liberal economic and civil rights policies at home but just as forcefully called for strong anticommunism in international and domestic affairs.

Finally, the Democratic commitment to expanding equal opportunity also drew in the neoconservatives. The Democrats believed that promoting overall economic growth would do the most toward achieving this goal, arguing that "a rising tide would lift all boats." At the same time, the liberal members of the party also pushed for social programs, including an expansion of social security, an increase in the minimum wage, and the provision of housing, that were specifically designed to open up more opportunities for marginalized Americans. The issues of civil rights and racial justice also received unprecedented attention from the Democratic Party in the postwar era. FDR had already persuaded African Americans to join the party fold when he built his New Deal coalition, but the liberal elements of the party wanted to go even further, insisting on a strong civil rights plank similar to that offered by the Republican Party. After Hubert Humphrey, the new Democratic senator from Minnesota, made his fiery appeal to the 1948 national convention, the Democratic Party pledged to commit "itself to continuing its efforts to eradicate all racial, religious, economic discrimination. . . . Racial and religious minorities must have the right to live, the right to work, the right to vote, and the full and equal protection of the laws on a basis of equality with all citizens as guaranteed by the Constitution." Southern Democrats accused the Democratic assembly of trying to "embarrass" their contingent and of practicing "totalitarian" behavior. These so-called Dixiecrats stormed out of the convention to form their own States' Rights Party with South Carolina Governor Strom Thurmond as their candidate.[19] The Democrats survived the Dixiecrat defection, and civil rights became a permanent fixture in the party's agenda, even though the platform itself was weakened during the next election cycle.

In moving to the right on big business and to the left on racial justice, the Democrats made substantial changes in the party, so much so that their policies actually resembled the Republican policies on those issues. Still, important differences existed between the two national parties, distinctions substantial enough that neither Heston nor the rest of the neoconservatives considered the GOP to be a viable alternative. Between the 1940s and the 1960s, the Republican Party had not yet modernized. It seemed overly tied to the business community and to small-town America, and a dearth of intellectualism only added to the party's woes. Furthermore, the Republican leadership had earned a reputation for isolationism and hostility to the New Deal in the 1930s and had difficulty overcoming its dour and old-fashioned image.

In fact, neither Heston nor the rest of the neocons seemed even to consider voting for a Republican presidential candidate, even when the Democrats stumbled and a number of new voices emerged in the GOP. After Truman's stunning victory in 1948, the president struggled in both domestic and international affairs. His Fair Deal never achieved legislative success, and his Loyalty Program was, Republicans charged, utterly ineffective in dealing with Communist subversion at home. Furthermore, his efforts to contain communism in Asia floundered when the Korean War stalemated without an apparent plan for either victory or disengagement. The Democrats' problems multiplied when General Dwight D. Eisenhower, fresh from his impressive command of Allied troops during World War II's D-Day invasion, declared his candidacy for president on the Republican ticket. The popular Ike won in a landslide, marking a rebirth for the GOP at the presidential level, and ushering in a Republican-dominated Congress.

The neocons might have been tempted to start voting Republican as early as 1952 if Eisenhower's nomination had indicated a substantial overhaul of the GOP. Alas, it was quite clear that the Republicans were not yet ready to modernize. Even though important Republicans, like New York Governor Nelson Rockefeller, proved capable of adjusting to the new role of the federal government in the economy and in international affairs, conservative elements of the party did not.[20] They still appeared overly hostile to the federal government, an outdated approach that seemed especially passé in light of the Keynesian success. Furthermore, they took the opposite extreme of their isolationist stance of yesteryear, proclaiming America's need to "roll back," rather than contain, communism, a notion that smacked of irresponsibility in the nuclear age. Therefore, a serious rift opened between the conservative and the moderate liberal wings of the Republican Party, a division that congressional Democrats masterfully exploited. Senator Lyndon Baines Johnson of Texas worked quietly to insert

Democratic language in key portions of Eisenhower's bills. When conservative Republicans fought the proposals, it looked as if they were squabbling with their own president and party. LBJ used such strategies to keep the Republicans divided, regain public favor for the Democrats, and set the mechanisms in place for his own subsequent rise to power. Indeed, by 1954, the Republican Party seemed in danger of imploding when McCarthy finally overreached himself and was censured by his Senate colleagues.[21] In 1956, the Democrats had regained control of Congress and retained the favor of the neoconservatives.

BEFORE HESTON BECAME A SUPERSTAR, he brazenly chastised actors who publicized their political opinions. After the release in 1952 of *The Greatest Show on Earth,* the famed gossip columnist Hedda Hopper quizzed him on the capability of films to provide broader messages beyond sheer entertainment. Heston replied that films should not have that responsibility but that he thought "a good film fulfills both purposes." He drew the line between a "message" and "politics," however, when he clarified: "Of course, if you mean a political message I would say no." Heston considered the silver screen an inappropriate place for partisan jostling and extended that sentiment to include the personal lives of performers. "Incidentally," he elaborated, "I'm supposed to be a rather outspoken individual, but I think actors, on any subject other than their own work, should keep quiet."[22] Considering the state of politics in Hollywood in the mid-1950s, it is not surprising that an up-and-coming actor would voice such an opinion, although it is amusingly contradictory to Heston's later views.

Heston reversed his apolitical stance within only a few years and for a variety of reasons. Hollywood had become a permanent residence for the Hestons, and local issues drew him into the political scene. After he was cast in *The Ten Commandments,* his status as an international star resulted in more publicity and more questions about his political views, questions that he increasingly felt comfortable answering. The heightened publicity also necessitated more mingling with the entertainment community, which itself became increasingly political after John F. Kennedy won the Democratic nomination for president in 1960. Furthermore, SAG asked

Heston to be on its board in 1960. This service exposed him to issues that he may not previously have considered and to a more politically minded group of colleagues. It appears that, because of these influences, Heston simply changed his mind about the appropriateness of actors in the political arena. He now began to view political activism as a responsibility. He told one filmographer that political engagements "are, you know, just things that everyone who is fortunate enough to have a successful career should undertake in my opinion."[23]

Heston made his first political statement with a letter to his local government. In February 1955, he appealed to the mayor of Los Angeles for a memorial in honor of the late Thomas Edison, proposing that the city enact the necessary legislation, and even offering his own monetary contribution to set the project in motion. "It is appalling," he wrote, "that nowhere in all Los Angeles—the world capital of the motion picture industry—is there a single lasting memorial to the man who invented the motion picture camera and projector."[24] It is not evident what accounted for Heston's zeal over a rather trivial issue. However, his encouragement of an Edison memorial expressed his willingness to use his name to influence government and his penchant for dramatic rhetoric.

As the press paid more attention to him, Heston was increasingly willing to discuss both politics and religion, revealing in the process ideas similar to those being cultivated by other neocons in the making. The media hype surrounding *The Ten Commandments* included multiple interviews in which Heston described the making of the epic and pontificated on the biblical prophet Moses' influence on the United States. Heston told one journalist that Americans owed their independence to Moses, arguing that the philosophies of the founding fathers stemmed from Moses' own beliefs in equality. In true neoconservative fashion, he encouraged posting the Ten Commandments in classrooms and in public buildings. He called the proposal "a fine idea" because the commandments promoted the "secular behavior of everybody not just in church," presumably meaning that one did not have to be a Christian to appreciate these standards. Heston's willingness to inject religious principles into the public arena mirrored that of the neoconservatives. They believed that politics could not survive without morality and that morality is derived primarily from Judeo-Christian beliefs, specifically from the principles laid out in the Ten Commandments. Kristol unhesitatingly claimed: "A profound consensus on moral and political principles is the first condition for a decent society."[25] Both Heston and the intellectual neocons would go on to make similar assertions over the course of their public careers.

The neoconservatives continued to support the Democratic Party in the 1956 presidential election. Heston joined with Democrats for Stevenson to campaign in the governor's second ill-fated contest against Eisenhower. His participation was limited, but at the least he signed a published petition indicating his support for the Democratic candidate. Not only did Heston agree with the party platform, but he was also drawn to Stevenson's style, finding him a very attractive speaker. Heston, although he was admittedly "very green" politically, simply found Stevenson the more attractive candidate, as did many of Hollywood's voters.[26] Only a few celebrities campaigned on behalf of Eisenhower, the most famous being John Wayne.

Stevenson's loss did not discourage Heston from participating in more public engagements. When, at Eisenhower's invitation in 1959, Nikita Khrushchev toured the United States, 20th Century Fox held a luncheon for the Soviet premier and expected the leading Hollywood entertainers to attend. Some actors, including Ronald Reagan, refused, stating that such a social gathering implied approval of and friendship with the Soviets. Believing, however, that it was the diplomatic thing to do, Heston opted to attend the luncheon, along with such leading figures as Bob Hope, Jack Benny, and Frank Sinatra. Although none of the men approved of communism in the least, they did not consider themselves compromised simply by meeting Khrushchev. Heston's refusal to join the boycott was a political act in itself. At the very least it indicated his support of President Eisenhower. Even though he had not voted for the president, Heston certainly wanted to support his commander in chief in matters of foreign policy. Snubbing Khrushchev would have been a slight to Eisenhower. In the midst of the Cold War, Heston believed it imperative to present a united front in dealing with the Soviets. This incident was among the first indicators of Heston's willingness to delve into controversial issues and pursue what he believed to be a moderate solution. The intellectual neocons encouraged such conciliation. Podhoretz, for example, "still thought that the Soviet Union was out to conquer the world and that only American power stood in the way" but "that it was up to us to take the initiative."[27] In meeting with Khrushchev, Heston was acting out Podhoretz's sentiments, albeit in a social situation.

In late 1959, members of the Hollywood community voted Heston into his first and only political office, that of honorary mayor of the city. Surprised by the announcement, his reaction to the news gave another clue to his conservative disposition. Not one to approve of unnecessary government bureaucracy, Heston accepted the position nevertheless. "I question the function of this office," he lightheartedly wrote in his journal. "But I'll operate on Jefferson's principle: 'The best government is the least government.'" Heston continued to repeat Jefferson's famous maxim throughout his public career. The actor believed in using the state to improve the lives of Americans but feared that excessive government would result in a loss of freedom. A ceremonial office seemed harmless enough, however, and Heston assumed his new position. Furthermore, he felt increasingly comfortable revealing his political beliefs to his admirers. For instance, he started publishing a fan-based newsletter that supposedly was confined to his movie career, but he could not resist making political observations on a regular basis. Heston had all but abandoned his apolitical stance when, in 1960, he attended the Democratic national convention, held that year in Los Angeles.

Heston was prepared to support Stevenson again, as were most of the neoconservatives. Indeed, it probably would not have mattered who the Democratic nominee was. The Republicans still showed no willingness to modernize, and as Podhoretz attests: "To me . . . the Republicans were at once the party of stupidity and the party of resistance to change."[28] Therefore, when John F. Kennedy, the young senator from Massachusetts, won the nomination, an impressed Heston comfortably changed his allegiance. The intellectual neocons, however, did not warm to Kennedy as quickly as Heston did. Actually, most scholars and academics held reservations about the nominee, so much so that Arthur Schlesinger Jr. took it on himself to sell JFK to the intellectuals. Still, the nominee won their ultimate support. A more enthusiastic Heston planned to work on JFK's campaign, but the filming of *El Cid* in Spain did not allow the time.[29]

Heston was considerably more approving of the party's nominee than of the "appallingly frivolous" convention that he attended. "Who was it that said, 'such a spectacle must offend the thoughtful and shock the fastidious'? It was like a giant premier party," he wrote in his journal, indicating early in his political career his disapproval of wasting money. What Heston seems not to have realized is that the pomp and circumstance resulted in part from the new role of the media in politics. After the major networks began televising the Democratic and Republican national conventions, American politics dramatically and permanently changed, as did the political connection with Hollywood. By 1960, 95 percent of American households owned at least one television set. During presidential campaigns, the major networks aired the conventions, the debates, and political advertisements, drawing even more attention to a candidate's image. Indeed, the age of television transformed political campaigns, which began to emphasize style as much as, if not more than, substance, creating a demand for articulate entertainers who knew exactly how to work the camera. Likewise, as politicians felt compelled to attempt their own hands at media posturing, Hollywood considered them less as impressive statesmen and more as awkward amateurs. As the dominating role of the media in politics became more inevitable, stars felt more comfortable with political participation.[30]

JFK made the merger between celebrities and politics possible for the first time since Roosevelt, although Kennedy himself did little to cultivate the connection. The senator fit Hollywood's image of the perfect American president because of his effervescent youth, stylish looks, and easygoing humor. Already possessing ample supplies of the money and style that Hollywood offered, he looked to southern California simply as a diversion, continuing his excursions to Los Angeles for play—meaning, women—but very rarely for politics. On at least two occasions, Kennedy was aware of the potential benefits that Hollywood offered, but the significance of these examples was somewhat limited. At one point, he hired television consultants for his live debates against the Republican candidate, Vice President Richard Nixon. They assisted with camera angles, lighting, makeup, and other media considerations. However, this concept was hardly new. Eisenhower had hired the actor Robert Montgomery for the same purpose in 1956. Additionally, Frank Sinatra campaigned faithfully for Kennedy, fostering an easy connection between the candidate and the stars, especially the legendary Rat Pack. Eventually, however, JFK felt compelled to sever his ties with Sinatra. Kennedy feared that the singer's connections with the notorious mobster Salvatore (Sam) Giancana could possibly damage his own credibility. Although Hollywood proved to be more enamored of JFK than was he in turn of the entertainment industry, the one-sidedness of this relationship does not negate its importance. Celebrity politics was back in the air, glamorous, attractive, and deemed a vital subject of conversation.[31]

Heston enthusiastically supported Kennedy's promise to connect American prosperity with the country's responsibilities abroad. JFK promised a more intense version of the postwar abundance and international superiority that Americans had come to expect, a message substantiated by his own youth and vigor. Nixon found himself saddled with his own conservative image as well as Eisenhower's grandfatherly persona. He, as part of the incumbent administration, was also blamed for the loss of economic momentum that had characterized the late 1940s and the early 1950s. The country experienced losses in economic growth that were small but noticeable enough for the Democrats to seize on as legitimate campaign issues. For instance, Kennedy pointed out that, while the gross national product grew at a rate of 3.8 percent between 1947 and 1954, it had risen only 3.2 percent between 1954 and 1960. He then proposed a platform that called for a 5 percent annual growth rate that would be produced by "Keynes-cum-growth" economics, in which the government pumped up demand through various tax measures. In other words, he would not rely solely on increased government spending to achieve growth. Kennedy vowed to "get the country moving again" on foreign policy issues as well. He accused the Eisenhower administration of allowing a "missile gap" to emerge between the United States and the Soviet Union and of practicing a rigid and tired old containment policy, a claim buttressed by recent Soviet achievements. The Soviets shocked the world when they launched the world's first intercontinental ballistic missile in August 1957 and then the world's first man-made satellite in October. Proposing a more aggressive version of containment, Kennedy pledged to build up the military and reach out to the Third World in a positive manner. In terms of racial justice, the Republicans appealed to some African Americans with their own civil rights plank, but the Catholic Kennedy eventually won over the largely Protestant black voters by reaching out to Martin Luther King Jr. and calling for the desegregation of federal housing.[32]

Although he ultimately embraced politics and used his celebrity status to his advantage, Heston did so with reservations about how much of a difference he could plausibly make and how much of an influence he, as an actor, should be allowed to exercise. In a jocular 1960 press release, Heston attempted to resolve the apprehension he felt about using his stardom for political purposes: "An actor pontificating on politics is about the equivalent of a high school boy describing the charms of Sophia Loren: he's just in way over his head." But he went on to defend an actor's right to lend his or her opinions to the public record. "It's a very old and very healthy American custom," he argued. Moreover, although an actor may be out of his or her league, the rest of the citizenry probably was, too, Heston assumed. "Hardly anybody DOES know anything about politics," he exclaimed. Even though he defended the right of actors to speak politically, he did not give much credence to their opinions, including his own, and encouraged Americans to think independently: "I think Frank Sinatra sings One More for My Baby better than anyone else alive, but I'd hate to think he was influencing all the people who agree with me on that as to which man to vote for on November 8th, because I don't think he knows that much about Presidents." He himself pledged not to be influenced by his fellow actors and approved of taking advice only from political experts, naming Walter Lippmann in particular: "They've been at it a long time and they know more about it than the rest of us, but beyond that I'd rather go it alone."[33] By releasing this self-deprecating statement, Heston attempted to resolve the tension between his earlier statements against entering politics and his seemingly contradictory work on Democratic national campaigns.

Once elected, Kennedy did not disappoint Heston. The youngest president-elect in U.S. history, Kennedy laid out an inspiring American mission in his 1961 inaugural address. "We shall pay any price, bear any burden, meet any hardship, support any friend, oppose any foe to assure the survival and the success of liberty," he pledged in a voice ringing with promise. Kennedy's economic policies enjoyed a successful start, although he would not live to see them to fruition. Between 1961 and 1965, the gross national product increased at a rate above the projected 5 percent, employment increased by 2.5 percent per year, and poverty dropped from 22.4 percent in 1960 to 14.7 percent in 1966. Kennedy oversaw the most enormous peacetime military buildup in U.S. history to that point, hoping to be able to handle any type of potential conflict—from guerrilla to conventional to nuclear warfare. Although the Kennedy administration's failure in the 1961 Bay of Pigs invasion was an international embarrassment, the president redeemed himself to Americans, including Heston, the following year during the Cuban Missile Crisis. Kennedy's willingness to stand up to Khrushchev so impressed Heston that he wrote in his journal: "I felt scared, and proud. It's been a long time since we took any initiative in the world."[34]

The burgeoning civil rights movement drew Heston into politics at the grassroots level, and, during his involvement with the campaign for racial justice, Heston largely acted out the sentiments of the intellectual neocons. The intellectual neocons showed their support for the civil rights campaigns in their writings; Heston did so by actually participating in demonstrations. The intellectuals articulated their reservations about certain policies and individuals associated with the movement; Heston demonstrated his uncertainties through his leadership and decisionmaking. Heston and the intellectual neocons are noteworthy not only because their ideas paralleled each other's but also because they lent their support to an unpopular cause. Even Hollywood, as enamored as it was of JFK, took significant prodding before becoming involved in the civil rights movement at the grassroots level. Heston was one of the first marquee players to lend his name to the cause.

The Supreme Court had banned segregation in educational facilities in 1954 with *Brown v. Board of Education,* a ruling that reversed *Plessy v. Ferguson* (1896) and, supposedly, overturned the system of de jure segregation that had become a way of life in the South after the Civil War. Hoping to accelerate the desegregation process, several organizations assumed leading roles in what is known as the modern civil rights movement, primarily the Southern Christian Leadership Conference (formed in 1957), the Congress of Racial Equality (founded in 1942 as the Committee of Racial Equality), the Fellowship of Reconciliation (founded in England in 1914), and the Student Nonviolent Coordinating Committee (formed in 1960). Adopting aspects of Gandhian thought, American pacifism, and Christian idealism, these organizations set the standard for nonviolent direct action that characterized the struggle. Public transportation systems across the South were desegregated with these methods, as were drugstore lunch counters.

Impressed with the civil rights movement in its early stages, both the intellectual neocons and Heston soon made their approval known. Podhoretz remembers: "I was enthralled by everything connected with the civil rights movement in this period of its history." And *Commentary,* the journal he edited, reflected those views. Likewise, when Heston learned that his friend Dr. Jolly West was involved with desegregation campaigns in Oklahoma City, he immediately wrote him a congratulatory note of support and soon became involved himself. "I guess it's time I did something about this kind of thing besides deploring it at cocktail parties," he wrote in his journal.[35] Civil rights activists had been organizing sit-ins in Oklahoma City since 1958, nearly three years before Heston got involved, and had made slow but steady progress in persuading local businesses to desegregate. Still, in 1961, plenty of establishments in that city remained segregated.

Clara Luper, the dynamic engineer of the demonstrations, noted the dramatic effect that Heston's presence had on residents of Oklahoma City, including the demonstrators themselves. She attests that news of Heston's arrival "had spread like wild fire and large crowds had assembled on Main Street to get a quick glimpse of the star." Heston accompanied West and Dr. Chester M. Pierce, an African American physician at the local Veterans Hospital, to lead eighty marchers through the streets of downtown where the three strongholds of segregation—John A. Brown's Department Store, Anna Maude's Cafeteria, and Bishop's Restaurant—were located. His placard read "All Men Are Created Equal—Thomas Jefferson" on the front and "Racial Discrimination Is Un-American" on the back. The three men inspired great bursts of applause, and Heston frequently stopped to shake hands with bystanders and talk with fans during the march. The integrationist forces attracted far more supporters than detractors and saw no violence, although Luper notes that a few hecklers singled out Heston with such denunciations as: "Go back to Hollywood, you Jew!!" (apparently confusing Heston's movie roles with his real life). Heston did not mention the hecklers in his journal or in statements to the press; however, he did note that they had not created the confrontation that they had expected and told a reporter the next day: "I suspect the next time I come to Oklahoma City, there won't be anything to demonstrate. The sentiments of the city are clearly in favor of desegregation." Indeed, Oklahoma City would continue to desegregate, although the integrationists would not achieve total victory until the 1964 Civil Rights Act. Even so, Luper gratefully claims: "Every step that Heston, West and Pierce took was adding tons of Freedom vitamins to our tired bodies that had been protesting for three years." Heston declared his "small civil rights activism" in Oklahoma "a significant milestone for me." Thereafter, he enthusiastically delved into a variety of public-sector issues, attributing his involvement to "a certain Scot's contrariness and a tendency to shoot my mouth off" but also to his "expanded persona, riding the tiger."[36]

Although Oklahoma City managed to avoid widespread violence, not surprisingly many Southern cities did not. Other civil rights campaigns— like one under the direction of the Southern Christian Leadership Conference in Birmingham, Alabama, in May 1963—resulted in highly publicized confrontations. Nonviolent protesters, including strategically placed schoolchildren, were attacked by the Birmingham police, who used clubs, fire hoses, and snarling dogs to force back demonstrators. The horrific scene was televised across America, the images, accompanied by similar displays of Southern resistance elsewhere, eliciting Northern sympathy for the movement. Only one month later, Alabama Governor George "Segregation Forever" Wallace physically barred two African American students from entering the University of Alabama. Appalled, Kennedy ordered the Alabama National Guard to protect the students and the next day went on television to ask for a federal civil rights bill.

Until this speech, JFK had avoided civil rights legislation for both personal and political reasons. As a moderate Democrat, he found executive action, presidential appointments, and the enforcement of existing laws more "personally compatible" with his style. He made more presidential appointments of African Americans than any previous president, and, under his guidance, the Justice Department actively promoted voter education projects in the South. However, the Democratic coalition was a precarious one, and he did not want to jeopardize his pending economic proposals by angering the South with civil rights legislation, especially when he felt that economic policy was the best approach to improving the well-being of African Americans. The violence in Birmingham and the theatrics of George Wallace eroded his resolve, and he began to consider the fight for civil rights a moral crisis in America. In his nationwide speech, Kennedy appealed to the minds of Americans: "Today . . . when Americans are sent to Viet-Nam or West Berlin, we do not ask for whites only. It ought to be possible, therefore, for American students of any color to attend any public institution they select without having to be backed up by troops." Then he appealed to their hearts. "The heart of the question is whether all Americans are to be afforded equal rights and equal opportunities, whether we are going to treat our fellow Americans as we want to be treated."[37] The president announced a bill that attacked segregation by barring discrimination in all public facilities.

Kennedy's bill immediately bottlenecked in Congress, but, because the fight against segregation in cities like Birmingham had captured the media spotlight, civil rights activists believed that the time was ripe to push the issue on Capitol Hill. The movement's leaders returned to an idea first proposed by A. Philip Randolph in 1940. The president of the Brotherhood of Sleeping Car Porters, Randolph had emerged as the leading figure in the black labor movement when he negotiated a contract for the employment of African Americans with the railroads in 1937. Noting the racism in New Deal programs and then the discrimination that excluded blacks from defense jobs during World War II, Randolph threatened FDR with a fifty-thousand-strong march on the nation's capital. Roosevelt acquiesced to Randolph's demands in June 1941 by issuing Executive Order 8802, which forbade discrimination by any defense contractors, and by establishing the Federal Employment Practices Commission. With this victory, Randolph canceled the march but kept in mind the powerful leverage that the threat afforded him. With black unemployment at double the rate for whites and the civil rights bill still unrealized in 1963, the seventy-one-year-old Randolph proposed a new march for "jobs and freedom"—what became known as the March on Washington. Randolph and longtime activist Bayard Rustin hoped to mobilize 100,000 participants for the unprecedented demonstration, and an overwhelming show of support came forth. Several of the movement's most respected leaders, known as the "Big Six," gathered and established the nature and goals of the march—to support Kennedy's legislation, demonstrate without civil disobedience, and encourage integration. Incidentally, these objectives were more moderate than Randolph and Rustin first intended.[38] Although JFK remained skeptical, a number of ad hoc groups popped up nationwide to organize their own Washington-bound contingents, one of which formed in Hollywood.

Heston joined the March on Washington Movement along with several other leading entertainers and liberals. The idea first arose in May 1963 when, after persuading craft guilds to open their ranks to black workers, Martin Luther King Jr. addressed a small group of well-known actors in Burt Lancaster's home. During his informal speech, King shared his personal experiences with racism. Appalled and sympathetic, the group donated $75,000 to King and moved to form a celebrity delegation to participate in the upcoming march. Calling themselves the Arts Group, the committee gathered at Marlon Brando's home on July 26, 1963, and "when the dust cleared" had elected Heston as its chair. Wary of this role, Heston commented: "I suppose I was elected chairman because of the time I put in with SAG . . . or maybe just because I'd gotten all those folks through the Red Sea." He did not mention his previous civil rights experience, also a likely factor in his selection.[39]

Heston recruited an impressive number of entertainers, providing leadership for a cause that many celebrities were unwilling to support. Only ten artists joined the original committee, including Brando, Peter Brown, Tony Curtis, Mel Ferrer, Tony Franciosa, Virgil Frye, Burt Lancaster, and Billy Wilder. However, by August 7, the committee had recruited at least sixty new additions, including Shirley MacLaine, Dean Martin, Frank Sinatra, Steve McQueen, Gene Kelly, Paul Newman, Joanne Woodward, Debbie Reynolds, Lena Horne, Sidney Poitier, Harry Belafonte, Sammy Davis Jr., Kirk Douglas, Judy Garland, Dennis Hopper, Eartha Kitt, and Pearl Bailey. This growth did not come easily or without detractors. For example, Heston could not persuade his friend George Stevens to join the committee at all, and Stevens almost talked Heston out of the whole endeavor because of their mutual suspicion of group action. Nor did most Americans approve of the proposed march. One Gallup poll revealed that two-thirds of Americans, in fact, disapproved.[40]

Indeed, large-scale civil rights activity had never taken a firm hold in Hollywood because the few African Americans who did work in the industry feared that they would endanger their careers by creating controversy. Studio heads had even urged Heston, in the middle of his indefatigable *Ben-Hur* run, to rethink his participation in the Oklahoma City picketing. They worried that he might "alienate moviegoers," a somewhat surprising concern since Heston had already won his Oscar for the movie and it had been playing in theaters for almost two years. Heston brushed off their warnings, but few African American actors could afford to do so. Black entertainers were well aware that "causing trouble" could spell the end of their careers. For example, the renowned Sidney Poitier joined some other black actors to petition the Actors' Equity Association regarding black employment, but they were rebuffed with threats of blacklisting. In fact, the head of the Negro Actor's Guild physically threatened Poitier for not being more "accommodating." Moreover, when the National Association for the Advancement of Colored People (NAACP) had attempted to instigate civil rights activity in Hollywood in 1951, its efforts fell flat with the black actors themselves. The NAACP imposed a censure on the popular radio-turned-television show *Amos 'n' Andy.* It applauded the show's all-black cast, and appreciated its popularity with African Americans, but condemned its blatantly stereotypical humor. Most African Americans in Hollywood, however, including the actors in the series itself, found the NAACP's censure antithetical to their interests. They considered the NAACP leadership a bunch of "naïve do-gooders" who had put the actors' livelihoods in jeopardy. The actors insisted that they should be able to choose their own roles without the interference of the NAACP.[41] The awareness that creating controversy could effectively end a career, as well as the disagreement over what was best for black performers, hampered civil rights activity in Hollywood. When the opportunity to address national civil rights concerns presented itself, however, many black actors did join the movement.

As the chair of the Arts Group, Heston made decisions that revealed his moderate approach, starting with the "statement of purpose committee" that he directed. The committee focused on legislative progress and the traditional functions of government, without resorting to radical solutions. First, the committee members made a general call for improving the proposed civil rights legislation pending in Congress. Second, they sought to "dramatize the issues for the general public" through peaceful demonstrations, meetings with members of Congress, and a conference with President Kennedy. Heston purposely avoided radical suggestions throughout the planning stages of the March on Washington, even voicing skepticism of group demonstrations in general, in spite of his leadership role in the Arts Group. He confided in his journal: "Instinctively I share [George Stevens's] opposition to group action. I don't like to follow other men's drums; I like to walk by myself, but here I am, ass-deep in a complicated, emotionally charged group action." He also pointedly informed the media that each of the artists involved was nonpartisan and acting of his or her own accord: "We're no organization, we have no name. This is all on an individual basis." When Heston flew to New York and temporarily abandoned his chairmanship a week before the march, he appointed James Garner to cochair with Marlon Brando, hoping that Garner's "cooler head" would prevail in his absence. While he was away, Brando and Newman fulfilled Heston's fears when they flew to Gadsden, Alabama, to attempt to mediate between city officials and civil rights groups during a demonstration in that city. After getting word of their unsuccessful trip, Heston fumed in his journal that Brando and Newman had gotten involved in Gadsden "without checking with me, or anyone else, as far as I can tell." His outrage continued: "This is the hook you hang on with a group. You can answer for what you do yourself, but how can you answer for what all the others do?"[42]

Heston's fears over group action stemmed largely from his unwillingness to engage in civil disobedience, a tactic entertained by some of the more liberal members of the Arts Group and a cornerstone of King's approach to the fight for racial justice. The Montgomery Bus Boycott of 1955, for example, which had elevated King to national prominence, was sparked by Rosa Parks's decision to break the city's bus laws. Moreover, King himself had spent time in jail for violating civil rights statutes. Still, Heston rejected civil disobedience as an option for the Arts Group. He believed that such a tactic should be avoided at all costs, especially since the leaders of the March on Washington had decided not to employ it. He explained his views in a later interview, saying that following the democratic processes guaranteed by the Constitution did not require resorting to civil disobedience. Heston considered civil disobedience extreme and unhealthy, even characterizing it as an option "only for dictatorships." Heston would not have joined the march had its leaders decided to engage in lawbreaking, and he tried to lead the Arts Group according to his own principles. He noted: "There were some of us who were primarily hooked on the drama of a civil rights demonstration, not on making it work. Our meetings were studded with rousing speeches about chaining ourselves to the Jefferson Monument and lying down on Pennsylvania Avenue." Paraphrasing a common expression, Heston vowed that as long as he was in charge: "We're doing it the way it says in the book." He worked for a balance between the naysayers, like Stevens, and those who promoted more dramatic action, like Brando. Therefore, he considered himself a centrist on civil rights issues, lamenting: "Moderates don't make themselves heard on public questions. It's too bad because moderates make a democracy work."[43] Heston would enter into many political frays seeing himself as an independent voice of reason.

His chairmanship of the Arts Group exposed Heston to the wide variety of opinions and policy proposals being discussed by African American leaders. Such conferences forced him to clarify his own opinions. Even though he strongly supported legislation prohibiting segregation, after accompanying King to a meeting between the NAACP and the Motion Picture Association of America (MPAA) Heston realized that he was skeptical of issues beyond the confines of the proposed bill. An Urban League dinner prompted similarly moderate views. "There were some very impressive people, though I can't agree with those who feel there's some sort of racial indemnity for the 'failures of the past,'" he confessed in his journal.[44] Heston supported the civil rights bill because he believed that it would open up equal opportunity for African Americans and allow them access they had previously been denied. However, he also believed that the federal government should be limited in scope and questioned the legitimacy and even the likelihood for success of its ventures into matters as personal as race.

Furthermore, Heston was prepared to distance himself from those activists who did not share his moderate ideas. When he learned that he would be reading a speech prepared by the author James Baldwin, he became quite concerned, especially because he would not be able to review it until the day of the march. Baldwin had willingly discussed "black rage" and possible revolution in such works as *The Fire Next Time* (1963), and Heston feared that those themes would pervade the piece he was scheduled to read. He even went so far as to write his own speech in case he deemed Baldwin's unacceptable. He was relieved when he found that Baldwin had "kept the nature of the event" in mind when composing his piece.[45] Heston's skepticism of Baldwin mirrored that of the intellectual neocons, especially Norman Podhoretz. Although Podhoretz respected Baldwin's "loyalty and courage," he had little sympathy for the black nationalism that Baldwin promoted. Heston ultimately approved Baldwin's speech, but he was ready to act on his reservations about the controversial author.

The march peacefully assembled black and white Americans for a common cause and is considered a high-water mark for the civil rights movement. On August 28, 1963, over 200,000 demonstrators gathered on the Mall in Washington, and all three major television networks broadcast all or parts of the event. Although the Arts Group was a comparatively small delegation, it drew significant publicity to the event and contributed to the day's positive ambience. The members of the Arts Group delivered speeches, provided entertainment, and, according to *Variety,* brought a "relaxed and peaceful 'country fair' mood to the huge demonstration." Ossie Davis emceed a preliminary show that included music by Joan Baez and Bob Dylan, statements of support delivered by Belafonte and others, and a presentation by Burt Lancaster of a scroll signed by fifteen hundred Americans living abroad. During the march itself, the actors carried no signs or placards and were not immediately recognized until a group of young girls called attention to the contingent by "shrieking at Lancaster, Belafonte, Poitier, Newman, and Heston." King easily transcended this excitement with his rousing "I Have a Dream" speech on the steps of the Washington Monument. Afterward, Kennedy received the Big Six at the White House, and the President told Rustin that he would throw his weight behind the pending bill to convince resistant members of Congress to vote for it.[46] The civil rights bill would finally pass the following year under Lyndon Johnson.

Heston was extremely proud of his participation in the march, and the event drew an unprecedented number of stars into politics. At day's end, Heston wrote in his journal that the march's execution "shows the strength of this country when our constitutional right to peaceable assembly can be exercised in such thousands, with such dignity and happy determination. Jefferson, whose monument was the last thing I saw tonight on my way to the airport, would have approved. Indeed, he would've said 'I told you so.'" The Washington event would be Heston's last civil rights march. He considered joining King in Montgomery in March 1965 for a demonstration to show support for three hundred marchers who had traveled from Selma to Montgomery and gained national attention after being attacked by the Alabama state police. Heston felt it both "meaningful" and "necessary" to attend but could not fit it into his schedule.[47]

The Selma march prompted President Johnson to propose the Voting Rights Act in 1965, and after its passage Heston did not consider joining any more civil rights demonstrations. With legal barriers out of the way, many white and black activists considered the struggle, at least in terms of securing federal legislation, to be over. Others, however, did not, and a number of activists turned their attention to social and economic discrimination in the North. Indeed, African Americans faced racism not just in the South. It was not uncommon for Northern cities to be segregated—a result of white hostility and black solidarity. Still, when the civil rights movement traveled north, the neoconservatives disagreed with many of the assumptions behind the shift. Podhoretz noted the failure of these more radical liberals to differentiate between the de facto segregation of the North and the de jure segregation of the South, an oversight that erroneously placed the North, which had passed laws prohibiting discrimination, on a par with the South. Furthermore, Podhoretz disagreed with the ongoing pursuit of integration. He noted that it was common for immigrant groups to be divided into ethnic enclaves. Why should it be any different for African Americans? Forcing integration with federal mandates seemed to him foolish and naive.[48] Heston illustrated the neoconservative beliefs through his inaction, that is, his decision to join no more demonstrations as they moved north and as the increasingly radical activists pursued goals beyond antidiscrimination laws. Instead, he became more heavily involved in SAG and in the Kennedy and Johnson administrations.

A distinctive mark of Kennedy's presidency was the sense of both cultural refinement and public service that he and the first lady brought to his administration, of which Heston became a part. The elegance of the inaugural ball foreshadowed the administration's interest in the arts, as did the Inaugural Committee's decision to specially invite prizewinners in the arts, sciences, and humanities to the swearing in. The ultrarefined, ultrachic Jacqueline Bouvier Kennedy brought glamour to the White House with her very presence. Furthermore, she launched a massive project to renovate the White House and make a distinct Kennedy imprint on the mansion. She solicited private donations of many of the mansion's original furnishings. She also organized the White House Fine Arts Committee, had the mansion declared a national monument, and incorporated the White House Historical Association.[49]

Heston took on a number of responsibilities in the Kennedy administration, responsibilities that revolved around art and film. In 1961, he acted as the official U.S. delegate and chair to the Eleventh International Film Festival in Berlin. Chosen by the Department of State, Heston attended the festival for two weeks along with MPAA President Eric Johnston and the director Billy Wilder. Heston's duties were not particularly tasking, but he was proud to have been selected as a representative of his country. The following year, Heston impersonated FDR in a series of films on the late president for the Defense Department. Although the scripts highlighted Roosevelt's relief programs during the Great Depression, they also emphasized programs, such as the Civilian Conservation Corps, that favored employment over cash payments. Heston could have been expressing his own sentiments when he quoted FDR's remarks about the harmful effects of government handouts. "When any man or woman goes on a dole, something happens to them mentally," he repeated. "The quicker they are taken off the dole . . . the better it is for them for the rest of their lives."[50] Heston's work for the Kennedy administration kept the actor aligned with the Democrats and made him feel like part of the administration. However, the projects were bipartisan in appeal and not solely confined to Democratic interests.

Kennedy was assassinated November 22, 1963, and his death deeply affected Heston. When CBS asked the actor to read a eulogy at the slain president's memorial service, he gratefully accepted, feeling that he had been "given a purpose to carry us through this dark weekend." After several days, Heston found that "the world, or at least my thinking of it, slowly began to return to normal, though the waste of that tough man's death still stabs as you pick up the threads you dropped on Friday."[51]

Kennedy and Heston shared a common approach to political problems and ideas. After the president's death, Heston continued to model himself after the moderate Democrat, while others got wrapped up in Kennedy's rhetoric and carried that energy further than the president had ever intended. The Kennedy biographer Herbert S. Parmet argues that JFK distinguished himself from his Democratic and Republican rivals by asking for sacrifices: "It was the missionary approach, the sailing-against-the-wind romanticism that conveys a masculine, messianic quality and portrays the stakes as choices between freedom and slavery, between extinction and survival." Kennedy's carefully cultivated image was similar to the persona that Heston conveyed as Moses and Ben-Hur, and his idealistic yet conservative nature was much like the philosophy that drove Heston's politics. Tellingly, Parmet concludes: "Kennedy was a Democrat by culture and geography only. Having come to power by that route, his only way to move ahead was by mobilizing the remnants of the New Deal, trying to resurrect and reorder that coalition through a style that fused moderation with idealism." Nor did Heston have an intense loyalty to the Democratic Party. It is this intriguing mix of moderation and idealism that perfectly captured the essence of Heston's political approach during the civil rights movement and in his other public involvements. Keeping one foot in reality illustrated the general strategy of the neoconservatives. In fact, Irving Kristol would later define neoconservatives as "liberals mugged by reality."[52] Eventually, the neoconservatives would believe that the Democrats had lost the ability to find verity.

Lyndon Johnson attempted to heal the nation by continuing Kennedy's programs, centering his legislative goals on unrealized bills instigated by the late president. Heston became even more involved in the Johnson administration than he was in Kennedy's, yet he continued to display his moderately idealistic nature and to shy away from any definitive party loyalty. For example, although he "rejoiced" at Johnson's landslide victory over the Republican nominee, Barry Goldwater, "with beans and beer," he found himself intrigued with the Arizona senator. Goldwater prided himself on "offering a choice, not an echo," to Americans in the 1964 presidential campaign. Whereas moderate and liberal Republicans had accepted the framework of the New Deal, Goldwater wanted to dismantle FDR's programs, reverse the Keynesian trend, and reduce the size and responsibility of the government. Each day, Heston passed a billboard proclaiming one of Goldwater's central campaign slogans: "In Your Heart, You Know He's Right." "I'd try not to look, or at least not think about it. But one morning there was a convoy of trucks coming through the crossroad," he later recalled. "As we waited, I experienced a true revelation, almost an epiphany, like St. Paul on the road to Damascus. I looked at that photograph of Goldwater and said softly, 'Son of a bitch . . . he is right!' And I knew he was."[53]

Of course, this "epiphany" was recounted in hindsight, and there were certainly aspects of Goldwater's platform with which Heston did not agree, namely, the candidate's opposition to the civil rights bill for which Heston had marched. However, trends in the national party alignment indicated that conservative Democrats like Heston, Kristol, and Podhoretz might very well find common ground with the Republicans in the near future. First, the intellectual base of the Republican Party had grown considerably larger since the mid-1950s and had finally succeeded in articulating a viable definition of conservatism. By 1964, such individuals as William Buckley, Russell Kirk, and James Burnham had risen to national prominence and succinctly explained conservatism as opposition to the growth of government power and the centralization of that power, to egalitarianism, and to containment (a policy they considered "appeasement"). Their hostility toward the state and toward utopian notions of equality resembled the skepticism that conservative Democrats held toward liberalism. Second, conservative Republican intellectuals voiced misgivings about the civil rights movement that resonated with conservative Democrats, and not just Southerners. Republican intellectuals also questioned the liberal focus on integration, believing that such an approach rendered the "multidimensional" race problem (which included such considerations as justice, the preservation of a federal system, and the maintenance of order) to a one-dimensional quandary. Addressing it as such was simplistic and possibly dangerous, said Republicans, sounding rather like Podhoretz.

Despite the signs that conservative Democrats and Republicans might eventually reach a mutual understanding, it was not yet to be. To the horror of many Americans, conservative Republicans persisted in their calls to roll back communism, even if it meant using nuclear bombs to do so. Furthermore, the Republicans needed an attitude adjustment. As the historian George Nash puts it: "The general mood was one of pessimism about the declining Old Republic." Indeed, Goldwater suffered a devastating loss at the polls, but election returns indicated that the Republicans had made significant gains in the South, previously a Democratic stronghold. Goldwater carried Louisiana, Mississippi, Alabama, South Carolina, and Georgia as well as his home state of Arizona.[54] Because of these heartening trends, the Right reenergized and determined to make the most of the defeat. It was not long before Heston and the neoconservatives found the conservative Republican agenda the more attractive platform.

Another trend highlighted by the 1964 election was the large number of celebrities involved in the campaign. Far more celebrities joined in the national election that year than had in 1960. Their partisan bias was clear. Democrats had seized the advantage in Hollywood because of JFK's reverberating appeal and the damage that conservatives had caused with the blacklist in the 1950s. This increased interest served many candidates well, as the exploding costs of media-driven campaigns forced more politicians onto the national campaign trail to raise funds. Hollywood, with all its glittering affluence, became an essential stop for any national candidate looking for treasure. However, it was moguls, not celebrities, who distinguished themselves as the most important fund-raisers in the 1960s. For example, Lew Wasserman of the Music Corporation of America and Arthur Krim of United Artists established the President's Club for the DNC in 1963, in which a $1,000 membership guaranteed the opportunity to brush up against the political elite. The President's Club foreshadowed fundamental changes in fund-raising, especially at the presidential level. First, the club attracted more Hollywood donors who expressed an increased interest in national political issues. Second, it emphasized the growing tendency to contribute to an individual candidate rather than to the party at large. Above all, Wasserman's President's Club helped realize the new expectation that movie executives would cultivate friendships with politicians.[55]

Despite the fact that Hollywood generally favored the Democrats, the Republicans enjoyed the support of Ronald Reagan, the most politically savvy movie star yet to hit the campaign trail for either national party. Reagan had hosted *General Electric Theater* from 1954 to 1962, a television variety show that also showcased an appliance-laden lifestyle. Indeed, the leaders of General Electric (GE) envisioned the program as a way to tout the merits of big business, and Reagan became a right-wing spokesperson when working for the company, delivering conservative speeches nationwide. After he left GE, Reagan continued to espouse what the historian Garry Wills calls "The Speech," a warning of the double menace of big government and insidious communism. In 1964, Reagan impressed the California Goldwater delegation when he made "The Speech" at a fund-raising dinner for the Arizona senator. The Californians arranged for Reagan to deliver it again on national television during the Republican national convention in Los Angeles. It was an unqualified hit. Reagan's magnificent delivery of a then-unpopular conservative message signaled to the party leaders that the actor had the potential to be an important force in the GOP. Reagan's successful oratory accomplished two things—it launched his own political career and demonstrated the importance of presentation. Reagan forced the parties to recognize the usefulness of celebrities who specialized in charming the camera and the audience alike.[56]

The Democrats also made greater use of celebrities. During the 1964 campaign, the Bi-Partisan Campaign on Arts and Communications formed in support of LBJ, and a number of entertainers campaigned on his behalf. During LBJ's second term, various administration figures encouraged the president to promote even more celebrity activism. In a memo written to Johnson and carbon-copied to Jack Valenti, the president's aide and conduit to the stars, the first lady's social secretary, Bess Abell, advocated using entertainers to act as "administrative spokes[persons] in much the same way [the stars] did during the campaign." Abell especially cited their potential assistance in publicizing "the President's program of economic opportunity, manpower retraining, [and] plans for progress." Johnson and Valenti saw the merits of Abell's memo, and they encouraged new levels of celebrity activism. Johnson invited celebrities to the White House on a regular basis, especially for events involving international guests or for matters concerning the arts. One friend of the Democratic administration, actor Gregory Peck, visited the White House seven times for such occasions, and another, Kirk Douglas, was received four times between 1964 and 1968. Peck and his wife even spent a long weekend at Johnson's Texas ranch in May 1968. However, these visits pale in comparison to the mogul Lew Wasserman's many meetings at the White House. According to the White House diary cards, Wasserman appeared at the Pennsylvania Avenue mansion no less than fifteen times, sometimes with the expressed purpose of discussing policy matters.[57]

One way in which Johnson recruited more celebrities was through an international cultural exchange system that sent various professionals overseas for an interchange of educational and cultural ideas. Kennedy had first set up the program when he signed the Mutual Educational and Cultural Exchange Act in September 1961. Presenting the act as a "component of our foreign relations," Kennedy asserted that such an exchange of people and ideas served as a "fundamental aid in developing understanding of each other's problems as well as consolidating existing friendship between the peoples of the United States" and those of other nations. By 1963, over ten thousand people from the United States had traveled to 130 countries and territories under this act, and the number continued to grow. In the fall of 1963, the Department of State reorganized the cultural presentations program to retreat from "its original competitive character" against similar Soviet endeavors and to better "reflect abroad the state of the performing arts in America" by selecting individuals and groups who displayed the "highest artistic quality."[58] Heston was chosen as such an artist when the State Department invited him to become involved in the cultural exchange program in 1965 and 1966.

Heston traveled to Nigeria, Egypt, Australia, and New Zealand for the United States, and these trips reinforced his commitment to the Johnson administration. In 1964, the program had newly emphasized smaller performing arts groups. Not only did they cost less, but visits by such groups also were more flexible, allowed for more personal contacts, and accommodated more widespread travel within a country. Heston's experience certainly illustrated these advantages. When touring Nigeria, Heston "spent a most interesting and I hope useful time" visiting the capitals of East and West Nigeria, Enugu and Ibadan, and a number of other cities to sign autographs and talk with everyday people. A presidential command performance of *Ben-Hur* to raise money for charity sold out and was the highlight of the trip. A reporter from *Variety* lauded Heston's efforts: "His poise and class did a lot for the much maligned motion picture industry and the 'ugly American' canard." Likewise, during his trip to Australia and New Zealand in 1966, Heston presented a number of readings and film screenings in Auckland, Wellington, Canberra, Melbourne, Perth, and Adelaide. Taking care to select his readings from both American literature and the literature of the country he was visiting, Heston again was a big success with these host countries, as was Kirk Douglas, who carried out similar missions to such exotic places as Morocco, Tunis, and Algeria. Heston relished these trips, proud of his representation of American culture and values. "I'm used to touring all over the world, but almost always either to make a picture or publicize one. To make a tour for the government is . . . different," he wrote in his newsletter in the fall of 1966. "You can't help thinking, 'What . . . me . . . for the whole UNITED STATES???'"[59]

As his comment about the cultural exchange program indicates, Heston demonstrated a charming and almost childlike exuberance for many of his civic engagements. That same year, he traveled to Lincoln, Nebraska, for a day of partisan pleasantries that could have been quite tedious to some Hollywood stars. Heston found them exhilarating. He, along with First Lady Lady Bird Johnson, attended the Nebraskaland Parade in support of the Democratic governor, Frank B. Morrison, who was running for the U.S. Senate that November. After the parade, local officials presented Heston with a cowboy award, a gesture that seemed to absolutely delight the actor, gauging by the pictures taken during the event. After receiving his trophy, Heston sat with it on his lap looking very much like a little kid on Christmas morning. At the end of the day, he wrote in his journal: "I rode in a parade, chatted with Ladybird, and dined with the governor (ahhh, the uses of power . . .). A long, western kind of day."[60]

Heston was not the only celebrity to feel this way; a small cadre of stars also became more politically active at the state level, particularly in California. For instance, in 1964, a number of high-profile entertainers rallied the vote against California Proposition 14, a proposal to repeal fair-housing legislation recently enacted by the state. Hoping to keep the fair-housing statute in place were such activists as Gregory Peck, Nat King Cole, James Garner, Frank Sinatra, Gene Kelly, Burt Lancaster, Billy Wilder, Elizabeth Taylor, and Richard Burton. Even Heston signed a petition encouraging voters to cast their ballots against the proposition. This position is surprising considering Heston's antipathy to government intervention. However, it is not evident that he put much thought into his public support for fair-housing legislation. He made no mention of the proposition in his journal. Furthermore, he was filming *The War Lord* (Franklin J. Schaffner, 1965) in northern California that fall and appears not to have actively campaigned against the proposition. This may have been an issue on which Heston did little research, violating his own credo to investigate every subject thoroughly before taking a public stand. Proposition 14 caused quite a public controversy, however, and it did not take long for celebrities to experience the dirty side of politics as well. After Lancaster had campaigned vigorously against Proposition 14, with numerous speeches, lunches, and television appearances, one of his opponents purportedly hired an African American to answer a "vacancy" sign at one of the actor's apartment buildings and report that he had been turned away.[61]

Negative experiences—real or merely alleged—did little to detract actors from politics, and it became evident that they could thrive in the public arena as politics increasingly became associated with the mass media. George Murphy, a former song-and-dance performer, made the advantages of such a background perfectly clear in his quest for a U.S. Senate seat in California against Pierre Salinger, the former press secretary to President Kennedy. Murphy, a charming and polished media veteran, appeared dignified during the campaign, whereas the more politically experienced Salinger seemed miscast as a statesman. Salinger could not win the trust of his audience, appearing, according to one journalist, like "a clown" at times and "a movie heavy" at others; as a result, he lost the election. Murphy's victory opened the door for other actors with political ambitions, and the need for money and media exposure to win only increased their chances. Two years later, Ronald Reagan won the California governorship without holding any prior office. Robert Vaughan, the star of the television show *The Man from U.N.C.L.E.* who himself nurtured political aspirations, sent a telegram of praise to the new governor: "It is to your credit that you have personally elevated the actor from a second-class citizen to a human being of dignity and respect in the social community."[62] Despite the success of Murphy and Reagan, few actors considered themselves potential political candidates. Certainly, Heston did not. However, many actors did feel that they could be positive and legitimate contributors to both the local and the national political scene.

Heston emerged as one of Hollywood's most prominent activists in the 1960s, and, in facilitating the rise of celebrity politics, he blurred the line between America's political and cultural realms. Whereas in the 1950s celebrities had been relegated to the national political stage only once every four years, by the 1960s they embraced a number of political responsibilities—from grassroots organizing to actually running for office. The Washington establishment took notice, recognizing Hollywood's stars as important assets, not just interesting spectacles at campaign time. Johnson was the first president to consistently use celebrities to promote policy initiatives, and stars would only continue to expand their presence. Even though Heston enjoyed "riding the tiger," he came to realize that his political inclinations, especially when compared to those of his fellow thespians, leaned toward the conservative. While he comfortably aligned himself with the Democrats during this period, that would not always be the case. Nor would Kristol, Podhoretz, and other intellectuals of their persuasion always feel at home with the party. These intellectuals continued to advance their ideas in the political realm throughout the 1960s. Heston acted out similar beliefs when working with the civil rights movement and when serving on the SAG and National Endowment for the Arts governing boards. The actor would continue to synthesize culture and politics, and as Podhoretz insightfully noted: "Politics itself was increasingly becoming a creature of cultural fashion."[63]

CHAPTER THREE

UNION LEADER

HESTON'S FIRST MOVIE CONTRACT PLACED HIM ON THE PATH TO INTER-national stardom; it also brought him into the fold of the Screen Actors Guild (SAG), an organization that consumed more of Heston's time and energy than any of his many other public endeavors. The Guild was an unavoidable organization—industry regulations required all working ac-tors to join the "union shop"—but Heston deepened his relationship with the union in 1960 when he filled a vacancy on the board. Heston quickly moved up the Guild's ranks, ascending to the presidency of the organiza-tion in 1965 and remaining there for six consecutive one-year terms until 1971. Despite the time and attention that his duties required, Heston con-sidered it a "responsibility" to get involved in the governing mechanisms of the Guild. Since he enjoyed the benefits that previous officers had won for actors, Heston believed it to be his duty to make similar contributions to the profession as well as to maintain the integrity and customs of the Guild itself.

Heston's sense of responsibility and tradition compelled him to em-brace the public activism that the Guild represented, and intellectual neo-cons have encouraged public service for largely the same reasons. In fact, as noted in chapter 2, intellectual neocons have developed a wide body of scholarship devoted to "mediating structures"—entities, including labor unions, that stand between the individual and the state. While Heston never contributed to the scholarly work about mediating structures, by taking on a leadership role in the Guild he animated the ideas championed by the intellectual neocons.

As president of the Guild, Heston pursued policies that exemplified the neoconservative approach. First, he closely followed the traditions of the Guild. For example, the founding members deliberately established mechanisms that kept the Guild focused on matters of wages, benefits, and working conditions. Heston conscientiously followed that framework and managed to achieve large gains for the Guild doing so. Second, he tried to find a balance between the individual rights of Guild members and the overall needs of the acting community. He took this community-minded approach even further by treating producers not as adversaries but as potential friends, calling his attitude "enlightened trade unionism."[1] Finally, he considered the government an important ally but generally sought policies that limited its involvement in union matters and in the film industry. For instance, when confronting the issue of pornography, he endorsed a rating system, as opposed to a government censorship scheme or no regulations at all. His leadership style generated criticism from those who expected more from their union, and some considered him too cozy with studio executives. However, Heston's neoconservative approach achieved considerable progress for the Guild, and he gained valuable experience there as an arbitrator, debater, and spokesperson.

Founded in 1933, the small Screen Actors Guild played a key role in the shaping of the film industry because of its high-profile membership. However, compared to other unions, the Guild was unique in that, at least until 1973, it promoted a relatively conservative agenda.

The Guild was actually a latecomer to union organizing in Hollywood. As early as 1916, the American Federation of Labor (AFL) attempted to bargain with the major studios over matters of artistic and industrial production. No union attempted to organize actors until the introduction of sound, when many members of New York's theater community relocated to Los Angeles. Coming from Broadway's strong union environment, many of these migrants attempted to organize the field under Actors' Equity. Perceived by many Hollywood veterans as an intruder, Equity could not rally the support of big-name stars or break down the recalcitrant producers. Actors from the silent era harbored suspicions of the New York invaders, while producers undermined Equity by offering actors lucrative contracts, thus discrediting Equity's insistence that Hollywood stars needed a strong union to protect them. When Equity persisted, the producers finally compromised by forming the Academy of Motion Picture Arts and Sciences (the Academy) in 1927, an organization to represent all aesthetic workers—producers, writers, directors, actors, and technicians—and to negotiate between the groups to solve differences and to avoid work stoppages. Actors were more receptive to the Academy than to the notion of organizing their own Equity affiliate. The producers agreed to cooperate with the Academy, whereas they promised to fight bitterly against Equity recognition. After the Academy successfully interceded to prevent salary cuts in 1927, those actors who had not already joined decided to enroll in the new organization, convinced that it would protect their interests. By 1929, the majority of actors belonged to the Academy, and Equity formally withdrew from Hollywood.[2]

The Academy represented Hollywood's actors for six years. Its leaders formulated a blueprint from which the Guild would pattern itself and committed mistakes that the Guild founders pledged not to repeat. The Academy won the first labor agreement, known as the standard contract, for freelance actors, an agreement that future negotiators could expand on. The standard contract specified certain work guarantees such as a six-day workweek, a definite starting date, and a guaranteed week's dismissal pay. Furthermore, through the Actors' Adjustment Committee, the Academy set a precedent for the "friendly adjustment of differences" with the producers. The ability to resolve problems before they escalated into openly hostile conflicts became a hallmark for the committee, and actors rarely appealed its decisions to a formal dispute resolution committee or to a court adjudicator. Actors soon discovered, however, that certain Academy practices tended to be overbearing. Run by "foundation" members named in the original charter, the Academy government proved itself highly oligarchic. At-large members could neither be elected to the board nor propose amendments to the constitution. Most significantly, with four other working groups to consider, the Academy was not devoted solely to the actors' interests.[3] Within only a few years, actors chafed under the Academy's restrictions.

The stock market crash in 1929 and the subsequent financial crisis that engulfed the nation further weakened the actors' relationship with the Academy. An emergency closing of the banks in early 1933 cut off the funds necessary to keep the studios functioning at a normal level. In response, the producers' association announced an eight-week salary cut of 50 percent in early March for most studio employees, including actors, as a way to deal with the decreased sales brought on by the Great Depression. The Academy convinced its producers to enact a sliding scale of cuts starting at 25 percent, instead of the proposed 50, to protect lower-paid actors. Nonetheless, this easy capitulation to the very idea of salary reductions incensed many actors. The organization's credibility suffered even more when the producers Jack Warner and Robert Goldwyn refused to resume full salaries on the date established by the Academy. In April 1933, six actors assembled at their fellow thespian Kenneth Thompson's house in Hollywood to discuss their future in the movie business. Their hopes rested on a self-governing organization as an alternative to their current company-controlled union.[4]

The antilabor climate in Hollywood reflected the mood of the nation at large and made the Thompson group's decision a bold one. The Los Angeles Police Department had proved itself notoriously both antilabor and anti-Communist, often linking the two even when no such ties were evident. Nor did the rest of Americans sympathize with organized labor, still resentful of the 4 million workers who, reacting to the financial crunch brought on by postwar demobilization, had launched over three hundred strikes in 1919. Most significantly, producers promised to blacklist anyone who defied their rules against union organizing outside the Academy. Thus, the Thompson group launched a "whispering campaign" to promote its cause. In June 1933, eighteen actors officially chartered the Guild and named Ralph Morgan its first president. The male members met at the

Masquers, a private men's club for actors, while the two women of the founding group colluded down the street at the Dominoes, the club's sister organization. The Guild founders used passwords, back rooms, and secret alleyways to elude the detectives the studios had hired in an effort to thwart union organizing before it started. This ragtag group set forth its goals—to correct the abusive behavior of producers and directors and to negotiate better wages and working conditions for all actors, from stars to extras. Although the Academy had secured the standard contract, actors had grown exasperated with long hours without breaks, uncomfortable and often dangerous conditions, low pay, and the generally unscrupulous behavior of their employers.[5]

Hollywood actors typically received a daily or weekly salary, as opposed to an hourly rate, so studio heads minimized costs by cramming the filming into exceedingly long days. Sessions that lasted from six A.M. to midnight were not uncommon, many times without breaks, even when the cast included children. Frank "Junior" Coghlan remembered one movie he did for Paramount: "We kids worked from eight A.M. to half past midnight." Fay Wray, of *King Kong* (Merian C. Cooper and Ernest B. Schoedsack, 1933) fame, worked twenty-two hours straight on one occasion. Despite such deplorable conditions, few actors dared to protest. Those who did were often threatened by the management, which unhesitatingly exercised its overwhelming power over the actors. One director jeered at Ginger Rogers when she protested his demand to return to the set in a mere four hours. "It's two o'clock in the morning. And they'd want me to do close-ups and I had to be back at the studio at six A.M.," she recollected in apparent disgust. "I said to the director, 'No you can't do that.' And he said, 'Yes, I can. Ha-ha!'" When Maureen O'Sullivan weepingly objected to similar circumstances, the director "said if I didn't pull myself together, I'd never work again."[6] Actors who loved their craft, and especially the many who lived precariously close to poverty, did not take these threats lightly.

Uncomfortable and even dangerous conditions compounded the strain of long hours, especially when on location. Some studios failed to provide basic comforts like restroom facilities, chairs on which to rest between takes, and private dressing rooms. Actors tolerated extreme weather conditions, and some shoots could actually be life threatening. Binnie Barnes waded through snake-infested water in *The Last of the Mohicans* (George B. Seitz, 1936), while Frank "Buddy" Ebsen, the original Tin Man in Victor Fleming's 1939 *Wizard of Oz,* "almost disappeared over the rainbow" because of the poisonous aluminum dust in his silvery makeup. Other shoots deteriorated into physically painful endurance sessions. The script of *Tillie's Punctured Romance* (Mack Sennett, 1914) called for Charlie Chaplin to slap the six-year-old Milton Berle across the face. "He hit me so hard I fell down," Berle recalled. Furthermore: "It took him eight times to get it right." Berle perceptively pointed out that actors' often fierce dedication to their craft compelled them to perform dangerous stunts even without the threats of a director. While he conceded that their working conditions needed significant improvement, he also argued that the management was not entirely to blame. "Actors are a strange breed because they'll do anything," Berle commented. "The actors don't know it, but SAG protects them from producers and directors and themselves."[7]

Despite their obsessive dedication, actors resented the poor compensation that they received and the treatment that they endured. Although salaries varied and those of some stars were impressive, 90 percent of actors received less than $5,000 in 1933, while 50 percent received less than $2,000. Extras, stunt doubles, and stand-ins fared far worse. Therefore, when the studios enacted the spring 1933 pay cut, the drastic measure threatened the actors' already unreliable income. Moreover, actors had become exasperated with the obnoxious and even cruel behavior in which their superiors indulged themselves. Dorothy Granger claimed that, in addition to being responsible for her own hair, makeup, and wardrobe, one studio expected her to brew the coffee for the rest of the crew. When Frank "Junior" Coghlan worked on a serial for Mascot Pictures in 1932, Nat Levine lived up to his nickname "the King of the Shoestring" by holding dangerous magnesium flares over his actors' heads rather than paying for the customary bulbs and generators to light the sets after sunset. Don Defore took objection to the assistant director Jack Sullivan's practice of "herding" the extras with a cane. Many, including Douglas Fairbanks, begrudged the browbeating techniques of studio executives, especially Jack Warner, whom he characterized as a "loud mouth bully." The director Cecil B. DeMille also piqued the bitterness of several actors. The child legend Dickie Moore recalled that, when he worked on *The Squaw Man* in 1931, DeMille "raised his riding crop to strike me" for insolence on one occasion; Moore was only five years old at the time. Luckily, Moore's "welfare worker and teacher interceded and told him she'd close down his set" before physical harm ensued.[8] Overall, actors and extras received little respect from the studios.

Actors had legitimate concerns, concerns that warranted unionization, but, in the spirit of the Academy, the charter members of the Guild felt it necessary not to appear overly bellicose in a business that relied on favorable public opinion. Thus, the choice to form a craft guild, rather than a union, was a deliberate move to avoid conflict. According to the historian David Prindle, the founders of the Screen Actors Guild were socially and politically conservative and "would have been uncomfortable in any group that featured 'union' in its title." Therefore, like the writers, the actors used the term *guild*, a title "that harked back to medieval associations of artisans."[9] Remembering Equity, the organizers knew that a controversial union would preclude the support of stars and aspiring actors alike if it compromised their chances of employment in a field dominated by conservative executives.

The nonmilitant strategy of the Thompson group allowed it to attract new recruits, especially stars. When the producers and the Academy continued to affront more and more actors, the Guild reaped the benefits. President Franklin D. Roosevelt had in June 1933 passed the National Industrial Recovery Act, which created the National Recovery Administration (NRA), in the hopes of achieving economic recovery through federally imposed regulation and competition. With this goal in mind, the NRA required written codes that focused on the production and sales of each ailing industry. However, representatives of the privately owned large corporations dominated the NRA, both in the writing and the enforcing of codes. The movie industry was no exception. The actors' branch of the Academy opposed the producer-dominated codes at the film industry's

NRA hearing, but the final draft of the codes revealed the actors' minimal influence. Not only did the draft include the two codes that the actors had opposed—the studios' right of first refusal after the seven-year contracts of their actors expired and the requirement that all agents be licensed by the studios—but the producers, confident of victory, also added a salary cap to the provisions. Furthermore, the producers ignored the labor codes that the government had written. For the first time, the federal government offered worker protection with Section 7(a), but many corporations, including the movie studios, refused to comply with the provisions that legalized bargaining rights, wage-hour protection, and the prevention of child labor. When the Academy, already suffering from latent distrust, seemed either unable or unwilling to contest the undesired code provisions effectively, the Guild seized the opportunity to further discredit the organization and establish its own legitimacy. When the Guild's representative, Eddie Cantor, presented the fledgling organization's case to Roosevelt over the Thanksgiving holiday in Warm Springs, Georgia, he persuaded the administration to incorporate the actors' suggestions into the NRA codes. This victory persuaded a significant number of actors to defect from the Academy in favor of the new, seemingly effective Guild.[10]

The highly recognizable stars who joined the Guild at the outset were especially successful at recruiting because their status reassured the lesser-known actors, who had less leverage with management. Well-known stars were prominent in Guild government. Mary Brian testified that the founding members took their new organization seriously and recruited aggressively. "I can remember hearing stories of Boris Karloff and Bela Lugosi recruiting fellow actors on the sets of their Universal horror movies. You can imagine the persuasive spectacle of Frankenstein's monster and Dracula in full make-up, bringing you an application and urging, 'Join the Guild now!'" And join actors did. Such high-profile celebrities as James Cagney and Douglas Fairbanks enlisted in the winter of 1933 and early 1934. As word spread among their fellow actors of the stars' backing, even more felt confident to sign up as well. "I knew that the big stars were backing the union, it was a who's who list of Hollywood," Ann Doran reminisced. "That gave me courage. If the stars believed in it, what kind of dope was I if I didn't believe in it?" Gloria Stuart became convinced of the Guild's integrity after hearing that Harpo Marx, Joan Crawford, and Edward G. Robinson all favored it. The unfair codes and the persuasive methods of early Guild members together resulted in hundreds of new recruits. The Guild quietly abandoned the Masques and Dominoes clubs in favor of an office at the Hollywood Center Building. Despite its growing popularity, the organization still operated secretly because the producers refused to bargain with both the Screen Actors Guild and the Screen Writers Guild (formed in 1934), threatening to blacklist anyone who joined either organization.[11] For the next three years, the Guild worked with the Roosevelt administration, the AFL, and the Academy to establish its legitimacy.

An amicable relationship between the Guild and the producers eventually ensued. In addition to recognizing the Guild as the exclusive bargaining agent for actors, the producers agreed to a basic minimum contract that specified shorter hours and more pay. The Guild celebrated guarantees for fifty-four-hour workweeks and assurances of twelve-hour rest periods, Guild access to the Call Bureau (the central placement agency for freelance players), and the entitlement of every actor to a written contract. In return, Guild leaders promised not to strike for the length of the contract, a compromise that minimized further agitation for the next nine years. The basic minimum contract set the stage for further contract negotiations, and the leaders of the Guild encouraged a generous view of the agreement. In the June issue of the Guild publication, *Screen Actor,* the board characterized the victory as "not a conquest of the producers by the actor; it is the triumph of an ideal—a victory for the entire industry." In an effort to prove that fair treatment from the producers would result in increased cooperation from the actors, Guild officers encouraged the organization's members to bear in mind their responsibilities to the industry as a whole.[12] The manifestations of this moderate temperament appeared time and again.

ACCORDING TO THE LONGTIME GUILD national executive secretary Jack Dales: "We were very conservative, actually." Indeed, the Guild displayed its conservatism through its bargaining practices and policies, which included a guarded stance toward strikes, bylaws limiting the political activities of the board, a loose relationship with other labor groups in Hollywood, and a strong anti-Communist sentiment. Prevailing until 1971, this conservative bent can be attributed to its founding members, many of whom were well-known celebrities who had no desire to align themselves with radical forces that could possibly compromise their public image. Foremost, they felt that the organization would be most effective if it maintained a moderate tone, a predilection similar to Heston's own personal values. In fact, two of the Guild's early presidents, Robert Montgomery and George Murphy, both belonged to the Alliance, a conservative organization formed during the 1940 election to eradicate communism, dismantle the New Deal, and rally support for the Republican presidential candidate, Wendell Wilkie.[13] This involvement in the Alliance is surprising considering that the New Deal had legitimated the very union that Montgomery and Murphy represented. Nevertheless, their politics differed from the ideology of most union chiefs who played an important role in the Roosevelt coalition.

The Guild founders first showed their conservatism by establishing mechanisms that would minimize strikes. For example, the 75 percent vote required to instigate a strike outweighed the simple majority needed in other unions and, thus, decreased the likelihood of a work stoppage. However, the Guild required only a small percentage of its membership to launch an initiative, referendum, or recall. Furthermore, the board and officers were chosen by the group at large, not by just a small fraction of the membership. Therefore, in direct contrast to the Academy, the Guild featured a more open democracy than most unions at that time.[14]

Second, the Guild bylaws forbade the union from endorsing political parties or particular candidates, preferring to keep its attention on matters directly related to the wages, benefits, hours, and working conditions of actors. These rules restricted the board's political activities to encouraging or opposing a particular piece of legislation or to providing financial support for other unions engaged in similar legislative efforts. The policy may seem extremely limiting, but it actually gave the Guild more choices in the long run since, by supporting no particular party or candidate, it was free to promote legislation in the best interests of its members no matter by whom proposed. Some actors requested more guidance in the political realm, but Dales testified that the board and the membership voted against the proposal. "In the main the majority of actors want it to be just that, a union that doesn't intrude into their political life," explained Dales. "They don't want to see the Guild too much into extraneous affairs that do not directly impinge on the actor, and that seems to be true of liberals or conservatives, oddly enough."[15] While Heston often informed the media of the candidates he supported, he did not announce his personal preferences as Guild policy.

A third mark of the Guild's conservatism was its independence. Dales recalls that neither the Guild's staff nor its actors "associated it too much with the labor movement" and that the leadership infused the union cause with a healthy dose of individualism. Considering his suspicion of group action and admiration of individualism, Heston could be comfortable with the policies and organization of the Guild. Dales maintains that the Guild founders did not want to unite with other aggrieved workers. "They just felt that they were on their own, separate and apart," he remembered. Guild members did not hold other guilds or unions in disdain, but, as artists, they did not feel that they had much in common with other laborers. Their different needs necessitated a separate course of action. The Guild wanted to concentrate on issues that affected actors directly and avoid extraneous matters, even if they were relevant to the industry at large. The conservative membership was chiefly concerned with the personal choice of the individual, not with the collective choice of the group. In fact, the potentially oppressive hand of organized labor seemed more threatening to many Guild actors than the possible domination of management.[16] Therefore, the Guild board rarely aligned with other unions on strike, instead allowing individual members to decide for themselves whether to cross picket lines.

The Guild demonstrated its loose and uneasy relationship with the rest of the labor movement during the prolonged struggle in the late 1930s and the 1940s between Hollywood's craft guilds and the International Alliance of Theatrical Stage Employees and Moving Picture Machine Operators of America (IATSE officially, but IA for short), an organization originally founded in 1896 to organize stagehands across the country. Since the early years of the twentieth century, the AFL had struggled to keep the peace between the IA, which organized on an industrywide basis, and the various craft unions, such as the International Brotherhood of Electrical Workers. Meanwhile, in 1922, the studio heads formed their own collective-bargaining unit, known at the time as the Motion Picture Producers and Distributors of America (MPPDA), and shrewdly played the hostile unions off one another. Finally, the pivotal Studio Basic Agreement (1926) allowed both the IA and the craft unions to negotiate hours, working conditions, and general grievances with the studios. However, all the unions struggled against both continued management hostility and internal strife. Then, in 1934, George Browne and Willie Bioff, two mobster hoods who would go on to collect bribes from studio bosses in return for suppressing labor agitation in Hollywood, seized control of the IA. In 1941, Browne and Bioff were indicted, leading to their expulsion from the IA, a move that supposedly rid the organization of its mob element. Meanwhile, the labor leader Herb Sorrell attempted to organize the craft unions into an umbrella organization, first with the Federation of Motion Picture Companies, then with the Conference of Studio Unions (CSU).[17] A number of Hollywood's Communists immediately began to align themselves with the CSU.

The Guild feared that the film industry might very well break down in the mid-1940s when Herb Sorrell amassed a federation of studio craft locals under the banner of the CSU with the specific intent of challenging the IA and winning recognition for the CSU as the crafts' proper representative. The Guild attempted to maintain its independence but twice sided with the mob-tainted IA rather than with the CSU, each time revealing the Guild's natural inclination to avoid strikes, respect the individual members of the group, and shun communism.[18]

Sorrell led the first CSU strike in the fall of 1944. Even though President Roosevelt had created the War Labor Board to establish guaranteed wages and avoid strikes, the spiraling cost of living outpaced established wages, and an unprecedented number of wartime strikes erupted nationwide, most noticeably in the coal industry. However, Guild leaders believed that Sorrell's actions were driven less by bread-and-butter issues and more by jurisdictional matters. Furthermore, the Guild had promised not to strike for nine years, and any vote to respect the CSU lines would, therefore, also have been a vote for no contract. Any sympathies that Guild members may have held for the CSU eroded almost immediately. The CSU first drew the ire of actors when it compiled its own blacklist of actors who crossed picket lines. Then, in December 1944, the Guild's extras left the organization, only to be taken under the wing of the CSU-backed Screen Players Union (SPU). The Guild ushered the extras into the Screen Extras Guild rather than lose them to an SPU/CSU alliance. Finally, the Guild grew increasingly suspicious that the CSU had been infiltrated by Communists. In March 1945, Guild members voted by an overwhelming margin of 3,298–96 to cross the CSU's lines.[19]

Guild suspicions that the CSU harbored Communists damaged the already precarious relationship between Sorrell and the actors even further. Throughout the CSU strike, the IA deputy, Roy Brewer, had alluded to the possible Communist infiltration of the CSU, an allegation that Guild leaders refused to dismiss. Brewer continued to make the accusation with increasing strength and frequency, at one point distributing anti-Communist propaganda that specifically targeted the CSU. A number of Hollywood labor historians characterize Brewer's behavior as politically motivated red-baiting, and Gerald Horne dismisses his charge that Sorrell was a Communist as "wildly inaccurate." Whatever Sorrell's party affiliation, it is clear from Mike Nielsen and Gene Mailes's study, which includes the verbatim testimony of one CSU activist, that a number of Hollywood's Communists aligned themselves with the CSU. Nielsen and Mailes even assert that the CSU became a base for Party operations.[20] Because of Brewer's charges and the Guild's suspicion that he was at least partially correct, the conservative board finally turned against the CSU outright, even more aggressively challenging Sorrell during his next strike, in 1946.

By this point, the war had ended, but prices had risen 15 percent, leading 5 million workers to participate in forty-six hundred strikes across the nation. Once again, however, Sorrell's strike was over jurisdictional matters, not wages, and the frustrated Guild leadership grew convinced that his ultimate purpose was to bring Hollywood to a chaotic halt. The Guild issued a statement almost immediately, encouraging actors to continue working, and lamenting the possibility of thirty thousand people being thrown out of work in a union controversy concerning 350 jobs. The Guild disagreed with a work stoppage and wanted to rely on the AFL to enforce a decision. Once again, the actors' decision to work overwhelmingly prevailed by a tally of 2,748–509. Following the Guild's lead, other craft unions also broke with the CSU and returned to work. Furthermore, Sorrell's equivocal behavior at negotiating meetings convinced the Guild that the CSU chief was taking orders from the Communist Party. Ronald Reagan, an ascending figure in the Guild, became even more convinced of the Communist infiltration of the CSU when, after encouraging actors to cross the lines, he received several threats against his life. Without the Guild's support, the CSU could not last, and, in February 1947, twenty-five unions representing twenty-five thousand workers and 75 percent of the Hollywood labor force signed a letter calling the CSU a "rump organization" that ignored AFL requests and tried to capture or destroy other AFL unions. In March 1947, more than three thousand carpenters, machinists, and painters were still on strike, but the lines dwindled, and the CSU gradually "dissolved," according to Reagan, "like sugar in hot water."[21]

The battle between the IA and the CSU had several significant consequences for the Guild. First, the IA firmly took control of the Hollywood crafts and organized them along semi-industrial lines, and it has not been seriously challenged since. Second, Reagan impressed the Guild board and membership with his negotiating style and articulate speech during the convention, and he won the presidency of the organization three months later. Foremost, the strike and behavior of Sorrell and others radicals convinced the Guild leadership that Communists had embarked on a plan to gain control of Hollywood's liberal organizations. This threat made the anti-Communist crusade a priority for the Guild's officers, especially Reagan, who wrote: "More than anything else, it was the Communists' attempted takeover of Hollywood and its worldwide weekly audience of more than five hundred million people that led me to accept a nomination to serve as president of the Screen Actors Guild."[22] Having ousted the CSU, the Guild willingly participated in the anti-Communist crusade that Washington brought to Hollywood.

The need to find Communists and root them out of government—and, indeed, out of all segments of American life—became a national issue by the 1946 midterm elections. For the first time in eighteen years, the Republicans won control of both the U.S. Senate and the House of Representatives. In May 1947, members of the House Un-American Activities Committee (HUAC) arrived in Hollywood to interview "friendly" witnesses who would be willing to name Communists in the film industry. Attention especially focused on the actors and writers whom HUAC believed could covertly insert Communist propaganda into their films. Jack Warner, in particular, called attention to the writers and supplied names of people he considered "un-American." The leaders of the Guild attempted to walk a narrow line in their testimony by acknowledging to the committee that the Communist threat was real but not so powerful that the current leaders of the industry could not keep it in check. Reagan, Murphy, and Montgomery did not want to agree with HUAC's accusations for fear that the government would involve itself in film censorship, studio administration, and union activities. However, denying HUAC's claims would only lead Congress to conclude that the men had been duped into obliquity. Therefore, Reagan testified that a small faction within the Guild did consistently oppose its policies, behavior that convinced him that this minority followed the Communist line. Still, he claimed, democracy overrode them, and Communist propaganda never reached the big screen. Ten "unfriendly" witnesses, however, refused to answer HUAC's questions about their political affiliation and, instead, responded with speeches defending their civil liberties. After HUAC cited the ten for contempt, fifty top Hollywood executives met at the Waldorf-Astoria in New York, deciding to fire the unfriendly witnesses and to deny work in the motion picture industry to suspected subversives henceforth. This pact became known as the Waldorf Declaration and led to the studio blacklist.[23]

The blacklist put the Guild in another precarious position, especially after Congress passed the Taft-Hartley Act (1947), a labor bill requiring all union officers to sign affidavits confirming that they were not Communists. Although Reagan instinctively felt that the blacklist was antidemocratic, he did worry about Communist infiltration of the Guild, and a sampling of actors' opinions indicated that many would willingly sign a non-Communist pledge. Reagan and the Guild leadership sympathized with the producers' concerns because, as high-profile stars, they understood that, if their politics were offensive to public opinion, then they would be unmarketable and without jobs. In 1948, the Guild voted 1,307–157 for a resolution requiring officers, directors, and committee members to sign individual affidavits swearing that they did not belong to the Communist Party, and, by 1953, all new members were required to make the same pledge. According to Dales: "We thought that this was a matter of patriotism and propriety."[24] The Guild's adoption of a loyalty program insulated it from accusations of communism, and the conservative leadership continued its domination of the organization with no serious challenges. Fervent anticommunism swept the movie industry, and, by 1950, every major studio echoed the Motion Picture Alliance for the Preservation of American Ideals (founded in 1944 by Sam Wood, Walt Disney, and Leo McCarey, among others, specifically to defend the industry against Communist infiltration) in its call for unqualified loyalty and militant anticommunism. Throughout the 1950s, believing that the film medium could be a powerful weapon against communism, studios ensured that films reflected this theme, as did Charlton Heston's *The Ten Commandments*.

AS NOTED EARLIER, THE SUCCESS OF *The Ten Commandments* and *Ben-Hur* catapulted Heston to international fame and established his persona as a moral and honest leader, and, in 1960, the Guild officers recruited the actor to serve on their board. Although the Guild proved unusually democratic compared to most unions, the board sought out replacement members and officers who would perpetuate conservative rule in what one historian has labeled an *oligarchy of ideology*. Those who served on the board worked to ensure "that a certain outlook and temperament dominated union policy," and they screened potential officers through both informal networking and a formal selection process. The informal networking occurred largely during the long breaks between takes necessitated by the nature of filming, breaks that allowed actors time to make acquaintances and casually discuss a number of issues, including one another's political outlooks. The formal selection process took place when the Guild's president appointed the committee chairs, including the heads of the Nominating Committee and the Board Replacement Committee. Both these committees used a "network of personal recommendations" acceptable to the current officers to replace vacant board seats between elections and to nominate "an invariably successful 'official slate'" each year. This system did not result in agreement on all issues, but it did guarantee that most who oversaw the Guild government operated from a conservative or moderate premise.[25] The board never knowingly drafted anyone on the opposite side of the political spectrum, so their interest in Heston meant they believed he shared their political outlook.

Heston stated that he agreed to serve on the Guild board because he had "received so much from my profession" and wanted to "repay others in the profession which has been so good to me." He certainly did not expect glamorous perks or financial reward. Governance duties within the Guild involved difficult and tedious labor, especially because of their intense demands on an actor's time. The bimonthly board meetings were only the beginning. Negotiating meetings often lasted all night during strikes, and strikes could last for weeks and even months. Furthermore, board members, and especially the president, had a number of additional responsibilities, including attending AFL conventions, testifying before Congress, and visiting Guild branches scattered throughout the country. By 1970, the Guild had branches or functioning offices in seventeen cities, including Atlanta, Philadelphia, and Minneapolis–St. Paul. The officers did not receive a salary, nor could they expect rewards in the way of movie roles. By the 1950s, "the glamour had worn off," claimed Dales. "In the 30s and early 40s, it was wonderful, but after that it was a damned chore, and you're fighting for your life; you're fighting your own membership. It isn't a job where you get too many cheers, even from your own members."[26]

Heston immediately became involved in pivotal negotiations with the studios concerning movie residuals. As Americans bought more and more televisions for their homes in the 1950s, networks developed new shows such as *I Love Lucy* (1951–57), *Father Knows Best* (1954–60), and *Gunsmoke* (1955–75), but they soon realized that the public also enjoyed viewing old movies long absent from the theaters. Because television had not existed when those movies were made, actors had no guaranteed residuals written into their film contracts, and, with the exception of MCA, which in 1952 had broken with the rest of the producers, studios had no intention of compensating them. For ten years, the Guild haggled with the producers, who had vowed never to pay residuals. By 1959, most studios had sold their entire film libraries, and, since almost any "talkie" could be seen on television, the Guild decided that the time had come for a showdown, even if it turned into a strike.[27]

Anticipating that residual negotiations could be a long and difficult contest, the board convinced Reagan, who had stepped down in 1952, to temporarily resume his former post as president. "We knew that was going to be a battle," Dales recalled, "there was no secret about it; the producers made no secret about it—so we wanted a strong leader, and everybody's mind turned back to Ronald Reagan." Indeed, its stiff demands required the best negotiator the Guild could summon. The Guild demanded that producers provide residuals for all movies made in the future, retroactive payment for all movies made in the eleven preceding years, and a health, pension, and welfare plan for its members. Throughout the thirty-six-day strike and extensive late-night sessions, Heston witnessed Reagan's negotiating style and adopted it as his own, although he conceded humbly: "No one could do it like Reagan." Still, "I began to realize," Heston remembered, "that grinding the other side down in argument isn't really the best tactic, though a lot of union negotiations are still carried on that way." He praised Reagan for being particularly adept at finding common ground and not treating management as an evil adversary, a concept that Heston found "painfully out of date." In the end, the Guild and the producers reached a compromise. The Guild agreed to sell all the television rights for the pictures made between 1948 and 1959 to the producers for a flat sum of $2.65 million, money that was then used to jump-start the Guild's first pension and welfare plan. For all the films made in 1960 and beyond, the producers agreed to the residuals that the Guild demanded. One star who would have benefited from the residuals of the pre-1960 films considered the agreement "a crushing blow to so many of us." Some even blamed Reagan for selling them out. However, those involved in the negotiations believed that the producers would never have agreed to retroactive payment and noted that the welfare and pension plan applied to all the Guild's actors.[28] Heston considered the compromise a victory and one of his proudest moments at the Guild.

This apprenticeship under Reagan shaped Heston's tactics as Guild president, and his and Reagan's shared sense of optimism further solidified their analogous approach to labor issues. Reagan's striking sense of optimism has been one of his trademarks. In contrast to the malaise that President Jimmy Carter brought to the White House, Reagan bragged during the 1984 presidential election: "It's morning in America again." This optimism appears to have been a natural instinct for Reagan, exhibited as a child and throughout the span of his political career. Completely confident in his acting abilities, Heston possessed this same sense of optimism about people, politics, and life in general. Just as political commentators have noted Reagan's "almost Pollyanna optimism," Lydia Heston has commented on her husband's. "He has a very easy-going, vigorous kind of temperament," Lydia once told an interviewer who had asked her about the personality differences between her and Heston. "He is extremely optimistic, he simply can't believe that anything bad is ever going to happen to him."[29] Heston himself admitted that, when auditioning, he never believed he would not get the part.

According to Martin Seligman, a cognitive psychologist who has devoted his life's work to identifying optimism and studying its consequences, optimists have an "explanatory style" that they use to rationalize both good and bad events—a style that characterizes their leadership. Seligman uses three factors to determine an individual's explanatory style: permanence, pervasiveness, and personalization. In a variant of the glass half empty/half full model, optimists view good events as the result of permanent factors diffused throughout their environment and especially due to their own personal set of qualities. When something bad happens, however, optimists explain those events with a set of premises in complete contrast to their method of explaining the good happenings. Bad events are temporary, specific to that situation, and external to their character. Whereas an optimist might explain a happy event with, "I always win good movie roles;

I am a good actor," he would explain losing a part with, "They wanted someone shorter than me, someone who would look good with that particular actress." Pessimists, on the other hand, would explain the situation in a completely different manner because they treat good events like optimists treat bad ones, and vice versa. A good event to a pessimist is temporary, its causes specific and external, while a bad event is permanent, pervasive, and personalized. After losing a part, a pessimist would say, "I never get the parts I want; I never can catch a break; I am a bad actor, a loser." If he did win the role, he would rationalize, "I just got lucky for once because the director wanted someone short like me, who would look good with that particular actress." Seligman notes the usefulness of pessimism, saying that it does "heighten our sense of reality and endows us with accuracy." However, he also insists that pessimism must be harnessed, for it promotes depression, produces inertia, gives one a low sense of subjective self-worth, and, therefore, results in the very consequences the pessimist fears. In contrast, optimists tend to be more successful in life, carry a strong sense of self-worth, enjoy better health, and prevail in politics—all characteristics that Heston most certainly displayed.[30]

The inherent optimism that served Reagan and Heston as a negotiating tool in the Guild would do so again in the national political arena. Optimists tend automatically to trust others until something proves that trust wrong, whereas pessimists are suspicious of others until something proves trust to be warranted. The optimist's tendency to be open and positive with people affected the way Reagan and Heston negotiated because they automatically assumed that the producers operated in good faith and could be relied on to find some middle ground. Reagan and Heston manifested this attitude in their analyses of situations in Hollywood as well, seeing the entertainment industry as basically good, marred only by temporary problems, not systemic flaws. Furthermore, optimists such as Heston and Reagan are more likely than are pessimists to win elections because voters want people who offer to solve their problems, to lead them. According to Seligman, an optimistic candidate evaluates a bad event but accompanies this analysis with a course of action to remedy the situation.[31] Heston's speeches as Guild president indicate this optimistic analysis of the issues.

His ability to work with producers and to inspire the confidence of the Guild membership resulted in five years on the Guild board and an additional six years as the organization's president.

As Guild president, Heston modeled himself after Ronald Reagan in his efforts to improve the security of actors in the profession, and he achieved considerable results without having to launch a strike. Only six months after taking office, he obtained additional benefits for actors and a year later won major wage hikes as well. In 1966, producers agreed to additional life and accidental insurance benefits, treatment for mental conditions, a hospital room and board allowance, and Medicare. By 1967, the Guild secured hikes in actors' minimum rates, residuals, and overtime wages and also won further improvements in pension funds, welfare plans, and safety requirements. Television, theater, and commercial actors all reaped the rewards of these added benefits, and Heston displayed a patient, moderate leadership in winning them. Throughout the negotiations, he treated the producers as parties with whom the Guild shared a mutual interest. "Our prosperity as performers depends on the producers' prosperity," he believed, and he made a deliberate effort to avoid a work stoppage during negotiations. An article in *Screen Actor* made sure to note: "These negotiations were the first in television since the advent of that medium in which the Guild has not been forced to take a strike vote in order to arrive at a reasonable agreement." The achievement was particularly attributed to Heston. Jack Dales told Guild members: "Chuck Heston has come to the meeting directly from the set—without dinner. He must report to the studio at 8:30 the next morning." Dales further congratulated the Guild president for not capitulating to anger and exhaustion when the two sides were at odds. "The easiest out in the world is to say 'No!' and call for a strike vote," he wrote.[32]

These contract improvements, Heston told Guild members, "represented standards of wage and working conditions that carry the actor, it seems to me, about as far as collective bargaining can carry him," and he thereafter turned his presidential attention away from bread-and-butter issues and toward industrial matters that affected actors. Much of Heston's tenure as president revolved around discouraging the overseas, or "run-away," production of American films. Although the Guild had "no part in securing employment for its members" and was "solely concerned with the wages and working conditions for actors when they are working," Heston considered overseas production part of the Guild's domain because it would indirectly be boosting employment. He was deeply concerned with the issue of runaway production, but he refused to confront the studios with demands or threaten to strike over it. Since Heston concluded that high domestic costs were the primary force driving producers overseas, he sought measures to reduce those costs, a technique that took the producers' needs into consideration as much as the actors'. Heston believed that he was practicing "enlightened unionism," constantly repeating: "Our prosperity is tied to the prosperity of the industry as a whole."[33]

From the first grumblings among actors that too many films were being made abroad, Heston placed the blame not on the studios but on the high cost of domestic production itself. In 1961, when he was third vice president of the Guild, he noted that, of the thirty-seven films being made that year, twelve were shot overseas and five outside Los Angeles. Searching for a reason, Heston told a House committee studying the impact of imports and exports on American labor: "I will turn for a moment to the villains in this plot. Unfortunately, I can't honestly say that I can find any. With the posse all saddled and ready to ride, we really should have some heavies to cut off at the pass, and I regret that I can't point eagerly and say 'they went thataway!,' but I can't." Not only did Heston refuse to attribute blame; he privately viewed those who did with sardonic dismissal. For instance, after one board meeting "fraught with concern with overseas production," he commented sarcastically in his journal: "O, brave new world . . . that hath such creatures in it."[34]

Heston himself made seven films that were shot entirely overseas, including his blockbusters *The Ten Commandments, Ben-Hur,* and *El Cid,* which were shot in Egypt, Rome, and Spain, respectively. However, he did not feel guilty for his participation in these productions. "I must tell you that, to the best of my knowledge, none of these films would have been made at all if it had not been possible to make them overseas," he explained to the Guild. Indeed, no studio could have afforded the cost of employing the enormous number of extras or building the grand sets the films required in the United States. Furthermore, the spectacular profits that *Ben-Hur* earned have been credited with saving the film industry, so perhaps overseas production should not always be considered harmful to Hollywood. Still, Heston was unwilling to stand by idly and wanted to engage in positive action that would persuade studios to make more movies at home. "To penalize pictures made elsewhere would merely further depress an already precarious industry," he warned. "We must encourage the making of more, not fewer pictures, by stimulating domestic production." Heston maintained this same attitude during the latter years of his presidency after spiraling inflation in the late 1960s heated the urgency of the debate. Whereas 34 percent of American films had been made abroad in 1960, 60 percent were filmed overseas in 1967.[35]

By 1968, Heston and the Guild openly fought against overseas production, but not before Heston had extinguished concerns regarding his potential conflict-of-interest problems. In 1956, the actor had launched his own production company, the Russel Lake Corporation, but any sort of producer status made him ineligible to be the Guild's president, much less one who was opposing certain production practices. After a concerned member wrote the Guild inquiring about the matter, in a closed meeting Heston reassured the board that his company made investments with the option to produce but had never done so. Although he frequently demanded approval of cast, director, or script, he did not consider those clauses to fall under the label *production*. He told the board that he was "keenly aware" of possible conflicts but that he had done "everything I can to diligently keep them separate and act only in the interest of the Board." Heston need not have worried. When he left the room to let the board discuss the situation freely, it gave him a vote of confidence, noting in the minutes: "The opinion was strongly expressed by many Board members that Charlton Heston is one of the most able and efficient presidents the Guild has ever had."[36]

Heston led the Guild as it developed and promoted a five-point plan to increase domestic production, a proposal particularly notable for its neoconservative tone—an emphasis on balancing the individual and the community and on pursuing limited government support. The first point of the plan was the elimination of "unfair" taxes, especially the Los Angeles County personal property tax, a feat that it accomplished almost immediately. Heston appealed directly to California State Senator George Moscone, the vice chair of the Revenue and Taxation Committee, to pass Senate Bill 393, eliminating this tax. "The studios of course are quite properly taxed in terms of the assessed value of their real and personal property, as with any other business," he wrote Moscone. "But to continue to tax them in terms of an additional assessment on the intangible value of all the scripts, unfinished films, and completed negatives they possess as of each March first is to smother the industry for at least three months of every year." According to Heston, the property tax was partially responsible for the sizable costs that producers faced and, thus, helped drive them out of the United States. Actors as well as the local economy suffered, Heston impressed on the senator, estimating that actors lost $1,295,000 in payroll because of this tax. Without that money being spent, Los Angeles as a whole bore the consequences. In the fall of 1968, the California legislature passed Senate Bill 393 and sent it to Ronald Reagan, elected the state's governor in 1966, to sign. Calling the new law "an outstanding victory," the Guild believed that the cessation of the tax would result in increased production in California and continued to work on the rest of its five-point plan.[37]

The second point of the plan proposed legislation that would distribute subsidies to the studios through a national film fund agency. The proposal involved collecting the proceeds of an excise levy on the public, commercial exhibition of motion pictures and prorating this fund among producers who abided by specific criteria. Heston and his colleagues considered a film fund to be one of the best ways to persuade producers to remain in the United States and not take advantage of the benefits available in foreign countries. Many European governments offered subsidies, including cash payments, low- or no-interest loans, tax rebates, advances of partial production costs, and private loan guarantees. The Guild hoped that a film fund would "equalize the competitive position of domestically produced motion pictures with foreign made motion pictures" by offering its own form of subsidy. Although the bill conservatively sought to help actors by improving the financial situation for producers, the Guild still sought out government intervention to do so, calling for even more government bureaucracy. The film fund would have required an independent agency in the executive branch with a three-person board of directors who served five-year terms with the assistance of full-time, salaried administrators. Every fifty-two weeks, the fund would determine which studios were eligible for payment.[38] By proposing the film fund, Heston sought government support, but, in a typical neoconservative approach, to only a limited degree.

The third point of the plan pledged a "committee review of the internal problems which may frustrate full production in Hollywood." The Guild considered the possibility that unions bore some responsibility for the "needless cost increases," although Richard Walsh of the IA denied that this was the case. The proposed review illustrated the Guild's desire to discover and then correct the problems causing such high costs, not just blindly blame some outside force. Displaying objectivity as well as maturity, the Guild announced: "We are prepared to explore any aspect of the problem with complete frankness and a willingness to accept constructive criticism." Additionally, the Guild sought to be open-minded about new forms of production such as small, independent filmmakers. An exploding number of low-budget independent films had hit the market, and they could not afford to meet Guild standards. Actors worked in these films illegally and outside their union contracts. Heston sympathized with actors' need to work but bemoaned the fact that "if they work bootleg they lose all the protections that SAG has built up over thirty-five tough years—not just salary, welfare, TV sale, and so on." Still, when Heston was obligated to chair a disciplinary meeting against John Cassavetes for making an independent feature outside his Guild contract, he privately thought the actor deserved some "elbow room" and was beginning to feel "uneasy about how well SAG was serving its working members by then." The Guild compromised on the issue by proposing that actors could initially work at half scale for movies budgeted under $50,000, deferring the other half until the movie made money, if it did.[39] This arrangement balanced the needs of the individual actors with those of the acting community as a whole.

The "self-help" review resulted in two new pursuits: the Guild's "come-back contract" and a federal tax bill. The comeback contract attempted to cut costs on actor contracts by "streamlin[ing] production in dramatic fashion." The Guild agreed to various changes in consecutive days of employment, the use of principal actors in preproduction, and the pay scale during makeup application, all of which would enable producers to save capital. The Guild members heartily signaled their approval. In a record vote of over 15,000 ballots, 14,903 voted to ratify the contract changes, while only 354 voted against them. Apparently, the Guild negotiated a retroactive clause because only a month later Heston wrote that under this contract: "Producers have shot nineteen films since February that either would not have been made at all, or would have been made out of the U.S." If these numbers are accurate, that is quite an accomplishment, and the contract itself is exactly the kind of "enlightened unionism" that Heston believed to be in the tradition of the Guild. "The Guild is proud of its responsibility as a moderating and reasonable force in the film community," he proclaimed. "We do not feel, as the old line thinking used to hold, that what's bad for management is good for labor."[40] Meanwhile, the Guild hired Thomas Kuchel, a former senator, as its "Washington consultant" in an effort to seek federal legislation boosting domestic production. After producer resistance forced it to drop the film fund proposal, the Guild searched for other mutually acceptable ways to cut costs.

The cost-cutting ambitions had a desperate air because production had slumped dramatically both domestically and abroad. Heston told the Guild membership in his sixth annual presidential address that "production around the world has fallen to its lowest ebb since I can remember." He informed them that, between 1955 and 1960, an average of 80 million people a week saw a film in the United States. In 1970, that number had dropped to 15 million per week. Heston encouraged the continued utilization of the comeback contract and more aggressive efforts to obtain federal assistance through a tax incentive. While he noted that it "reject[ed] any kind of restrictive legislation such as tariffs, or quotas," the Guild still pursued direct tax deductions for producers and even enlisted the help of Ronald Reagan to do so. Echoing Heston's disapproval of trade barriers for fear of emotionally charged retaliations from foreign countries, Reagan urged President Richard Nixon to pass legislation calling for a 20 percent tax break on the gross income earned by the motion picture industry. By the end of 1971, these various ideas had come to fruition, most notably with the Tax Reform Act of 1971. The new reforms offered studios a 7 percent investment tax credit and a tax provision called the *domestic international sales corporation* that allowed the use of moneys, tax deferred, from 50 percent of the earnings of pictures exhibited abroad when reinvested in domestic production. The Guild hailed these measures as precisely the boost that producers needed, a claim seemingly proved correct by Universal's addition of five more domestic features to its 1972 agenda. Although it is not clear just how much responsibility the Guild could claim in increasing domestic production, the issue was important because of the innovative, yet conservative, strategies that Heston used in attacking the problem.[41]

The fourth point of the plan included working with international unions. In 1970, the Guild joined the International Federation of Actors in an effort to help overseas unions achieve parity with the contracts that the Guild had negotiated. Heston hailed this nontraditional step as "one of the most effective tools we have in redressing the markedly lower production cost in foreign jurisdictions that is such a factor in taking production out of the country."[42] Heston hoped that producers would avoid going abroad so frequently if the actors in foreign countries demanded wages on par with those of American actors.

In the fifth and final point of the plan, Heston and the board encouraged the development of cutting-edge technology. Heston implored the federal government to open the airwaves for subscription television in the hopes of stimulating new job opportunities for actors. Although theater owners opposed such a development, the board voted unanimously to "affirm . . . its support of the development of subscription television." When presenting the resolution to the Guild membership, Heston presented the matter as one "of vital interest to our citizenry and the free enterprise system," the same argument that he later made when testifying to Congress. Heston also promised Guild action on what he anticipated as "the biggest prize package opened in Hollywood since sound came in . . . video cassettes." The Guild would fight for residuals from this medium, just as it did for residuals from films shown on television. If recalcitrant producers resisted, Heston declared: "Personally, I am prepared to sacrifice almost anything to this end. It could well become a basic strike issue. If so . . . so be it. I'll look to you for support when that time comes."[43] Heston's efforts to obtain additional benefits and videocassette residuals illustrate that the Guild did not lose its militant edge and negotiating power under his presidency, while his work on runaway production indicates his willingness to cooperate with producers. This combination very much followed the pattern that the Guild had established in its formative years and illustrated Heston's neoconservative inclinations.

While his goals as Guild president when dealing with bread-and-butter issues were fairly progressive, when dealing with social and cultural issues, Heston maintained fairly traditional positions. Still, he was always willing to compromise. For example, as he worked for a solution regarding runaway production and production cuts, he realized that a fair amount of the Guild membership relied on television to employ them. He deplored the quality of programming on television, however, considering it a sunken medium in its current state, compared to his days on *Studio One*. While he had enjoyed the opportunity to perform live Shakespeare, television actors during his presidency appeared chiefly in situation comedies and variety shows. "We feel that the networks have completely failed in their responsibility to the viewing public and the performer," he told the *Los Angeles Times*. Disgusted with the networks' "utter disregard for any standard of excellence," Heston turned to a traditional form of compensation—large paychecks. "If the networks cannot shape a medium in which the performer can take some pride," he said dryly, "we can at least make it sufficiently lucrative for the performer." He reported to the Guild in his 1967 presidential address that actors had made an unprecedented $100 million in the preceding year and that two-thirds of those earnings came from television and largely from commercial advertising.[44] He promised to improve those earnings even more.

Heston struck similar middle ground with debates over censorship in the late 1960s. The MPPDA had actually established its own voluntary production code in 1922, and the Hays Office enforced its rules with the threat of $25,000 fines. This self-regulating system crumbled after independent producers refused to adhere to what they considered rigid codes, a position upheld by the Supreme Court in 1952 on the basis of free speech. At the same time, studio heads did not want to compromise their sales by offending audiences. In 1968, Jack Valenti, the head of the producers' association, which by then was known as the Motion Picture Association of America (MPAA), devised a rating system that did not restrict speech yet prepared audiences for potentially offensive material. The Code and Rating Administration (CARA) rated movies "G" for general audiences, "PG" for parental guidance recommended, "R" for restricted to consumers under the age of seventeen without an adult, and "X" for adults only. Heston immediately offered the Guild's support for the CARA venture. Because the CARA system served as a guideline and not a restriction, Heston announced: "I think the [MPAA] rating system is as good a solution as can be devised for the problem of protecting both rights of the filmmakers and the audience." Heston pointed out that mature adolescents would be denied access to well-made films because of their age and that some poor films could actually succeed because of the extra publicity garnered through an X rating, two consequences he believed to be flaws of the new system. However, he felt Valenti's proposal to be a workable solution to a complicated problem. "Only a fool rejects the best solution to a problem because it is an imperfect one," he preached. "In an imperfect world, there are even some problems for which there are no solutions at all!"[45] This sort of nondogmatic approach aptly characterized Heston's attitude toward Guild matters during his presidency. He was tied less to ideology than to what worked.

The Guild position regarding minority issues both shaped and reflected Heston's attitude toward civil rights, discrimination, and affirmative action. The Guild already possessed a relatively admirable record toward minority issues before Heston came into office, largely because Reagan had initiated communication with African American actors during his presidency in the 1940s. The National Association for the Advancement of Colored People (NAACP) had long advocated better Hollywood jobs and more respectable screen images for African Americans, an appeal ignored by the Guild and resisted by black actors, both of whom worried that the elimination of stereotypical roles would result in no jobs at all. Reagan took interest in this debate, and, in September 1946, the Guild adopted an antidiscrimination resolution and established a committee to monitor its progress. Wanting to keep black actors working, the Guild did not demand elimination of secondary or demeaning roles. It simply asked that producers treat those black actors respectfully. Producers considered the Guild's recommendations and, in March 1947, agreed on three new practices: parts written for blacks would be played by blacks and not white actors made up in blackface; consideration would be given to hiring more blacks for crowd scenes and similar environments; and blacks would, henceforth, be portrayed as ordinary people, not caricatures. Beginning in 1952, Reagan continued to work with the board to find methods of spurring black employment, a practice the Guild continued after Reagan stepped down from the presidency.[46] These efforts established an early precedent within the Guild to encourage progressive measures on race but to respect the individual choices of African American actors.

Although the producers promised to portray black characters in a better light, their agreement with the Guild did not establish any accountability or monitoring system. Hence, civil rights organizations continued to accuse Hollywood of treating blacks as "invisible" and as "caricatures." In 1963, Martin Luther King Jr. stepped in, representing the national office of the NAACP. King was actually in town to discuss the issue of black employment in Hollywood's unions. Since the Guild allowed anyone of any race who obtained a job to become a member, King enlisted Heston's help to encourage the craft unions to open up their all-white membership rolls. King's presence in Hollywood also inspired a discussion of the portrayal of blacks on the screen, a negative image that many actors blamed on producers, who, in turn, placed the onus on New York financiers, who supposedly believed that African Americans could not produce good returns at the box office.[47]

Heston attended a meeting on what actions to take to prevent discrimination in the craft unions and how to achieve a more favorable on-screen image of blacks. He was the first prominent actor to voice his opinion on both matters. Although he led the arts contingent at the March on Washington, he had never called for radical action on civil rights matters, and this meeting was no exception. His comments were strikingly moderate. He encouraged other organizations to use the Guild's antidiscrimination policy as a model and noted that the craft guilds discriminated against everyone outside their family circles, not just blacks. In making this point, Heston echoed a number of intellectual neocons, who also noted the strength of family-oriented professions and pointed out that powerful ties, such as family, ethnic, or religious loyalties, complicated visions of racial progress. In terms of how blacks were portrayed onscreen, Heston conceded that "films have borne [a responsibility] over the years in making this image [of minorities] an unjust and unsympathetic one," but he never advocated ethnic casting quotas or affirmative action to correct those mistakes. Heston arranged meetings between King and other craft guilds and producers to promote the use of antidiscrimination clauses in employment and to improve the portrayal of blacks and Hispanics in films. However, he believed that the best actor should be hired for a role with little concern for race. In other words, the designation of "black roles," "white roles," or "Hispanic roles" seemed wrong to him. Indeed, Heston himself played the role of a Hispanic detective in Orson Welles's *Touch of Evil* in 1958, a plum job "I'd have been damn sorry to have been denied."[48]

Heston was not the only actor to feel this way. A number of performers wrote to *Screen Actor* complaining about the results of ethnic quota casting. The Guild member Bernadette Hale believed that some minority groups received more attention than others and complained: "The demands and pressures exerted by these groups of producers, directors, and writers have reached a level which has become ridiculous." Likewise, Noel de Souza, an actor "of East Indian origin and skin type," had customarily played Latin characters but complained that the lobbying pressures of African American and Hispanic groups no longer made these roles accessible. "I am not alone in this situation," Souza told the Guild, "and the reason I write about it is because I feel that while correcting one wrong, we are creating another injustice to many devoted people in the profession." On the other hand, the actors Iron Eyes Cody and Kid Chissell complained that "everybody is playing Indians" except Indians. Heston took the conservative side of the debate, arguing that the Guild "cannot make actors totally interchangeable and cannot deny the producer the right to cast the actor he thinks is right for the role." Heston's was a judgment with which the neocons would have agreed. Indeed, they frequently pointed out that every human activity involved discrimination of some sort.[49]

Despite the controversial issues and the inevitable internal disputes that he faced, Heston enjoyed immense popularity as Guild president because of his talents as an able and competent leader attuned to the actors' needs. According to Dales, actors have an informal set of criteria when deciding on who their leaders will be, and Heston qualified on all counts. In addition to a "certain charisma," Dales argued, the Guild president also needed a basic knowledge of the issues most important to actors. Whereas Dales, a nonactor, automatically believed salary to be the primary issue when first coming to the Guild, he soon realized that sometimes other matters loomed just as large, such as working conditions during voice looping or a television station's right to colorize films originally made in black-and-white. Dales broke it down into three main requirements. "They want an actor who knows his profession," he explained. "They want an actor who is not singleminded to a particular kind of actor; that is to say, the contract actor versus the freelance actor. And I think most of all, they want an articulate leader with whom they can identify; not a white knight necessarily, but a man who can say to the public and back to them, what they would say if they were there."[50] If these are the qualities that appealed to actors, then it is evident why Heston enjoyed their support. In addition to the automatic respect that he received as an immensely successful actor, Heston proved himself an able and articulate spokesperson, not only in Guild meetings, but also as the acting profession's representative to the outside world. Furthermore, he honestly explained what he perceived as the biggest threats to actors but optimistically proposed solutions to those problems.

Heston also possessed an astute sense of perspective as Guild president. When presiding at meetings, he opened the floor to discussion but ruled with a strong gavel so as not to lose track of the point at hand. Even so, after the thirty-fifth annual meeting, the Guild member Paul Ehrman wrote a letter to *Screen Actor* addressed to Heston. "Your own courtesy during the floor discussion period was impressive, even moving, but it's too much," he complained. "That is, there's obviously a tradition that encourages a lot of people to stand up and talk about themselves at great length." Indeed, Heston himself grew weary of the constant pontificating, characterizing one meeting in his journal as the "usual large amount of tommyrot (with now and then a grain of sense, mind you)." He refused to become mired in extraneous issues and focused ably on the issues that he perceived to be the most important. Many Guild members appreciated his efforts, including Eugene Francis, from the Guild's New York national board, who commented at Heston's last meeting as Guild president: "I believe as thoroughly as I think you do in the democratic principle, the majority must be served, although the minority must be protected. . . . Having watched all the presidents that have gone before us—and some of them have been great ones—none of them, in my humble judgment, have been equal to the dedication, the compassion, nor have they given the sacrifices made by Charlton Heston."[51] Although Francis's praise received a standing ovation, not all Guild members were as pleased with Heston's leadership.

Near the end of Heston's reign, an insurgent movement arose to shift the political tenor of the Guild to the left. The officers who ran the Guild saw themselves as highly democratic, and, when challenged, they pointed out that the Guild had more member mobility and more turnover of board members than other unions. Indeed, compared to other labor organizations, the Guild was more democratic, but, compared to other public service organizations, the participation of the rank and file was quite limited. The historian David Prindle argues that the Guild's critics were largely correct because the defining characteristics of a truly democratic union are participation by the membership at large and closely contested elections. Until 1971, the Guild had neither.[52] Indeed, no incumbent officer had even been mildly threatened by an unseating, but this situation soon changed. By 1970, a small number of insurgents had emerged with specific demands over membership and residuals. In 1971, they had formed the Concerned

Actors Committee (CAC) with the hopes of opening the Guild to greater rank-and-file participation. At this point, Heston had joined the National Council on the Arts of the National Endowment for the Arts as well as the American Film Institute board and was also attempting to star in and direct the 1972 *Antony and Cleopatra,* a complicated project that consumed much of his time. Heston felt that it was time to step down from the Guild presidency, and he did so in the summer of 1971.

No unslated candidate could have defeated an incumbent of Heston's stature, so the timing of Heston's decision could not have been better for the CAC. The disgruntled members planned to make a legitimate grab for power in the next election. The CAC founders, Charles Briggs and Michael Vandever, assembled a slate with a common platform, coordinated mailings and public appearances, centralized financing, and handpicked a spokesperson. With a platform that focused on democratizing the Guild and increasing film production in the United States as well as a slate that included the well-known actor Donald Sutherland, the CAC immediately captured the attention of the Guild membership. Taken by surprise, the Guild's slated nominees, including the presidential contender John Gavin, quickly regrouped and campaigned more aggressively than in years past. Even Heston, who had originally planned on keeping his preference for Gavin quiet, announced his backing of the slate after the CAC mavericks made their intentions clear, claiming that they were running against not only the official slate of 1971 but also the past administrations of the Guild as well. The slated nominees—or, in Heston's mind, the "good guys"— handily defeated the CAC nominees, but the episode foreshadowed an upcoming revolution in the Guild. Set against the national turmoil of the early 1970s, the campaign and election prompted Heston to look within and clarify his political and cultural positions.[53]

HESTON'S NEOCONSERVATIVE APPROACH toward labor issues meshed well with his own union as well as with the labor movement in general. The founding members of the Guild established a conservative organization that stood removed from party politics, and Heston repeatedly pursued policies that would honor and maintain that tradition. Heston worked to strike a balance between individual rights and the common good and to develop creative ideas that maximized government support without sacrificing the independence of the Guild. Heston's neoconservative method bore fruit. The Guild enjoyed significant gains in terms of bread-and-butter issues. Plus, Heston found a reasonable middle ground on complicated and emotional issues like runaway production, television standards, minorities in film, and a ratings system. His methods also resembled the moderate stance taken by labor as a whole. Despite labor's earlier flirtations with socialism and communism, by 1948 and 1949 it had abandoned social reform In exchange for economic security, pursuing that goal through a private and depoliticized system of collective bargaining. FDR had ushered labor into the Democratic fold. Big labor went on to approve of the Cold War liberalism of the Democratic Party and similarly made Keynesian economics and anticommunism central elements of its approach. Like other unions, the Guild prioritized economic security, but, unlike the United Auto Workers, for instance, it did not align itself with the Democrats.

At the end of Heston's presidency, the CAC challenged the Guild's traditions and Heston's neoconservative approach, saying that it wanted to "democratize" the union. Heston rejected the CAC for several reasons. First, it had more on its agenda than met the eye. For example, one of its founders wanted to restrict the labor pool by making it harder to become a Guild member through higher dues and more extensive training.[54] Second, it wanted to overturn Guild traditions, customs that Heston believed important, not only because of his natural reverence for the past, but also because he believed them superior to other alternatives. The Guild was, indeed, more republican than democratic in nature. Like the intellectual neocons, Heston preferred an organization that was representative—and led by enlightened individuals—to an all-out democracy. Kristol pointed out: "[America's] Founders thought it appropriate that popular sentiments should be delayed in their course, refracted in their expression, revised in their enactment, so that a more deliberate public opinion could prevail over a transient popular opinion."[55] Heston wanted to run the Guild in the same way, believing a full democracy to be more messy and time-consuming and to hold a real potential for mob rule. Therefore, he and the CAC disagreed in ideological terms on how best to run the Guild: as a republic or a democracy. Heston's position came under attack, especially in the late 1960s, as the champions of participatory democracy began to challenge traditional institutions—a trend that Heston fought against both in the Guild and on the National Council on the Arts.

CHAPTER FOUR

ARTS PATRON

CHARLTON HESTON'S ACTING CAREER CONTINUED TO FLOURISH DURING the late 1960s and the early 1970s. Between 1965 and 1972, Heston starred in fifteen feature films, directed one of his own, narrated documentaries on Franklin Delano Roosevelt and Martin Luther King Jr., and returned to the stage for several theatrical productions. But the actor craved public service as well. During that same period, he presided over the Screen Actors Guild and steadily increased his presence in Washington, DC. President Johnson had noted the contributions of celebrity activists to his 1964 landslide victory and increasingly utilized well-known stars to promote his Great Society, especially endeavors dealing with the arts. Heston participated in the White House Festival of the Arts, served as a member of the National Council on the Arts of the National Endowment for the Arts (NEA), and chaired the American Film Institute (AFI). Meanwhile, a number of intellectual neocons also became deeply involved in Johnson's domestic agenda, particularly the War on Poverty. Despite Heston's support of Johnson, he grew skeptical of the president's ever-proliferating programs. The intellectual neocons became similarly doubtful, and for largely the same reasons as Heston, despite their lack of an actual relationship with the actor.

Three developments particularly struck Heston and the rest of the neocons as rendering Johnson's initiatives problematic. First, a number of Great Society programs became politicized, initially over the Vietnam War, and then regarding cultural issues. Second, the Great Society seemed in danger of becoming not a unifying but a dividing force in America, especially along racial lines. Third, the Great Society contributed to an even larger federal government, a trend abhorred by the neocons, especially because of the increased bureaucracy that accompanied it. The intellectual neocons came to these conclusions primarily through observation of and participation in the War on Poverty, while Heston's judgments derived from his involvement in the president's arts programs. Heston's experience with federal arts initiatives between 1965 and 1972 typified the overall disillusionment with the Great Society experienced by visceral neoconservatives and intellectual neocons alike. When Heston confronted what he considered to be the problematic aspects of the NEA, he tapped into a larger political and cultural critique of the Democratic welfare state and positioned himself on the conservative, traditional side of the emerging battle for American cultural authority.

Heston and several other actors, such as Kirk Douglas, had participated minimally in the Kennedy administration, but Heston did not become a permanent feature on the White House legislative and cultural scene until Johnson's presidency. Considering Hollywood's awe of JFK, it is ironic that Johnson outdid Kennedy in making use of the newfound celebrity activism emanating from Hollywood. As celebrities reached out to the new president, the administration searched for creative ways to tap into these potential gold mines of publicity.

One of Johnson's most enthusiastic supporters was Gregory Peck. A celebrated actor known for such hit productions as *Roman Holiday* (1953), *Moby Dick* (John Huston, 1956), and *To Kill a Mockingbird* (Robert Mulligan, 1962), Peck worked with Heston on the set of *The Big Country* in 1958. The two remained friends and became fellow public servants. Indeed, through his energetic work for President Johnson, Peck created opportunities for other politically minded celebrities, including Heston. After Peck narrated a film for the State Department, George Stevens of the U.S. Information Agency's Motion Picture Service encouraged Jack Valenti, a special assistant to the president, to cultivate a relationship between Peck and LBJ. For instance, when Peck was in Washington, DC, in January 1964, Stevens requested that Valenti arrange for the possibility of Johnson's "saying hello" to Peck. Immediately after this meeting, Peck sought to further his connection with LBJ. The actor informed the administration that he would soon be honored at the Annual Headliners Banquet in Austin and offered to relay "anything that the president would like me to say on his behalf." A few weeks later, Peck wrote Valenti: "If there is ever an occasion when the President wants to reach out for someone who has no political ambitions or axe to grind; someone who would be glad to use his capabilities on a diplomatic errand, a special mission, or a chore of any description, I would be proud to serve."[1] Indeed, Peck participated in rallies for Johnson during the 1964 campaign, and, afterward, the administration continued to cultivate the enthusiasm of Peck and other celebrity admirers of Johnson. Johnson's arts legislation offered an opportunity to further this connection with Peck and between Washington and Hollywood in general.

Johnson had already used his dramatic ascension to the presidency to his legislative advantage. Kennedy's assassination in November 1963 had thrust the nation into mourning, and LBJ used this grief to push the late president's domestic agenda and then some—from civil rights legislation to the War on Poverty. As Johnson shaped domestic programs to his own liking, he fit them into the larger agenda of his Great Society, first presented in the spring of 1964. Sustained economic growth had turned the nation's sights toward new matters of concern. With the country no longer fixated on the creation of wealth, experts believed that America's riches should be used to improve the quality of life for its citizens. Despite its obvious usefulness, wealth could also degrade humanity through consumerism, materialism, and damage to the environment. Echoing those concerns, Johnson proclaimed: "The challenge of the next half century is whether we have the wisdom to use that wealth to enrich and elevate our national life and to advance the quality of our American civilization." Not only did the Great Society "rest on abundance and liberty for all," but it was also "a place where every child can find knowledge to enrich his mind and to enlarge his talents. It is a place where the city of man serves not only the needs of the body and the demands of commerce but the desire for beauty and the hunger for community." As more Americans enjoyed significant amounts of leisure time, Johnson argued that they had a responsibility to use this time constructively. The arts would be the perfect arena in which to do so, breathing life into the souls of Americans, and rounding out the goals of the Great Society.[2]

Unable to predict how long his liberal consensus would last, Johnson pushed Congress to pass a host of legislative reforms that seemingly included something for everyone.[3] Johnson enjoyed immediate success with the Civil Rights Act of 1964. In 1965, major legislative victories included the Elementary and Secondary Education Act, the Voting Rights Act, the Immigration Act, Medicare, and the National Foundation on the Arts and the Humanities Act, which established the NEA. The Arts and Humanities Act grew out of the National Arts and Cultural Development Act, which LBJ had signed in September 1964. The earlier act had established the National Council on the Arts as a twenty-four-member body charged with proposing methods to encourage private initiative in the arts and conducting studies "with a view to formulating methods by which creative activity and high standards and increased opportunities in the arts may be encouraged and promoted in the best interests of the Nation's artistic and cultural progress." A precedent was, thereby, established on which additional legislation could build, but alone the National Council on the Arts was purely advisory and had no financial support.[4] When Johnson signed the Arts and Humanities Act into law on September 29, 1965, creating the National Endowment for the Arts and providing for twenty-six citizens to serve as advisors to the agency as members of the National Council on the Arts, he transformed the weak National Council on the Arts into an institution with significant funding and a relatively permanent base. In so doing, he established an unprecedented role for the government in the arts sector.

The relation between the federal government and the arts had, until that point, been limited and somewhat troubled. The question of government funding to the arts had first been addressed by George Washington and Thomas Jefferson, who called for the federal government to support artistic endeavors. The majority of Revolutionary Era Americans viewed art and its trappings as elitist, however, and this suspicion of the arts would become even more entrenched in the nineteenth century with President Andrew Jackson. "Old Hickory" lauded the humble origins of the common man, creating a long-standing political tradition in which art was dismissed as an outmoded aristocratic pastime.[5]

Not until the turn of the twentieth century did the federal government become involved with artistic endeavors, at least on a minor scale. President Theodore Roosevelt established the thirty-member Council of Fine Arts to buy art for federal buildings, and his successor, William Taft, strengthened and modified those initiatives when he formed his own Commission of Fine Arts. Reacting to the concern that federal money had been wasted on worthless pieces of art, Taft appointed the commission to provide guiding expertise in purchasing quality pieces. Important as they were, these efforts confined federal arts endeavors to the nation's capital and did not encourage large-scale national support of artistic production. In fact, the most important arts legislation to come out of the Progressive Era proved to be the income tax and inheritance tax legislation passed in 1913 and 1916, respectively. These new laws offered tax deductions for charitable giving and opened up support for nonprofit organizations, including arts groups. The federal government, however, did not undertake any new arts programs until the 1930s.[6]

President Franklin Delano Roosevelt included the arts sector in his efforts to create jobs during the Great Depression. Although his New Deal seemed like an opportunity to forge a permanent relation between the government and the arts, FDR's agencies left a bitter legacy among artists and New Deal opponents alike. Under the authority of the Works Progress Administration (WPA), the New Deal included four special projects for artists: the Federal Art Project, the Federal Music Project, the Federal Theater Project, and the Federal Writers Project. Between 1935 and 1943, the federal government pumped $160 million into these "Federal One" programs.[7] Such legendary artists as Aaron Copeland, Jackson Pollock, John Steinbeck, Robert Frost, and Orson Welles found employment through the WPA and eventually went on to become major cultural figures in the

United States. Despite the success of these individuals, tension frequently arose between the Roosevelt administration and the projects' artists. Whereas FDR developed the New Deal to inspire confidence in Americans, the artists themselves were primarily committed to artistic freedom. Federal One artists sometimes reflected the antibusiness, prolabor sentiment of the Depression-ridden 1930s, and several eventually clashed with the administration or with congressional critics.

The most famous conflict revolved around the brilliant but cantankerous Orson Welles. In June 1937, Welles and John Houseman attempted to stage Mark Blitzstein's *The Cradle Will Rock,* a musical supportive of union organizing in the steel industry. Sensitive to the concerns of the nation's steel barons but unwilling to censor Welles openly, Congress informed the WPA that, owing to budget cuts, no plays could be staged until the following year. To enforce this decision, authorities sealed off Maxine Elliott's Theatre in New York City, the play's original venue, in case Welles disobeyed their orders. Welles, in turn, arranged for the nearby old Venice Theatre to stage the production instead and dramatically marched his audience to the new location. Because the government restricted project actors from performing, Blitzstein told the story line sitting onstage atop a beaten-up piano while the actors shouted their lines from various points in the audience. Welles ran the Spartan production for two weeks and subsequently cut ties with the WPA, thus becoming a symbol of the artist's struggle for independence from government interference.[8]

The WPA's projects faced even more intense scrutiny between 1935 and 1938 when the House Un-American Activities Committee (HUAC) began to look into the agency's arts programs. Under Chairman Martin Dies, HUAC found Communists on the Federal One employment rolls. Because of this revelation as well as the controversy already surrounding the program, the Federal Theater Project was abolished in 1939, and the remaining Federal One programs came under state control during World War II. Meanwhile, the WPA was gradually phased out of existence.[9] The Federal One programs did not establish a permanent role for the federal government as a supporter of the arts and very likely had a negative effect on public opinion and the artists themselves.

After a decade-long hiatus, the federal government slowly reintro-
duced itself to the arts world. Concerned about a balanced budget, Dwight
Eisenhower often preached government retrenchment and fiscal conservatism. However, Ike had other worries as well. As the historian David
Smith notes, Eisenhower "was deeply concerned about the virtue and soul
of his nation, especially in the face of the rampant materialism that seemed
to so characterize the 1950s."[10] Ike believed that art had the potential to inspire Americans but grew concerned about the increase in commercial art,
which was at the mercy of profit-seeking advertisers and less likely to provide that inspiration. Therefore, Ike considered the relation between the
government and the arts an important one, and he took steps to strength-
en their connection.

Ike's emphasis on fiscal conservatism and belief in the healing power
of the arts is an important combination to note because it paralleled Heston's attitude. Although Heston always called for the prudent spending of
public money, he also vigorously encouraged government involvement in
the arts, believing that the state could promote art for the nation's benefit.
Heston himself later noted that public money had funded some of the
greatest artistic works in history. He pointed out to one congressional
committee: "The King James translation of the Bible was produced by a
royal commission appointed by and paid for by the royal treasury. The finest work of Michelangelo, some of the Sistine ceiling and the like were created under the patronage by the Vatican." Heston also echoed Ike's concerns
about commercial art. He believed that commercial television had declined in quality since his *Studio One* days, consistently featuring mediocre
work, a problem for which he blamed advertisers. He told Congress that
television might as "well be called an adjunct or subsidiary of the advertising
business." Even during financially difficult times, Heston encouraged the
government to find a way to support artistic ambitions. In 1973, when the
country suffered from debilitating inflation, Heston testified in favor of extending the NEA's charter. "It may seem strange to plead for the arts when
children are hungry and families homeless. I submit that the feeding of the
spirit has a priority, too. I believe the programs you have funded have done
that. If they are continued, I think our country will be richer for it."[11]

The fact that in the 1950s some fiscal conservatives found government intervention important and even necessary marked a turning point in the government's provision of assistance to the arts and planted a seed that would bloom in the 1960s. These conservatives believed that government intervention would be beneficial to the overall health of the nation. Furthermore, they hoped that federal subsidies would guarantee a higher quality of works than would result from the narrower commercial pursuit of artistic interests. Americans would have access to more sophisticated works of art and would, therefore, be more spiritually enriched by their contact with the world of culture.[12] Eisenhower hoped to increase the government's role in the arts with his proposed Federal Commission on the Arts and National Cultural Center. Congress approved the cultural center in 1958 (the center was renamed the John F. Kennedy Center for the Performing Arts in January 1964, two months after JFK's assassination), but the federal commission had to wait until 1963.

By the 1960s, two trends convinced a variety of intellectuals that the quality of American art had declined considerably. First, fine art had been popularized. For example, Sears, Roebuck had hired Vincent Price to assemble an art collection of original works in the late 1950s. Soon enough, Sears showrooms across the country included the paintings of Chagall, Goya, Picasso, and Rembrandt. Second, there was a noticeable decline of the elitist monopoly on art. As fine art became more popular, many Americans decided to try their own amateur hands at the artist's block. From the late 1950s to the early 1960s, the number of amateur artists exploded. They even published their own magazine, *American Artist,* and formed their own association, the Amateur Artists Association of America. While amateur artists hoped for a government program that would foster their interests, the elite artists looked to the state to revitalize their monopoly on the art world. Since both groups clamored for government support, the time seemed ripe for federal intervention.[13] However, the fact that professional and amateur artists fostered opposing goals for government assistance would lead to difficulty for the NEA, and for Heston, throughout the period.

When President Kennedy established the Advisory Council on the Arts in 1963, he made his primary interest in the professional artist quite clear. While he encouraged "widespread public interest" in the arts, he did not promote increased amateur participation in the production of art. "I emphasize the importance of the professional artist because there is danger we may tend to accept the rich range of amateur activities which abound in our country as a substitute for the professional," he explained. "Without the professional performer and the creative artist, the amateur spirit declines and the vast audience is only partially served."[14] Kennedy's council was purely advisory, and he was largely interested in expanding opportunities for the professional artist, not the amateur.

Johnson, however, focused on the amateur artist when he proposed the Arts and Humanities Act. Ironically, it may have been professional artists who prompted LBJ to aggressively pursue arts legislation in the first place because the insecure president wanted to prove to them that he could outdo his predecessor on cultural matters. The East Coast intellectual establishment had been enthralled with Kennedy but held little regard for the coarse Texan who had just assumed the presidency. However, since LBJ did not feel comfortable with the exclusive-minded individuals in the arts world, he did not focus on them in the proposed legislation. He envisioned federal involvement in the arts as a way to improve the lives of average citizens, not further the careers of professional artists. He hoped that federal support of the arts would "make art more widely available to millions of Americans." Therefore, his sponsorship of the NEA departed from Kennedy's narrow, elitist focus, embodying instead Johnson's own populist inclinations.[15]

Heston's tempered support for a federal arts endowment reflected the neoconservative attitude toward the Great Society in general. When Heston was summoned to Capitol Hill to testify on the proposed arts legislation, he expressed his reservations. He worried about the increasing reach of the federal government and the problems sure to arise when the goals of the artists conflicted with the aims of the endowment. However, Heston was also deeply concerned about the individual artist. He and Lydia had once struggled to make livings as actors. Furthermore, Heston was well aware of the dismal unemployment rate in Hollywood, even though he made clear "that my statements today are made as a private individual . . .

I cannot today speak for the Screen Actors Guild officially." Therefore, in his testimony, Heston supported the creation of an arts endowment but also noted the risks that the government would be taking. "I can say that I view the possibility of the legislation that you are considering with mixed emotions," he testified. "On the one hand, as a citizen who subscribes to the Jeffersonian theory that the best government is the least government, it might be said that any legislation would give me pause. On the other hand, as an artist I am delighted at the prospect." Heston even predicted that an endowment would clash with individual artists, saying that some would probably rebel against the agency. But, he said: "That is the nature of the human animal. And my own feeling is that although there would be problems, certainly, there would be instances of rebellion and contention, but on the whole it would be an excellent thing for the artists."[16] Heston ultimately came down in favor of the legislation because he thought that it would help professional artists and, therefore, improve the quality of the arts in general.

HESTON JOINED A NUMBER OF OTHER artists in an effort to drum up support for the proposed legislation. Eric Goldman, a special consultant to President Johnson, proposed a "White House Festival of the Arts"—eventually held on June 14, 1965—that would simultaneously build support for the legislation and offer "an outgoing, warm, colorful White House salute to the Americans who were building up the museums and symphonies in the local communities, organizing reading and discussion groups, [and] staging their own art festivals." It would be the first time the White House would pay tribute to so many forms of American art, including ballet, photography, drama, classical music, prose, poetry, and jazz. Arts supporters composed the bulk of the guest list, but Goldman also invited a number of prominent intellectuals and artists to contribute to the festival program with readings, sculptures, and other artistic displays. The organizers of the festival originally slated Peck to close the daytime program by reading the narration for a compilation of five "great" American films made since World War II. When scheduling problems forced Peck to decline, the White House then invited Heston to weave together a series of clips from *North by Northwest* (1959), *On the Waterfront* (Elia Kazan, 1954), *Shane* (George Stevens, 1953), *Friendly Persuasion* (William Wyler, 1956), and *High Noon* (Fred Zinnemann, 1952).[17]

It was during the planning of the festival that the first problematic aspect of the Great Society became evident—the programs could be politicized. Earlier that spring, Johnson had ordered the continual bombing of North Vietnam. Some actors, such as Peck and Heston, offered their support for such action, but the bombing prompted fierce criticism among a number of artists. Robert Lowell was the first to decline his invitation to the festival on the grounds that he opposed Johnson's military policies. Lowell's decision brought negative attention to the event since he declined in an open letter to the press only a week after he had first accepted his invitation. Lowell explained that he had "accepted somewhat rapidly and greedily" in the excitement of artistic celebration but, after a moment's pause, had realized that "every serious artist knows that he cannot enjoy public celebration without making subtle public commitments." Even though Lowell viewed LBJ's Great Society with enthusiasm, the president's foreign policy left him "with the greatest dismay and distrust." He worried that his attendance at the festival would imply his support of American efforts in Vietnam. Lowell's announcement prompted several other artists, including the playwright Arthur Miller, to refuse their invitations. The situation quickly gained the attention of the press, especially after it was rumored that Johnson was so offended by Lowell's actions that he was considering skipping out on the festival himself. Only after some skillful persuasion on the part of Jack Valenti did Johnson finally deliver brief remarks at the festival. However, he did so in the absence of eighteen of the original invitees, an unusually low acceptance rate for a White House event, but perhaps fairly impressive considering how emotionally charged the issue of the Vietnam War was.[18]

Indeed, the president's Vietnam policies troubled a number of the artists who decided to attend the festival, but they did not want to miss such a prestigious event, especially if they could use it to make a public statement. John Hersey informed the festival chair, Eric Goldman, that he would be reading an excerpt from his 1946 novel *Hiroshima,* a work detailing the effects of the first atomic bomb dropped by the United States on Hiroshima to end World War II. Hersey planned to tell the gruesome story of Miss Susaki, a woman injured by the blast of the bomb. While Goldman considered Hersey's reading legitimate artistic criticism, he was outraged by the actions of Dwight Macdonald, a writer for the *New Yorker* and a film critic for *Esquire*. Although he accepted his invitation "with pleasure," Macdonald warned that he shared Lowell's disapproval regarding Johnson's foreign policy. Macdonald surprised and repulsed the festival's organizers when he brought to the actual event a petition of protest that stated: "We should like to make it clear that in accepting the President's kind invitation to attend the White House Arts Festival, we do not mean either to repudiate the courageous position taken by Robert Lowell, or to endorse the administration's foreign policy. We quite share Mr. Lowell's dismay at our country's recent actions in Vietnam and the Dominican Republic."[19]

Macdonald managed to embarrass most of the festival's guests with his frenzied efforts to obtain signatures on his petition. According to one of the event's organizers, "most of the guests, myself included, were so struck by [Macdonald's] actions that they were too paralyzed to react," with the exception of Heston and maybe one other person, "the only people of the day that stood up to him." When the disheveled Macdonald approached Heston in the Rose Garden and the actor refused to sign his complaint, Macdonald reportedly called Heston "a lowbrow lackey of Hollywood." Defending himself, Heston cited his record of civil rights activism. "But that really isn't the point," Heston continued. "Having convictions doesn't mean that you have to lack elementary manners. Are you really accustomed to signing petitions against your host in his home?" Jack Valenti remembered, to his "undying pleasure," that Heston "just ate [Macdonald's] ass out" for his lack of "propriety": "And then he gave Macdonald precise directions as to what he could do with this petition, and they were very precise." The two argued only momentarily but managed to attract the attention of several members of the press. Macdonald continued to express his contempt for the president, the festival, and its participants, going so far as to sneer at the exhibits. Meanwhile, Heston remarked to a *Newsweek* reporter: "He belts me in his movie reviews. Why should I sign his lousy petition?" Heston made no mention of his confrontation with Macdonald in his journal. He wrote only that he was "proud" to be a part of the White House event. The skirmish reveals several key aspects of Heston's political personality. First, he did not want to see the festival politicized, and, second, he was willing to stand up to anyone trying to do so. Finally, even though he was clearly disturbed by Macdonald's behavior, he casually made light of his disapproval to the press, even going so far as to be self-deprecating about his film career.[20]

Despite Macdonald's shenanigans, the festival continued smoothly, and Johnson made his brief appearance. The festival organizers felt vindicated the following September when Congress passed the Arts and Humanities Act, or what Kirk Douglas called "the emancipation proclamation for the arts in America." With Gregory Peck, Agnes DeMille, George Stevens, and Lew Wasserman in attendance, Johnson signed the act in a ceremony at the Rose Garden, the locale of Heston and Macdonald's toe-to-toe, eyeball-to-eyeball confrontation. Valenti claimed that, after the festival, Johnson began to "feel a sense of wariness about academia and whether or not you could trust people to be civil," but he had no aversion to Hollywood luminaries. In fact, the festival further solidified the connection between movie stars and the White House, and Johnson would invite them to shape the new agency.[21] Still, the politicization of the festival foreshadowed similar splits over the political and cultural implications of the NEA's arts programs in the future.

The nature of the NEA's founding allowed for considerable interpretation by its council and staff members. The Arts and Humanities Act established the National Foundation on the Arts and Humanities as an independent agency in the executive branch. The agency was composed of the National Endowment for the Arts, the National Endowment for the Humanities, and the Federal Council on the Arts and the Humanities. Each of the two endowments would have a national council, that is, a policy board consisting of a chairperson and twenty-six private citizens appointed by the president, as well as a staff of administrators. The NEA's objective was fourfold: to make art more widely available to millions of Americans; to preserve America's cultural heritage for present and future generations; to strengthen cultural organizations; and to encourage the creative development of talented individuals. The NEA would attempt to achieve these goals by giving grants to official state arts agencies, nonprofit tax-exempt organizations, and individuals of exceptional talent. The only qualification was that grants had to be for programs, projects, or activities to be specified in the grant application. The NEA could authorize no money for the purposes of debt retirement, construction, or general administration, nor would it provide more than 50 percent of a grantee's budget.[22] All grant seekers were required to find matching funds from an outside source, a rule designed to spur private support of the arts. Because the NEA's goals were so broad and its guidelines so few, its national council had considerable latitude in shaping the character of the agency. The NEA would, thus, vary significantly from year to year, depending on who served as chair and on the board.

Heston served on two very different boards during his tenure at the NEA and believed that the distinctions between the two made for serious political and cultural connotations. The original chair of the council, Roger Stevens, perceived the council, and his management of it, as restricted by certain bounds. Stevens and the rest of the council immediately confronted two questions in deciding the character of its agency: whom the NEA would prioritize for funding and what the role of the artist should be in society. On both these issues, the council came down on the conservative side of the debate, tending to subscribe to JFK's presumption that professionals, not amateurs, should receive the bounty of the NEA. The NEA's working assumption became that the agency had been established to save art from commercial enterprise. The council saw its role as promoting elite and cutting-edge tastes and, at the same time, as "build[ing] a more appreciative audience for the arts." Therefore, the first round of grants went primarily to professional artists "of great talent." As for what role the artist should play in society and whether the NEA should fund artists who considered themselves "social critics," the council decided that artists who wanted to overturn "conventional" tastes clashed with a program created to promote excellence in the traditional sense. The council came to both conclusions partly out of financial considerations—the NEA had a relatively small budget with which to work, only $10 million. And Stevens did not try to overrule it. He attested: "Unless there was very substantial agreement among members of the Council, I didn't try to put a project across." He believed that with "so many things to do and so little money to do it . . . there was no point in getting into a project that the Council wasn't really sold on."[23]

These predilections still dominated the NEA when President Johnson swore in Charlton Heston as a member of the National Council on the Arts on February 1, 1967. Heston easily fit in with the Stevens council. Heston wanted to "feed the soul of the nation," but he was more interested in providing funds for individual professional artists than in democratizing art. There were two different ways of looking at how best to feed the nation's soul. One was to provide quality art to audiences through professional artists of excellence. Another was to let everyone become an artist through educational programs. Heston chose the former and believed that his preference corresponded to the original purpose of the NEA, likely remembering Kennedy's intentions rather than Johnson's. He also disagreed with programs that had a purpose beyond pure art. For the actor, anything that was educational or political in nature seemed inappropriate for agency funding, so he was not likely to support an artist who was also a social critic. In pursuing these goals, Heston constantly looked for ways to slash wasteful spending.

Heston's preference to fund professional artists and to avoid social criticism stemmed from concerns over the NEA's limited budget, his own experiences as an actor, and his general cultural beliefs. He was keenly aware of the NEA's budgetary constraints and wanted its limited resources to be awarded to professionals rather than amateurs. Furthermore, Heston believed that professional artists needed extra financial support so that their work would not be diluted by commercial considerations. Despite his successes in commercial film, Heston believed that the stage more consistently offered a higher-quality experience for both the audience and the actors. He constantly struggled to find meaty movie roles and often felt compelled to return to the stage when the film industry failed to offer impressive parts. He explained: "You look to the film work to increase your net worth and maintain your public identity, keeping your eye open for the now and then very good film. The stage, well, that's to keep your muscles stretched and, once in a while, take a shot at the real mankillers." He especially loved performing Shakespeare, an activity that he referred to as "waltz[ing] with the old gentleman."[24] Therefore, he wanted to keep the professional theater alive. Finally, Heston came to his conclusions about the NEA because of his cultural views. He believed that art should be dominated by certain standards of beauty, truth, and excellence. He did not want those ideal principles compromised by amateurs or by those out to make political statements.

The effects of Heston's frugality and cultural beliefs soon crystallized. On the day he was sworn in, he wrote in his journal: "I can't remember what it is we swore to do. Not waste the public money I hope." Heston tried to carry out this pledge of prudence throughout his tenure on the council, immediately gaining notoriety as the group's "hit man." At his first set of meetings in Tarryton, New York (a favorite council venue), Heston discovered that New York's Lincoln Center had lost $750,000 the previous year on productions alone. He did not hesitate to vote against its next grant application, hoping that the rejection of the fiscally irresponsible group would send a message to future applicants. "I don't want to reward that kind of profligacy with the public's money," he wrote in his journal, "not in the spotlight that shines on the Lincoln Center."[25] The council agreed with him, and Lincoln Center was not funded that year.

On the second day of meetings in Tarryton, Heston continued his hatchet work, this time taking on a program that he believed to be inappropriate, and likely too liberal, for the NEA agenda. Ted McIlvenna, the director of community development for the Glide Urban Center in San Francisco, informally requested $10,000 for a cultural center in the Haight-Ashbury district. McIlvenna proposed to use this money for the purchase of artistic materials, classes, art shows, and "mixed media performances including varieties of 'happenings' for young people living in Haight-Ashbury." The council did not approve the grant, and Heston credited himself with persuading the rest of the group to turn down the proposal. He recorded in his journal: "On the surface, it seems a plausible idea, but I read a letter from within the community that indicted the whole thing . . . a cry for help, really. I read it aloud, complete with scatological syntax, and pointed out my conviction that the problem was a medical one, to be solved by juvenile aid, not cultural encouragement."[26] Since Haight-Ashbury was the most famous of the hippie enclaves, Heston probably did not believe that much in the way of artistic excellence would come out of such a program.

Heston's proclivities did not clash dramatically with those of the rest of the council as long as it was under the direction of Roger Stevens. Generally, Heston's preference for individual artists and conservative programs seemed to be shared by the group. What set Heston apart during his first year's tenure was his strict attitude toward spending. His parsimonious ways did not seem to provoke hostility between Heston and Stevens or any other member of the council, however. In many ways, the council worked in unison. Stevens's deputy chief, Livingston Biddle, characterized it as "a small family, developing close ties."[27] Heston's easy relationship with the rest of the council dissolved when Richard Nixon appointed Nancy Hanks as the new chair in 1969. With a degree from Duke University, Hanks numbered among her credentials participation in an arts study for New York Governor John Rockefeller and leadership of the American Council for the Arts (now Americans for the Arts). Clearly, Hanks was eminently qualified, but she and Heston disagreed on who deserved top priority for funding, which programs to fund, and how much to spend. Whereas Heston preferred, as has been noted, to focus on professional artists, conservative programs, and cost-effective grants, Hanks favored institutions, liberal programs, and grants with large budgets. Furthermore, she was not as willing to defer to the council as her predecessor had been. In order to achieve her vision, she had every intention of taking charge of the council and willingly sparred with its members over projects she favored.

The NEA became a much larger agency under Hanks's guidance. Not only did she possess the political skill to win congressional support, but President Nixon expressed his willingness to greatly increase the agency's funding as well. After meeting with Nixon for the first time, Hanks discovered that they shared the same attitude about the future of the NEA: they both wanted to extend the arts to middle America and the nation's young people and to encourage all Americans not just to appreciate art but to produce it. This vision, however, demanded a larger budget for the endowment. Hanks told Nixon that she needed $20 million to achieve her ends, but Nixon far surpassed the new chair's request. He asked Congress to authorize $40 million for fiscal year 1971 and to extend the life of the National Foundation on the Arts and Humanities for another three years beyond its expiration date, scheduled for June 30, 1970. Hanks personally visited 150 members of Congress in 1970 to persuade them to vote for the president's programs. Hanks and Nixon succeeded in their efforts. By 1978, the NEA budget had grown to over $123 million. Many NEA insiders considered the Nixon years the agency's golden age.[28]

Nixon surprised many arts supporters when he called for the largest budget expansion in NEA history, an act that legitimated the agency as never before. Not only was Nixon a Republican, but he hardly seemed the arts connoisseur. In fact, his aversion to modern art was so well-known that the State Department took down most of the modern pieces that adorned the American embassy in Paris before his visit to France in 1969. However, Nixon possessed definite convictions that explain his purpose for expanding the NEA's budget so dramatically. He believed that the American soul was under fire, threatened by the corrosive moral relativism of the hippie counterculture and the growing acceptance of obscenity. The new president believed that uplifting cultural expression through federal arts programs could counteract these trends, but he did not believe that America's intellectual establishment could lead the way, having long mistrusted intellectual elites. He preferred to rely on nonacademics for the nation's future. Thus, his argument to democratize the arts—"to enhance the quality of life for all Americans"—fit in with both his desire to promote spiritual uplift through the arts and his unwillingness to use intellectuals to promote the arts.[29] Although Heston certainly agreed with the idea of spiritual uplift through the arts, he did not agree that such an undertaking should be entrusted to amateur artists. Hanks did, however, and the two would clash repeatedly for the remainder of Heston's tenure on the council.

Under Stevens, the council had preferred to direct "assistance directly to artists 'based on a criteria of exceptional talent plus some need.'" Under Hanks, this pattern would change, the new chair's preference being to channel support to institutions and, through them, to amateurs. In October 1970, Hanks launched an initiative to expand NEA programs—including the controversial Museum Program, intended to support, among other things, conservation and renovation—and, in the process, break down the boundaries between the arts, the sciences, and the humanities solidified by the creation of separate arts and humanities endowments. As she divulged privately to Michael Straight, her deputy chair at the NEA: "I have had in mind, since I took the Chairmanship, that our pattern of support should be, first, to pick up the orchestras, then the operas, . . . then I figured we'd move on to museums and eventually to restoration. I believe that museums, orchestras, and community cultural groups are parts of the whole fabric of what we call our cultural resources."[30] Even without knowing her full intentions, Heston viewed Hanks's proposals with skepticism. For one thing, he feared that, even in its newly augmented form, the NEA budget could not afford the expansion. For another, he feared that such expansion, focusing as it did on institutions, would draw attention away from the artists themselves. The White House too opposed her initiative, and in 1976 Hanks was forced to settle for a compromise under which the Museum Program was abandoned and the Institute for Museum Services (now part of the Institute of Museum and Library Services), to be run by the Department of Health, Education, and Welfare (HEW), was established. Undaunted by this setback, Hanks continued her attempts to refocus NEA funding, and Heston found that he could do little to stop her.

Under Stevens, the council had primarily funded conservative programs that focused on quality art, but Hanks wanted to liberalize the agency's programs to focus on social goals. Her intentions were most apparent in the Expansion Arts Program. This program had initially been launched in 1968, under Stevens, as the Inner City Summer Arts Program. While its advocates thought the program would be "useful in alleviating inner city problems during the coming summer," its primary focus was on encouraging artistic excellence. The major NEA "concern was that assistance be provided for projects of *artistic quality,* particularly for workshops which might discover and develop new talent." In fact, only six months later, in January 1969, the council clearly limited the program to budding professionals, excluding amateurs. In a discussion of how to create an "intellectual underpinning" in American society, the council did concede that the NEA could have a role in such an endeavor. However, it wanted to keep any such effort tightly focused. "We have 'Art for Art's Sake' and 'Art for Life's Sake,'" the council stated. "The latter emphasis does not necessarily mean that if we boldly embark on programs that directly involve the non-academic writer . . . in teaching programs at every level, we embrace 'Art for Therapy's Sake,' or in the case of what we call Inner City Programs, 'Art to Keep 'Em off the Streets.'"[31] Thus, the Stevens council clearly limited the purpose and focus of the original Inner City Summer Arts Program. The Senate Appropriations Committee did not renew the program's funding for fiscal year 1969, probably because of concerns regarding the cost of the expanding war in Vietnam.

When Hanks revived the program as the Expansion Arts Program, it soon became a social program for amateur artists despite Heston's discomfort with such a scheme. He confessed in his journal: "I'm deeply concerned over the degree to which an increasing proportion of the funds we vote are granted to programs primarily social in purpose. This is totally against the theory of the legislation as I understand it, and certainly beyond the scope of our funding." These words stemmed from a long debate Heston undertook with the NEA council and staff following Hanks announcement that she was expanding the Expansion Arts Program and dividing it into several components, including Instruction and Training, Arts Exposure Projects, Education and Social Goals Projects, and Neighborhood Arts Services. Heston had requested that the program director, Vantile Whitfield, explain the program's purpose. Whitfield stated that he chose the term *expansion* because he "felt the program is to help people expand their national consciousness and perceptions through the arts, and to use the arts in life services." Whitfield and others on the council saw the Expansion Arts Program as a way to bring art to a wider range of Americans. Indeed, many of the programs it sponsored, such as one in Mobile, Alabama, called "Culture in Black and White," had been established specifically to include people who had received little exposure to art, especially children. The Mobile program offered "training in art, ceramics, dance, drama, music, and creative writing to 150 youngsters aged 7–18 whose public and parochial schools provide no art, music or other cultural instruction at all." The classes also included field trips to artistic institutions in the Mobile area that students might not have been able to attend on their own.[32]

Not all Expansion Arts programs catered to schoolchildren, however, and Heston questioned the practice of involving the NEA in what were called *life services,* especially in programs targeting troubled elements of the population. Heston pointedly second-guessed funding arts programs for prisoners and drug abusers, such as New York's Street Theatre, an NEA grantee that performed for and worked with prisoners across the country. Many council members considered such programs as worthy of support because they, like LBJ, saw the NEA as an instrument for bettering the lives of all Americans through government action. One council member told Heston that the actor mistakenly viewed "the program as an educational tool" rather than, more appropriately, "as support for art of a certain type of lifestyle, and support of the creation of art within the lifestyle." Another council member admitted that he "thought that expansion arts is really what the Endowment is about and that the idea of this program is not really all that new." It appeared that a majority of the council had adopted Hanks's position regarding the NEA's mission; Heston's was now a minority view.[33]

Those who strongly supported the Expansion Arts Program were more in tune with Johnson's vision when he created the NEA. However, Heston considered it the NEA's primary purpose to assist individual artists who harbored creative potential, not the throngs of amateurs across America who wanted recreational inspiration or needed social improvement. Heston elaborated on his opposition to the Expansion Arts Program in 1976: "I was coming to feel that the limited funds the NEA had were going to projects and programs that while basically admirable (street dancing, finger painting, and so forth), were primarily designed to meet social needs, not creative ones." He continued: "It seemed to me and it still does, that the Department of Health, Education, and Welfare, which has the largest share of the federal budget, should assume these responsibilities, and leave the NEA to fry other fish." Heston conveyed his views to Congress in 1978. Even though his council term had expired, he testified concerning a proposal that President Carter call a White House conference on the arts. He supported the idea of a conference but qualified his endorsement by testifying: "I would hope as well that this conference might attempt to establish a precedent between the social value of art as opposed to its permanent creative value." Again, the actor suggested HEW as the proper manager for "social" programs.[34]

Heston resisted programs like Expansion Arts that were social in nature because he believed that they could easily be politicized. For example, after a council meeting in November 1971, Heston complained in his journal: "This was a wasted day. I worked as hard as I could, spoke as resourcefully as I was able, on a subject I feel very strongly about: the gradual dilution of the arts program away from quality to a politically diluted program." He believed: "The staff's instincts for a *big* agency and the political choices necessary to sustain it, combined with the councillors' knee-jerk impulse to approve any program labeled socially good defeated my best effort."[35] Not only did Heston regret the growth of the agency, but he also feared its politicization. Resisting such changes proved to be a frustrating experience for him.

While Heston was resisting the dilution of standards in the artistic fields, the intellectual neocons were protesting similar changes in academe. Norman Podhoretz wrote a controversial indictment of American intellectuals in *Making It,* a book in which he accused academe of foolishly capitulating to political and cultural radicalism. The majority of intellectuals were coming to what he considered two misguided conclusions: in terms of foreign policy, the United States was bloodthirsty and pursuing world domination; in domestic matters, it was becoming a "sick society" because of its unbridled pursuit of money and success. Podhoretz believed that this generally adversarial posture led intellectuals to take similarly hostile stances toward a number of academic traditions. He woefully took note of a new trend among intellectuals, known as *against interpretation.*

The academic and writer Susan Sontag particularly took the lead in this shift in her repudiation of the teaching of classic, canonical texts. Considering that tradition "elitist," she instead turned to popular culture, including music, television, and comic books, for inspiration. Citing the new notion of *relevance,* Sontag and her allies dismissed writers of the past who did not immediately interest students or, even more worrisome to Podhoretz, did not serve a useful political purpose. Because of these developments, the intellectual neocons began turning against their fellow members of the intelligentsia, a divorce that brought Podhoretz "the special happiness that comes from breaking out of a false position and giving free rein to previously inhibited sentiments and ideas."[36]

Despite the fact that President Nixon, Heston, and the intellectual neocons shared a common mistrust of artistic and academic relativism, they came to different conclusions as to how best to remedy the situation. Nixon looked toward the middle class in general and, in the case of the NEA, to amateur artists. However, the neocons did not approve of this solution. In Heston's eyes, amateurs simply could not promote artistic excellence. Furthermore, mainstream America, too, had fallen prey to relativistic countercultural tendencies. Irving Kristol cleverly pointed to the absurdity of suburban fathers flocking to see *The Graduate,* Mike Nichols's 1969 hit movie starring Dustin Hoffman and Anne Bancroft. The film explored the illicit affair between a bored housewife and her daughter's boyfriend, a recent college graduate who disdains the middle-class lifestyle but seems inept at discovering a better alternative.[37] Indeed, countercultural values seemed to be flooding the American marketplace in movies, music, and advertising. Therefore, the neocons called for the revitalization of traditional standards in the arts and academe to confront the weakening of American culture in general. They willingly fought for their conservative beliefs—Heston in National Council on the Arts meetings; the intellectual neocons in their written diatribes.

ANOTHER ASPECT OF THE 1960S WELFARE state that came to trouble the neocons was the divisions that it seemed to exacerbate; the neocons believed that government programs actually increased tensions between different socioeconomic classes and racial and ethnic groups. By promoting separatism and exercising special privileges for minorities and the poor, the government, the neocons charged, not only increased hostility between groups but also violated the ethos of equal opportunity once revered by the Democratic Party. Furthermore, multiculturalism began to take hold in a number of social programs, a policy the neocons abhorred.

The intellectual neocons focused their disapproval on Johnson's War on Poverty and, because of the problems associated with it, indicted much of the Great Society. The War on Poverty was only one part of the Great Society, which included over sixty pieces of legislation tackling issues ranging from health care, to highway beautification, to highway safety, to farm subsidies. Even though Great Society programs mainly benefited middle-class whites, Johnson spoke repeatedly and passionately about helping the poor through the War on Poverty. Thus, LBJ's special attention to the poor allowed the War on Poverty to become a centerpiece of the Great Society, and the backlash against the antipoverty program came at the expense of Johnson's entire domestic agenda.[38]

Indeed, in his complaints against LBJ's domestic agenda, Irving Kristol treated the War on Poverty and the Great Society as essentially interchangeable, hardly bothering to distinguish between the two. In one essay, he complained: "The centerpiece of the War on Poverty was the sociological fantasy that if one gave political power to the poor, by sponsoring 'community action,' they would lift themselves out of poverty at the expense of the rich and powerful." Kristol considered such a mentality to be dangerously close to socialism and, in fact, accused the entire Great Society as "coming out of class struggle." In another essay, he lamented the Great Society as being too selective and as failing to be universal. In fact, the Great Society was so expansive that LBJ happily believed it offered something for everyone. However, the president's constant rhetoric about helping the poor actually sabotaged his own intentions, and a number of Americans began to view his domestic agenda as being one big handout.[39]

Even after LBJ's presidency, when the Great Society as such was no longer being pursued, enough of the programs remained in place to allow for an explosion of government bureaucracy. A "new class" of professionals—one consisting of scientists, lawyers, city planners, social workers, educators, criminologists, sociologists, public health doctors, and others—had become entrenched in the public sector, warned Kristol. "Though they continue to speak the language of 'professional reform,'" he charged, "in actuality they are acting upon a hidden agenda: to probe the nation from that modified version of capitalism we call 'the welfare state' toward an economic system so stringently regulated in detail as to fulfill many of the traditional anti-capitalist aspirations of the left." Kristol and the rest of the neocons believed that a certain degree of state intervention was acceptable and even necessary. However, they increasingly believed that the Great Society had gone overboard and was actually turning into a socialistic enterprise. Socialism took from the "haves" to give to the "have-nots" and, according to Kristol, engendered class struggle along economic divisions.[40]

While the intellectual neocons focused on the class divisions that they believed the Great Society promoted, Heston encountered another form of division at the NEA—racial conflict. The separation of the races seemed to characterize a number of government programs, including the NEA's Expansion Arts Program, which allowed for minority groups to be set apart from other grantees. For example, instead of granting money to the Capitol Ballet Company, also known as the "Black Ballet," under the auspices of the Dance Program, the NEA funded the dance troupe through the Expansion Arts Program. Likewise, the Afro-American Total Theatre Arts Foundation and El Nuevo Teatro Pobre de America were not funded under the Theater Program, and the Community Radio Workshop was not funded under the Public Media Program.[41] They, too, fell under Expansion Arts. Proponents of the Expansion Arts Program argued that historic discrimination toward minority groups necessitated such a practice. However, the neocons believed that it smacked of "separate but equal," a concept so recently reviled for the inequality it advanced in practice.

Racial separation, the neocons charged, led to the extension of certain privileges to some groups at the expense of others. Not only was this practice unfair, but it also came at a moral and psychological cost because minority groups were often held to inferior standards. Lowering the bar gave the impression that certain groups were not capable of excelling without special help. As Norman Podhoretz noted: "Benign discrimination still was a form of discrimination—of, that is, special treatment—and not even its generous intent could altogether conceal the inexorable implication it carried that on the whole and as a group Negroes were inferior to whites."[42] Furthermore, lower standards for minorities echoed the new relativism that academics were increasingly promoting, and that neocons were strongly resisting, because the slackening indicated that traditional standards of excellence were no longer worthy of pursuit.

Despite the opposition of the neocons, racial separatism became ingrained in government programs and led to the widespread practice of multiculturalism. The NEA embraced multiculturalism—the celebration of many cultures—in the late 1960s and early 1970s. Vantile Whitfield, the director of the Expansion Arts Program, particularly encouraged multiculturalist expression. Michael Straight testifies that, after Whitfield's appointment, "unfamiliar types wearing Afros and dressed in dashikis began to move through the halls of the Endowment." Heston and the other neocons appreciated the variety of cultural beliefs and traditions practiced in the United States but disapproved of the growing tendency among multiculturalists to tout the superiority of particular groups, reject the dominant culture, and resist assimilation. For example, the National Black Theater in Harlem focused explicitly on achieving a black consciousness. The theater's director, Barbara Ann Teer, developed "liberation" classes and told one journalist: "We have tried very hard not to be influenced by Western techniques." Over time, the neocons grew increasingly critical of and hostile to multiculturalism and its presumptions. Heston later wrote with incredulity: "How did we get . . . to the point where the ethical foundations of Western Civilization are now in question?" Irving Kristol damned multiculturalism even more harshly, calling it "a desperate—and surely self-defeating—strategy for coping with the educational deficiencies, and associated social pathologies, of young blacks."[43]

As noted earlier, the neocons grew skeptical of the Great Society for what they considered the easy politicization and the divisiveness of its programs; but what underlay both these trends and troubled the neocons the most about LBJ's domestic agenda was the tremendous expansion of the federal government that accompanied it. The neocons had always been suspicious of big government in an abstract sense, but, as participants in the Great Society, they encountered particular problems that led them to sharpen their critiques. To the neocons, one of the most insidious consequences of the Great Society was the increase in bureaucracy that it engendered. The intellectual neocons scrutinized the bureaucratic structure of the War on Poverty, while Heston focused on the NEA, and they all came to the same conclusion: that bureaucracies should be kept to a minimum. They were expensive and meddlesome and frequently produced unintended consequences that were more troubling than the ones they had originally been created to solve. This realization proved to be a significant milestone for the neocons. The intellectual neocons founded the *Public Interest* in 1965, a journal that was originally designed to explore possible social reform initiatives but that soon emphasized the "limits to social policy" almost exclusively. Meanwhile, Heston defied Nancy Hanks and her bureaucratic allies in the public arena, a confrontation that marked the initial steps of his newly evolving political personality.

The intellectual neocons quickly noted the unintended consequences of the War on Poverty. The sociologist Nathan Glazer originally had hoped to "rationally and pragmatically attack our domestic problems" and, thus, participated as a writer and consultant in Johnson's administration. Glazer and his like-minded colleagues soon began developing a new point of view, however. They feared that government programs actually weakened traditional ways, such as neighborhood associations or churches, that people had previously used to handle distress. The neocons considered traditional institutions important to maintaining bourgeois principles and beliefs. When they voiced their concerns, they found themselves at the mercy of the bureaucrats, who had achieved a stronghold in government agencies and who discounted the very structures that Glazer, Kristol, and the others deemed critical to a healthy society.[44]

For example, Daniel Patrick Moynihan released *The Negro Family* in 1965, a study in which he argued that the black community was dividing between a "stable middle-class group that is steadily growing stronger and more successful and an increasingly disorganized and disadvantaged low-er-class group." Moynihan stressed the black family—intact and disintegrating, respectively—as the key difference between the two groups and recommended that the government find ways to strengthen it. Moynihan's unflattering depiction of the poor black family—and its increasing rates of marital dissolution, female-headed homes, out-of-wedlock births, and welfare dependency—met with strong resistance from black and white liberals, especially those involved in the War on Poverty. They accused Moynihan of racism, claiming that his own bourgeois perspective led him to deem such trends as female-headed households pathological when they really were strengths. Revisionists discounted the need for the nuclear family of the "white" tradition and praised the extended family of the "black" tradition as an acceptable, and even superior, replacement, with or without fathers. Glazer and his allies were furious with the "liberal collapse" around Moynihan and the bureaucrats' willingness to promote a welfare system that seemed to reward fatherless households. As more and more people got on the welfare rolls, the expansion of the welfare state became even more unsettling, its growth seemingly connected to such problems as increasing rates of juvenile delinquency, drug use, and crime. The neocons' fears of big government were fulfilled when they saw the strength and influence of the bureaucrats in the War on Poverty and their unwillingness to take account of the unforeseen consequences of their actions. Irving Kristol pointedly questioned the motivations of the professional class. "If you want to work with poor people, go out and work with poor people. I have great respect for people who do that," he remarked. "But when people start becoming bureaucrats of compassion and start making careers out of compassion—whether political, journalistic or public entertainment careers—then I must say I suspect their good faith."[45]

Heston also found himself battling bureaucracy, as he struggled with Nancy Hanks over the future of the AFI. Whereas the intellectual neocons felt that bureaucrats in the federal government weakened families with welfare policies, Heston felt that bureaucrats in the NEA undermined the strength and potential of the AFI. Heston had been involved with the film agency almost since the beginning. The AFI had not been included in the original legislation that created the NEA, but Johnson mentioned the idea for a film program when he publicly introduced the endowment, proclaiming: "We will create an American Film Institute, bringing together leading artists of the film industry, outstanding educators, and young men and women who wish to pursue this twentieth century art form as their life's work." The call for the AFI surprised Roger Stevens and Livingston Biddle, both of whom had worked on the legislation, but they certainly welcomed the addition. The two spokespersons for film on the first NEA council, George Stevens and Gregory Peck, also strongly supported the idea. At their urging, the NEA paid $91,019 to the Stanford Research Institute (SRI) to advise the endowment on the establishment of the AFI. Working under Peck's supervision, the SRI conducted interviews and undertook studies to determine the appropriate nature of the proposed film industry. In August 1966, the SRI invited Heston to attend an advisory meeting, where he "unburdened . . . my thoughts, random and otherwise, on what the shape of the projected AFI should be." Thus, when the actor joined the National Council on the Arts in January 1967, his interest in the AFI had already been established. Later that year, the SRI recommended that the AFI be directly aligned with the NEA in terms of funding and programming, but it also urged that it remain a separate entity. President Johnson agreed with the SRI's findings. He praised Peck: "I think your organizational approach is a sound one. Operating as a private nonprofit, nongovernment corporation supported by funds from the National Endowment for the Arts, and private moneys, the American Institute will have the necessary support as well as the essential freedom of action which a creative venture of this nature requires."[46]

It was regarding the AFI's "essential freedom of action" that Heston clashed with the NEA bureaucracy. During Roger Stevens's tenure, the AFI enjoyed considerable latitude concerning its budgeting and programming. The AFI undertook major programs in five distinct areas and established a $5 million budget to meet its needs. Stevens immediately allotted $1.3 million in endowment funds over the next three years for the AFI, and the Ford Foundation and the Motion Picture Association of America (MPAA) both pledged equal amounts. Stevens also wrote Peck a letter saying: "It is reasonable to expect that approximately 10 percent of the [NEA's] available funds will be available to aid the Film Institute in the future."[47] The AFI board operated under the assumption that it would not be subject to the same financial restrictions—requirements for matching funds and not receiving more than 50 percent of its budget from the NEA—because of the nature of its founding, the scope of its projects, and Stevens's generosity. Furthermore, Stevens automatically forwarded all film applications to the AFI and did not question the film board's decisions in accepting or rejecting those projects.

Under Hanks's leadership, the AFI did not enjoy the freedom that it once had. Financial troubles partially provoked the change. The Ford Foundation did not renew its grant, and the MPAA never fulfilled its $1.3 million pledge. Therefore, Peck presented Hanks with Stevens's letter and expected the NEA to pick up the slack. Hanks, however, had doubts about the AFI. Her skepticism revolved around two concerns: the AFI's emphasis on Hollywood productions and its lack of financial accountability. Critics charged that the AFI was too Hollywood oriented. Indeed, when its funding collapsed, the AFI was forced to prioritize its programs within a limited budget, at least for the time being. The AFI board chose to concentrate money and attention on its archives and education programs, rescuing classic movies that had been fading on crumbling nitrate film and holding training seminars led by Hollywood notables. Because of these priorities, independent filmmakers felt especially slighted, as did many film educators and critics outside the Hollywood establishment. What appeared to be financial recklessness worried a number of the AFI's critics as well. Outsiders were suspicious of George Stevens's ability to manage a budget and especially disapproved of his salary, which far surpassed that of the rest of the AFI and NEA staff. Rumors of Stevens's frivolous spending rippled through the film community, and, when the AFI moved its headquarters to the regal Greystone mansion in Hollywood, the critics howled. Although Beverly Hills charged the AFI only one cent per year in rent, the mansion's steely walls and imposing manner contributed to the AFI's elitist Hollywood image. Above all, the AFI seemed inaccessible.

Hanks proposed new guidelines for the AFI in an effort to include non-Hollywood artists in the public media program and to establish some financial controls. At her first meeting in October 1969, from which Heston was absent, Hanks won council approval for the new terms that she proposed for the AFI. First, she wanted to halt the customary practice of forwarding applications for film projects directly to the AFI without council review. Instead, she suggested that the council be the first to review those applications and "entertain future requests for film projects." Furthermore, the council decided: "The Endowment may suggest AFI as an alternative source of support. Interesting projects, particularly those which might not be considered within AFI's structure, should be considered by the Council and Endowment." On the face of things, it appeared that the council was to be competing against the AFI. However, Hanks's real purpose was probably to provide funding for groups, outside the Hollywood establishment, that the AFI had, she felt, ignored in the past. In addition, the council established a liaison between the NEA and the AFI to oversee the AFI's financial transactions. Since Heston did not attend the October meeting, he could not oppose these changes, and for the next year no problems arose between the AFI and the NEA.[48]

In the meantime, however, Hanks secretly recruited a new employee to help her revamp the AFI's Public Media Program, and Heston would be unhappy with the results of their efforts. Hanks hired Chloe Aaron, a film and television critic, to write a special report on organizations that did not receive support from the AFI but that in her opinion deserved funding within the NEA's Public Media Program. Aaron presented her report to the council in February 1971 at Greystone. Heston had been invited to be on the AFI board only one week earlier, so he had a significant interest in Aaron's conclusions. Aaron argued that, of the five major program areas the AFI had undertaken, only three had been successful—Archives and Preservation, Filmmaker Training, and Education. "There are two areas, however, that would appear to be seriously in need of additional funding," she continued. "The two complaints most frequently heard from independent filmmakers are 1) insufficient funding for the production of short, innovative films and 2) insufficient outlets for independently produced short or feature length films." The AFI had a program for independent filmmakers but had responded to only 6 percent of the applicants. Aaron proposed that the NEA take responsibility for the production and distribution of independent films. Hanks immediately announced her intention of creating a $1 million pilot program to implement Aaron's proposals.[49]

On hearing the Aaron/Hanks plan, Heston and Peck sat "silent and motionless when . . . all the other members of the council applauded." It seemed to Heston and Peck that the bureaucrats were infringing on their territory. They found it maddening that the NEA chair and her staff would designate a $1 million budget for themselves in an area that was under the jurisdiction of the AFI. True, some of the AFI's programs had received more attention than others. A brand new entity, the AFI could not possibly have satisfied all its potential beneficiaries, especially after its funding from the Ford Foundation and the MPAA collapsed. Heston and Peck did not believe that the AFI should be reviewed by the NEA media staff; they thought that it should be required to answer only to the National Council on the Arts itself. The council was a "who's who" of successful artists; the NEA staff was not. Heston and his allies did not believe that the Public Media Program would provide quality work. In fact, Peck braved a New York snowstorm to travel to Tarrytown and inform the council that he had attended a Public Media subpanel session in California and had been "shocked by the poor quality of the applications and by the way in which they had been approved."[50] Finally, the AFI board worried that the NEA's Public Media Program would siphon away funds that would normally have been allotted to the AFI. Peck, Stevens, and Heston denounced the Aaron/Hanks plan, ready to take opposing measures if necessary.

Heston emerged as the leader in the struggle between the AFI and the NEA. "Halfway through an AFI Board meeting [in December 1971], I went to the men's room," he wrote in his journal, "and came back to find I'd been elected chairman. There is a really serious fund-raising problem, which is not something I'm good at. Well, what the hell . . . it'll be interesting."[51] Heston immediately sought ways to raise funds for the AFI. The film agency started its Lifetime Achievement Award, which included a fund-raising banquet, as well as a Film Day, in which participating theaters donated a percentage of their sales to the AFI. Heston solicited donations from Hollywood moguls, companies, and directors and also bargained with Hanks over funding for the next two years. However, in his negotiations with Hanks and her staff, it became clear that the gulf between them was widening, not narrowing, and much of the difficulty stemmed from their disagreement over the appropriate role of the bureaucrats.

Heston believed that LBJ had founded the AFI for a specific purpose—to serve as the premier agency for the film medium—and feared that the NEA staff was weakening the AFI in its attempt to tailor the NEA to particular political and personal agendas. The AFI board hoped that the institute could rise as a preeminent agency and believed that such a goal required the selective production of professional works that could be understood and enjoyed by the general public. Despite his skepticism of commercialism, Heston believed that a Hollywood-based agency was best equipped to realize the AFI's goals because filmmakers could receive government support while also learning from respected professionals and working with the latest equipment. Heston believed that, as a result of the easy way in which it distributed money through its Public Media Program, the NEA was in danger of supporting obscure or low-grade work. He noted that, if, like the NEA's Public Media Program, the AFI became "unwieldy" and passed cultural judgment only "in theory," it would not be taken seriously and would be unable to solicit funds from private donors. Even though the AFI was, indeed, selective, admitting only a handful of fellows each year, Heston still worried about the quality of the work they produced. He rejoiced over the particularly good ones but ruminated over the implications of the less successful. For example, Jack Warner had recently donated $250,000 to the AFI for a film theater in the Kennedy Center when he was invited to a dinner and showing at Greystone. "He failed to be impressed by two films we made by AFI Fellows," Heston noted. "'Jesus *Christ,* but those are lousy,' he said. 'What the hell ya gonna *do* with that crap!?' 'Jack,' I said, 'please don't take your money back.'"[52]

As Heston continued to pursue his agenda, the chasm between the AFI and the NEA widened even more. Heston privately summed up his perception of the conflict: "We're really in a confrontation with them, and I'm clearly one of the running dogs of Hollywood in their eyes. Obviously, the current bunch at [the NEA council] doesn't view the AFI warmly." He continued: "To the bureaucrats, we're a bunch of dirty elitists. (Since when did a commitment to quality mark you as a bad guy?)" The Hanks staff was "well aware of the importance and the creativity of the commercial film world," countered Michael Straight. "But it was not our world." Straight believed that the AFI should received NEA money only for the "educational and archival aspects of commercial film-making" and that the NEA should direct its resources toward the non-Hollywood segment of the film constituency. Straight complained about Heston and his colleagues: "They had joined the AFI board as a patriotic duty. They saw us as meddlesome bureaucrats." "As for our panelists," he went on, "they were insignificant failures. If they had been any good, they would have made their fortunes in Hollywood. The notion that we and our advisers would sit in judgment upon their decisions seemed to these men to be preposterous. They maintained . . . that we should be grateful to them for giving up their valuable time to guide the AFI."[53]

Heston bargained with Hanks over NEA funding for the AFI over the next two years but without realizing an agreement. Believing that it was time for the two entities to go "head-to-head," Heston began shopping his idea "that it might eventually be best to separate the AFI from the National Council on the Arts, since they seem to make uneasy bedfellows." Because such a separation would require Congress to amend the original NEA legislation, Heston approached Representative John Brademas of Indiana, "one of the most active men on the Hill," to air his grievances with the Hanks council and staff.[54] Congress held several hearings to consider separating the AFI from the NEA and allowing the AFI to receive its funding directly from Congress.

During his testimony regarding the AFI, Heston presented a workable solution, denied the bureaucratic nature of the AFI, and tried to appease his antiestablishment critics. He proposed a new system of financial support in which two-thirds of the AFI budget would come directly from Congress and one-third would be raised in the private sector on a matching basis. The plan appealed to Heston because the AFI had no ticket sales to rely on for support yet needed stable funding. Interestingly, he did not think of the AFI as being as bureaucratic as the NEA. He argued: "We would not be demanding a corner of the Rayburn Building or indeed any other government structure."[55] Heston was able to deflect most of the charges of elitism directed at the AFI by responding that the institute would be better equipped to reach independent filmmakers and other discontented groups if it received the amount of money the SRI had originally recommended. He argued that the AFI had not been attempting a "dismissal of their [the independent filmmakers'] values" but that it could not do everything at once. He balked at cutting back the AFI's responsibilities, hoping instead that the film institute could maintain its original programming.

A striking aspect of the AFI negotiations was the deference with which Heston was treated by Congress while testifying on the institute's behalf. Jack Valenti commented that, when the actor appeared in one House committee meeting, "a reverent hush" fell over the audience until, "out of the quiet," a "shrill piping voice" said, "Holy Smokes, it's Moses!": "It brought the house down." Several times, members of Congress noted on the record how honored they were to meet him. After Heston had testified that separation "seems the only option remaining, if we are not to wither on a vine," Senator Claiborne Pell immediately took to the defense of the AFI. Despite his own instinctive discomfort with splitting the endowment, he accused the NEA of being "niggardly" in its approach to the AFI. Pell even went so far as to openly worry about who would run the institute when Heston and Stevens decided to retire from its service. When Stevens and Heston suggested that they would prefer that the AFI stay within the NEA if the agency could guarantee the institute's financial security, Pell immediately placed the onus on the NEA, remarking: "The Endowment of the Arts is making a fundamental mistake in error in not having worked out some understanding with you in this regard."[56]

Another notable aspect of the AFI tale was Heston's increasing willingness to take on his critics in the public arena. Not willing to compromise in backroom negotiations, Heston actively publicized the AFI's problems in an effort to win public sympathy. His willingness to fight for his convictions remained evident in his public life—from his uncompromising leadership of the National Rifle Association to his permanent role in the culture war. For conservative groups, Heston was an irreplaceable ally: Moses or Ben-Hur, incarnate, a hero who will conquer the opposition. His adversaries, however, considered him as stubborn and uncompromising as those characters. After the AFI disagreement, Straight wrote: "[Heston's] film roles consisted of a series of confrontations between the forces of righteousness and the forces of evil; they were tailored to his personality, and, in turn, his personality conformed to his roles."[57] In the eyes of both friends and foes, Heston's public image as an actor was becoming intertwined with his political roles.

Congress finally rejected the AFI's request for independent status in 1975. Senator Pell, a sponsor of the original NEA legislation and one of Heston's fans, led the opposition to the split because he ultimately did not find enough justification for it. In fact, Heston did not expect to win, but he had hoped to amass enough publicity to relieve the AFI of its pressing financial concerns. Although the AFI did not receive additional funding from the NEA, Hanks did agree to transfer review of the institute to a newly formed panel as well as establish a new liaison, moves that eased the tension between the two entities. Meanwhile, the AFI board found ways to raise more money in the private sector, taking on, for example, a commission to make a film for the National Bicentennial Celebration—"the best thing to happen to the AFI," according to Heston. The board also decided to make the Lifetime Achievement Award an annual event. Heston considered the first presentation of the award, the 1973 tribute to the director John Ford, "something of a smash": "It seemed to me better than the Academy show. . . . It was well and enthusiastically attended." Ford also received the Presidential Medal of Freedom from President Nixon at the ceremony, which, as Heston put it, "tends to hold your attention." And it seemed meaningful to those who were honored. Heston was convinced that Ford was "pleased with the tribute paid him, though he is now very old, very sick. This will be his last appearance, I think. I'm glad we brought it off."[58] Since then, the AFI has honored such esteemed figures as James Cagney, Orson Welles, William Wyler, and Bette Davis, and the AFI's Lifetime Achievement Award has become the highest honor for a career in film.

The Institute continued to grow and flourish, and Heston continued his association with its leadership. He served as chair of the board of trustees until 1982. He then became president of the AFI, a position that he held until his retirement from public life in 2002. He was then given the title chair emeritus, and the following year the AFI established a new award in his honor—the AFI Charlton Heston Award, established to "acknowledge individuals who have made distinguished contributions to both the film and television communities and to the American Film Institute." Heston was the first recipient of the award. George Stevens subsequently left the AFI to move into independent producing and directing, and Jean Picker Firstenberg is the current director and CEO of AFI. Tensions remained, however, between the so-called Hollywood set and the rest of the film community. For instance, John Frohnmayer, the NEA director during the late 1980s, received complaints from independent filmmakers concerning Hollywood's AFI "stranglehold" on the NEA's Public Media Program even before he had moved into his new office.[59]

HESTON'S EXPERIENCE WITH FEDERAL funding for the arts illustrates the general neoconservative frustration with the Great Society and its problems, particularly the politicization, divisiveness, and bureaucratization that it fomented. The neoconservatives' struggles with the Great Society indicated that politics, at least if big government prevailed, would increasingly have cultural implications, and not just in an artistic sense. Questions concerning traditional artistic standards as well as bourgeois values, foreign policy decisions, and social trends became inexorably intertwined in a complicated political, cultural debate. Heston continued to support the NEA as a legitimate organization, even when he did not totally agree with its policies, because he agreed with the general principles from which it was founded. However, he proved that he would stubbornly fight for certain standards. Likewise, despite their disagreements with certain elements of the Great Society, Heston and the rest of the neocons continued to endorse the Democrats until 1972. But, as the Democratic establishment began to lose its grip and the party platform shifted, the Democrats would no longer be able to count on Heston and the neocons for support.

CHAPTER FIVE

DEMOCRAT FOR REPUBLICANS

CHARLTON HESTON HAD TAKEN ON SO MANY PUBLIC SERVICE COMMIT-ments during the late 1960s and early 1970s that he could not help but comment: "I'm not an actor anymore, for God's sake . . . I'm an activist."[1] Heston's core beliefs did not vary during this period, but America's political and cultural landscape did undergo tumultuous transformations. Cultural and political radicals contributed to major changes in two institutions that had once seemed profoundly stable and constant—the Democratic Party and the American middle class. As the Democrats adopted a series of liberal reforms and the middle class absorbed countercultural sensibilities, Heston, Irving Kristol, and other like-minded Americans resisted these changes. It was during this period that Heston and Kristol realized that they were no longer liberals, or even dissident liberals, but cultural, and even political, conservatives. In fact, it was at this point that Kristol and his intellectual allies became known as *neoconservatives,* thanks to the sociologist Michael Harrington. Harrington did not intend this term to be a compliment. Indeed, he was so disgusted with the rightward drift of his fellow thinkers that he focused solely on intellectuals when affixing the *neoconservative* label. However, Heston's beliefs and actions unmistakably paralleled those of the intellectual neocons during this time period—so much so that it is clear that neoconservatism was not just an intellectual movement but one that included a number of Americans like Heston who believed that the bourgeois ethic was under assault, America's position in the world was in danger, and the Republican Party was best prepared to deal with these problems.

Even though Heston did not actually work with Kristol, Norman Podhoretz, or any of the other intellectual neocons, the actor similarly bemoaned the implications of the Democratic reforms undertaken after the 1968 election and the ascension of the hippie counterculture. Heston and the intellectual neocons rejected the assumptions that drove a new group of Democrats, led by Senator George McGovern of South Dakota, in restructuring the party. The McGovern Commission, among other things, installed affirmative action into the platform of the Democratic Party and replaced party stalwarts on the Democratic National Committee with delegates who had been chosen on the basis of their race, gender, or age. McGovern ushered in a decidedly leftist ideology that would dominate the Democrats for years to come. Heston and the intellectual neocons vehemently opposed these measures and considered them a betrayal of the party. Podhoretz and Heston both remarked that McGovern's nomination as the Democratic presidential candidate in 1972 represented a direct challenge to everything the party had stood for under John F. Kennedy. Meanwhile, the Republican candidate, Richard Nixon, contained the rising conservative forces in the GOP and presented himself as a moderate with populist appeal. Kristol, Gertrude Himmelfarb, Heston, and a growing number of neoconservatives voted Republican in a presidential contest for the first time when they cast their ballots for Nixon in 1972. At the same time, Heston and the intellectual neocons unequivocally rejected countercultural assumptions. They worried about the effect of cultural radicalism on the American lifestyle and on Americans' perceptions of society. Kristol and Heston were particularly concerned that the military and big business were no longer seen in a positive light. And both Heston and the intellectual neocons noted the importance of the cinema in shaping American culture and spreading countercultural beliefs. For example, both Podhoretz and Heston singled out the movie *One Flew over the Cuckoo's Nest* (Milos Forman, 1975) for propagating the "repugnant" message that the "world's an asylum, the inmates are sane, and the keepers are mad."

While Heston and the intellectual neocons shared similar political and cultural beliefs, the methods that animated their views were quite different. The intellectual neocons relied on the power of the pen in the world of ideas with their editorials, magazines, and books. Podhoretz, for example, conducted a "no-holds-barred campaign" against the counterculture in his magazine *Commentary* between 1970 and 1973. Heston, however, conveyed his sentiments through his actions, most of which, owing to his superstar status, were publicized by the media. He resisted the counterculture by choosing movie roles that conveyed his own bourgeois ethics and principles and turning down offers that violated them. He also revealed his beliefs through political action, particularly at the grassroots level with the Screen Actors Guild. In the early 1970s, the Hollywood union reflected the political and cultural trends of the nation when a new upsurge of young radicals attacked the leadership and very organization of the group. The reform efforts of these mavericks resulted in the so-called Revolution of '73. Within a few years, a new set of staff and officers replaced the old guard and was determined to shape the Guild into an activist, politically liberal union. Heston disapproved of the Guild's new direction and attempted to halt the young turks' influence. The early 1970s proved to be epiphanic years for both intellectual neocons and visceral neoconservatives alike, who concluded that their bourgeois, traditional beliefs had to be defended in both the political and the cultural arenas.

THE JOHNSON-HUMPHREY COALITION THAT won the greatest presidential victory in American history disintegrated almost immediately. In 1966, the tortured president watched his approval ratings plummet, and a "dump LBJ" campaign emerged within the Democratic Party the following year. The historian Allen Matusow argues that the Democrats' stunning collapse was the fault of the liberal New Deal coalition that dominated party policymaking. Liberals themselves were to blame, Matusow concludes, not only because their policies were ineffective, but also because they seemed to be responsible for causing even more problems abroad and at home.[2] First, the Vietnam War produced increased casualties without an honest assessment of American policy from the Johnson administration. Second, civil rights measures did not meet the expectations of economically and socially outcast African Americans, many of whom acted out their frustrations in urban riots. Finally, LBJ's controversial War on Poverty appeared to focus on race more than class and alienated many Democratic Party regulars. Critics on the left accused LBJ of not doing enough, while conservatives charged that the president's policy failures invited increased crime and lawlessness, which, by 1967, would be the number one domestic concern among Americans. As both the Left and the Right leveled charges against the moral integrity of liberalism, the traditional Democratic establishment struggled to maintain control of the party's agenda.

The Vietnam War tore Democrats apart during the Johnson presidency, and dismay with American policies in Southeast Asia underlay a political and cultural revolt that would affect the entire nation. U.S. involvement in Vietnam had begun immediately after World War II, but it was under Johnson's leadership that the war became "Americanized." In August 1964, LBJ pushed through Congress the Tonkin Gulf Resolution, which allowed the president to "take all necessary measures to protect American troops and prevent further aggression in Vietnam." Hoping to demonstrate American determination to defend South Vietnam, LBJ authorized bombers to unleash sustained air attacks on North Vietnam under Operation Rolling Thunder in February 1965. The following month he deployed troops to guard air bases and serve as an emergency reserve. In July he sent fifty thousand more soldiers at the request of General William Westmoreland, the commander of U.S. forces in South Vietnam. Privately, LBJ agreed to ship an additional fifty thousand troops by the end of the year, all of whom would be operating independently of the South Vietnamese army.[3]

These developments signaled a distinct shift in policy, yet LBJ managed to Americanize the war without alerting Americans. Rolling Thunder launched the pattern of deceit that would cripple LBJ's presidency. When the president portrayed the air campaign as merely "tit-for-tat" retaliation, he deceived Americans about Rolling Thunder's true nature, as he would with a number of future operations. Adding to this deception, he downplayed the new role that U.S. troops had assumed and manipulated the budget to avoid having to enact a truth-exposing war tax. With these duplicitous acts, LBJ set the stage for an inflation crisis and the downfall of liberalism.[4]

LBJ used gradualist methods (i.e., incremental steps instead of drastic policy changes) to augment American support of South Vietnam for several reasons. First, he did not want to put the country on full war alert because doing so would jeopardize financial backing for his Great Society programs. To Johnson, being candid about the cost and scale of the war would have justified either the demand of the doves that he withdraw from Vietnam or that of the hawks that he scale back reform efforts and give the war his, and the nation's, full attention. Second, LBJ believed that gradualist methods would result in fewer American lives lost. Third, he wanted to minimize the risk of drawing Communist China, or even the Soviet Union, into the war. Above all, LBJ believed that gradualist methods were all that were necessary to defeat the small, technically inferior nation.[5] This underestimation dictated the methods with which the war would be waged and, eventually, drew protest from hawks and doves alike.

Heston and the intellectual neocons were similarly skeptical of U.S. involvement in Vietnam, especially after the war became Americanized. Heston divulged to the fans who received his quarterly newsletter that he worried about both "the integrity of our purpose" and "the depth of personal commitment held by the troops."[6] Likewise, Norman Podhoretz and others who normally followed a strong anti-Communist line feared that America's attempt to install democracy halfway around the world would prove impossible.

Because of his doubts and concerns, Heston decided to fly to South Vietnam to assess the situation himself, a decision that reveals an important aspect of his character—confidence in his own judgment. Seeing himself in the tradition of one of his heroes and role models, Thomas Jefferson, Heston considered himself an independent thinker looking out for the public good. And Heston, like Jefferson, had the access to financial and political power to carry out his reconnaissance. As was his style, Heston traveled to Vietnam alone, not as part of a celebrity entourage, so that he could probe the dark recesses of the jungle where isolated troops rarely saw USO productions. He admitted: "I flew to the Far East filled with the misgivings and apprehensions that colour the thinking of every American these days."[7]

On January 15, 1966, Heston arrived in Saigon, where he hopped a military flight to Danang to join a Special Forces mission. The actor stayed busy, calling on two to twenty outposts per day. His tour included visits to an advanced field hospital and a Special Forces gunship. At the end of his two-week expedition, Heston even had a meeting with Westmoreland. "Since I could travel both light and alone, I was able to go to fairly remote areas," he wrote in his journal. "Though I'm sure they'd rather have seen Bob Hope and the girl singers, at least I was able to let some of the men in the boondocks know they weren't forgotten . . . by me anyway." No doubt, many soldiers appreciated Heston's forays into the backcountry and visits to hospitals. One wounded soldier (who had first met the actor at a surgical unit near Danang) was so inspired by Heston that he sought him out at a book signing several years later to tell him: "I'd been hit seventeen times, and they thought I wouldn't make it. I'll always believe I made it because of what you told me that day." It is very likely that Heston was the only actor to penetrate so deeply into Vietnam, his travels paralleled only by those of Jimmy Stewart, who flew on a bombing mission over Cambodia before his son was killed in the war.[8]

Heston's self-appointed mission to Vietnam erased his doubts about American involvement there. Immediately after he returned to the United States, he shared his opinions with the public. First and foremost, Heston called the loved ones of each of the troops with whom he had spoken in order to deliver their personal messages and assurances. This was a gesture for which he neither sought nor received publicity—and one that must have been quite a surprise to the recipients. Then he reassured those who received his newsletter that he was "impressed beyond measure" with U.S. troops and convinced that the American presence in Southeast Asia was justified. "The war in Vietnam is neither showy, nor easy but the men who are fighting it made me believe we are undertaking a job no-one else is equipped or inclined to do, and I think perhaps we can," he wrote. Heston voiced his approval of the war to the general public by making a special appearance on *The Tonight Show* regarding his trip and filming a U.S. savings bond commercial encouraging Americans to support "the servicemen in Vietnam." Not only would a bond eventually bring profit to the buyer, Heston proclaimed, but it would also "keep America strong and help defend the cause of freedom everywhere."[9] As this patriotic commercial indicates, the Johnson administration had clearly recognized the draw of a celebrity spokesperson and was using Heston's support to its advantage.

Most neocons did not come to the same conclusions as Heston; in fact, only Irving Kristol lent his support to the war effort. Kristol believed it was America's responsibility, as the most powerful nation in the world, to police the globe. To dodge such a responsibility, he proclaimed, "is one form of the abuse of power." Furthermore, Kristol feared that withdrawing from Vietnam would make America appear vulnerable, a dangerous consequence in the context of the Cold War. Since the neocons were divided on the appropriateness of American intervention in Vietnam, it is not surprising that Hollywood celebrities, too, came to opposite conclusions.

A number of entertainers coalesced around both sides of the debate and tried to rally support for their respective positions. Actors of both the hawk and the dove persuasions believed that their respective sides were exposing the "truth" about the nature of the war. In 1967, Heston joined such well-known stars as Henry Fonda, James Garner, and Bob Hope in staging an Independence Day television special "to explain U.S. goals in Vietnam." Believing that the media had not accurately informed the public regarding either policy or troop morale, these actors worked with the military and the State Department to correct the "misunderstandings."[10]

Far more stars spoke out against the war, the most vocal of whom being Jane Fonda. Fonda also traveled to Vietnam, and, despite the fact that her father, Henry, supported the war, she formulated a much different opinion after her visit. Horrified by the devastation of the Vietnamese countryside caused by U.S. bombing runs, she transformed her disenchantment into what Heston considered a simplistic glorification of the Communist North. Fonda came to be known as "Hanoi Jane" after she perched atop a North Vietnamese tank pointing toward the South. Undaunted, Fonda brought her message back to the United States, where she joined Donald Sutherland, Peter Boyle, Barbara Dane, Dick Gregory, Gary

Goodrow, and Swamp Dogg in an antiwar review called "Free the Army." Staged twenty-one times to over sixty-four thousand U.S. servicemen, the purpose of the show was to inform the armed forces about "the truth" of the war and turn them against it. Fonda stirred up hostility with the review and generated more controversy and outrage in 1972 when she called American prisoners of war "liars and hypocrites" for claiming that the North Vietnamese had tortured them.[11] Fonda's disgust with the war led her to question American Cold War policy as well as her own faith in the American system.

The media attention accorded the hawks and the doves obscured a third view of the Vietnam War, a view that came to be shared by the majority of Americans, including most of the neocons: that American involvement in Vietnam had been an error but that it was not a mistake that indicted America's entire foreign policy. The majority of Americans believed that the United States had been well-intentioned in going to Vietnam but, as the casualties mounted and the price tag rose, began to wonder whether it was worth the expense. They eventually believed it to be a mistake. Still, they considered American involvement in Vietnam an altruistic enterprise. Podhoretz called it an "excess of idealism."[12] Thus, as debates over the Vietnam War brought up the related issues of patriotism and anticommunism, some, like Fonda, came to doubt these values, while others, like Podhoretz, continued to embrace them, even if they disagreed with the war itself.

The Democratic Party experienced further inner turmoil regarding the civil rights movement. Tensions had festered between King and the Student Nonviolent Coordinating Committee (SNCC) since at least the March on Washington in 1963. The demonstration at the Mall was a glorious day for Heston and many others, but some black activists resented King's efforts to march for Kennedy's civil rights legislation instead of for A. Philip Randolph's originally proposed agenda calling for "jobs and freedom." The charismatic Stokeley Carmichael personified SNCC's discontent with King, and the two activists struggled over the movement's future agenda. King continued to utilize nonviolent tactics, encourage integration, and target legal and political issues in an effort to effect social change, but Carmichael questioned these methods. Carmichael and King subsequently clashed over such projects as the Mississippi Freedom Democratic Party (MFDP), a civil rights delegation sent to the 1964 Democratic national convention in Atlantic City, and the Selma march in 1965.[13] Indeed, many leaders in the movement, individuals who had endured their share of racist violence and planned their own grassroots projects, grew tired of King's dominating presence in the movement. These more radical activists referred to King derisively as "de Lawd!"

Heston lost touch with the movement not only because he disapproved of the radicalism exhibited by the increasingly influential Carmichael but also because King moved to the left. To be sure, there were important differences between the two civil rights leaders. Most significantly, King maintained his basic values regarding nonviolence and integration, while Carmichael embraced black nationalism. Carmichael started an all-black political party called the Lowndes County Freedom Organization in 1966 and in May of that year was elected president of the SNCC. In office, Carmichael broke from his predecessor, John Lewis, to repudiate nonviolence, call for "Black Power," and limit the role of whites in the previously integrated organization. Predictably, Heston approved of King's tactics far more than he did Carmichael's, but King's actions after Johnson signed the Voting Rights Act in 1965 indicated that the movement was shifting to the left. For instance, King spoke out against Johnson's handling of the Vietnam War and participated in antiwar marches in 1967.[14] King's opposition to the war further worked to alienate Heston from the movement.

Moreover, Heston did not agree with King's approach to the War on Poverty. The "color-blind" nature of the War on Poverty as LBJ presented it—a program focusing on self-help and equal opportunity—seemed compatible with a movement calling for integration and nondiscriminatory policies and corresponded to Heston's own beliefs. LBJ's program encouraged individualism and identified with the work-oriented approach of the New Deal. However, it was almost immediately criticized by most black leaders. Because of the unique nature of black poverty, even King indicated his approval of singling out blacks in an economic program when he urged LBJ to enact a "G.I. Bill of Rights for the Disadvantaged." Opportunity, King argued, was not enough. Blacks needed some sort of economic guarantees, or rights, to make up for years of marginalization in American society.[15] Heston greatly admired King, but he would not approve of a program that singled out race.

Liberal welfare reformers agreed with King, however, and almost immediately transformed the language of the War on Poverty by denouncing "opportunity" and demanding "entitlement." As the civil rights movement moved to the North, where marches and programs proved ineffective at securing better jobs, housing, and schooling, a number of moderate blacks and welfare reformers distanced themselves from the White House and joined militants in their critique of an America dominated by racist people and institutions. Welfare reformers fought the Johnson administration through community action programs (CAPs), which were financed by the federal Office of Economic Opportunity. Exploiting the program's "maximum feasible participation" clause, CAP reformers taught methods of direct action protest to the urban poor across the country. The political implications of using public funds for protest-training workshops devastated the reputation of the War on Poverty and infuriated Johnson. His exasperation with the hard-line radicals climaxed at the White House antipoverty conference "To Secure These Rights" in the spring of 1966. The leftists insisted that traditional liberal values impeded social and racial justice and that economically disadvantaged groups should have unconditional rights to welfare payments, without government requirements in terms of work or behavior. Realizing that his accomplishments and programs had been discounted and manipulated, an outraged LBJ considered his civil rights efforts exhausted, and he no longer personally engaged in the antipoverty debate.[16]

The reformers' emphasis on entitlement and protest realized the neoconservative fear of "compassionate" reform. The neocons believed that a "new class" of professionals—social workers, lawyers, city planners, educators, scientists, sociologists, and others who found their careers in the public sector rather than the private—was growing in strength. They feared the influence of this new class for three reasons. As a group that emphasized the limits and unforeseen consequences of social policy, the neocons believed that some naive segments of the new class had little awareness of such constraints. Kristol believed that some involved in the War on Poverty "had been dazzled by trendy sociological theories" and had, therefore, lost touch with reality.[17] The neocons also feared that many in the new class were more self-interested than they let on, representing themselves as concerned with the public good (especially of the poor and blacks) but really just wanting to aggrandize themselves. In other words, they worked to expand their agenda so that they would have jobs and could influence public policy through those jobs.[18] Finally, the neocons feared that some of the new class harbored what Kristol called "a hidden agenda": "to propel the nation from that modified version of capitalism we call 'the welfare state' toward an economic system so stringently regulated in detail as to fulfill many of the traditional anti-capitalist aspirations of the left."[19] Socialism, the neocons suspected, was the ultimate goal.

Despite LBJ's inability, or perhaps unwillingness, to rein in programs gone awry, the neocons continued to support the president because they considered him loyal to and representative of the traditional New Deal Democrats. Orthodox liberals, including the neocons and LBJ, struggled to reclaim the Democratic focus on individualism, equal opportunity, and coalition politics. However, a group of burgeoning leftist Democrats was simultaneously trying to push the party toward an emphasis on the equality of results and ideological politics. Many who had formerly been a part of the New Deal coalition would soon move into open opposition to LBJ, citing as their primary motivation his mishandling of the Vietnam War and the War on Poverty. Their search for a "New Politics" meshed with the increasing radicalism of American young people and would, ultimately, make the Democratic Party repugnant to the neocons.

The New Left grew from a small group of disenchanted political misfits to a mass movement of student radicals that increasingly interacted with the civil rights movement, the counterculture, the antiwar movement, and the Democratic Party as it gained influence. Many within the liberal establishment, like Heston and the rest of the neocons, would bemoan the influence of the New Left, while others considered it their political and personal salvation.

Students for a Democratic Society (SDS) emerged as the primary vehicle of the New Left in 1962 when Tom Hayden, the organization's leader, drafted the Port Huron Statement, an ideological critique of Cold War America. A supposedly democratic nation, America was not living up to its ideals, SDS charged, pointing to evidence of racial bigotry, atomic weaponry, and poverty that contradicted the quest for equality, peace, and prosperity. Worried that consumer-oriented Americans were "in withdrawal from public life, from any collective effort at directing their own affairs," SDS called for peaceful and "participatory" democracy and designated students as the agents of change. Promoting campus free speech and protesting the Vietnam War proved to be the two issues on which SDS made the most impact. SDS activists at the University of California, Berkeley, established their campus as the focal point of political radicalism in the fall of 1964 after they attempted to disseminate political information there. The university prohibited all such activities, liberal and conservative alike. SDS then staged sit-ins at Berkeley and soon attacked almost every aspect of university authority, but particularly state-sponsored research related to the Department of Defense. In the spring of 1965, SDS took a leading role in antiwar protests and university teach-ins across the country, and the number of people identified with the organization rose from twenty-five hundred in December 1964 to ten thousand in the fall of 1965.[20]

However, the New Left lost credibility with moderates as it became increasingly radicalized. Heated confrontations with authorities tainted the SDS agenda. Furthermore, as the New Left's anger over the American presence in Vietnam mounted, many student radicals abandoned their commitment to peaceful dissent and directed their hostility toward American imperialism and hegemony. This new focus led the New Left to identify with Viet Cong "revolutionary guerrillas" in Vietnam and African American "urban guerrillas" in American cities. Student radicals argued that they themselves were also victims, only of abundance rather than deprivation. Most American citizens considered the New Left's self-identification with oppression outrageous and disapproved of the students' inclination to pursue power without any particular goals in mind. For example, the seizure of Columbia University in 1968 seemed to be a senseless act of hostility, and the growing obsession with the Communist leaders Mao Zedong, V. I. Lenin, and Karl Marx was disturbing. When these student "revolutionaries" turned to violence as a legitimate means of radical change, they delivered the most detrimental blow to the New Left's quest for legitimacy.

Despite its excesses, the New Left formulated a political challenge that forced the Democrats on the defensive. Some, like the neocons and President Johnson, stood their ground and maintained their commitment to authority and coalition politics. Others, inspired by the concept of participatory democracy, began to think in ideological terms and reevaluate their political traditions. In the process, such converts became more receptive to the critiques of modern American life expressed by the counterculture. The distinction between political and cultural radicalism soon blurred, making the youth culture's impact on the Democrats even more significant.

The counterculture had very different roots and values than the New Left, but the hippie assault on the prevailing culture was just as insulting to the neocons' politics and as offensive to their sensibilities. What the historian Allen Matusow calls "the hippie impulse" was a set of youthful challenges against the traditional values of bourgeois culture. The bourgeois elite traditionally emphasized reason, progress, order, achievement, social responsibility, materialism, competition, a work ethic, hygiene, monogamy, and the subjection of nature. The counterculture rejected all these middle-class norms. Hippies celebrated experimentation, cooperation, nature, passion, and the destruction of all traditional standards.[21] They established communes across the country but settled most heavily in urban enclaves in New York and California. Their appearance was distinctive because of their long hair and tie-dyed clothes, and they also experimented with LSD, marijuana, acid rock, and "living in the moment." At first blush, the countercultural ideology appeared innocently benign. The hippie impulse was only in the interest of personal reconstruction, not yet to be used for transforming the world. Hippies primarily wanted to change their own personal experience of reality and life. Still, the hippie lifestyle was appalling to the neocons, especially Heston, a man whose career and credo rested on responsibility.

Meanwhile, several wings of the Democratic Party openly rebelled against LBJ, tearing apart the New Deal coalition. In the summer of 1967, the president called up forty-five thousand more troops and finally asked for higher taxes. In response, thousands of student protesters vilified him. Additionally, a number of leftist intellectuals, like Noam Chomsky, abandoned their rhetorical condemnations of the war to encourage outright resistance. This disobedience included such measures as refusing to pay the percentage of taxes apportioned for the military, promoting draft resistance, and aiding those who did evade the draft. Likewise, a number of influential Democratic leaders turned against LBJ. The president's war measures had garnered support in 1964, but even then several Democrats harbored private concerns about his policies. By 1968, these senators willingly expressed their mistrust of LBJ. For instance, William Fulbright, chair of the powerful Senate Foreign Relations Committee, called the war "unnecessary and immoral." The country "sickens for lack of moral leadership," he accused. The dissatisfaction expressed by the students, intellectuals, and Democrats inspired Allard Lowenstein of Americans for Democratic Action to instigate a "Dump LBJ" effort. Senator Eugene McCarthy of Minnesota and Senator Robert Kennedy of New York both announced their candidacies based on antiwar agendas. Governor George Wallace of Alabama emerged from the conservative wing of the party to announce his candidacy as an Independent. Wallace also criticized LBJ's handling of the war, but the governor mocked peace, recklessly promising to bomb Vietnam "to smithereens." The Democrats were divided, and leftist radicals were poised to overrun LBJ's agenda.[22]

Feeling betrayed by his own party and overwhelmed by the domestic consequences of the Vietnam War, LBJ withdrew from the 1968 presidential contest in the hopes of redeeming his legacy. Concerned about American political stability and not particularly impressed with McCarthy or Kennedy, Heston considered the president's decision "a mistake." Meanwhile, LBJ pledged to turn his full attention to finding peace in Vietnam, and, thus, at home, goals that seemed achievable when he started negotiations with America's Communist adversaries in Vietnam. However, within only a few weeks, the nation was engulfed in even more chaos. In April, the administration's attempts at peace in Vietnam fell apart. And, on the sixteenth of that month, a white ex-convict shot and killed Martin Luther King Jr. in Memphis. Urban neighborhoods erupted into agonizing displays of frustration, and, by the end of that week, riots had broken out in over one hundred cities.[23] Only three months later, another assassination shocked the nation when a disenchanted Arab émigré shot Robert Kennedy the night he won the California State primary.

Troubled by these murders, and worried about the moral implications of black poverty and the war, Americans turned to large questions: Had something gone wrong with America? Was it a morally flawed society, intoxicated by its own power and success? Was it a perpetuator of violence, inherently sick? It was in answer to these questions that the differences between the New Democrats and the orthodox, including the neocons, became quite apparent. While some liberals came to the conclusion that, yes, America was a morally flawed society, Heston denied that it was. In fact, he addressed these concerns explicitly in his journal, writing: "No, I don't think Robert Kennedy's death reveals a hidden core of violence in the American spirit . . . simply that [violence] runs like a red thread through the heart, or the reflexes of the human animal." Furthermore, he thought that Americans needed to recognize that a nation that allowed and encouraged dissent would have to face violence occasionally, not because the society was sick—a society that allowed dissent was actually a healthy one—but because some individuals were disturbed. To Heston, "the fact" was that "dissent breeds disorder, and disorder breeds violence, and violence breeds murder." But these were risks a free society took in order to be free.[24]

Likewise, the Johnson administration also denied that a sickness was afflicting American society. The White House took specific measures to arrest the rapidly developing sense of national guilt and improve the Democrats' deteriorating reputation on crime control. The presidential aide George Reedy urged LBJ to treat Senator Kennedy's assassination as a "great personal tragedy" but not a societal sickness, concluding: "This nation cannot afford to wallow in another orgy of self-flagellation." Echoing Reedy, LBJ told Americans that it was "wrong" and "self-deceptive, to conclude from this act that our country is sick."[25] The president designated June 9, 1968, as a national day of mourning for the slain senator, appointed the National Commission on the Causes and Prevention of Violence, and attempted to strengthen the gun control portion of his proposed Omnibus Crime Control and Safe Streets Act. With these measures, he hoped to allay the hysteria over the assassinations.

LBJ had actually been trying to pass comprehensive gun control measures since learning that President Kennedy had been shot with a mail-order rifle. In 1965, he had introduced to Congress a bill that prohibited the interstate mail-order sale of handguns, rifles, and shotguns; outlawed the over-the-counter purchase of handguns by nonresidents; and regulated the importation of surplus military firearms into the United States. However, the bill died in Congress, largely, according to the Department of Justice, "due to the opposition from the NRA [National Rifle Association]."[26] The NRA accepted regulatory procedures for the sale of handguns, but the organization's lobbyists vehemently opposed the same restrictions on rifles and shotguns, arguing that mail-order catalogs provided the only access to long guns that rural hunters had. In fact, LBJ's general philosophical approach to crime prevention differed dramatically from that of Republicans and the NRA. The president focused on gun control, while conservatives emphasized the harsh punishment of criminals. These competing philosophies made it difficult for the parties to agree on crime legislation, and, therefore, their negotiations on gun control achieved little progress between 1965 and 1967.

When the political tenor of the country changed dramatically in 1968, LBJ exerted new pressure for gun and crime legislation. Not only had the Republicans made significant gains in the midterm congressional elections of 1966, but from 1964 through 1967 the country had also witnessed a historic number of urban riots. The White House knew that, in preparing for the 1968 national election, the Democrats needed to bolster their reputation on crime in order to compete with the Republicans. Indeed, a

Gallup poll conducted in February 1968 confirmed the administration's suspicions when it revealed that "crime and lawlessness" was the top domestic concern of Americans while poverty was second to last.[27] These changes indicated to LBJ that he had a reasonable chance of passing gun control measures.

Johnson introduced his safe streets bill in the spring of 1968 and attempted to strengthen the gun control portion of the bill by imposing the restrictions on rifles and long guns that the Senate had failed to enact in 1965. However, in May 1968, the Senate again thwarted LBJ's efforts by shifting the focus of the bill to the training and assistance of law enforcement officers. Not until Robert Kennedy's death, when a new outcry of support poured forth for stricter gun control laws, did the regulation of shotguns and rifles appear possible. In the wake of the assassination, LBJ received five thousand letters and telegrams favoring by a margin of nine to one strong gun control legislation. He castigated the Senate for ignoring rifles and shotguns and renewed his effort to include those weapons in a gun control bill. The Senate's regulation of handguns was only a "half-way measure," according to LBJ. "Weapons of destruction can be purchased by mail as easily as baskets of fruit or cartons of cigarettes," he charged. "We must eliminate the dangers of mail-order murder."[28]

Johnson believed that more guns equaled more risks and, ultimately, more crime, and he used this philosophy in attempting to sell his legislation to the public. The statistics regarding the use of firearms seemed to support the administration's claims that handguns were not the only weapons of choice. According to White House records, rifles or shotguns were used in 30 percent of firearm murders, and 25 percent of law enforcement officers killed between 1960 and 1965 were felled by those types of guns. Furthermore, John F. Kennedy and Martin Luther King were both victims of long guns, and authorities had even concluded that the firearm used by Lee Harvey Oswald against Kennedy was purchased by mail order.[29] * LBJ used these statistics to try to persuade the public of the merits of his case, hoping that he could force Congress to include rifles and shotguns in the gun control bill. A number of celebrities, including Heston, supported the president and repeated his statistics in their own statements to the press.

The Johnson administration welcomed the celebrities who joined the

*which was stated earlier

gun control debate and guided their efforts. The actor Hugh O'Brien instigated perhaps the most aggressive and clever publicity campaign for LBJ's
legislation. O'Brien called the White House on June 10, 1968, to present his
idea. He told the administration that masculine actors whom the public
identified as justice-wielding gun brandishers or outdoorsy hunters would
forcefully dramatize the issue. O'Brien had played the part of Wyatt Earp,
and he and Jack Valenti found four more "cowboys" to join in the campaign—Gregory Peck, Jimmy Stewart, Kirk Douglas, and Charlton Heston. Larry Levinson, special assistant to the president, prepared a "very
tough statement" and "'slipped'" it to Hugh O'Brien through Jack Valenti,
the president's Hollywood connection.[30]

O'Brien's group issued the Johnson administration's statement in a
variety of public forums, all the while emphasizing their commitment to
the rights of the lawful gun owner. They delivered the same speech to both
the Associated Press and United Press International in Los Angeles; attended a Hollywood luncheon, thrown "at the President's suggestion,"
where they repeated their appeal; and even appeared on *The Joey Bishop
Show*, a late-night television talk show, to bring attention to the legislation.
In their statement, the so-called cowboys argued that restricting the sale of
weapons would result in less crime and murder without limiting the rights
of the law-abiding gun owner. They charged that American gun laws were so
lax "that anyone can buy a weapon . . . the mentally ill, the criminal, the boy
too young to bear the responsibility of owning a deadly weapon." The actors told Americans that sixty-five hundred murders were committed each
year and stressed the dangers of long guns as well as pistols. They reassured their audience that LBJ's bill was not designed "to deprive the sports-
man of his hunting gun, the marksman of his target rifle, nor would it deny
to any responsible citizen his constitutional right to own a firearm." They
characterized the provisions of the bill as "three sensible and realistic rules"
banning mail-order traffic in rifles, prohibiting the sale of rifles to minors,
and allowing sales to consumers only in their state of residence. The group
concluded dramatically: "In the name of humanity . . . in the name of conscience . . . for the common safety of us all . . . for the future of America, we
must act . . . it is up to you . . . you alone and the time is now!"[31]

When Heston joined Hugh O'Brien's "cowboy committee," he did so with a hint of reservation. In fact, he later claimed that Peck was such an imposing figure that he simply followed his lead. Indeed, Heston sounded less than enthusiastic in his journal when he wrote: "Before taking off [from a National Endowment for the Arts meeting] I spent some time this morning on this committee I somehow got involved in, supporting the administration's position on gun control legislation." This tepid attitude likely stemmed from exhaustion over a crowded schedule rather than from a fundamental disagreement with the details of the bill, which he characterized in his journal as a "good one." The bill did call for restricting rifle sales, but it did not demand the licensing or registration of firearms, something anathema to Heston even then. At the time, Heston deemed Johnson's proposals a reasonable compromise and, because of his experience as a hunter, believed that he was one of the best-qualified celebrity spokespersons for this specific issue. "You've got to have the moderate opinions heard on this," he wrote. "Somehow, on any public issue, you hear only the wild-eye screamers on both ends of the spectrum." He decided, somewhat condescendingly: "I'd rather stand up and be counted on it than have some of my colleagues display their emotions on the subject."[32]

At this point, the cowboy committee could not convince Congress to pass LBJ's proposals. In fact, the cowboys received very little press because, on the day of their press conference, Congress had already sent the bill to LBJ. The gun control portion had been struck from the legislation. Even so, the president signed the Omnibus Crime Control and Safe Streets Act of 1968 having obtained no substantial control over the sale of long guns. Johnson decided "that this measure contains more good than bad and that I should sign it into law."[33] Meanwhile, he planned on presenting even stricter gun control legislation to Congress.

Heston did not, however, lend his support to Johnson's subsequent gun control efforts. Immediately after LBJ signed the Safe Streets Act, he asked Congress to "go further to give Americans . . . elementary protection" with a bill devoted solely to gun control. This time, the president had a new set of demands, including the strict control of the interstate and mail-order sale of guns, the registration of all guns, and the licensing of all those who owned or used guns.[34] A number of actors and other prominent

American figures formed the Emergency Committee for Gun Control to support the president. The committee, chaired by the celebrated astronaut Colonel John H. Glenn Jr., instigated a national write-in campaign targeting Congress. A number of actors and entertainers, including Lauren Bacall, Warren Beatty, Sammy Davis Jr., Janet Leigh, and Cary Grant, joined the committee, but Heston did not. He was not even swayed by the fact that fellow cowboys Peck and Douglas did. Obviously, he was willing to withhold his support for a president with whom he normally agreed.

In fact, Heston's position on gun control in 1968 largely matched that of the NRA. "What I regard as a moderate position on gun control does not include either registering or confiscating all the firearms in private hands," he wrote in his journal. Heston resisted these provisions because he had hunted and used guns since childhood and, "in my view, the Constitution establishes certain rights in this arena not granted to citizens of other countries." The NRA also opposed the licensing and registration of guns and lobbied against that portion of LBJ's bill. The final Gun Control Act that the president signed into law on October 22, 1968, actually matched Heston's original position with the cowboy committee, and the NRA believed it a reasonable compromise as well. The most comprehensive gun bill passed in the United States to that date, the law prohibited the sale of all guns by mail, established an age requirement for gun purchases, and established controls over gun imports. The registration portion of the bill did not pass, a weakening of which "cowboy Heston" could approve.[35] However, Heston and the NRA would both eventually conclude that their support of the measures included in the 1968 bill was a mistake.

Even in its weakened version, Johnson's crime and gun control legislation represented an important victory for the Democrats, but the triumph did nothing to repair the rifts that had opened up within the party. These divisions revolved around two types of competing political styles that emerged among the Democrats—orthodox liberalism and "believer" politics. Both John F. Kennedy and Lyndon Johnson were orthodox liberals and sought to maintain the New Deal coalition built by President Franklin D. Roosevelt. Kennedy and Johnson both relied on compromise, coalition building, and bargaining in order to make progress, settling for the most they could get through these means. Before his assassination, Robert Kennedy had begun to distance himself from orthodox liberalism, moving toward a more ideological brand of politics. This new ideological approach, which came to be known as the New Politics, stressed the immorality of compromise. Furthermore, New Politics leftists were ideologically committed to the notions that American society was sick and the American people selfish. They strove to build a new political force representative of the young, disadvantaged, oppressed, and well educated.[36]

The New Politics agenda was energized by antiwar protest, and the leftists hoped that their ideology could become an enduring vision. However, the sentiments embodied in their agenda did not correspond to those of most Americans, including Heston. In 1968, for example, 67 percent of Americans favored the continued bombing of Vietnam even though they wanted the war to end. Furthermore, standard liberal issues languished at the bottom of the list of "problems most worrying the American electorate." The public's top five concerns included ending the Vietnam War, preventing crime and juvenile delinquency, maintaining a strong military, curtailing urban rioting, and preventing World War III. The issues of least concern included such liberal causes as improving education, reducing poverty, alleviating racial problems, and providing medical care for low-income families.[37] Even so, New Politics liberalism would replace Great Society liberalism as the party's focus but, as would be shown in future national elections, would receive less mainstream support and pave the way for a neoconservative defection.

THE FIRST STEP TO BECOMING A neoconservative was questioning one's loyalty to the Democratic Party. As New Politics liberals gained influence over the party platform, the New Deal coalition finally succumbed to years of battering. White, Southern Democrats had abandoned the party during the 1966 midterm elections because of racial and states' rights issues. After the 1968 presidential election, culturally conservative Democrats left the party as well, believing that it had reversed course and was acting in opposition to such party heroes as Franklin D. Roosevelt, Harry S. Truman, and John F. Kennedy.

The 1968 Democratic national convention in Chicago highlighted the split within the party over Vietnam and the public disapproval of the burgeoning New Politics and, furthermore, gave little hope that the party's problems could be solved easily and in a timely manner. The death of Robert Kennedy established Vice President Hubert Humphrey as the frontrunner for the nomination. Humphrey faced serious opposition, however, from leftist radicals, who threatened to picket the convention because of the candidate's ties to White House war policies. Chicago Mayor Richard J. Daley attempted to discourage the leftists' plans by beefing up the city's convention security plans. Undaunted, leading radicals mobilized at least five thousand protesters, some committed to nonviolence, and others envisioning more apocalyptic scenarios. The struggle between the authorities and the protesters finally erupted outside the Hilton Hotel on the third night of the convention. The national networks aired the melee. The Democrats did not appear capable of agreeing on a Vietnam policy or anything else for that matter. The convention's aftermath illustrated the public disapproval of the leftists. A national poll conducted immediately after the convention disclosed that 71 percent of Americans considered Daley's security measures justified and 57 percent maintained that the police had not used excessive force.[38] Mainstream Americans also expressed vehement disapproval of the militant and confrontational antiwar movement in general. For example, in one 1968 poll, 83 percent of Americans believed that "radicals who create violence in the streets" contributed most appreciably to the violence that seemed to beset the country. Perhaps the leaders of the Democratic Party, concerned about relating to mainstream voters, were correct in their desire to mute antiwar protest.[39] But the party was at a crossroads, and forging a compromise acceptable to all Democrats was a tricky business indeed.

The neoconservatives lent their support to Hubert Humphrey in the vice president's campaign against the Republican candidate, Richard Nixon. Heston had long admired Humphrey for the Democrat's passionate defense of civil rights. Furthermore, Humphrey called for a halt to the bombing in Vietnam, but he did not advocate the unilateral withdrawal that the leftists demanded. Humphrey's position was, to Heston's mind, a

reasonable compromise. Likewise, Kristol, Podhoretz, and other intellectual neocons voted for Humphrey, as the candidate represented the orthodox liberalism and the moderate welfare state that they supported.

Meanwhile, Nixon was able to exploit the damage that the leftists had
caused at Chicago. The Republican pointedly campaigned to mainstream
Americans, framing the issues to appeal to a middle class that daily grew
more conservative and alienated. However, he repudiated liberalism without appearing reactionary. Nixon skillfully reassured Americans that he
had a "secret plan" to end the war in Vietnam and avoided the incendiary
statements that Wallace was prone to make. Regarding race, Nixon expressed compassion for oppressed minorities but encouraged the private
sector and black enterprise to lead the way in rebuilding the inner cities.[40]
Overcoming the public relations catastrophe at Chicago, Humphrey ran a
surprisingly strong campaign and barely lost to Nixon in the November
general election. It was the first time in twelve years that Heston voted for
the losing candidate. Nixon's moderate approach, however, indicated that
Heston would find him an acceptable leader.

In the meantime, Heston flirted with the idea of running for political
office himself. After the political success of the actors George Murphy and
Ronald Reagan, the notion of an entertainer becoming a politician was not
just possible but encouraged, especially as the stature of actors had risen
while the reputations of politicians had declined. Actors enjoyed name
recognition and seemed to have the ability to manipulate the media, both
crucial aspects of modern politics. An actor such as Heston, with a strong,
moral screen presence and a history of political activism, stood a good
chance of winning an election. Accordingly, both national parties courted
Heston to run for a seat in the U.S. Senate. Surprised by such a proposal
but instinctively opposed to it, the actor mulled the possibility of such a
move over anyway, feeling: "It's the kind of thing you can't just brush off."
A number of friends, including his fellow civil rights activist Jolly West,
encouraged Heston to pursue a candidacy, but his wife, Lydia, opposed the
idea. The fact that winning an office could effectively end his acting career
especially discouraged Heston. It made more sense for him to satisfy his
taste for politics on his own time and under his own terms so that he would

not have to choose one vocation over the other. He considered the idea for several weeks, likening it to "a boy masturbating . . . you know it's pointless, but it *feels* so good." Ultimately, however, he "had to dispose of my non-blooming political career." To Lydia's relief and the disappointment of both parties, he decided: "I want to act. I know it's trivial but there it is."[41]

The Democrats also underwent political introspection. The radical protesters outside the 1968 Democratic national convention had garnered the most publicity, but disruptions on the convention floor actually had the most impact on the Democratic agenda. A significant number of young antiwar delegates had traveled to Chicago in the hopes of nominating McCarthy, and they bucked at the tight yoke imposed by the party regulars at the convention itself. Johnson insisted on the strict management of the convention, for he was not willing to allow his own party to denounce his policies before he finished serving his term. Democratic regulars, too, had resisted a McCarthy nomination, partly because they feared for their own positions at the local level. The regulars had worked, instead, to insert a peace plank that would energize the Humphrey candidacy but still respect the Johnson presidency, hoping that this strategy would bridge the major divisions within the convention. However, the young antiwar delegates tended to adhere to the New Politics agenda and mistrusted the efforts of the party regulars to compromise. Several fistfights had actually broken out between the regulars and the antiwar delegates on the convention floor. New Politics liberals left Chicago feeling marginalized and were convinced that the Democratic Party's system of governance needed to be reformed. They began to focus on what Podhoretz considered a "revolutionary" concept, the "equality of results."[42]

The new chair of the Democratic National Committee, Senator Fred Harris of Oklahoma, appointed Senator George McGovern as chair of the Commission on Party Structure and Delegate Selection in February 1969 to investigate the complaints of the antiwar delegates. McGovern's commission examined the party's state laws and regulations and held hearings in seventeen cities, where they interviewed over five hundred Democrats. These hearings led McGovern to believe that the nominating process had been so "perverted" as to render the full participation of all Democrats impossible. He further believed that the Chicago convention would not have been such a debacle had the party responded to the groundswell of support for McCarthy and other antiwar candidates. Therefore, the commission restructured the nominating process with the hopes of achieving full participation of the Democratic rank and file in the next presidential election. Most significantly, these reforms set quotas for minorities, young people, and women on behalf of each state for the next national convention, assuming that age, sex, and race translated into unique political perspectives—in effect instituting the affirmative action for which the New Democrats had been calling. Moreover, the commission implicitly believed that the party no longer needed labor unions, a group once considered an integral part of the New Deal coalition. In the minds of New Politics liberals, labor was no longer a leftist group because it had achieved its goals and become a conservative entity of proprietary privilege. Labor certainly did not pass the New Politics test of ideological purity. Therefore, the new affirmative action policies complicated the goal of achieving the full participation of all Democrats.[43]

The McGovern commission so dramatically influenced the proceedings of the 1972 Democratic national convention as to make the party uncongenial to those with neoconservative inclinations. The reforms made delegate selection more systematic, but the new rules did not make the convention more widely representative of the American population. Instead, the reforms overwhelmingly favored New Politics activists, causing further disagreements between the reformers and the regulars. Problems abounded. First, 80 percent of the delegates attending the convention were there for the first time. Second, many delegates failed to represent accurately their home states. For example, the Iowa delegation did not include farmers or any representatives over the age of sixty-five. Third, Democratic regulars were pushed out. The most extreme example was that of the prominent statesman Averell Harriman. A respected official in several Democratic administrations and a former governor, Harriman was beaten out for a seat on the New York delegation by a nineteen-year-old novice. Furthermore, McGovern forces unseated fifty-nine Chicago delegates, including Mayor Daley, claiming that they had been "improperly slated." Finally, the new delegates tended to be affluent liberals who appointed themselves to represent a particular constituency—blacks, young people, women, and other minorities—or who otherwise adhered to the New Politics ideology. Culturally conservative white males, such as Heston, became objects of disdain. This shifting and categorizing actually made the national convention less representative and more fractionalized than it had ever been.[44]

Celebrities enjoyed a new political prominence after the reforms of the McGovern commission. Since private caucuses held by party leaders had been outlawed, all Democratic voters, including celebrities, had a say in who would be the nominee. After McGovern won the Democratic nomination for president in 1972, celebrities thrust themselves into the publicity-driven political fray. For example, Shirley MacLaine doggedly campaigned for McGovern for seven weeks, earning the cover of *Newsweek* for her efforts. Likewise, Warren Beatty organized five concerts to raise funds for the candidate with such high-profile entertainers as Barbara Streisand, James Taylor, Carole King, Simon and Garfunkel, and Peter, Paul, and Mary. These crooners in support of McGovern contrasted markedly with those of the old Hollywood, including Frank Sinatra and Bing Crosby, who were singing for Nixon.[45]

The support of celebrity activists did little to help McGovern during his disastrous and self-defeating campaign. He promised to end the Vietnam War, reform welfare, and create more job opportunities, but he offered an unpopular program to achieve these goals. McGovern presented American extrication from Vietnam as a deserved defeat and praised draft evaders who had fled the United States. His welfare reform involved a $6,500 *demogrant*, or guaranteed basic income, thus promoting an even more extravagant notion of entitlement and, in turn, abandoning the focus on individualism and the work ethic that voters preferred. McGovern also championed affirmative action policies in employment. Furthermore, the Democrat became saddled with the catchphrase "amnesty, abortion, and pot," even though he had gone on the record against all three. Voters shared McGovern's concerns about the issues. In achieving these aims, however, Americans preferred the stability offered by Nixon to the ideological crusade promised by McGovern.[46]

Nixon is best known for his foreign policy endeavors as president, but, during his first term, he actually launched a number of positive programs that especially resonated with Heston. Nixon supported the tax credit for which Heston, on behalf of the Screen Actors Guild, had lobbied. He also authorized dramatic budget increases for the National Endowment for the Arts. In civil rights, Nixon boosted minority enterprise and accomplished what LBJ had not, the desegregation of schools in the South. Nixon also sought to streamline the federal government and curtail the ever-growing bureaucracy through welfare reform (a job he assigned to the neoconservative Daniel Patrick Moynihan) and revenue sharing between the federal government and the states. In foreign policy, Nixon extended this reform-minded approach by opening up communication with the Chinese and the Soviets. Although the Vietnam War had not been resolved by the 1972 election, Nixon had muffled the antiwar movement by phasing out deferments, terminating Vietnam duty for new draftees, and ending conscription in 1972.[47] Nixon introduced these measures with the intention of invigorating society by means of moderate reform, and, in so doing, he easily countered McGovern's campaign.

The neoconservatives believed that McGovern's influence on the Democratic Party was a direct threat to many of the values that had brought them into the Democratic fold in the first place. Since at least 1965, Irving Kristol had been feeling that the Democrats were "taking" his "bourgeois values for granted." But it was not until McGovern's nomination that he left the party for good, concluding finally that it was "not hospitable to any degree of conservatism." Heston experienced a similar revelation over Memorial Day weekend in 1972. "I saw the JFK documentary I narrated for him a year ago," he wrote in his journal. "How unacceptable his voice and his views would be to the party that has defied him." Likewise, Norman Podhoretz was appalled at the New Democrats' claims that orthodox liberalism had failed and achieved no fundamental change in society since the end of the New Deal. Furthermore, he noted, the radicals attacked the notion of economic growth as the downfall of the world. "Armed with such ideas," Podhoretz observed, "the New Politics movement took a position that amounted to so complete a reversal of the theme of John F. Kennedy's New Frontier that it might have campaigned under the slogan, 'Let's Stop the Country from Moving Again.'"[48]

The year 1972 marked a turning point for the neoconservatives. Irving Kristol, Gertrude Himmelfarb, and Heston all voted Republican. When Heston announced his support for Nixon, he echoed the intellectual neocons in his critique of the New Politics agenda. Facing reporters on his ridge in Beverly Hills, Heston made the personal significance of his choice quite clear. "As an individual voter I have all my voting life cast my ballot for the Democratic candidates for the presidency of the United States," he announced. "I didn't vote for President Nixon in 1960 or in '68, but I'm going to vote for him this fall." Heston then outlined the reasons for his choice. First, the actor felt that Nixon had done a good job during his first term, especially in light of "the enormous problems this country faces" at home and abroad. Second, Heston thoroughly disapproved of the McGovern coalition, believing it to be overly critical of American society and policy. He explained: "I am sick to death of the doom-watchers and the naysayers. I think this is a good country." With this pronouncement, Heston summed up the neoconservative critique in a message suitable for the camera. He resembled Kristol and Podhoretz in condemning the nihilistic and adversarial postures that the new class had taken. Just as Podhoretz had called out political radicals for spelling America *Amerika* to suggest an association with Nazi Germany, so too did Heston. He concluded his press conference with characteristic drama. "I know you don't spell America with a *K*," he said with a flourish.[49]

By beseeching Heston to hold a news conference announcing his preference for Nixon, the Republicans upstaged the Democrats in terms of celebrity activism by stealing one of their own. Heston noticed that other Democratic regulars "seemed busy dissociating themselves from McGovern" as well. Heston attended fund-raisers for both parties, including a celebrity-studded gathering at Nixon's home in San Clemente, but his attention was obviously turned toward the GOP. After endorsing Nixon, Heston read a prayer for prisoners of war at the Republican national convention and attended Nixon's inauguration. By this point, Heston had grown accustomed to the national political scene, but he certainly did not take it for granted. At the GOP convention, he was impressed by the "spectacular water transfer" he made "with Lydia to a yacht full of governors on parade," an event he considered "superior to the kind I've done so often in the back of convertibles." Furthermore, Heston seemed to have little intimation of what was in store for him in terms of future political activism. On inauguration day, he commented: "It's the kind of thing you only do once, I guess, but it's worth the fuss and discomfort." Little did Heston know that he would be attending more inaugural balls and becoming even more engaged in political affairs in the coming decades.[50]

The rest of the intellectual neocons did not start voting Republican just yet, but they did try new means of political activism starting in 1972. To be sure, they held a low opinion of McGovern and were unhappy with the Democrats, but many of them were not mentally prepared to vote for the GOP. The Republican Party still had no evident vision, no overarching blueprint. The Republicans, like the Democrats, were in transition, their future agenda muddled. Furthermore, Nixon, known for his red-baiting tactics in the 1950s and nicknamed "Tricky Dick" by critics, was not exactly a likable figure. Even Heston, despite his endorsement, "voted, with some misgivings but a wholer heart than I'd thought I'd have, for RMN."[51] Therefore, it would be several more years before the rest of the intellectual neocons would follow Kristol's and Himmelfarb's leads. Until then, they sought to combat the New Democrat radicals through other political channels. For example, Podhoretz hoped to keep anticommunism in the Democratic Party's vernacular by "joining a number of unrepentant hawks in founding the Coalition for a Democratic Majority [CDM]." The CDM drew from FDR, Truman, JFK, and LBJ in setting its agenda, calling for internationalism, equality of opportunity, government action to end discrimination, and further economic growth. It supported Daniel Patrick Moynihan in his New York senatorial bid in 1976. After Moynihan won on a platform stressing family, individual initiative, hard work, and a strong military, Podhoretz hoped that the rest of the Democrats would follow suit. He soon realized, however, that, while some individual Democrats did maintain their commitment to the values of the New Deal coalition, the party as a whole would not.

Heston, not Podhoretz, reflected the beliefs of most voters. While Podhoretz was still willing to fight for the Democrats, most Americans were not so game. An exasperated populace did not consider McGovern's

Heston and Judith Evelyn in a performance of *Macbeth*, December 22, 1951. It was during an earlier production of *Macbeth* that the producer Hal Wallis first discovered the actor. (Screen Actors Guild Archives.)

Heston as Moses in *The Ten Commandments* (1956), the Cecil B. DeMille production that made the actor an international superstar and led the public to identify Heston as a moral, authoritative figure. (Motion Picture and Television Archive.)

Heston in the most celebrated stunt sequence in film history, the chariot race in *Ben-Hur* (1959). (Motion Picture and Television Archive.)

Heston kissing his wife, Lydia, while imprinting his hands in the wet cement at Grauman's Chinese Theater in 1961. This ritual memorialized Heston's status as a Hollywood heavyweight. (Motion Picture and Television Archive.)

Heston holding his son, Fraser, at the Lincoln Memorial in Washington, DC, in 1960. (Photograph by Lydia Heston; courtesy Charlton Heston.)

Heston, Dr. Chester M. Pierce, and Dr. Jolly West demonstrating against segregation in Oklahoma City in 1961. This protest was Heston's first civil rights march and what inspired him to "ride the tiger" and get more involved in political affairs. (Photograph courtesy Charlton Heston.)

Sidney Poitier, Harry Belafonte, and Heston at the March on Washington, August 28, 1963. Heston helped organize the Arts Group, a cadre of Hollywood personalities who brought added publicity to the event. (National Archives.)

(Left) Heston, James Baldwin, and Marlon Brando at the March on Washington, August 28, 1963. Heston read a piece penned by Baldwin at the event. (National Archives.)

(Below) Heston proudly holds a cowboy award he received when campaigning with Lady Bird Johnson at the Nebraskaland Parade in Lincoln, Nebraska, June 15, 1966. Heston portrayed several cowboys throughout his film career, including the lawman Wyatt Earp. (Photograph by Robert Knudsen, Lyndon Baines Johnson Presidential Library.)

Heston and President Lyndon Baines Johnson at the unveiling of the Franklin D. Roosevelt Portrait at the White House on January 31, 1967. At the unveiling, Heston presented the painting, a perk of becoming a White House insider during the Kennedy and Johnson administrations. (Photograph by Robert Knudsen, Lyndon Baines Johnson Presidential Library.)

Ricardo Montalban, Sally Blane, Ann Doran, Ronald Reagan, MacDonald Carey, and Heston at the "End Strike Meeting" at the Hollywood Palladium during a Screen Actors Guild strike against producers for residuals on old movies rerun on television, April 18, 1960. Impressed with Reagan's negotiating style, Heston would seek to emulate it during his own years of service as president of the Screen Actors Guild. (Photograph by Gene Lester, Gene Lester Collection, Screen Actors Guild Archives.)

(Above) Heston at a special Screen Actors Guild meeting at the Hollywood Palladium in 1963, when he was Guild second vice president, with Guild Executive Secretary Jack Dales, William Walker, and Ann Doran. (Below) Heston and Ronald Reagan at the 1966 annual meeting of the Screen Actors Guild, during Heston's first term as Guild president. Heston and Reagan shared an easy relationship and a similar optimistic approach to political affairs, even though at that point they were affiliated with different parties. (Photographs by Gene Lester, Gene Lester Collection, Screen Actors Guild Archives.)

(Above) Karl Malden, Edward G. Robinson, and Heston at the 1969 annual meeting of the Screen Actors Guild. Edward G. Robinson received the Guild's Annual Award that year. He and Heston costarred in *The Ten Commandments* and would go on to work together in *Soylent Green,* Robinson's last film, in 1973. (Below) Heston and Gregory Peck at the 1970 annual meeting of the Screen Actors Guild. Heston presented Peck with the Guild's Annual Award that evening. The two starred in *The Big Country* together in 1958 and remained friends and fellow public servants throughout their careers. (Photographs by Gene Lester, Gene Lester Collection, Screen Actors Guild Archives.)

(Above) Heston delivering a speech about "runaway production" at the 1970 annual meeting of the Screen Actors Guild. Runaway production was a vexing issue on which Heston focused much attention during his Guild presidency. (Photograph by Gene Lester, Gene Lester Collection, Screen Actors Guild Archives.)

(Right) Heston narrating a film montage at the White House Festival of the Arts in 1965. The festival was a precursor to the establishment of the National Endowment of the Arts. Heston would serve on the National Council of the Arts from 1967 until 1971 and continue a long-standing affiliation with the agency. (Lyndon Baines Johnson Presidential Library.)

(Above) Heston chats with Lady Bird Johnson at the White House Festival of the Arts in 1965. (Lyndon Baines Johnson Presidential Library.)

(Right) Heston and President Richard Nixon honoring the director John Ford at the American Film Institute Life Achievement Award ceremony in 1973, at which Ford also received the Presidential Medal of Freedom. Heston served as chairman of the board and then president of the institute from 1971 until 2002. (National Archives.)

(Above) Heston visiting U.S. troops in South Vietnam. Heston traveled to Southeast Asia twice during the war. (Photograph courtesy Charlton Heston.) (Below) Heston and President Nixon at a fund-raiser in San Clemente, California, in 1972. Heston had publicly endorsed Nixon a few months earlier, the first time the actor had endorsed a Republican presidential candidate. (National Archives.)

(Above) Margaret Thatcher, President Reagan, and Heston at a state dinner for the British prime minister at the White House in February 1981, soon after Reagan's inauguration. Heston went on to become increasingly involved with the Reagan administration. (Ronald Reagan Presidential Library.)

(Below) Barbara Bush and Lydia and Charlton Heston at the Vice Presidential Residence, Naval Observatory, Annapolis, Maryland, March 9, 1981. Heston was a frequent guest of Vice President Bush, and the two often played tennis. (George H. W. Bush Presidential Library.)

Heston and President Reagan at a meeting of the Presidential Task Force on the Arts and Humanities in the Cabinet Room at the White House, June 15, 1981. Heston cochaired the task force and recommended continued federal support of the National Endowments for the Arts and the Humanities. (Ronald Reagan Presidential Library.)

Heston at a protest in 1988 for Actors Working for an Actors Guild, a caucus group within the Screen Actors Guild that worked to redirect the Guild's agenda away from liberal political causes to its traditional focus on wages, hours, and working conditions. (Motion Picture and Television Archive.)

Phil Gramm, Heston, and President Bush at a fund-raising dinner for Gramm in Houston, Texas, December 7, 1989. Heston became increasingly involved in fund-raising events for the GOP throughout the 1980s and 1990s. (George H. W. Bush Presidential Library.)

(Above) Heston interviewing President Bush for a documentary about Air Force One at the Old Executive Office Building in Washington, DC, September 28, 1990. (George H. W. Bush Presidential Library.)

(Left) Heston and President Bush joking after the interview for the documentary about Air Force One. Heston and Bush shared a similar sense of humor and a close relationship. (George H. W. Bush Presidential Library.)

President Bush and Heston in the Oval Office before the signing ceremony for the *Beck* Executive Order, which required federal contractors to inform union employees of their financial core rights, in 1992. During the Rose Garden ceremony, Bush singled out Heston for his heavy lobbying in support of the order. (George H. W. Bush Presidential Library.)

Heston delivering a speech about the Second Amendment to the National Press Club in Washington, DC, in 1998. Heston impressed National Rifle Association members with his forceful defense of gun rights. (Photograph courtesy Charlton Heston.)

(Above and below) Heston and National Rifle Association members at the organization's Oklahoma City campaign rally, 2002. Heston was beloved as the organization's president and served a record five consecutive terms. (Photographs courtesy Charlton Heston.)

Heston shaking hands with National Rifle Association members at the organiza-tion's annual meeting in Reno, Nevada, April 26, 2002. (Photograph by Emilie Raymond.)

proposals, such as unilateral withdrawal from Vietnam and redistributive taxation, acceptable remedies to America's problems. Nixon's pragmatic traditionalism overwhelmingly prevailed over McGovern's New Politics. The historian Godfrey Hodgson sums up the Republican victory: "It wasn't that the majority liked Nixon; its members just didn't feel that things were bad enough that you had to put up with McGovern."[52]

The Democrats' ability to elicit confidence at the presidential level was effectively ruined, and it would be difficult for the party to regain the public's trust since the new liberals consistently rejected coalition building. The Democrats had already lost the South, and, after the 1972 election, the party could no longer count on the support of labor or the middle class for its presidential nominees. The Democrats identified with ideas that did not have public approval, and, therefore, the party appeared beholden to extremist interest groups. The more the Democrats were identified with the radicals, the less the party's chance in the next presidential election. Despite this readily apparent problem, the liberal elite continued to identify with the radical minority, and, throughout the 1970s, they attacked mainstream American society together. Moreover, because of the radical liberals' association with drugs, free love, and confrontational politics, Democrats were vulnerable to Republican accusations that the party was responsible for the "domestic corruption" of American culture.[53] New Politics liberals gained more influence over the Democratic agenda as the moderates fumbled for composure and the rest of America continued its exodus from the party.

McGovern's attempt to integrate previously marginalized groups into the party's leadership was certainly pragmatic and admirable, but he did so at the expense of white, male traditionalists, such as Heston. The affirmative action policies were implemented at the expense of other constituents who provided the necessary numbers and moral credibility to win elections. The new liberals formulated categories of people whom they deemed to be oppressed, but the radicals failed to recognize that other groups, such as working-class males, dealt with their own oppressive forces. Arguing that, because she was female, a rich woman was more oppressed than a working-class man struggling to feed his family was unconvincing. More important, the categories designated for affirmative action quotas required delegates to identify themselves solely in those terms. The party assumed that only individuals who were themselves of a particular minority could represent the interests of that group.[54] Heston certainly did not fit within these bounds.

The Democrats also lost constituents as the party's moral credibility in domestic and international matters plummeted. New liberals presented themselves as morally superior because of their sympathies toward minorities and their hostilities toward American power. Many mainstream voters, however, considered the new liberals depraved for defending draft dodgers, calling for the legalization of marijuana, and promoting abortion rights. The liberal Democrats slipped and lost touch with family and community concerns. Liberal attitudes toward welfare measures illustrated their repudiation of community obligations. By 1972, liberals demanded direct cash entitlements but considered it reprehensible for the government to demand any sort of reciprocity in terms of work or behavior. Furthermore, the Democrats moved to the left on foreign policy, seemingly unconcerned about the threat of communism.[55] Americans did not trust that the Democrats could handle the nation's problems, especially foreign threats. Clearly, the *neoconservative* label should not be limited to intellectuals but expanded to include the many middle- and working-class Americans who repudiated radicalism, abandoned the Democrats, and began voting Republican because of their bourgeois cultural sentiments and anti-Communist beliefs.

Just when Heston and other neoconservatives lent their support to Nixon, the right wing of the Republican Party was questioning the president's leadership. Nixon had successfully courted moderates and conservatives to win the nomination in 1968, but the Right only grudgingly accepted him as the Republican leader. By the time Heston came to support Nixon in 1972, the Right had rejected the president for his moderate welfare state, détente with China, fiscal "insanity," and wage and price controls. In fact, Young Americans for Freedom (YAF), an organization for students on the right, actually refused to back Nixon after he won the Republican nomination for a second term. Instead, it put its energy into a

Youth against McGovern campaign.[56] However, the very moderation that turned the Right against Nixon eased the path for disaffected Democrats, like Heston, to vote for him. The conservative position that the YAF advocated would not be found appealing by the majority of Republicans—indeed, the majority of Americans—until Ronald Reagan, with his sunny optimism, made it attractive. Therefore, Nixon became the optimal transitional figure to draw Heston—and his kind—to the party that he would soon call his home.

THE SECOND STEP IN BECOMING A neoconservative was to reject the counterculture. During the same period that the neocons battled political radicals, they also found themselves combating the hippie influence. Even though the New Left and the hippie counterculture had different origins, the neoconservatives recognized the New Left as a cultural movement masquerading as a political one.[57] The neocons considered both movements dangerous because of what they believed the groups had in common: an unwillingness to take political responsibility and a contemptuous view of American society and culture. Indeed, by the early 1970s, the two movements had intertwined. Not only had they succeeded in overhauling the Democratic Party, but their potential influence over mainstream American culture was seen as a threat by the neocons. The neocons condemned the hippie impulse and resisted it through a variety of means—the intellectual neocons through writings and think tanks; Heston through movies and political activism.

The neoconservatives themselves had criticized the rampant materialism and conformity of the affluent 1950s, but, when faced with the countercultural critique, they did not accept the hippie solution, as Timothy Leary put it, to "tune in, turn on, and drop out." Confronted with free-wheeling hippies who celebrated the expansion of the mind through LSD, sexual promiscuity, acid rock, and Zen, the neocons realized that, as Kristol put it, they "had been cultural conservatives all along." As Heston explained in an interview in 1977: "Although anyone could find valid examples of [countercultural criticisms], basically I oppose it myself." Kristol made a similar point: "Oh, yes one can cull 'insights,' as we say. . . . But the inmates of any asylum, given pen and paper, will also produce their share of such 'insights'—only it doesn't ordinarily occur to us that this is a good way of going about collecting our insights."[58] While neocons willingly conceded the pitfalls of the bourgeois lifestyle, they also considered the bourgeois ethic responsible for an increasingly prosperous, just, and advanced society. To ensure a safe and secure future, the bourgeois principles of family, work ethic, delayed gratification, and obligation to society needed to remain in place. Neocons looked to Christianity in particular to nurture those values.

Whereas the neocons believed that society had improved because of bourgeois principles, the cultural radicals saw any positive changes as having taken place *in spite of* the obstinacy of the middle class. The cultural radicals focused on the dangers of middle-class culture. The family could be dysfunctional, the work ethic unrewarding, delayed gratification repressive. The hippies believed in nurturing and maximizing the self to achieve human potential, as opposed to looking to the community. Indeed, cultural radicals found the suburban enclaves where they were raised and the corporate businesses in which their fathers worked to be devoid of individual creativity. The counterculture advocated throwing off restraint and questioning the very standards that the neocons considered vital to a healthy society.

The neocons deplored the spreading influence of the counterculture, believing that, if gone unchecked, it would poison American society and result in intellectual and moral anarchy. As Heston put it: "If there are no valid concepts—which is the ultimate view of the counterculture, that nothing is valid, that nothing is worth being—then what are you living for?" He went on to explain: "Of course a concept can be challenged; a commitment can be reexamined, but to say there are no qualities of human nature that are, per se, admirable, that there are no point of views [*sic*] or ethical concepts that are simply of themselves good as opposed to other point of views, is futile." Without a basic set of values from which everyone drew on, society could not function. Kristol noted that, as Americans increasingly rejected or ignored bourgeois values, toleration, pluralism, and relativism took their place—three trends he believed to be "a prescription for moral anarchy."[59]

Despite the warnings of the neoconservatives, the hippie ideal reverberated across the country. While only a tiny percentage of Americans actually lived in communes or tried psychedelic drugs, many shared the motivations and ideas that prompted those experiments. Mainstream society easily reconciled with the counterculture. The nation's young people adopted hippie fashions such as blue jeans, tie-dyed shirts, and love beads. Even their middle-class parents were more willing to experiment with sexuality and personal liberation. The historian Allen Matusow characterizes hippies as "only a spectacular exaggeration" of trends already evident in the larger society. The very qualities that drove modern consumer capitalism—materialism and self-indulgence—also undermined the values of hard work, delayed gratification, and submission to social discipline that made this type of economic system triumphant in the first place. After capitalism solved the problems of want, Americans reveled in its bounty and abandoned restraint.[60] Therefore, the American mainstream eagerly co-opted the counterculture. Middle-class society robbed the hippies of their radical edge by modifying their anticapitalist undertones and, in the meantime, absorbed their dress, language, music, self-indulgence, and antiauthoritarian impulses.

Because of the ready influence of the counterculture, what the neocons predicted as the two worst consequences of cultural radicalism soon became evident—moral relativism and an increasing lack of respect for institutions. According to the hippie mentality, people should be free to make their own morality, but the neocons believed that certain standards still had to be upheld. Irving Kristol compared the moral situation to a garden: "Different gardeners will have different ideas, of course, but there will be a limit to this variety. The idea of a garden does not, for example, include an expanse of weeds or of poison ivy. And no gardener would ever confuse a garden with a garbage dump."[61] By the mid-1970s, the "weeds" and the "poison ivy" were beginning to take their tolls on the United States. Drug use, STD and abortion rates, and out-of-wedlock births were all on the rise. But, without the moral language to condemn these trends, the prospect of arresting them seemed dim.

The neocons were also concerned about the increasing lack of respect for institutions and authority. The church, corporate business, the government, and the military were all being drained of their legitimacy. Whereas such institutions had once commanded respect and even reverence, these sentiments were no longer assured. Instead, these entities were increasingly seen as harmful to American society. For example, Vietnam veterans often found themselves facing a hostile antiwar movement. The assumption that the military was a twisted and dangerous institution, full of psychopathic warmongers, became commonplace. In fact, the whole idea of insanity had been turned on its head. Cultural radicals accused standard American institutions of being so heavy-handed that they were actually driving people crazy. As the Beat writer Allen Ginsberg put it, the "best minds" of his generation had gone mad, victims of oppressive institutions.

The neocons considered the entertainment industry particularly culpable for spreading countercultural notions and ideas. Books, television shows, movies, and other forms of entertainment all have the potential to significantly influence the way people view themselves and their place in the world. While some chastised the neocons for taking amusement too seriously, Kristol countered: "If you believe that no one was ever corrupted by a book, you also have to believe that no one was ever improved by a book . . . that all education is morally irrelevant. No one, not even a university professor, really believes that." Movies, with glamorous stars and mass audiences, could be especially influential. Concerned about the new views of insanity, Podhoretz called out Ken Kesey and Norman Mailer for celebrating the psychopath. In such works as Kesey's *One Flew over the Cuckoo's Nest* (1962) and Mailer's *The Armies of the Night* (1968), the idea of "insanity as redemption" was popularized. In both books, it is the authorities—either the nurses and doctors or the cops and marshals—who seem truly insane with their masochistic and authoritarian behavior. Podhoretz found these ideas "repugnant" and, with *Commentary* magazine, engaged in a three-year "no-holds-barred" campaign against radical political and cultural ideas and the literary and intellectual figures who celebrated them.[62]

What the intellectual neocons did not, perhaps, realize was that they had a friend in the entertainment business. That like-minded individual was, of course, Charlton Heston. Heston was also concerned about Hollywood trends. The movie roles that he accepted and rejected during the 1960s and 1970s reflected his dissatisfaction with the political and cultural radicalism that seemed to be gaining infinite momentum. By retaining the trademark characteristics of masculinity, individuality, and responsibility that he had first presented to the public in the 1950s, Heston demonstrated that he still preferred these traditional values. Even in the futuristic *Planet of the Apes* (1968), in which he launched himself as a modern-day action hero, he displayed this conventionalism.[63]

In *Planet of the Apes,* Heston's character, George Taylor, is deeply critical of American society, yet he defends humanity when it is in danger, thus reaffirming the actor's traditional public persona. From the opening scene, Taylor's caustic demeanor is inescapable. One of four astronauts on a space-exploration mission gone awry, Taylor wastes little time disparaging the planet from which they traveled. He sarcastically quips about the mixed-up values that he knew on earth and laughs wretchedly when a fellow astronaut plants an American flag in the soil where their shuttle crashed. When attacked by the apes ruling the planet on which they have landed, however, Taylor boldly and decisively rises to defend mankind in a dramatic chase sequence, during which he utters lines that are among Heston's most famous: "Get your paws off me, you damn, dirty ape." Even though Taylor is finally captured, Heston's masculinity is implicit since the loincloth that he is forced to wear exposes his muscular stature. Indeed, his virile body is far more impressive than what the apes have to offer. He wins the companionship of another imprisoned human, the silent but beautiful Nova (Linda Harrison), and even one of the apes has a crush on him. Taylor reasserts man's superiority over the apes, successfully proving that humans had existed on their planet for millions of years and were not primitive animals. When Taylor discovers the Statue of Liberty washed ashore, he realizes that he is actually on his own earth, years into the future. He cries, "You did it! You really did it! God damn you to hell," condemning humans for destroying themselves. However, Taylor does not rejoin the apes but rides into the sunset with Nova, presumably to start humanity all over again. Heston represented renewal, masculinity, and responsibility in this box office smash.[64]

Heston also made his preference for traditional standards and moral heroes quite evident when he starred in Boris Sagal's 1971 film *The Omega Man,* a hit that, like the *Apes* films, went on to become a cult favorite. Heston played Captain Robert Neville, a full-blown traditionalist by the terms of the 1960s. Neville is a scientist in the military, and his hobbies include playing chess and collecting expensive art. His favorite piece is a bust of Julius Caesar. However, scientific achievement also led to the horrific environment in which Neville lives. In a deserted New York City, Neville appears to be the only human being left alive after terrorists waged germ warfare on the United States, destroying the population of the earth in the process. The only other living creatures are nocturnal ghouls who prey on the city and, paralleling the counterculture, seek to destroy all things modern. They hold feverish book burnings and relentlessly pursue Neville in an effort to kill him. Neville eludes the ghouls and vows to survive. Eventually, he discovers that a few other humans remain alive as well.

In this contest between traditional values and the counterculture, Neville continues to adhere to his scientific principles, administering to the sick survivors a serum that he has invented. When one of his patients expresses sympathy for the ghouls, Neville sermonizes about the primitive behavior and inherent corruption of their inferior way of life. As the critic John Bell noted: "This underscores the . . . elitism of the Doctor. Only those things that are best are worthy to survive. There is no leveling here, there is no quailing in the vision of what the nature of evil is."[65] Indeed, the ghouls kill the young sympathizer. Neville dies heroically at film's end, but he has treated enough patients for his values to persevere. He sets the standard, and the survivors pledge to start humanity over again, patterning their new society after Neville's principles. Neville's values, at least for the time being, endure.

Heston also resisted political and cultural radicalism by rejecting certain roles. In 1975, MGM sent Heston a script that he described as a scenario "in which a homicidal maniac is the hero [and] the U.S. government is the heavy." Not accepting the role, he commented, "gave me a high moral feeling of achievement." Likewise, Heston dismissed another "fashionable kind of countercultural piece" in 1976 when he turned down a film that portrayed the world as an asylum, where "the inmates are sane, the keepers are mad." In this particular film, the U.S. Army was to be the "asylum." As a former soldier, Heston did not believe such a film to be a correct depiction of the armed forces and said: "At this time in the twentieth century, given the realities of the world, I don't care to make that point." "Besides," he concluded, "the part's not that good."[66] Had Podhoretz only known of Heston's decision regarding the asylum film, the intellectual most surely would have been impressed.

Heston's decision to turn down the asylum film in 1976 and star in the patriotic movie *The Battle of Midway* instead exemplified his rejection of the counterculture and adherence to traditional values. An old-fashioned war epic celebrating the American victory over Japan at the Battle of Midway in 1942, the film focuses on the unflinching heroism of the men who gave their lives in the conflict. Heston played Captain Matt Garth, the only fictional character in the movie, who proves to be the most heroic soldier of them all. After U.S. intelligence learns of a Japanese-planned surprise attack at the American-held Midway Island, the naval forces orchestrate their own preemptive strike. The navy successfully protects the American landing strip on Midway but needs to destroy the four Japanese aircraft carriers from which the imperial army launches its fighter pilots. Three of the carriers are destroyed, but the United States loses a significant number of men in the process, leaving just a few pilots to attack the last ship. Even though Garth is a top-ranking captain, he unhesitatingly flies a plane and bombs the final carrier. Garth heroically destroys his target, dying in the process. This battle proved to be the turning point for the United States in the Pacific theater. This patriotic, traditional film corresponded to Heston's public persona and his personal beliefs.

That the intellectual neocons did not look to entertainers as allies may have been an error—and an error of pretension at that. Even though the intellectual neocons recognized the importance of the mass media in shaping the American culture, as Mark Gerson attests: "Neocons do not respect the intelligence of movie stars."[67] Indeed, neocons did not align themselves with or even take note of Heston. The intellectual neocons' failure to collaborate with Heston also stemmed from their views of their roles in society. They saw themselves as writers, responsible for proposing, defending, or rejecting ideas, not as activists. Therefore, aligning with anyone who was not an intellectual would have seemed unnecessary. Consequently, the intellectual neocons and Heston never joined forces in a concrete way during the 1970s.

Nevertheless, like the intellectual neocons, Heston believed that ideas had consequences, particularly in shaping America's political culture. Therefore, he chose movie roles that, at least to some extent, reflected his traditional bourgeois values and rejected the counterculture, sometimes quite explicitly. While he did not want to overestimate the power of an actor's personal views, he felt that, as a public figure, his actions were not trivial either. Heston believed, and hoped, that an actor could, "perhaps, provide a reasonable example of behavior or standards or goals to people who admire him, and to whom this may have some meaning."[68] He may not have been working with neocons in a coordinated effort, but he reacted to political and cultural radicalism with similar revulsion and believed it his responsibility to reject radicalism in a public forum. By utilizing the silver screen in this effort, Heston was able to reach much broader audiences than were the intellectual neocons.

Meanwhile, the notion of participatory democracy would transform the character of the Screen Actors Guild and prompt Heston to resist radicalism at the grassroots level as well. From its founding in 1933, the Guild had been dominated by conservatives, including Heston. As noted in chapter 3, when Heston relinquished his presidency in 1971, progressive insurgents under the umbrella of the Concerned Actors Committee (CAC) used the opportunity to present their own slate and platform attacking the old regime. The slated presidential contestant John Gavin won the election by a two-to-one margin, but the insurgents rallied enough enthusiasm to alert the old guard. Sensing the winds of change, Gavin initiated several reforms and concessions. These changes, however, did not satisfy Guild progressives, who, resembling New Politics radicals, rejected compromise in favor of ideology. The CAC's efforts to loosen the old guard's stranglehold on the Guild leadership bore fruit in 1973, when the progressives' ally Dennis Weaver ran victoriously on an independent ticket.

Weaver's triumph marked the first time that a nonslated nominee had won the Guild presidency and indicated a new direction for the Guild. Guild members referred to Weaver's victory as the "Revolution of '73" and "an exercise in democracy." The progressives remained in the minority since conservatives, including Heston, who remained the vice president, dominated the rest of the board. Even so, Weaver's leadership style fore-shadowed major changes for Guild politics. Wanting to exhaust the full range of Guild member opinion, Weaver held long and frequent board meetings and expanded the number of people on board committees. Weaver's weak gavel reflected his intention to promote the participatory democracy newly popular in political and social organizations. Thereafter, the Guild changed from what the historian Steven Prindle characterized as "a relatively streamlined institution under the control of the president to a large, noisy and willful tangle of individuals pursuing their personal agendas."[69] Furthermore, Weaver spearheaded a drive to reverse the bylaw requiring Guild members to repudiate communism. When longtime executive secretary John Dales retired, the void allowed for new staff leadership to be installed as well. The Guild was poised for a new era.

Kathleen Nolan, Weaver's successor, transformed the tone of the Guild with both the issues that she pursued and her personal style. For example, Nolan did not trust either the federal government or big labor and publicly called for an overhaul of the telecommunications industry in particular and the American economy generally. The Guild founders, on the other hand, accepted capitalism and avoided matters not directly related to actors. Furthermore, Guild policies forbade the board from political campaigning, but Nolan flagrantly used Guild funds to pursue issues, such as women's rights, that were important to her personally. Nolan again broke from her predecessors when she presided over board meetings as a passionate advocate rather than the neutral arbitrator that Heston strove to be. She argued strongly for the position she preferred and sometimes burst into tears or used profanity during debates.[70] Thereafter, the activist style of Nolan became the norm, a legacy propagated by the Guild's new staff.

Feeling useless and ideologically outcast, Heston left his position on the Guild board in May 1975. He explained this decision in his journal, saying that the board had "changed radically recently, and I've become a surly curmudgeon, bitching about policies they go ahead and vote through anyway." Nolan took Heston by surprise when she boldly attempted to reshape the Guild into an activist, politically liberal union. Heston felt that these changes would no longer allow him to enjoy serving on the board. He commented in his journal: "I'll miss it, but I can no longer serve effectively enough to be worth the irritation and time it takes."[71] Heston's disapproval of the Guild's new style would only grow in the future, and, eventually, he would be unwilling to simply step aside.

HESTON AND THE INTELLECTUAL NEOCONS unwittingly walked in lockstep during the late 1960s and early 1970s as they took the two crucial steps toward neoconservatism—rejecting both political and cultural radicalism. The fallout from the Vietnam War and the civil rights movement exposed a power vacuum in the Democratic Party. This void was filled by insurgents who pulled the party to the left, and the McGovern commission solidified those changes. Consequently, the neocons spiritedly defended the bourgeois ethic and realized their conservative inclinations, finally concluding that they no longer fit comfortably within the party.

Heston and the intellectual neocons reflected the general sentiments of the American public. Nixon won reelection in 1972 in a landslide, and conservative grassroots organizations gained considerable momentum during the 1970s. These groups would contribute to a conservative resurgence in the 1980s. The fact that much of the American public seemed to be moving in the same direction as the neocons actually caused the neocons to rethink their attitudes toward the masses. Whereas both Heston and the intellectual neocons had once held somewhat elitist attitudes toward average Americans, this was no longer the case. The neocons broke with the so-called experts and put their faith in the rank and file. As Irving Kristol put it: "It is the self-imposed assignment of neoconservatives to explain to the American people why they are right, and to the intellectuals why they are wrong."[72]

CHAPTER SIX

REPUBLICAN IDEOLOGUE

CHARLTON HESTON DEVELOPED A NEW PUBLIC PERSONA BETWEEN 1972 and 1992. Not only did he emerge as one of Hollywood's most prominent modern action heroes, but he also became a leading spokesperson for conservatism. Heston's basic political beliefs did not change. He continued to champion individualism, responsibility, and anticommunism. However, the methods that he used to express and advance his ideas changed markedly. The actor became more ideological and partisan, finally dropping his Independent status to formally register as a Republican in 1987. Heston had always prided himself on being a moderate. Throughout the course of the 1970s and 1980s, however, he increasingly asserted unyielding political beliefs that constituted, he felt, a moderate stance but that were, in essence, conservative. Furthermore, he no longer confined his political criticisms to his journal but willingly voiced his discontent in the public arena. He became an ideologically driven public force for several reasons. First, the national political climate had increasingly come to emphasize ideology. Second, Heston became more involved in special interest groups in which firm, ideological positions were encouraged, even mandatory. Third, his attempts to compromise in the 1970s and 1980s often left him frustrated. Finally, when he did decide to take a noncompromising stance, he tended to get his way, thus, in his mind, vindicating his hard-line position.

Heston's new political personality represented a general conservative drift in the American populace, a trend that Irving Kristol approvingly designated *the new populism*. Kristol noted a new wave of conservative activism and believed it to be a commonsense reaction to the mistakes committed by the liberal new class elites regarding foreign, economic, and social policies. The reason Kristol so appreciated the new populism was that its adherents so greatly resembled the intellectual neocons. In devising the *new populism* label, Kristol only partially captured the characteristics of the movement. As he accurately conveys, it was composed of everyday Americans who largely operated from an emotional standpoint. However, his catchphrase did not effectively impart the origins or conclusions of this group. The new populists were former Democrats who, in reaction to political and cultural radicalism, began voting Republican in the 1970s and 1980s and relied on traditional bourgeois values in their policy prescriptions; in other words, they were visceral neoconservatives.

Neoconservatism—both visceral and intellectual—composed only one aspect of a general conservative mobilization in the 1970s and 1980s but offered a distinct approach. The New Right, the Religious Right, and big business all effectively organized during this time period. However, all three could be alienating in their appeals. Neoconservatism set itself apart from these groups and seemed to offer a middle ground between the Right and the Left by coming to the same conclusions as conservative organizations but offering them in a more evenhanded and, thus, convincing approach, by continuing to advocate a partial welfare state, and by offering new ideas that helped reinvigorate the Republican Party. Heston exemplified all these characteristics. He served as a spokesperson for somewhat controversial conservative groups, but his salesmanship of their positions was so well articulated that it seemed practically unreasonable *not* to agree with him. He also continued to advocate several government programs, particularly the extension of the National Endowment for the Arts (NEA). Finally, he offered new ideas regarding environmental and labor policies that indicated that he wanted not simply to support the Republican Party but to shape it as well. Likewise, the intellectual neocons made coolheaded appeals for conservatism in their columns, advocated the continuation of

Medicare and social security, and helped reinvigorate the GOP by promoting economic growth through supply-side economics.

The visceral neocons were likely influenced by the intellectual neocons, perhaps even subconsciously, but also acted on their own terms. Kristol was particularly impressed by the new populist reaction to liberal education policies that allowed the teaching of sex-education classes but prohibited the posting of the Ten Commandments. "School prayer then appears to offer an antidote to the corruption of our educational ethos," he wrote. "The un-wisdom of our elites is what accounts for the populist rebellion against our current educational practices—a rebellion whose demands are basically commonsensical, not at all extreme." Heston's newly assertive stance toward the Guild leadership typified the approach that Kristol found so endearingly practical: a reasonable reaction to the unmindful policies of the liberal union leaders. In the 1970s, the Guild leadership had been captured by more liberal actors who wished to expand the union's activities into social and political channels not directly related to the job of acting. In the 1980s, the Guild's leadership became even more militantly liberal. The resulting policy shifts provoked a reaction from Heston and a number of other conservative actors. Between 1980 and 1992, Heston led the conservatives in a successful campaign to return the Guild to its original policy focus, shaping federal labor policy with his efforts. This twelve-year struggle with the Guild leadership illustrates Heston's influence as a visceral neoconservative and his new political personality as a conservative ideologue.

BEFORE HE TOOK ON HIS NEW political personality, Heston assumed, as has been noted, a new screen persona, that of a modern action hero. The American public increasingly saw less of Heston in epic films and more of him in everyday roles. Between 1966 and 1976, he starred in twenty films, only three of which were set in the distant past. He accepted parts playing an airline pilot, a quarterback, an astronaut, a conductor, an architect, and a police detective.[1] These characters often possessed human flaws that were atypical of Heston's past roles, but, ultimately, the actor continued to display heroism and responsibility even as the movie industry came to embrace countercultural values. In the 1950s, Heston's traditional virtues and patriarchal authority had been much admired. Those qualities had fallen out of style in the 1970s. For example, one of the most critically acclaimed movies of the decade was *One Flew over the Cuckoo's Nest* (1975), which celebrated the defiance of authority. Furthermore, the sensitive antihero, personified by such actors as Alan Alda and Dustin Hoffman, emerged during the 1970s. These actors played characters who were polar opposites of Moses and Ben-Hur. Throughout this period, however, Heston, albeit in contemporary costume, continued to play the conservative, masculine authority that audiences had come to expect.

Heston starred in a number of disaster films, a newly popular genre in the 1970s that depended on that very persona. He described these pictures as featuring a "disparate group of people, most of them strangers to each other, thrown suddenly into a life threatening situation." The films usually focused on the special effects of the calamity itself and the characters' reaction to it, in the process allowing limited time for character development. Therefore, the casting in disaster films depended on what Heston called an "iron mandate" for easily identifiable stars with established personas. Heston accepted roles in four disaster films in the 1970s: *Skyjacked* (John Guillermin, 1972), *Earthquake* (Mark Robson, 1974), *Airport 1975* (Jack Smight, 1974), and *Two-Minute Warning* (Larry Peerce, 1976). In all these pictures, Heston played the strong and masculine hero who helps avert danger. These movies allowed Heston to preserve his identity with the public even though he stopped performing his epic roles.[2]

Furthermore, Heston personified traditional masculinity in the science fiction pictures he made during the 1970s. As has been noted, in *The Omega Man* (1971), Heston played Captain Robert Neville, presumably the last human on earth after a germ warfare attack. Neville scours the city for supplies during the day, proving his virility by running a four-minute mile and stripping off his shirt to expose a well-muscled frame. When he finds that other humans do, in fact, exist, his authority is so impressive that one child asks: "Are you God?" Naturally, the only adult female in the group becomes Neville's lover, a character played by Rosalyn Cash, who shares one of the first interracial onscreen kisses with Heston. Likewise, in *Soylent*

Green (Richard Fleischer, 1973), Heston played Police Detective Thorn, a hardened operative investigating a murder. Throughout the course of the investigation, Heston's character exudes the traditional masculinity that characterizes his other roles, but he is far more brutish. Thorn independently pursues the moral course of action regarding the case but simultaneously humiliates the women, known as "furniture," with whom he interacts. Shirl, Thorn's love interest in the movie, must beg him to make love to her, and he angrily strikes a female suspect later in the film. Despite the dark cynicism of these movies, Heston's character offers humanity renewal in the final frames, promoting traditional masculinity as the key to this regeneration. The modifications of Heston's screen presence foreshadowed the changes in his political persona.

Heston's new approach was partially influenced by the overall political climate. As Irving Kristol commented: "For better or worse, ideology is now the vital element of organized political action." Both national political parties had abandoned coalition building to pursue their respective agendas. Special interest groups, which could naturally be more idea oriented anyway, grew further apart and hunkered down into distinct ideological camps as well. Indeed, a new era of ideological politics had begun.

The Democrats had changed as early as 1972, with the rise of the New Politics liberals and the reforms of the McGovern commission. Throughout the 1970s, the Democrats were generally associated with group rights, countercultural values, and the accommodation of communism. Jimmy Carter, a moderate Democrat elected president in 1976, did not necessarily embrace the new Democratic agenda. In fact, he consistently battled the party's liberal wing. However, he could not prevent the Democratic National Committee from adopting a liberal economic platform when his strict budget failed to cure the nation's economic woes. Furthermore, Carter himself argued that the United States should accept a more conciliatory stand toward the Soviet Union and draw a harder line against anti-Communist right-wing dictators who had committed human rights abuses.[3] Indeed, the Democratic Party was one that stressed ideology and failed to achieve peace within its own ranks, much less with the Republicans.

The GOP also became more ideologically driven. Richard Nixon had attempted moderate reform during his first term, thus prompting Heston to vote for him in 1972. Nixon strove to build a New Republican majority and reached out to new constituents, such as African Americans and Hispanics. Indeed, he employed coalition building as his main tactic in revitalizing the party. To Heston's disappointment, many of President Nixon's programs failed. The president's economic initiatives, which employed wage and price controls, collapsed, resulting in what would come to be known as *stagflation*. In 1972, Nixon signed the first Strategic Arms Limitation Treaty with the Soviets, an agreement for weapons control that had unforeseen results. The treaty froze the deployment of only certain weapons and actually established goals, not limits, for the two superpowers to pursue. Moreover, Nixon's "secret plan" to end the war in Vietnam was, in the words of the historian Stephen Ambrose, a "disastrous choice, one of the worst decisions ever made by a Cold War president."[4] Nixon's strategy certainly did not prevent the Northern Communists from sweeping South Vietnam in 1975.

Furthermore, several of Nixon's initiatives were manipulated by bureaucrats and resulted in policies that Nixon and Heston actually opposed, corroborating the neoconservative fear of the powerful influence of civil service workers. For example, the Bilingual Education Act of 1967 required that non-English speakers be taught in their own languages until they became fluent in English. Nixon authorized increased funding to implement the act. However, the Office of Civil Rights (OCR) and the Department of Health, Education, and Welfare (HEW), the federal agencies under which the program fell, intruded into local schools to enforce the act. The historian Gareth Davies remarks: "The disdain with which the OCR now treated the nation's school districts contrasted markedly with its elaborate deference to minority-rights activists."[5] Indeed, the bureaucrats in the federal OCR used the 1964 Civil Rights Act to pursue a liberal agenda without the president's approval. Thus, the balkanization of America and its division into rights-demanding ethnic communities actually found sanction during the Nixon administration, a trend of which the president himself and the neocons certainly did not approve. Heston went on to scathingly condemn such attention to ethnic difference when he established his voice in the culture war in the 1990s.

Nixon's moderate reforms suffered from problems even before being tainted by his trail of political sabotage, and the neoconservatives would look to the Republican Right for leadership after Nixon was forced to resign. At first, it appeared that Watergate would help the Democrats. In 1974, Americans sent to the nation's capital the most Democratic Congress since the Goldwater debacle. Identification with the Republican Party was at an all-time low, and the political tenor of the country remained fairly liberal. Over time, however, Watergate actually helped the Republicans because it forced a realignment within the party. Watergate marked the death knell of the liberal Republicans and allowed the conservative Right to take control of the party's agenda and achieve long-term success. Despite the neoconservatives' concern about political "responsibility," Nixon's "dirty tricks" did not cause them to reject the GOP. Heston remarked: "In the aftermath of Watergate, I'm often asked what I think of my virgin Republican vote. I feel the way Chevalier said he felt on reaching the age of eighty. 'When you consider the alternative, I feel fine.'"[6] Heston went on to participate in a number of conservative causes that contributed to the Republican comeback.

The formation of the New Right, the growth of the Religious Right, and the mobilization of big business breathed life into the GOP. The New Right was led by longtime conservatives who found new issues on which to build as the social context changed. Such figures as Richard Viguerie knew that increased crime, pornography, drug use, promiscuity, and divorce rates were trends that disturbed many Americans in the 1970s. New Right leaders also attacked the concept of a "controlled society" run by "social planners," thus opposing such measures as busing and affirmative action plans.[7] Viguerie and his allies formed political action committees (PACs) and used direct mailings to publicize the detrimental effects of liberal policies and raise funds for conservative candidates. Meanwhile, a revival of religious sentiment that some have characterized as yet another Great Awakening facilitated the ascension of the Religious Right. As mainline churches lost numbers during the 1970s, evangelical and fundamentalist Protestant churches grew, and their membership became more middle class. Especially emblematic of this growth was the "superchurch," with charismatic ministers, thousands of members, enormous edifices, and programs on cable television. Leaders on the Religious Right were concerned with the same trends that galvanized the New Right but tended to blame the "tide of permissiveness and decay" on the "ungodly minority" of "secular humanists" who were, evangelicals believed, gaining prominence in educational and media outlets. Ministers like Jerry Falwell, of the Moral Majority, and Pat Robertson, of the television show *The 700 Club*, argued that churches should infuse the political order with Christianity and particularly advocated that religious leaders should attend the Republican national convention.

As the New Right and the Religious Right gained momentum, business leaders organized as well. Corporate business felt impotent against a political system that had been largely influenced by the Democrats. Believing that high government spending, deficits, and regulatory agencies weakened the viability of the private sector, corporate business leaders set out to convince Americans of the advantages of free enterprise by forming a loosely organized business roundtable, creating PACs, funding conservative think tanks, and developing advertising campaigns. By 1975, the roundtable represented 160 companies, including the ten largest, and made particular use of task forces and high-profile executives, instead of paid lobbyists, to sell its ideas. In 1984, corporate PACs outpaced labor by a whopping four to one. The American Enterprise Institute (AEI), the flagship of conservative think tanks, saw an increase in its budget from $0.9 million in 1970 to $10.6 million in 1983, largely because of its six hundred corporate sponsors.[8]

Heston and the intellectual neocons often agreed with the conclusions of these rightist groups but continued to maintain their own identity as neoconservatives. The New Right primarily focused on hot-button issues to raise money for conservatives and, according to the historian Bruce Schulman, could be "overzealous" in their appeals. The neoconservatives considered themselves moderate voices and, instead, usually relied on more reasoned logic to win people to their positions. The intellectual neocons also did not join up with the Religious Right in an organized fashion. While they similarly lamented the dominance of "secularists," as a largely Jewish and Catholic force they would not be a natural fit with the Protestant Religious Right. Furthermore, the Religious Right could be a bit too fervent for any number of Protestant Americans, especially nonevangelicals. The neocons would not find their political home in conservative business organizations either. Even though Heston and the intellectual neocons often defended corporate interests, the neocons were not businessmen in their own right and did not advocate the free market policies typical of corporate capitalists.

In fact, the groups on the right seemed to recognize that, despite their momentum, they were not yet mainstream, and they recruited neocons to improve their images so that they could better relate to the public. Through out the course of the 1980s, Heston would work with various Religious Right leaders, New Right groups, and corporations to strengthen the steadily growing Right. He made several appearances on Pat Robertson's television show *The 700 Club*. Moreover, he contributed to the mobilization of big business when the Anheuser-Bush Brewery hired him as a spokesperson. Heston narrated five ads for Anheuser-Bush's "It's a Good Part of the Good Life" series of commercials. The publicity campaign attempted to legitimize beer as part of American culture. In one commercial, Heston told viewers that beer has "figured prominently throughout our nation's history." It was present on the Mayflower and served at the first Thanksgiving. The Puritans drank it, as did many of the nation's founding fathers. In fact, George Washington had his own recipe for beer, Heston lectured. More important, Anheuser-Bush wanted the television-watching public to appreciate the company's contribution to the economy. In another advertisement, Heston informed viewers that the company provided $10 billion in salaries and $15 billion in tax revenues to the economy and paid $600 million to farmers for the ingredients of their brew. While Heston spoke, scenes portraying factory workers, farmers, the Lincoln Memorial, and the Washington Monument dramatized his message.[9]

While Pat Robertson and Anheuser-Bush recruited Heston, the AEI brought prominent intellectual neocons into its ranks. Irving Kristol became the first neoconservative resident scholar at the AEI and was later followed by Michael Novak, Nathan Glazer, Seymour Martin Lipset, and others. The AEI of the 1960s had been a right-wing exponent of free enterprise. By inviting neoconservatives to the think tank, the AEI gained credibility. Not only did the neocons provide an intellectual component that the AEI had thus far been missing, but they brought new ideas to what had been a single-issue organization. Kristol, in particular, became more interested in economic growth policy after joining the AEI.

In fact, both the visceral neoconservatives and intellectual neocons brought attention to issues and ideas that helped the Republican Party. During the late 1970s and early 1980s, the visceral neoconservatives led tax and gun revolts, with the result that both taxes and gun control became prominent issues for the GOP. The most significant tax revolt took place in California when Proposition 13, which called for a cap on property tax rates in the state, passed on June 6, 1978, presaging a "taxpayer revolt" throughout the country. The revolt had populist roots, but conservatives parlayed Californians' discontent into a Republican issue by attacking big government as a cesspool of waste and corruption. Only two years later, the Republican candidate for president, Ronald Reagan, professed the sentiments of the tax rebels when he declared: "Government is the problem." Indeed, the taxpayer revolt is considered one of the crucial factors contributing to Reagan's victory in 1980.[10]

Visceral neocons also led a gun revolt in California and recruited Heston for support. Californians against the Gun Initiative (CAGI) organized in 1982 in reaction to Proposition 15, a gun initiative that called for freezing the number of handguns in the state at their then-current level and requiring their registration. While Proposition 15 did not call for the confiscation of any firearms, CAGI feared that its sponsors intended to gradually ban all handguns. Early polls indicated that the initiative enjoyed a two-to-one lead. Therefore, CAGI, with the support of the National Rifle Association (NRA), raised over $5 million to fund a "statewide education effort" to defeat Proposition 15. CAGI recruited several celebrities in its media deluge, but Heston proved to be its most active and effective spokesperson. He narrated a thirty-minute documentary produced by the gun coalition specifically attacking Proposition 15. The video featured various police officers, criminologists, lawyers, and sociologists who concluded that gun control did not control crime. In fact, they argued that Proposition 15 would actually undermine law enforcement by requiring burdensome paperwork and, thus, deferring resources from the pursuit of "real" criminal activity. Other celebrities joined Heston against the bill, most notably the actor Roy Rogers, whose cowboy credentials were well established. Rogers had a horse named "Trigger" and a dog he called "Bullet," he reminded the press. "They'll have to shoot me first to take away my gun," he vowed. California voters defeated Proposition 15 in November 1982, and gun control would become a central Republican issue—and, of course, a central issue for Heston.[11]

In the meantime, the intellectual neocons brought new ideas to the GOP, ideas that helped strengthen the party, most significantly its position regarding economic growth. During his tenure at the AEI, Irving Kristol grew more interested in economic policies. While Kristol had been a long-time defender of capitalism and the Keynesian approach, he had come to believe that, in the face of stagflation, Keynesian economics was no longer a suitable policy. Furthermore, he believed that the Keynesian focus on consumer demand and fulfillment had negative cultural consequences. He became intrigued with a new economic growth theory advocated by Arthur Laffer and Jude Wanniski called *supply-side economics*. Laffer and Wanniski argued that the key to prosperity without inflation was to expand the nation's supply by increasing the incentives for individuals to work, save, and invest. The role of the government was, they maintained, to provide those incentives by cutting corporate and individual taxes. The supply-siders asserted that the growth generated by their policies would make up for lost tax revenues. Kristol saw the supply-siders' emphasis on working, saving, and investing as analogous to the virtues that he wanted to resuscitate in American society. To that end, he help promote Laffer's and Wanniski's ideas. Kristol published Wanniski's first article on supply-side economics in the *Public Interest* and secured grants for Wanniski to write *The Way the World Works*. Furthermore, Kristol became an intellectual mentor to Representative Jack Kemp of New York, who would be one of the prominent political proponents of supply-side economics.[12] The neocons would have a similar influence on the Republican Party regarding welfare reform and foreign policy, particularly through the neoconservative-laden Committee on the Present Danger.

Ronald Reagan's campaign for the presidency practically revolved around the neoconservative agenda. Reagan promised the "three R's": the restoration of America's military strength and international prestige; the revitalization of the U.S. economy; and the reversal of the ballooning federal government. He offered specific methods to carry out these goals. Accusing Carter of allowing a "window of vulnerability" to emerge between the United States and the Soviet Union, Reagan called for an increase in military spending to destroy what he believed was "the evil empire." He promised that he could raise the funds for such an undertaking through the supply-side approach. Supply-siders asserted that, after their tax cuts took effect and the economy grew, Reagan would have the revenues for a modest increase in military spending. Moreover, Reagan promised to continue the deregulation of industry and the slashing of social programs that Carter had initiated. This, Reagan predicted, would reverse the growth of the federal government and actually allow him to cut the budget. Furthermore, Reagan's message was peppered with a healthy dose of moralism as he attacked welfare abuse and condemned abortion.

Heston and the intellectual neocons endorsed Reagan for president and believed that they had played an important role in his victory. Owing in part to their efforts, they proclaimed, Republicanism had modernized and usurped abandoned Democratic traditions. Apparently, Reagan himself was convinced of their contributions as neoconservatives received the spoils of victory. Heston played a starring role in Reagan's inaugural gala at the White House, where he presented a series of dramatic readings. Only a few weeks later, Heston attended a state dinner for British Prime Minister Margaret Thatcher at the White House. More important, he and the rest of the neocons would play important roles in Reagan's administration. More than fifty members of the Committee on the Present Danger received federal appointments during the Reagan years. Irving Kristol never actually held a government post, but his lobbying helped secure positions for his neoconservative allies, including William Bennett, who became the chair of the National Endowment for the Humanities (NEH) (and secretary of education during Reagan's second term), and David Stockman, who became Reagan's director of the Office of Management and Budget.[13] Heston, too, enjoyed a close relationship with the president, and he carried out a number of duties for the Reagan administration. Heston's work for the Reagan White House solidified his relationship with the GOP and illustrated his newly evolving political personality.

Reagan first requested Heston's assistance when federal funding of the arts came into question. Reagan had promised increased funding for the NEA in his 1980 campaign, but the new president's chief budget officer, David Stockman, horrified the arts community when he proclaimed that both the NEA and the NEH were ineffective and, therefore, of low priority to the administration. Arguing that American artists relied too heavily on the federal government as their financial patron, Stockman believed that they had grown used to the largesse of the NEA and failed to pursue outside sources of funding. That dependence, Stockman argued, discouraged private individuals and corporations from seeking opportunities to support artists. He announced that he was considering cutting NEA budgets by at least one-third so that the private sector would again promote artistic endeavors.[14]

Reagan appointed Heston to serve on a task force to directly assess Stockman's concerns. Heston, representing the arts sector, cochaired the study with University of Chicago President Hanna Gray, who spoke for the humanities, and the newly appointed ambassador-at-large for cultural affairs, Daniel Terra, who represented the administration. Reagan charged the task force with discovering methods to encourage private support, increasing representation of nongovernment opinion on cultural matters, and improving the management and structure of the endowments themselves. After holding six hearings across the country in the spring of 1981, the task force strongly endorsed the NEA and its structure. It recommended neither a reorganization of the agency nor a budget cut. Instead, Heston and his colleagues claimed that Stockman was wrong. The report noted that, because of the matching-fund requirement, private support for the arts had actually increased dramatically after the initial legislation of 1965 had passed and concluded that "federal funds have encouraged private support" rather than discouraged it, as Stockman had claimed. Furthermore, the task force maintained that the NEA had been crucial to the livelihood of small arts institutions and individual artists. It argued that substantial tax credits and strong presidential leadership could possibly achieve even more private funding. With this report, Heston helped shape Reagan's federal arts policy, thus bringing him closer to the president. Furthermore, he illustrated the neoconservative approach by promoting federal programs that boosted private funding.

While Reagan was pleased with the efforts of the task force, the experience proved frustrating and somewhat eye-opening for Heston. He felt that the arts community and the media did not treat him fairly during the hearings. The longtime arts supporter Livingston Biddle admitted that, because of Heston's close friendship with Reagan, many assumed that the committee was assembled with the consequences preordained: to dismantle the NEA. Heston blamed the media for this perception, claiming that, during the hearings, "the informed were vastly outnumbered by the uninformed, most of them with media credentials. They had determined before our first session that the president had convened a new Spanish Inquisition. I had been appointed Lord High Executioner with a predetermined mandate to cut off some heads."[15] Heston had once enjoyed an amicable relationship with the press, but his misgivings about the role of the media in American life would grow as he vocalized his conservative inclinations. However, his frustration did not dissuade him from working with the NEA in the future. Only four years later, he returned to chair the NEA's Twentieth Anniversary Committee. In light of his experience on the task force, Heston made it his goal to increase the public's understanding of the agency's work.

Heston became further entrenched in the Reagan White House when he volunteered to work on a variety of special film projects for the administration. The actor narrated several films to be shown to the general public and worked on internal, classified productions as well. For instance, Heston provided the voice-over for a 1981 film explaining the U.S. Farm Export Education Project to the public. The following year, he narrated a recruitment video encouraging exceptionally motivated individuals to apply for the White House Fellows Program. Heston became even more of an insider when, in 1983, the Department of Energy recruited him to narrate six classified productions for employees involved in nuclear weapons programs. In order to employ Heston's famous voice, the government authorized the actor to receive "Q Clearance," the highest level of top secret clearance in the military. It is no wonder that Robin Leach, host of the popular television show *Lifestyles of the Rich and Famous* and accustomed to the privileges of celebrity, commented that Heston was the first star he met who was "buzzed by the Pentagon" during a meeting.[16]

Heston also embarked on several international trips representing the Reagan administration. In 1982, he met the French culture minister, Jack Lang, in Mexico City, Paris, and Brussels to debate the power of film and politics. While Lang argued that the United States used film to impose its popular culture on a defenseless world, Heston countered that "the success of American films throughout the world was not a question of cultural imperialism but of cultural internationalism," thus defending trends toward globalization. The actor also visited U.S. Marines in Beirut in 1984 and joined a Red Cross delegation to Ethiopia in 1985 to study the famine situation in that nation. These trips differed from Heston's work in the cultural exchange program in the 1960s because he could actually influence Reagan's policy decisions. Indeed, the Ethiopian delegation reported to the president upon its return so that Reagan could "review America's substantial commitment and announce any additional initiatives."[17]

Heston impressed a number of Republicans with his newly partisan persona. His work inspired Mrs. Alfred E. Meyer, a ninety-one-year-old woman from Florida, to write President Reagan. "You have a sincere friend in Mr. Charlton Heston," she informed the president. Impressed with Heston's intellect and skills as an orator, Meyer suggested that Reagan appoint the actor as ambassador-at-large. The White House never employed Heston, but he undertook an incredible amount of work for the GOP, a fact not unnoticed by other party supporters. In 1986, he served as the master of ceremonies for the Tenth Anniversary Ethics and Public Policy Dinner honoring William Buckley. Republican Senator Phil Gramm wrote a letter of support to Reagan on behalf of Heston regarding the actor's nomination for a Medal of Freedom. A note from then Vice President George Bush to Heston indicated similar admiration for the actor. Bush reminded Heston: "The Heston memorial guest room—with full access to the V.P. tennis court—is ready for you whenever you get back to Washington." Heston was considered an important friend of the administration, and he grew increasingly partial to the GOP throughout both of Reagan's terms.[18]

In 1987, Heston finally announced that he had registered as a Republican. In doing so, he made it a point to comment that the "Democratic Party moved, I didn't." The decision to formally become a member of the GOP made sense on one level. To be sure, Heston's political philosophy was compatible with the Republican platform. Furthermore, he took on a number of causes that were part of the conservative agenda and not simply Reagan initiatives. At the same time, his decision to declare himself a Republican was uncharacteristic. Heston had always been proud of his Independent status. Indeed, not having a partisan affiliation sometimes added credence to his political positions. However, Heston attested that Reagan inspired this decision.[19] It is possible that Heston was a bit starstruck by Reagan. Nevertheless, he never looked back and has remained aligned with the Republicans ever since.

Heston's increased involvement with the Republican Party was not the only factor contributing to the changes in his political personality; equally important was his heavy participation in the activities of special interest groups, in which ideological, noncompromising approaches were the norm. A special interest group formed around a single issue or idea. Such a group often lobbied to protect or sell its position and compromised only as a last resort. This tactic was the opposite of that which Heston had employed when conducting negotiations at the Screen Actors Guild. As Guild president, he negotiated for change and frequently compromised, calling a strike only when all possible options had been exhausted. However, between 1972 and 1992, he began joining new interest groups. In doing so, he displayed his neoconservative beliefs by continuing to preach a hard line against communism and by looking for new solutions to vexing problems. But he also became more dogmatic in his activism.

Heston's heightened involvement in special interest groups signified a larger trend in national politics. As John Judis points out in *The Paradox of American Democracy*, lobbyists and special interests grew increasingly powerful in postwar America. For instance, between 1955 and 1980, federal employment grew by less than 20 percent, but the number of lobbyists sextupled, indicating that the postwar era was dominated not by the rise of big government but by K Street.[20] A weakening of party identification further affected the growing impact of special interests. Less loyalty to a particular party allowed for increased split-ticket voting. For example, although Reagan won the presidential election in a landslide—with 489 electoral votes to Carter's 49—Democrats retained a majority in the House of Representatives. The general decline of stable party loyalties left elections largely unpredictable. Indeed, effective special interest groups could, ultimately, decide an election, a prospect that inspired even more single-issue groups to form. As the number of special interest groups proliferated and special interest groups gained increasing power, the trend for celebrities to enter politics thrived as well.

Special interest groups often recruited stars to promote their respective causes, and celebrities found the prospect of working with such groups quite attractive. First, a special interest lobby did not demand as much time from a celebrity spokesperson as a political party did. Stars could greatly increase their levels of political participation and, with such a narrow issue, not be forced to abandon their more lucrative day jobs. While most celebrities did not have the time or the inclination to become full-time partisan fund-raisers, a special interest lobby that required appearances on television or occasional testimony to congressional committees could more easily attract a famous spokesperson. Second, a particular issue was more likely to appeal to a celebrity's emotions than the platform of a seasoned politician. Third, special interest groups also allowed celebrities to become more involved in fund-raising, an area in which the moguls had generally dominated. Finally, becoming a spokesperson for a cause could, in turn, attract publicity to a celebrity.

As Heston became increasingly involved in special interest groups, so would a myriad of Hollywood luminaries. Reagan's foreign policy initiatives especially prompted celebrity activism; whereas Heston used special interest groups to defend Reagan, most celebrities participated in such groups to attack the president. Under Reagan's leadership, the arms industry became the leading growth sector in the United States, elevating the level of weapons production to unprecedented proportions. Heston applauded Reagan's tough rhetorical stance toward the Soviets and his dramatic escalation of the arms race. Reagan's military spending alarmed many Americans, however, who worried that more nuclear weapons only increased the chances for world annihilation. In 1982, a grassroots organization, which came to be known as the Nuclear Freeze Movement, popularized the concept of a freeze on weapons arsenals. In June of that year, over half a million Americans gathered in New York City's Central Park demanding that the United States halt weapons production indefinitely. The largest political rally ever held to that date, the New York protest inspired a subsequent demonstration at the Hollywood Bowl in Los Angeles. A number of celebrities and Reagan's own daughter spoke out against his policies.[21] Also in that year, members of the California-based Nuclear Freeze Initiative spearheaded State Proposition 12, which demanded that President Reagan suspend the development and deployment of nuclear weapons. Proposition 12 drew a number of liberal celebrities to the freeze cause.

Heston believed that, if enacted, Proposition 12 would make the world a more dangerous place than Reagan's nuclear buildup ever could. Therefore, the actor made television commercials for Californians for a Strong America, a special interest group opposed to a freeze, in order to attack Proposition 12 and defend Reagan's nuclear program. Furthermore, Heston accepted a seat at a roundtable discussion at the Strom Thurmond Institute and appeared on Pat Robertson's television talk show *The 700 Club* to denounce Proposition 12. Heston's publicity circuit was highlighted by a skirmish with his fellow superstar Paul Newman. Newman advocated a bilateral freeze between the Soviet Union and the United States that would include on-site inspections, saying that the Soviets "kept treaties as well as anybody." Heston held his own press conference in which he insisted that a bilateral freeze was impossible, and he berated Newman for thinking that the United States could trust the Soviets. Heston correctly pointed out that the Soviet Union had incurred more than two dozen treaty violations in its brief existence. "If Paul had taken the time to read a little history," Heston chided, he would know "they don't keep their treaties. You can't trust them." Finally, the two actors debated each other on the ABC news program *The Last Word.*[22] Clearly, Heston was growing more combative and vocal, and his work with special interest groups and access to the media allowed him to behave in such a way.

In 1985, Heston joined forces with another interest group that further contributed to his new public persona. The American Security Council (ASC) had been founded in 1955 to promote anti-Communist and pro-military policies in the United States. Reagan himself was a longtime member of the organization. When the president presented the Strategic Defense Initiative (SDI), a controversial proposal for a nuclear defense system, his critics derided the plan as a "Star Wars" fantasy. However, the neocons supported the president. Heston worked with the ASC to rally national support for the president, defending his proposal, and raising money on his behalf. In one commercial, the actor told listeners that "Tip O'Neal [a Democrat and the House Speaker at the time] and his anti-defense friends" were attempting to destroy the initiative before it even had a chance. Therefore, the president "urgently" needed the public's assistance. "Join with me," Heston implored, as he encouraged listeners to pledge money to pay for more commercials supporting SDI. "With your help," Heston rumbled, "we can work to end the terrifying possibility of nuclear war forever."[23] Heston's efforts with Californians for a Strong America and the ASC demonstrated his newly partisan and combative persona.

Yet another interest group recruited Heston in the 1980s, and, again, he demonstrated a dogmatic attitude, even criticizing President Reagan. In 1984, Heston joined the former U.S. Congressman John LeBoutillier to publicize Skyhook II, a project that raised funds to find the twenty-five hundred Americans who were listed as missing in action in Vietnam. The Reagan administration refused to support Skyhook II. Heston told one journalist that Reagan and his predecessors "have chosen to ignore" the issue because "it's embarrassing and destructive to international relations." Nevertheless, Heston contributed to the effort by recording a "fiery" telephone pitch to solicit donations.[24] Heston's political evolution stemmed in part from his involvement with special interest groups, not just from his relationship with Reagan and the Republicans.

To be sure, Heston did not become a wanton and obsequious supporter of the Republican Party. His work with environmental conservation groups proved that he could still participate in bipartisan endeavors and that he looked for new solutions that were not exactly in the Republican mainstream. For instance, in 1981, concerned that America's dependence on oil was compromising the country's security, Heston converted his Chevrolet Corvette to run on methanol fuel. In October 1983, the tenth anniversary of the Arab oil embargo, Heston donated that same automobile to the solar lobby's education-oriented affiliate, the Center for Renewable Resources, to set an example. Heston joined Republican Senator James McClure of Idaho and Democratic Representative Jim Wright of Texas in this effort.[25]

In fact, Heston's environmental activism paired him with several celebrities with whom he was not normally associated. In a lighthearted promotional for the U.S. Space Foundation's Environmental Impact Project, Heston teamed with the feminist pioneer Gloria Steinem to promote the use of space satellites to monitor soil erosion and other forms of environmental degradation. The ad cleverly played on Heston's and Steinem's ideological differences to demonstrate the bipartisan nature of the project:

HESTON: We disagree on most things,

STEINEM: I agree with that,

HESTON: But when they asked us to talk about how the peaceful exploration of space benefits *all* men,

STEINEM: *All* people,

HESTON: We agreed.

In a similar vein, Heston joined the singer John Denver in a televised spot for the National Arbor Day Foundation and encouraged Americans to plant trees. He also became a spokesperson for Forests Are Us and for An-heuser Bush's wildlife programs.[26] Not all Heston's work through special interest groups resulted in partisan bickering, as his participation in the environmental endeavors illustrates.

Heston's interest in the environment stemmed from his long-standing concern about the world's resources. One issue that Heston found particularly ominous was the world's growing population. He and his wife, Lydia, had adopted their second child, Holly, and were devoted supporters of several family-planning organizations. The movie *Soylent Green* conveyed Heston's environmental concerns in a most dramatic fashion. Set in New York City in 2022, *Soylent Green* depicts the city—and, presumably, the rest of the world—suffering from a massive population crunch. Only the elite live in comfort. The vast majority of people are packed like vermin into stuffy underground rooms, where they live in dirty conditions and sleep in bunk beds. Even worse, there is not enough food available to feed everyone. Only the extremely wealthy can afford fresh fruit, red meat, and plentiful supplies of water. Everyone else is forced to rely on rations, particularly the "soy-based protein bar" Soylent Green. When resources are in especially short supply, garbage trucks simply scoop the terrified masses off the streets and carry them to their deaths. As a policeman investigating the murder of a wealthy man, Heston's character, Detective Thorn, enjoys certain luxuries for the first time, like a $250 jar of strawberries and a hot bath, but his investigation eventually leads him to the horrific truth. Soylent Green is not a plant-based product. "Soylent Green is people!" an agonized Thorn cries in the film's famous final scene. *Soylent Green* is the only film that Heston made with the express purpose of advancing a political message. The fact that it was a movie about the population boom illustrates how important Heston perceived the issue to be.

Despite his bipartisan approach to environmental matters, Heston became increasingly affiliated with the Republican Party, and celebrities working on the other side of the aisle became more ideological as well. Indeed, there were far more liberals living in Hollywood than conservatives. As Heston himself commented: "The Hollywood community is probably as liberal as any community outside the university faculty." The journalist

Ronald Brownstein's study on the "general ideological positioning" of Hollywood affirms Heston's assertions. Of the Hollywood "opinion leaders" surveyed by Brownstein, 60 percent considered themselves liberal, while only 14 percent claimed to be conservative. Hollywood clearly did not represent the American public, 30 percent of which considered themselves liberals and 43 percent of which claimed to be conservatives.[27]

Like the conservative Heston, liberal celebrities joined a number of special interest groups in the 1980s. Andy Spahn successfully formed the Democratic Entertainment Industry Project with the assistance of the leftist political veterans Tom Hayden and Jane Fonda. The short-lived project spawned two important star-studded political groups, Network and the Hollywood Women's Political Committee (HWPC). Both Network and HWPC gained influence in the 1980s, and they fulfilled two distinct roles in the Hollywood political scene. In an effort to counteract Ronald Reagan's appeal to younger voters, Network especially catered to younger stars. Fifty actors, including Tom Cruise, Rob Lowe, Eric Stoltz, Daphne Zuniga, and Rosanna Arquette, publicized Democratic causes and candidates. Network did not engage in fund-raising, but the group gained a reputation for its assertive and vocal liberalism.[28] The primary strategy of the HWPC, on the other hand, was to circumvent the media and raise large stocks of cash to advance liberal policies.

These groups encouraged an ideological and radical agenda, annoying many Democratic candidates from middle America. Brownstein comments that the HWPC "operated on the explicit conviction that politicians could learn from listening to their Hollywood donors" and that many members were pushing Democratic candidates to "return to their sixties roots" and embrace liberalism. HWPC members seemed domineering and somewhat naive to moderate Democrats, but the vast wealth behind the organization inspired many candidates to find common ground with the group. Not all politicians, however, felt that the potential donations would be worth the political cost of associating with the HWPC. For instance, when Barbara Streisand held a concert at her home to raise money for the Democrats, neither Pat Leahy of Vermont nor Harriet Woods of Missouri attended for fear that the glitzy soiree would alienate them from their constituents. In fact, Woods would not even accept any of the money raised at the event.[29]

After the 1988 election, in which the Democratic candidate Michael Dukakis paid little attention to Hollywood, liberal celebrities evaluated their roles within the party and oriented themselves even more determinedly toward special interest groups. Convinced that most politicians accepted their donations with little intention of actually addressing their concerns in Washington, liberal celebrities outmaneuvered the party and used the media to sell liberalism straight to the public. A number of organizations, including the Creative Coalition, the Earth Communications Office, the Environmental Media Association, and an ad hoc American Civil Liberties Union defense group all formed using this straightforward strategy. Most significant was the Hollywood Policy Center, an organization that grew out of the HWPC after Hayden and Fonda left that organization. The center immediately absorbed Network, thus combining fund-raising and publicity in one organization. The center first worked for abortion rights but soon branched into a variety of different fields. For example, it sponsored events, in conjunction with the group Medical Aid for El Salvador, to raise awareness about El Salvador's ten-year civil war and to support its leftist guerrilla insurgents.[30] These special interest groups assumed a heightened public role in the liberal camp while Heston increased his campaigning for conservative policies and ideas.

A third reason that Heston evolved politically was that his attempts to compromise often left him frustrated. For example, during his tenure on the National Council for the Arts, he attempted to negotiate with his colleagues over the growth of the Expansion Arts Program. However, he could not convince the council of the validity of his position, and he was forced to relent as the NEA turned Expansion Arts into a social endeavor. Indeed, Heston never came to embrace the program. As late as 1981, he expressed his desire to relegate the "recreational" Expansion Arts to HEW.[31] Moreover, when he tried to accommodate himself quietly to developments with which he disagreed, he found himself feeling equally dissatisfied. For instance, after Kathleen Nolan assumed the presidency of the Guild, Heston grew aggravated with her policies and governance, and he resigned his board seat. However, simply stepping aside contradicted the motto that brought him to activism in the first place: "to stand up and be counted." Whereas he had been willing to compromise with producers as Guild president, he became less inclined to do so when his suggestions were rejected by the board itself and he was forced into silence.

The final reason that Heston became a publicity-seeking champion of hard-line conservatism was the success that he achieved when he refused to compromise. If, after his attempts to negotiate failed, he then tried to achieve results through a dogmatic approach, he generally got his way. For example, he disagreed vehemently with the reforms that Nancy Hanks proposed for the American Film Institute (AFI) in the early 1970s. He and Gregory Peck attempted to negotiate with Hanks for nearly two years regarding the institute's access to funding and its relation with the NEA. However, when the discussions collapsed, Heston refused to step aside. He purposely sought publicity in the hopes of garnering sympathy for the AFI and was willing to go "toe-to-toe" with Hanks. Furthermore, he wanted to amend the original legislation so that the AFI would be independent of the NEA but still receive direct funding from the federal government. Congress ultimately rejected Heston's proposal. However, the actor's militant and vocal approach forced the NEA to loosen its hold on the AFI. Thus, his willingness to reject compromise was reinforced by his own success, and he increasingly took a firm position in policy debates.

Heston's activities at the Screen Actors Guild between 1981 and 1992 typified his populist zeal as a visceral neoconservative and helped solidify his new political personality. Heston had disapproved of the liberal Guild leadership at least since he resigned from the board in 1975. At that point, he confined his complaints to his journal, but in 1981 he broke his silence. On finally expressing his discontent, he continued to criticize the Guild leadership until he finally forced it into acquiescence in 1992.

The tension between Heston and the Guild leadership grew especially strained after Ronald Reagan's election to the White House. The liberal Guild board took little pride in Reagan's status as commander in chief and made no effort to establish a relationship with the organization's former president and negotiator. Within several months of Reagan's inauguration, the press noted the lack of harmony between the president and the Guild. A reporter for *Variety,* for instance, noted that the Guild supported the Equal Rights Amendment but that Reagan opposed it. Furthermore, the Guild annually honored a member who, "by example or deed, fostered the finest ideals in the acting profession," but it had yet to so honor Reagan.[32]

In late 1981, the Guild Awards Committee met and nominated three persons for the award, and Reagan won the contest by what one witness called a "comfortable lead." The committee subsequently sent a letter to Reagan, notifying him of the honor, and inviting him to the Guild's annual meeting to accept the award in person. Customarily, the award remained undisclosed until it was revealed to the rest of the membership at the presentation. However, Kim Fellner, information director for the Guild, defied tradition. Conceding "that confidentiality is the rule, and autonomy for the Awards Committee is customary," Fellner nevertheless felt obligated to notify the Guild Executive Committee about Reagan's forthcoming receipt of the award, hoping that she could urge it to revoke the honor.[33]

Fellner argued that Reagan's recent handling of the Professional Air Traffic Controllers Organization (PATCO) strike made it impossible for the Guild to reward Reagan and maintain its credibility with the rest of organized labor. Indeed, the AFL-CIO had cut ties to the Reagan administration in August 1981 when twelve thousand unionized air traffic controllers violated a no-strike clause in their contract and walked off the job. The controllers voiced legitimate complaints about their difficult duties and understaffing problems, but, nonetheless, they had promised not to strike. Reagan ordered them to honor their no-strike pledge or face dismissal. After the deadline passed, Reagan fired them all and won the overwhelming support of the American public for what was considered his tough and decisive exercise of presidential authority.[34] Since the Guild had authorized that $5,000 be given to a fund for the assistance of the strikers and their families, Fellner implored the Executive Committee to intervene in the award situation. She was convinced that giving the award to Reagan would "alienate us from the rest of the labor movement, subject us to embarrassment and ridicule, and cause severe and unhealthy disruptions within the membership."[35] But most unions had not actually supported the controllers. Labor was generally unwilling to support an illegal strike staged by federal employees. Moreover, many unions lacked sympathy for the controllers, who received high salaries and had ignored most of their union fellows in the past.[36]

Despite the general unpopularity of the PATCO strikers, the Guild board followed Fellner's advice. It voted to override the Awards Committee and suspend the award for the year and then promised to keep quiet about the covert measures. However, Fellner's action did not remain a secret. The board's decision to revoke the award infuriated the members of the Awards Committee who had chosen Reagan in the first place. Isabel Boniface, the chair of the committee, wrote a scathing letter to Fellner on learning of the information director's intervention. "How dare you, a paid employee, take it upon yourself to act in such a manner as to substitute your narrow, uninformed and biased mind for that of a duly appointed committee," Boniface raged. "When you think that your personal political philosophy is more important than your job," she continued, "you should resign." Then Fellner herself leaked the story to the press, hoping to embarrass Reagan. Indeed, the media reveled in the fact that the only labor leader ever to be elected president of the United States had been repudiated by his own union.[37]

The bungled award and the overt activism of the staff and officers unleashed a fury in Heston, and he subsequently took the lead in publicly criticizing the Guild leadership. Heston immediately condemned the board and echoed Boniface in his statements to the press, calling Fellner's actions "a grievous error" that politicized the union and warranted her dismissal. He considered the board's interest in politics and social issues "an indulgence our priorities cannot justify." Noting the chronic unemployment unique to the acting profession, Heston pointed out that using the members' "hard-come-by dues to give $5000 to striking air controllers who make ten times what they do, doesn't help them [actors]."[38] Heston believed that recent technological changes, such as cable television and VCRs, necessitated focused leadership from the Guild board. He argued that the current board's decisions to boycott Nestlé (for allegedly distributing inferior baby formula to the countries of the Third World) and to support multilateral nuclear disarmament indicated that it was not focused on issues relevant to the acting profession. These political activities distracted and weakened the Guild as a governing body, Heston believed.

Heston used the conflict over the Reagan award to formulate broad critiques of the Guild, but he insisted that the president was not personally involved in any of his public actions. Heston told one historian: "I was at great pains never to discuss it with the president. It came up once or twice talking to Nancy. That's just sort of private pal kind of conversation. But I was determined to say I've not discussed this with the president and I never did." White House records, however, indicate that Heston was not quite as noble as he claimed and that he most certainly kept the Reagans abreast of the situation. On January 13, 1982, he wrote the president and first lady a letter thanking them for a telephone call in which they had expressed appreciation for his support. Heston also forwarded the Reagans a letter he had written to the board regarding his disapproval of its actions. He told the couple, "I'm trying to keep as much heat on the current SAG leadership as I can. I did a wire service interview with [the Associated Press] which should break tomorrow, and plan a network tv interview on the subject, focusing not on the Guild's foolish rebuff to you, but on the politicization of the union, which is of course the basic issue."[39] While these exchanges certainly do not indicate any sort of conspiracy between the former Guild leaders, the subject of the award was not just casual conversation either. Heston made sure to inform the president of his actions, and he was willing to go to the press to air his complaints.

Furthermore, Heston unhesitatingly personalized his critique of the Guild leadership. He focused on Ed Asner, the Guild president at the time, when he denounced the politicization of the board. Best known for his role as the gruff but lovable Lou Grant on television's *The Mary Tyler Moore Show,* Asner attempted to turn the Guild further to the left during his presidency. Asner had made his disapproval of Reagan well-known and had even picketed on behalf of the striking air controllers. Heston insisted that, during his own years as Guild president, he had pointedly kept his personal political activism and his Guild activities separate. Asner, he charged, was imposing his political views on the membership. This willingness to publicly single out his rivals was a marked change from his earlier style. Heston certainly did not disparage individual white racists when he marched for civil rights; nor did he use the press to personally denounce any of the antiwar protesters with whom he disagreed. However, beginning in the 1980s, he frequently singled out his political foes and publicly criticized them.

Heston's disapproval of Asner heightened in February 1982 when the Guild president announced his intention to merge the actors' union with the Screen Extras Guild. Asner hoped that such a merger would raise the status of extras, benefit actors on the margins who sometimes worked as extras, and strengthen the clout of the union. Believing that recent mergers, such as that between the Coca-Cola Company and Columbia Pictures, would allow producers extra bargaining leverage over the actors, Asner argued that one large entertainment union with coterminous contracts could help neutralize management's growing strength. Heston immediately voiced his opposition to the proposed union merger and began to rally other like-minded actors to vote against it. "Shocked" that Heston would not want a bigger, stronger union, Asner accused him of working as a "stooge" for Reagan to punish the Guild for rescinding the award.[40]

What was sure to be an ugly public controversy became more complicated when Asner held a press conference—only a few days after publicizing his merger plans—in which he presented a $25,000 check to the leftist group We the People. The money, Asner announced, was to be used for medical aid for El Salvador's Communist guerrillas. He criticized Reagan's firm anti-Communist line in Central America, particularly the government's aid package to the right-wing military government that was suppressing Communist incursions in El Salvador.[41] The national outcry over Asner's left-wing sympathies only fueled Heston's opposition to the Guild president.

Heston was the first to castigate Asner for his support of Salvadoran guerrillas, claiming that his argument was not with the Guild leader's position but with Asner's failure to disassociate himself from the Guild when presenting money to We the People. "Obviously, he has the perfect right to give money to El Salvadoran guerrilla rebels for money or arms or anything he wants," Heston told one journalist. The iconic actor was angry, however, because Asner failed to specify that his donation was a personal one and not a gift from the Guild. "I've been fielding calls . . . all day long, all because Ed Asner didn't make it clear he wasn't speaking for the S . . . A . . . G," Heston growled. He warned: "The next time he better goddamned well take time to make it clear."[42]

Asner further personalized the debate—and in a much uglier manner—drawing more attention to his disagreement with Heston and compromising his own leadership. Asner called Heston a "scumbag" at a press conference and, allegedly, a "cocksucker" at a board meeting. The latter comment prompted Heston to write a letter to Asner that, naturally, made its way to the press. "I'm only sorry you can't understand how deeply demeaning this is to you, to your office, and our Guild," Heston wrote in disgust. Asner did not publicly apologize for either epithet, but he did admit his "goof" in not distinguishing his personal views from Guild policy. He joked about the situation, telling *Newsweek:* "I now have a button which will identify me as a private citizen for such [political] occasions." Being labeled the "Jane Fonda of Central America" only evoked sarcasm. "I had no idea I was so cute," he deadpanned.[43] Still, Asner's position as Guild president only became more tenuous. In only a short time, he became the target of death threats, hate mail, and public protests. Furthermore, his blithe attitude toward Heston's complaints and derogatory comments about Heston's character would lead Heston to abandon his rhetorical critiques in favor of more serious pressure.

A month after the El Salvador controversy, Heston continued to use the press to challenge Asner's merger proposal and leadership style. He appeared on *The Phil Donahue Show,* a daytime talk show, explaining his disagreements with Asner. Heston argued that it was not in the best interest of the Guild to absorb extras. He refuted Asner's contention that merging with them would strengthen the Guild. He believed that actors retained more power and choices when their union remained an independent entity. Furthermore, Heston criticized Asner's negotiating strategies. He believed it necessary to move away from Asner's "confrontational" style, telling Donahue that the Guild "need[ed] negotiation, concession, seeking agreement, not standing out in the streets with your sleeves rolled up saying, 'Strike! Strike! Strike!'" Heston called the current Guild president an "extremely angry and short-tempered man" whose style would "not serve the Guild well in the office he holds."[44]

One member of the Guild board echoed Heston's critiques. Don Dubbins resigned his position on the board, citing as his grievances the hostile attitude of the board and the leadership's intolerance of dissent. The "Revolution of '73" was supposed to "democratize" the union and facilitate new ideas, but, Dubbins believed, the opposite had resulted. Deeply dissatisfied, he complained of a "terrible, disagreeable polarization that now prevails in the present board, a destructive one in which profanity and labeling of dissenting members is rampant." Furthermore, he indicated that, while the conservative ideology may have changed, the leadership's "oligarchy" had not disappeared. According to Dubbins, the board maintained its control by appointing like-minded individuals to serve as alternates, with the intention of nominating and electing the alternates to office (a practice likely copied from the Guild's preceding conservative system). Thus, the board perpetuated its domination of the Guild's agenda. Indeed, the board's liberal ideology and informal conduct during this period indicate that it had been infused with radicals devoted to participatory democracy. Dubbins described the board in its early years as "dignified, hard-working, sensitive, listening, and accomplished." He complained that the board he was leaving had transformed into the opposite: "a verbose, carping, complaining, accusatory, sniping, manipulating, insulting mob." Likewise, one historian compared Ed Asner's board meetings to "college bull sessions."[45]

As more Guild members broke with Asner, Heston created a small-scale special interest group to pressure the leadership to turn the Guild's attention back to its traditional focus. He even rejected an Asner-sanctioned offer in early 1982 to serve on the board. Heston claimed that he preferred to exercise his views as a "normal member."[46] However, his subsequent actions were certainly not characteristic of a regular Guild actor. In response to the merger proposal, Heston gathered with other members opposed to Asner's initiatives at a North Hollywood high school to discuss their future in the Guild. Furthermore, Heston privately worked with several other Guild conservatives to organize a caucus group in opposition to the board. Out of these meetings, Heston organized Actors Working for an Actors Guild (AWAG), a group that immediately attempted to block initiatives it considered beyond the scope of wages, benefits, and working conditions. AWAG's long-term goal was to unseat, or at least break the monopoly of, the activist and confrontational Guild leaders.

AWAG immediately worked to defeat the merger proposal and to attract new recruits. Heston's coalition of actors filed a suit in California Superior Court to stop the balloting already in progress, claiming that the ballots and accompanying merger information were "invalid." The merger proposal suffered defeat, however, so the suit proved unnecessary. AWAG celebrated the victory and finally held its first formal meeting on June 13, 1982, at the Masquer's Club, the locale of the original Guild founding. Morgan Paull chaired the meeting, which was attended by Heston, Robert Conrad, Don Dubbins, Marie Windsor, Donald Galloway, Anthony Carreso, Bob Herron, Renee Wedel, and other influential Guild members. AWAG purchased advertisements in the trade papers to rally support. "We are not elitist, not union busters, not anyone's stooges, not McCarthyites, not red baiters, not blacklisters, not liberals or conservatives, not 'scumbags' and *we are not extras* . . . we are actors," they proclaimed.[47] The new group boasted 250 members.

AWAG set two immediate goals: to block yet another Asner proposal and to challenge the current board in the next election. Earlier that year, Asner attempted to overturn a long-standing Guild policy by proposing an initiative that would allow the board to formally endorse political candidates. On June 22, 1982, AWAG led the drive in killing that proposal. By the end of that year, AWAG was viable enough to present its own set of candidates to run against the Guild's formal slate of officers. Unfortunately for AWAG, the official slate swept all thirteen seats, and Asner claimed it a victory that would buoy his personal program. An optimistic Heston, however, predicted that the small but viable support for AWAG's candidates marked the first step in the reversal of Asner's policies.[48]

Indeed, over the next two years, AWAG amassed considerable momentum by calling for the Guild to return to what Heston called "an apolitical and nonconfrontational" stature. In a mass letter to the Guild membership, AWAG claimed that "SAG has slipped from its place as a cornerstone of the film community" and blamed "our Board's focus on issues outside filmmaking" for the decline. AWAG listed several issues on which the Guild should be reoriented, including establishing contracts regarding "Pay TV," promoting more jobs for all actors (without relying on affirmative action resolutions), and abstaining from partisan politics. AWAG used several examples to dramatize its platform. Regarding affirmative action, AWAG promised that "more films made in this country will create more parts for every ethnic, religious, and sexual category within our membership than all the 'Affirmative Action Guidelines' you can file away in forty feet of file cabinets." Likewise, it discussed the pursuit of a liberal political agenda in personal terms. For instance, the board had lent its support to a rent-control initiative instigated by the Coalition for Economic Survival. Not only did AWAG consider the initiative completely beyond the Guild's interests, but the group also believed it an "affront" to any Guild member who owned, rented, or otherwise managed property.[49] AWAG's conservative agenda appealed to many disenchanted Guild members.

AWAG gained even more support when an overly confident Asner presented the extras merger proposal to the Guild membership for a second referendum in 1984. AWAG designed a flyer urging members to vote no, and Heston pointedly made an example of Asner. In Asner's most recent address to the Guild, Heston charged, the president talked "about nothing but the extras and called everyone who disagrees with him Nazis." "I truly don't understand the Board's hysteric commitment to this merger," Heston complained. Other prominent actors contributed their opinions. Tom Selleck warned that the merger would "disenfranchise the working actor," while Lynn Redgrave promised that it was the "union's integrity at stake." Jimmy Stewart argued: "We must not be so vain as to think we can speak for the needs of all workers." Robert Conrad pointedly condemned the proposal. "It's an awful idea," he wrote. "Whoever dreamed it up is more interested in power by numbers than in actors." Meanwhile, the Guild board distributed its own flyer entitled "Actors: Do Not Be Deceived." The flier called AWAG "producers with management interests" and "union busters," in fact illustrating the very heavy-handed behavior that Heston had condemned. AWAG proved victorious again. The seeming wastefulness of asking members to vote on an initiative that had so recently been defeated struck many actors as a sign of contempt for their decisionmaking abilities. Indeed, Guild members rejected the merger initiative a second time by an even more resounding margin.[50]

The indisputable strength of AWAG forced Asner's board to negotiate with Heston and the disgruntled actors, and subsequent meetings between the two groups fostered peaceful coexistence. For example, AWAG asked the board to consider amending the Nominating Committee procedure in order to ensure the participation of the rank and file in determining the slate. The board subsequently agreed to change the nominations so that two-thirds of the officers would be chosen at random or elected by the whole membership. In the 1984 elections, AWAG won one-third of the seats on the board, claiming fifteen hundred supporters with thirty committed activists. Heston had high hopes for the year ahead and stepped away from the front lines of controversy. Despite a few instances of open warfare between the liberals and the conservatives over the next six months, the election of the well-known actor Patty Duke to the presidency further advanced conciliation. Committed to healing the wounds of the Guild, the liberal Duke kept her personal views to herself. In 1986, Heston told one interviewer: "Miss Duke has proved excellent; she's disavowed the social agenda which upset so many."[51] Thus, Heston's newly combative and vocal militancy achieved the results he wanted. But the truce would not last.

IN JUST A FEW MONTHS, THE GUILD BOARD and AWAG once again found themselves at odds; in the subsequent clash, Heston became even more dogmatic and turned to new measures to pursue his agenda. The fundamental differences between the Guild's liberals and conservatives dramatically resurfaced during joint contract negotiations with the American Federation of Television and Radio Artists. The Guild's liberal negotiators agreed to a contract that pledged the Guild's "non-negotiable" right to go on a sympathy strike with the Screen Extras Guild. AWAG felt betrayed. Heston considered the agreement against the spirit of the recent negotiations between the Guild and AWAG and in violation of the rules of the National Labor Relations Board. He immediately called a press conference and announced that he, and presumably the rest of AWAG, could not support a clause obligating the Guild to a strike. Forced to capitulate, the Guild leadership deserted the extras, but the board, no longer considering AWAG to be "loyal opposition," resumed its political activism in liberal social issues.

The conservatives did not attempt to reconcile with the board and, instead, searched for ways to disassociate from the Guild. The new AWAG chair, Mark McIntire, began promoting the idea of becoming "Buckley members," or part-time members. Buckley members would pay for their share of expenses for collective-bargaining purposes. However, they would not be required to join a union or pay full dues if they did not want to participate in or fund activities that fell beyond that scope. Meanwhile, another concept, known as the *right to work,* gained support. Since the Guild was a closed shop, it could prevent any actor who was not a member from working. A right-to-work law would outlaw compulsory unions and allow members of AWAG to leave the Guild without jeopardizing their careers.[52]

Frustrated with the Guild leadership and confident that he could force the board to surrender, Heston campaigned for right-to-work laws in 1986. The actor served as the spokesperson for Idaho's "America Is Watching" campaign, and played off his film career to convince Idaho voters to support Referendum 1, the state's right-to-work initiative. "I've played men like Thomas Jefferson, Andrew Jackson, Lincoln—all of them heroes in defense of American freedom," he told voters. These patriotic references, combined with his position as a former union leader, lent added power to his message. "We're all watching, Idaho. Strike a blow for freedom and vote 'yes' on Referendum 1," he encouraged, as an eagle soared across the horizon. Not voting for right to work seemed unpatriotic in such a context.[53] The majority of Idaho's voters agreed and confirmed the resolution. Heston conducted similar campaigns in New Mexico and California that year as well.

His right-to-work campaigning did not indicate that Heston had betrayed the Guild or that his beliefs had changed in a dramatic way. As early as 1968, he had believed that the Guild should allow independent filmmakers more leeway in allowing actors to work outside the Guild contracts. Furthermore, his belief in the purpose of the Guild remained unchanged. He consistently maintained that the Guild needed to focus on wages, benefits, and working conditions. In fact, during the same period that he campaigned for right-to-work laws, he lobbied to win new tax breaks for artists, earning the praise of the Performers' Union Coalition. The organization purchased a full-page advertisement in *Variety*, thanking Heston for his "extraordinary efforts" to successfully lower tax rates for artists. "Your letters and telephone calls to Treasury and the Conference leadership in the House and Senate have been invaluable," the advertisement praised. Likewise, Heston urged Congress to establish actors' royalties on VCR tapes. Heston's right-to-work campaigning did show, however, that the way in which the actor expressed his views had changed. Negotiating with the liberal board was no longer an option for him. He employed ideological, noncompromising, and confrontational tactics to force the Guild to adopt his position. He did not consider his position extreme, however. Considering himself "the cool voice of reason in a cacophony of animal cries," he defended the right-to-work proposal as a mechanism that would protect the Guild. He believed that such a policy would force the leadership to "be more responsive" to its members and to abandon its political agenda.[54]

Heston's promotion of right-to-work laws troubled many Guild members, however. Fearing that a right-to-work law would lessen the power of, and possibly destroy, the Guild, between three and four thousand of the Guild's sixty thousand cardholders voted in 1986 to censure Heston for his "antiunion" activities. Heston admitted: "It's uncomfortable to suffer the disapproval of several hundred of my fellow members and most of all our board." "But," he continued, "I'm even more disturbed that their censure challenges the First Amendment of the Bill of Rights of the Constitution of the United States, a document generally cherished by Americans." Conservative stars such as Clint Eastwood, Jimmy Stewart, Tom Selleck, and Chuck Connors spearheaded a letter-writing campaign backing Heston's position and his right to speak freely. Even the liberal actor Richard Dreyfuss defended Heston's right to air his political opinions, no matter how "bizarre and distasteful" they were and "however big a damn fool he may be."[55]

The Supreme Court effectively settled the debate between Heston and the board in 1988 and, in Heston's mind, vindicated his tactics. In *Commu-*

nications Workers of America v. Beck, the Court upheld Section 8(a)(3) of the 1935 National Labor Relations Act, which permitted unions to enter into an agreement requiring all employees in the bargaining unit to pay union dues even if they chose not to join the union. However, the Court ruled that unions could not exact dues from nonmember employees for activities unrelated to collective bargaining, on the basis of the employees' right of free speech and the union's duty of fair representation. The *Beck* decision meant that the Guild could continue to run a closed shop but that it also had to allow its members to adopt "financial core status" if it continued its political activities. The board responded by banning political discussion, and, in a letter to Guild Secretary Ken Orsatti, Heston suggested that the staff pass out cards that the board members could use to keep the meetings focused on matters directly related to actors. Referring to an old tradition, Heston encouraged Orsatti to print slips of paper reading: "Mr. President, I point out that the issue on the floor has nothing to do with wages, working conditions, or negotiations, which is the proper and sole business of this body. I move the agenda." Doing so, Heston predicted, would preclude members from opting for financial core status (a 20 percent reduction in dues) and, thus, retain more money for the Guild coffers.[56]

The *Beck* decision also brought Heston closer to the Republican Party. Heston encouraged Elizabeth Dole, secretary of labor in the Bush administration, to flex her authority and live up to her "responsibility to workers" by requiring "all signatories to any collective bargaining agreement to properly and fully inform all affected workers of their court-protected financial core rights." Not every union had a person such as Heston in its membership reminding it to comply with recent Court rulings. Therefore, he feared that most workers probably did not even know their new rights under the *Beck* decision. Commenting "how effectively the media . . . eliminated this reality by ignoring it," Heston urged Dole to provide information on *Beck* to all union members, noting that such a move would likely weaken the bond between organized labor and the Democratic Party. "To diminish that power by even a tenth would alter the political landscape overnight," he predicted.[57]

Heston increased his pressure on the Bush administration when the Actors' Equity Association of America ignored his attempts to assume financial core status a few months later. Heston had launched his acting career on the stage, so the theatrical union Equity was the first that he had joined. Forty-three years later, he adopted financial core status because of the union's affirmative action policy. Equity encouraged hiring more minority actors and required that a part representing a minority be played by an actor of that particular descent. The policy justified Equity's decision to ban the British actor Jonathan Pryce from playing a Eurasian role in the musical *Miss Saigon*. When Heston learned of what he considered to be "blatant racist preference," he protested to Equity. "As actor and director, I thought the idea was to get the best actor for the part, no matter what color, or religion, or politics. . . . How naive I was," he wrote. Heston posed several scenarios questioning just how far the union was willing to carry its policies. "Equity would now prohibit Laurence Olivier from giving us his Othello, widely regarded as the best performance by any actor in any part of this century. Dustin Hoffman gave us a memorable Shylock; does that mean now only Jewish actors can be cast in the role?" he asked. "Because Sean Connery and I are Scots, are we the only actors who get to play Macbeth?" Citing *Beck*, Heston demanded that Equity "supply me with a lower dues rate and a proper accounting of same, deducting the costs of political actions like this vote, with which I disagree."[58] When Equity did not conduct an internal audit or grant Heston the lower dues rate that he requested, he pressured Secretary Dole to inform unions about the legalities of the *Beck* decision.

Heston warned Dole that enforcing *Beck* was "going to be a very public conflict" and advertised the case to President George H. W. Bush as a "major Republican issue." However, the Bush administration skirted the issue over the next two years. The president first tried to couch *Beck* in a general campaign finance reform package in order to avoid alienating the union leaders from whom he hoped to gain endorsement. Finally, in April 1992, he signed an executive order requiring federal contractors to inform employees of their financial core rights under *Beck*. Not only was the order what Heston had been demanding, but Bush invited the actor to the signing ceremony and singled him out for his efforts on right to work. While taking note of Heston's leadership at the Guild, Bush also praised him for standing guard over "a union's individual freedom of conscience," calling the actor a "crusader for individual rights."[59] It was already illegal for unions to contribute funds directly to a candidate's treasury. Because of Bush's order, associations like Equity were required to tally the currently unknown portions of their dues that were spent on such partisan political activities as newsletters, telephone banks, and get-out-the-vote drives. Undoubtedly, the financial limitations necessitated by *Beck* lessened union mobilization for the Democrats to some extent. Heston felt that his public, noncompromising tactics were finally validated, and he would go on to utilize similar methods at the NRA and in the upcoming culture war.

As the signing ceremony in the Rose Garden suggests, Heston and President Bush enjoyed a relationship every bit as warm as the one Heston shared with President Reagan, if not more so. Heston worked on various film projects for the Bush administration, including narrating a tape of the 1989 Bush-Gorbachev Malta Conference that was given to Soviet Premier Mikhail Gorbachev and participating in the Heroes/Rewards Campaign against Terrorism for the State Department. Just as he did Reagan's, Heston publicly supported Bush's foreign policy. He appeared on *The Phil Donahue Show* and defended the president's decision to use armed force against Iraq in 1991 and, for probably the first time in his public career, endured a chorus of boos from the studio audience. Heston and Bush actually seemed more friendly than Heston and Reagan. Heston was given permission to make a documentary about the presidential plane Air Force One (with Elliot Sluhan of Sluhan Productions) and even interview Bush for the project. Furthermore, the two men frequently wrote notes to one another and shared a similar sense of humor. For example, after Bush revealed to the press that he did not care for the taste of broccoli, Heston wrote the president: "I want you to know I'm with you all the way on the Broccoli Policy." Paraphrasing John F. Kennedy, Heston pledged: "I will go anywhere, bear any burden, pay any price to reduce the finite permanent supply of broccoli drifting around the United States, re-heated, re-served and ignored night after night." An amused Bush reciprocated by sending Heston a broccoli T-shirt.[60]

HESTON EXPERIENCED AN IMPORTANT transition during the 1970s and

1980s. He evolved from a political activist who focused on negotiating and avoiding dramatic public conflict to an outspoken ideologue who battled his rivals in the media in order to force them into acquiescence. He retained many of his same beliefs, and, therefore, he underwent this transition without admitting, or maybe realizing, that he had changed. He continued to believe that he was a moderate and not one of those "wild-eyed screamers" he so detested. Indeed, he presented his ideas in a way that upheld his assumption. In the true mark of a neoconservative, Heston continued to be well mannered, chivalrous, and moderate in tone, even when presenting controversial material about which he felt passionately. These tactics left his political foes bewildered as to how effectively to contest him. Meanwhile, he won several awards that indicated his close relationship with the Right and his impact as a visceral neoconservative. For example, the Washington Institute for Policy Studies honored him at their fifth annual meeting and dinner in 1991. Heston joined the conservative icons Barry Goldwater and William Buckley as the organization's special honorees.[61]

His own political experience led Heston to make this transformation, as did two general trends—developments within the two major national parties and the rise of special interest groups. The Democrats moved prominently to the left, while the Republicans moved noticeably to the right, leading Heston to become more ideological and partisan. Furthermore, the rise of K Street in the 1980s was as significant to the celebrity activist as the use of television had been in the 1950s. Television was the first step in leveling the playing field between politicians and stars, blurring the line between entertainment and politics. Former actors who successfully competed in the political arena, such as Reagan and George Murphy, further solidified the Hollywood-Washington connection. Moreover, Lyndon Johnson's duplicity regarding Vietnam and Nixon's attempts to cover up the Watergate break-in lessened the respect that politicians had once commanded in Washington and eased the way for more celebrities to enter the political arena. The growth of special interest groups in the 1980s allowed even more celebrities to become effective activists, and stars enjoyed the benefits of this type of political engagement. Special interest celebrity activism did not become a highly prominent trend until the 1990s, but it is important to note its beginnings in the Reagan years. Once again, Heston was at the forefront of this trend. He became most heavily involved in his preferred single-issue group, the NRA. As he rose in the ranks of the NRA, the gun control debate became a microcosm of celebrity activism.

CHAPTER SEVEN

GUN GURU

ON A LATE SUMMER MORNING IN 1987, A SMALL CONTINGENT OF WEALTHY guests and Hollywood celebrities gathered at Orange County's Coto de Caza desert resort and eagerly anticipated their host's arrival. At precisely 11:45 A.M., a helicopter landed, and the boot-and-jean-clad star emerged to greet those participating in his Charlton Heston Invitational Celebrity Shoot. Designed to woo large donors to the NRA-ILA—the Institute for Legislative Action (ILA) of the National Rifle Association (NRA)—the shoot-out permitted a number of wealthy corporate leaders to mingle with such television stars as Jameson Parker of *Simon & Simon*, John James of *Dynasty*, and Martin Kove of *Cagney & Lacey*. The event not only raised money for the NRA but also forged a new relationship between the gun lobby and Hollywood, piquing the interest of like-minded supporters the organization never even knew it had. Thereafter, celebrities, most especially Heston, assumed a more prominent role in the NRA, and entertainers increasingly aligned themselves on either side of the debate about restrictions on gun sales and ownership.

Founded in 1871 to promote gun marksmanship training, the NRA enjoyed a "mom and apple pie" reputation for nearly a century.[1] It focused primarily on shooting, hunting, and safety programs and devoted little attention to partisan politics. Even so, the NRA established a legislative platform early in the twentieth century. It explicitly committed the organization to advocating the harsh punishment of criminals and protecting the rights of the lawful gun owner. It was only in the 1960s, when the NRA believed that individual gun rights were in jeopardy, however, that the organization formally engaged in the political process. Finally, in 1975, in response to a series of gun control measures passed during the Johnson and Nixon administrations, the NRA established the ILA as a separate lobbying unit. The ILA achieved substantial legislative success in the 1980s, and many Americans agreed with the concept of harsh punishment of criminals that the NRA touted. However, the organization gained an unseemly reputation for its uncompromising and punitive tactics. By 1987, the NRA needed to improve its image and, thus, welcomed Heston's celebrity shoot, promoting it as an annual event. Heston subsequently endorsed the gun lobby in a variety of forums during the next decade. However, the organization committed a series of political blunders, and divisive internal squabbles undermined its efforts to reenter the political mainstream.

The NRA board skillfully restored the integrity and credibility of the organization in the 1990s by recruiting Heston to move well beyond his intermittent role as spokesperson and assume the presidency of the organization. The Heston regime succeeded in reunifying the organization, increasing its membership, and improving its relationship with mainstream Americans. Doing so, however, exposed Heston to widespread criticism. The actor had once been held in high regard by the press, but, as the NRA president, he suddenly became a subject of media ridicule. Heston considered this treatment an obvious sign that a cultural division existed in American society. He had struggled over cultural issues at the National Endowment for the Arts and with the Screen Actors Guild. In the early 1990s, he was ready to address such issues on a much larger scale. When he assumed the presidency of the NRA, he defended not only the Second Amendment of the U.S. Constitution but also the traditional cultural values for which the organization stood. As NRA president, he finally held a position from which to launch the full-scale cultural assault for which he had long, perhaps subconsciously, been preparing. It was from his post as NRA president that Heston became the most prominent of the visceral neoconservatives.

IN THE IMMEDIATE AFTERMATH OF THE American Civil War, Colonel William C. Church and General George Wingate openly complained about the poor marksmanship exhibited by their own troops during combat. These Union veterans worried what this lack of skill could mean for the country's future safety. Church and Wingate firmly believed that well-armed and properly trained citizen soldiers had won America's freedom from Great Britain during the Revolution and would be necessary for protecting America's borders from international encroachment in the future. Dramatic postwar disarmament especially alarmed Church and Wingate, who noted that national guard duties at that time were largely ceremonial. Some recruits served out their entire enlistments without ever firing their guns.[2]

Inspired by the formation (in 1859) of the National Rifle Association of the United Kingdom, Church and Wingate received a charter from the state of New York on November 17, 1871, to establish a similar organization in the United States. Calling itself the National Rifle Association, the new group stated as its central objective: "to promote rifle practice, and for this purpose to provide a suitable range or ranges." The charter allowed the NRA to introduce "a system of aiming drill and target firing among the National Guard of New York and the militia of other states." Fifteen men attended the first NRA meeting and elected the organization's charter officers. It was at this inaugural meeting that the NRA established the practice of having one ceremonial president and one workaday vice president, a tradition that continues today. For the president, the NRA installed General Ambrose E. Burnside, a former commander of the Union Army and the governor of Rhode Island, who was capable of attracting publicity. Church served as the organization's vice president, actually running the meetings and taking care of everyday details. Burnside and Church immediately raised the necessary funds to construct a rifle range on Long Island, which was finished and named Creedmoor in 1873.[3]

For the first quarter century of its existence, the NRA concentrated on shooting contests and matches and gained widespread public approval. The organization maintained a solid reputation as it expanded its rifle programs. As early as 1903, for example, the U.S. Congress worked with the NRA to create the National Board for the Promotion of Rifle Practice

(NBPRP). The NBPRP encouraged the NRA to extend its training to everyday citizens and more military, state reserve, and national guard members. By 1906, the armed forces had revised their shooting requirements and built ranges according to NRA standards. The NRA further improved its reputation by fostering an amicable relationship with local governments. In the 1920s, for instance, it affiliated with urban police forces for marksmanship-training courses. It worked with the NBPRP to design a range known as "Hogan's Alley," featuring mock buildings and disappearing targets that simulated realistic conditions. Immensely popular, Hogan's Alley was copied across the country and is now a standard part of many police ranges. The NRA continued to cooperate with local governments in the 1950s, devising its Hunter Safety Training Program to assist sportsmen in obtaining newly required state licenses. The program, which also offered the necessary instruction for hunters under seventeen to receive game permits, had expanded nationwide by 1953. These developments worked to improve the organization's standing with the American public.[4]

Indeed, by the mid-twentieth century, the NRA was a mainstream organization that had received the accolades of a number of American presidents for its purpose and programs. Ulysses S. Grant was the first president to join the gun enthusiasts, and, in 1883, the NRA elected him president of the organization. Theodore Roosevelt, whose big game hunting excursions were well-known, paid a $25 fee for an NRA life membership in 1907. Dwight D. Eisenhower and John F. Kennedy also joined as life members, with Ike speaking at the seventy-fifth annual meeting in 1946. Those U.S. presidents who were not members of the NRA also paid their respects to the organization. For example, the NRA collected thousands of rifles, pistols, ammunition cartridges, and binoculars to send to British soldiers before the United States joined them in World War II. After the war, President Harry S. Truman expressed his hope that "the splendid program which the [NRA] has followed during the past three-quarters of a century will be continued."[5] The NRA enjoyed this glowing presidential attention without sacrificing its legislative agenda.

The NRA had developed its political agenda in the early twentieth century in response to a wave of gun measures passed during the 1910s and

1920s. Until then, only a general prohibition on concealed weapons had existed. This all changed in 1911 when Timothy Sullivan, a New York State legislator and political boss, convinced his colleagues to pass what is known as the Sullivan Act, a bill requiring gun owners to obtain police- or court-issued licenses for their firearms. The NRA looked with dismay on what it considered "dozens of injustices by overzealous police and prosecuting attorneys" under the Sullivan Act. The NRA documented dozens of erroneous arrests to illustrate the weakness of the statute. For example, in one case, a young woman who found a gun and turned it over to the nearest police station was jailed for carrying a concealed weapon.[6] Despite its problems, the Sullivan Act was the only gun law on the books, and, as crime rose steadily during the 1920s and 1930s, other states moved to copy the New York statute. NRA opinion hardened against subsequent firearms legislation that restricted gun ownership by law-abiding citizens. After a federal law was passed in 1927 prohibiting the shipment of pistols through the mails, the NRA became more politically aggressive.

In 1927, the NRA formulated a general policy regarding firearms legislation and established a presence in Washington. Karl T. Frederick and Major General Milton A. Rickford represented their organization on Capitol Hill. They emphasized the tough punishment of lawbreakers who used guns but called for the liberal availability of weapons to law-abiding citizens. The NRA's basic platform in 1933 differed little from its stand under Heston's leadership. The organization opposed four types of gun control measures: (1) those limiting the sale of rifles, shotguns, pistols, and revolvers (but not machine guns); (2) those requiring a concealed-weapons permit to transport guns for lawful purposes; (3) those requiring identification files for bullets; and (4) those attempting "by any means to deprive the honest citizen or to make it unduly difficult for the honest citizen to obtain pistols, revolvers, rifles, and shotguns." At this point, the NRA declared itself "not opposed to Federal or State Legislation requiring the manufacturer, jobber and dealer to maintain a permanent record showing the make, model, and serial number of guns sold and the name and address of the purchaser," although it would later resist such a registration scheme. The question of licensing or taxing guns had yet to become an issue. The platform of 1933 was the basis from which the organization devised its policies on subsequent firearms legislation.

The philosophy driving the NRA's platform rested on two basic principles. First, legislation should target criminals, not law-abiding gun owners. Second, the government was not to be trusted in matters of gun ownership. Instead, the NRA insisted that tough, enforced laws against criminal action, as well as an armed citizenry, would do more to deter crime than restrictions on gun ownership. According to the gun organization, the criminal would either ignore gun control laws or "depend more on heavy lethal weapons such as the blackjack and sling shot and on edged weapons such as the sword cane and stiletto—weapons which are still and always will be available to him." Ultimately, the NRA feared that strong gun control measures, even when proposed in good faith, could, ultimately, result in the seizure of such weapons. It was the government's responsibility, the organization believed, to punish criminals, not interfere with gun ownership, especially since most gun owners obeyed the law. "The gun has always been more important as a law-enforcement than as a law-breaking weapon, and *it has been the progressive disarming of the honest citizen, coupled with the progressive development of the automobile and the airplane, which has coincided with the growth of criminal aggressiveness and criminal power in this country,*" the NRA proclaimed in 1933.[7]

In 1934, the NRA formed its Legislative Affairs Division, which utilized direct mailings to inform members of legislative matters and to encourage their political involvement. In the fliers, the NRA advised its members not to be apprehensive about writing their political leaders. If gun owners expressed their opinions, the NRA encouraged: "You will find that in ninety-nine cases out of a hundred he will appreciate your interest and assistance, will tell you so, and will do his level best to get what you want." The NRA also included its platform in the circulars and then offered alternative reasons for incidents of crime, usually focusing on permissive cultural attitudes and poor enforcement of the law. Finally, the mailings listed bills currently under debate followed by the official NRA position on each.[8] The NRA was a national organization, but it was through the local post office that the group achieved its grassroots effectiveness.

As early as 1933, the NRA found itself fighting the assumption that eliminating guns would greatly reduce crime. However, it claimed victory with legislation that punished gun-wielding criminals and maintained the rights of lawful gun owners throughout the 1930s. For instance, it "enthusiastically" supported the final form of the 1934 National Firearms Act, which imposed taxes and regulations on fully automatic weapons, sawed-off shotguns, short-barreled rifles, mufflers, and silencers and also required dealers to pay an occupational tax. The NRA also endorsed the 1938 Federal Firearms Act (FFA), which made it a federal offense for anyone under indictment or convicted of a felony to transport, ship, receive, or carry firearms across interstate or international borders. Both these acts targeted criminals, and neither placed undue restrictions on lawful citizens. However, the NRA vigorously opposed the Alco Crime Prevention Bill of California, proposed in 1934 as an amendment to the FFA, and endorsed by U.S. Attorney General Homer S. Cummings. If passed, the Alco proposal would have outlawed any weapon capable of being concealed.[9] After the defeat of the Alco Bill, the NRA faced few new challenges to its agenda over the next two decades.

It was not until 1957, when proposed changes in the FFA conflicted with the NRA platform, that the organization became seriously involved in the national political debate once again. The NRA believed that the proposals "would have amounted virtually to a federal firearms registration system." Furthermore, the organization objected to the inclusion of an entirely new provision that would have allowed the secretary of the Treasury, as opposed to the U.S. Congress, to prescribe the rules and regulations to carry out the FFA. The NRA considered this provision outrageous, saying that it allowed a cabinet member too much leeway and even the ability to bypass the legislative branch. None of the provisions that the NRA opposed were included in the new FFA regulations, but the skirmish prompted the organization to strengthen its political apparatus for future battles.[10]

The 1958 NRA platform regarding gun control legislation echoed many of the sentiments first articulated in 1933, but this later version tolerated fewer controls and was more stern rhetorically. The NRA had grown even more wary of government intervention. "The inevitable result" of licensing, it argued, "is to vest the arbitrary power to say who may and who may not own a gun in the hands of an appointed or elected official." The NRA's suspicion of government interference in private gun ownership led it to oppose registration of any sort. "Regardless of professed intent," the NRA prophesied, "there can be only one outcome of registration, and that is to make possible the seizure of such weapons by political authorities, or by persons seeking to overthrow the government by force."[11]

The NRA clarified its position at a pivotal time, for, although Congress struck the Treasury clause from the Federal Firearms Act of 1958, that initial skirmish was only the beginning. The 1960s saw a host of new firearms laws proposed, the most significant of which was Lyndon Johnson's gun control bill of 1968. The NRA had fought off Johnson's initiatives earlier in his presidency and was especially opposed to this last effort, which called for the registration of all guns. However, LBJ could not push the bill through Congress. A weakened version was, as discussed in chapter 5, signed into law, limiting the importation of inexpensive firearms, and restricting the sales of guns through the mail and to minors.

Nevertheless, the Gun Control Act of 1968 was considered a watershed in the history of the NRA because it highlighted two changes for the organization. First, the act brought thousands of new members to the organization, increasing its rolls to over 1 million men and women. Second, and most important, the debate over the legislation exacerbated a split between the sportsmen and the politicos in the organization. Even though the NRA had been politically active since the 1930s and had always focused on marksmanship and shooting, one camp of sportsmen wanted the NRA to be considered a sports league, with less emphasis on guns. The executive vice president of the NRA, General Franklin Orth, even testified in favor of the Gun Control Act because he shared this sentiment. Another faction of politicos, under the leadership of the charismatic Harlon B. Carter, disagreed vehemently, believing that gun control efforts would eventually restrict all varieties of gun ownership, including that of the sportsmen. The politicos opposed the Gun Control Act, although they were forced to consent to its final compromise. These internal divisions brewed over the next decade and became especially apparent when the

NRA attempted to name its proposed rifle range and recreation center in New Mexico. While the NRA politicos wanted to call it the National Shooting Center, the sportsmen preferred to call it the National Outdoor Center, claiming that it would be recreational and that shooting would be only one of many activities enjoyed there.[12]

Carter pulled the NRA toward an increasingly active political agenda. He was the most influential figure in the politico camp and shifted the NRA's focus when he helped establish the ILA in 1975. There was little doubt in what direction the NRA was moving when, the following year, the organization created the Political Victory Fund, a political action committee (PAC) designed to support and elect progun candidates at all levels. Still, it took a full-fledged coup for Carter and the politicos to extinguish the influence of the sportsmen once and for all. In the fall of 1976, in a true tale of subterfuge and intrigue, Carter schemed to stage an insurrection, but his plan was unveiled before he could execute it. In what was known as the Weekend Massacre, the NRA terminated seventy-four of Carter's cohorts who worked at the organization, and he resigned in protest. Six months later, Carter made a dramatic appearance at the NRA's annual meeting in Cincinnati and, using parliamentary means, changed the bylaws to nominate himself for the position of executive vice president. Carter easily won this contest and assumed an even more prominent role in the organization. The so-called Cincinnati Revolt completed the organization's evolution into a politically active gun lobby.[13]

THE NRA ENJOYED TREMENDOUS GROWTH in the 1970s, but its newfound status as a legislative lobby thrust the organization into a public role that included more than just politics. Poised against a more seasoned political foe in the New Politics liberals who dominated the Democratic Party, it soon discovered that gun control legislation was not the only policy about which the two groups disagreed. They also emphasized two different sets of values. As Edward Leddy, an intellectual in the progun movement, puts it: "What the NRA and much of America sees as virtuous—self-reliance, courage, strength, independence, and patriotism—the new adversary culture sees as faults: an outmoded and offensive male image, violence, chauvinism, and anti-intellectualism." Leddy labeled New Politics liberals the *adversary culture* and noted that that culture was "guided by different principles and admire[d] different virtues" than the NRA.[14] Indeed, the NRA viewed the adversary culture's bohemianism with the same disdain that the neoconservatives did, and both emphasized the resuscitation of bourgeois values as the key to a stable and healthy society. This cultural schism led the NRA to defend not only gun rights but also many traditional mores and standards. Heston would bring these same qualities to the NRA through his masculine and conservative public persona.

Heston had participated in NRA-sponsored shooting matches as a young man, but he did not become a member of the organization until 1978. He first felt compelled to speak out on gun rights four years later when he participated in the NRA-supported Californians against the Gun Initiative, a group that formed to defeat Proposition 15 (discussed in chapter 6). Even though the NRA claimed victory, it faced real difficulties during the 1980s on the public relations front. One historian blames this problem on the NRA's own "rhetorical overkill."[15] The NRA-driven media onslaught surrounding Proposition 15 was one example of this tendency. Furthermore, the NRA often issued overly dramatic statements that played on the fears of its members that one gun control initiative would lead to the termination of all gun ownership. The NRA's problems were not entirely self-inflicted. Antagonism by many within the liberal establishment toward the NRA contributed to its image problems. The NRA often found itself the target of liberal newspapers and journalists, which frequently depicted it as extremist.

To combat its unseemly image, the NRA designed the popular "I'm the NRA" campaign. These advertisements featured a cross section of average, nonthreatening Americans, especially women and children, who explained why they owned guns and how they practiced safety. For example, one ad featured an eight-year-old boy who cradled a BB gun and explained how much he looked forward to going hunting with his grandfather. Another featured a man sitting in a wheelchair. Positioned across each ad were the words: "I'm the NRA." The NRA ran the ads in over forty-five magazines, prompting favorable attention, and drawing new recruits to its cause.[16] The ads highlighted the diversity and everyday appeal of its members but did not insulate the lobby from problems on Capitol Hill.

The Firearms Owners Protection Act of 1986, better known as the McClure-Volkmer bill, was one important triumph for the NRA that simultaneously tainted the organization because of the mistakes made in securing its passage. U.S. Representative Harold Volkmer of Missouri, a Democrat and lifelong hunter, teamed with Republican Senator James McClure to overturn Johnson's Gun Control Act of 1968. The 1968 act barred the mail-order and interstate shipment of firearms and ammunition and allowed for a wide range of other restrictions that frustrated gun owners and dealers. The NRA argued that the law was full of loopholes and left so much room for interpretation that it could easily "be used or manipulated by an anti-gun Administration, President or bureaucrat to restrict your gun rights any way they please." Therefore, the McClure-Volkmer bill focused on three key elements: allowing purchasers to obtain guns in other states (if the sale was legal in both states); exempting small-scale hobbyists from dealer requirements; and outlawing any future attempts to register firearms and ammunition. The NRA sent flyers to its members in support of McClure-Volkmer and whipped up support for the bill by publicizing alleged abuses under the Gun Control Act.[17]

The NRA was so committed to overturning the 1968 Gun Control Act that it single-mindedly worked to pass McClure-Volkmer, with little regard for the long-term consequences of its actions. Furthermore, it would go on to compromise on future legislation, including that involving armor-piercing bullets and Glock 17s, in its efforts to pass McClure-Volkmer. The NRA leadership knew that it had to put up a militant front, however, in order to appease its hard-liners. A number of firebrands had long complained that any concession to compromise was a betrayal of the organization. Thus, the leadership attempted to appease the militants with rhetoric. The NRA publicly denounced compromise and unleashed vicious attacks on its enemies but, ultimately, had to settle for halfway measures on many of its bills anyway. This mindless strategy alienated the organization from both the public and its own members, thus weakening its legislative success.

The NRA's self-destructive approach was highlighted in the debate over armor-piercing bullets and Glock 17s, two of the most controversial gun-related issues of the 1980s. Both these issues emerged while the NRA was working on McClure-Volkmer. In 1981, police unions across the country endorsed a legislative ban against armor-piercing bullets that had the ability to rip through the protective vests that the police wore while on duty. Even though few manufacturers made the Teflon-tipped bullets, the NRA opposed such legislation. The lobby worried that such restrictions would set a bad precedent and also argued that the bill was too broad. Indeed, a considerable amount of ammunition for hunting and sporting purposes would also have fallen under the ban. However, the emotionalism over the ammunition, which had been labeled *cop-killer bullets,* took its toll on the NRA, eroding the organization's traditional bond with the police. Furthermore, in order to save McClure-Volkmer, the NRA was forced to compromise on the armor-piercing bullets, even accepting provisions that it had originally opposed. Therefore, the NRA damaged its reputation with the public by opposing the bill and then alienated its militant faction by settling for an attenuated version of the legislation.[18]

The NRA suffered further damage in 1986 during a heated public battle over the Glock 17, a gun made primarily out of plastic. Targeted because it could supposedly pass through airport security undetected, the Glock 17 was the object of a congressional ban, and police groups across the country endorsed the measure. The debate over armor-piercing bullets had motivated the police to organize their own lobby, the Law Enforcement Steering Committee (LESC), which was especially effective during the plastic gun debate. LESC touted the merits of the legislative ban and berated the NRA for supporting the surreptitious weapon. The NRA vowed not to compromise and attacked LESC leaders with a vengeance, accusing the coalition's most outspoken members of being the naive stooges of gun control organizations. For example, after Joseph D. McNamara, the chief of police in San Jose, California, complained about the NRA to the press, the gun lobby conducted a particularly vicious public relations assault on him. It purchased advertisements in *Time, Newsweek,* and *USA Today* claiming that McNamara could not be trusted and falsely accused him of wanting to legalize drugs. Furthermore, the NRA unleashed its character-istic mail and telephone barrages against other Glock-banning police of-ficers across the country. Such personalized attacks further marred the NRA's image—and, once again, to little avail. The gun lobby was, ulti-mately, forced to compromise in order to save McClure-Volkmer; plastic guns were banned, but the detectability standard was lowered from the original 8.5 ounces to 3.7 ounces.[19] McClure-Volkmer passed with very little adulteration of its original wording, but the NRA's missteps regarding armor-piercing bullets and Glock 17s severely crippled the organization's reputation.

The NRA realized that the viability of the organization was in jeop-ardy but seemed unable to address the problem's underlying causes. The lobby's tendency to reject compromise and punish opponents had become a habitual, almost compulsive tactic. Furthermore, factional infighting un-dermined the potential for a strong guiding force in the organization. Hes-ton's first annual celebrity shootout in 1987 partially counteracted the organization's tarnished reputation since it brought gun enthusiasts "out of the woodwork," giving the NRA a new celebrity base from which to work.[20] After the notorious battles with law enforcement, however, the NRA's problems were immense. They certainly could not be solved by a group of wealthy socialites and entertainers who raised money on an annual basis. The NRA's self-righteous behavior and lack of leadership were problems that actually worsened in the short run.

The Brady bill initiated a vicious battle between the NRA and gun control advocates that would not be resolved until the mid-1990s, after the gun organization had alienated some of its most important supporters. Introduced in 1987, the Brady bill was named for James Brady, the presi-dential aide who was severely wounded in 1981 during an assassination attempt on President Reagan. When first proposed, the bill called for a seven-day waiting, or "cooling-off," period between the time firearm sales were initiated and the time they were finally concluded. During the span of debate, however, the legislation became the subject of several significant amendments. The NRA opposed the bill, claiming that the waiting period would do little to decrease crime and that the paperwork would be a burden to police officers and lawful gun owners. The NRA's opposition to the legislation hardened in 1988 when the Brady bill became part of the administration's War on Drugs and was tacked on as an amendment, along with a federal ban on assault weapons, to the House Omnibus Drug Bill. The NRA feared that this statute's prohibition of what it broadly defined as an *assault weapon* could, ultimately, be taken as referring to almost any type of firearm.[21] Congress agreed to temporarily shelve Brady for a year, during which time it would undergo a special study.

In the meantime, however, the NRA's behavior during a congressional debate over semiautomatic weapons permanently estranged the organization from some if its strongest allies. Congress banned the import of five types of semiautomatics in 1989 in response to the Stockton Massacre, in which an assailant murdered five schoolchildren in Stockton, California, with a semiautomatic Soviet AK-47. Senator Howard Metzenbaum, a liberal Democrat from Ohio, subsequently introduced an anti–assault weapons bill in the Senate that banned even more imported and domestically produced weapons and would have confiscated any such weapons that had already been sold. The NRA opposed the ban, arguing that the assailant at Stockton should have been in jail already. Before his murderous rampage, he had been arrested at least nine times for petty crimes and miscellaneous offenses. One NRA ally, Senator Dennis DeConcini (D-AZ), attempted to stake out a "reasonable middle position" between Metzenbaum and the NRA. He introduced a bill that banned future sales of several domestic and imported semiautomatic weapons but allowed present owners to keep their guns.[22] The NRA attacked both Metzenbaum and DeConcini despite the Arizona senator's longtime ties to the organization.

DeConcini had once been named the NRA Person of the Month, but, when he proposed his compromise legislation, the NRA turned on him. The organization mailed fifty thousand letters to its Arizona members, warning that the bill would eventually lead to the confiscation of all their guns, and urging them to contact DeConcini's office with their complaints. In a later letter, it compared the Arizona senator's bill to despotic tactics in the Soviet Union, likening the consequences of his legislation to gun confiscation in Lithuania. As both DeConcini's and Metzenbaum's bills slowly worked through Senate channels, the Brady bill again came up for a vote. Finally convinced that it could not alienate its allies and still have a chance of defeating Brady, the NRA took a different approach and enlisted Heston to address the organization's problems.

First, the NRA used Heston to instill pride in its membership and encourage unity. The organization honored Heston in 1989 by naming him the keynote speaker for its 118th members banquet in St. Louis. In his speech, Heston reminisced about hunting in the Michigan woods and explained the necessity of firearms in a free society. He also highlighted his activities in support of the Second Amendment, and he made sure to note the "media bias" against the gun lobby. "I went to the war they asked me to go to. I raised my family, none of them are in jail. I pay my taxes, I contribute to charity, I vote in every election," he told the audience. "Now, because I support the Bill of Rights, I am a zealot? Like hell!" he exclaimed. The drama continued at the speech's finale when, on receiving the handmade musket given to all NRA annual honorees, Heston held aloft the rifle and growled: "From my cold, dead hands." Heston's speeches for the NRA followed this pattern, down to the last thunderous vow, throughout his leadership of the organization. The NRA was delighted with his speech, praising it as "what most observers considered the most stirring and forceful address they had heard."[23]

Second, Heston concentrated on rectifying the NRA's public reputation. In April 1989, he was the first celebrity to grace the advertising pages of the "I'm the NRA" campaign. Although it was first undertaken to showcase the average citizens who composed the majority of NRA members, the campaign was redirected to publicize celebrity supporters. By advertising the fact that a moral traditionalist such as Heston embraced the organization, the NRA helped boost its credibility with Americans. Furthermore, Heston filmed a series of commercials discrediting the whole "gun ban approach" and especially singled out Metzenbaum, the NRA's bête noir, for his bill banning semiautomatics. The advertising series set Heston in Washington, DC, against a darkened wall covered with graffiti while sirens wailed in the background. "This is the most dangerous place in America," Heston told viewers. "These streets once ruled by Jefferson,

Lincoln, Truman are now ruled by criminals. I'm one of 70 million gun owners who want to stop crime," he told the audience. "Tough judges and jail time will do that. Senator Metzenbaum's gun ban approach won't."[24] In addition to these commercials, Heston appeared on the television news program *The McLaughlin Group* to articulate the NRA's platform in a debate against Michael Beard of the Coalition to Stop Gun Violence.

Heston's appearance on *The McLaughlin Group* made clear to the NRA the advantage of having a celebrity spokesperson. Heston received far more attention from the show's host and its audience than did Beard.[25] The gun lobby frequently complained about the media bias against the organization. However, celebrity favoritism, as the *McLaughlin* segment indicated, worked to the NRA's advantage when Heston campaigned for the organization. The media were consistently biased in the attention devoted to celebrities, as opposed to everyday citizens, and the NRA capitalized on this fact. The NRA's opponents caught on to this phenomenon as well, making for interesting debate as the gun control battle continued unabated. Gun control groups could not counteract Heston, however, who trumped almost any other celebrity because of his legendary and iconic status.

Even with Heston's support, the NRA faced grave problems in the early 1990s. First, the organization feared a massive weakening of its power if it could not stop the Brady and semiautomatic weapons bills from being passed. At the same time, the lobby realized that it had to tone down its criticism before the legislation became a referendum on the organization itself. A relatively subdued strategy was especially imperative after former President Reagan publicly spoke in favor of the Brady bill in the spring of 1991. Later that year, the NRA's concerns were eased when Congress failed to pass either Brady or a ban on semiautomatic weapons.[26] Yet, even as the lobby celebrated its narrow victory, it had two other problems about which to be concerned. The NRA's membership roles had declined from 3 million in 1989 to 2.3 million in 1991. Furthermore, several gun control groups gained new members and made logistic and organizational improvements to more effectively counteract the grassroots and financial strength of the NRA. Indeed, they recruited their own celebrities in the hopes of offsetting Heston's influence.

Celebrities on both sides of the aisle became increasingly involved over the course of the 1990s in the gun control debate. This trend could be spotted almost anywhere, even in a women's fashion magazine. The editors of *Elle* invited Heston and Beau Bridges, who won an Emmy for his portrayal of James Brady in Michael Toshiyuki Uno's 1991 HBO film *Without Warning: The James Brady Story,* to articulate their respective positions in the pages of the publication. Bridges argued that "responsible gun-safety legislation" would both prevent armed criminals from acting out their felonious fantasies and still respect the responsible gun owner. Heston, relying on the "irrefutable adage" that "guns don't kill people, people kill people," countered that such legislation would not dissuade criminals. Only the prospect of the armed citizen, he argued, would decrease the crime rates by reducing the vulnerability of the criminal's intended victim.[27] As the issue of gun control gained headlines, more celebrities would become part of the debate in the most surprising of forums.

Meanwhile, national political developments once again looked ominous for the NRA. As Reagan's vice president, George Bush had received the organization's enthusiastic endorsement for the presidency in 1988. Disappointment with Bush's ambivalent policies toward the organization while in office, however, prompted it not to endorse either him or the Democratic contender, Governor Bill Clinton of Arkansas, in 1992. Instead, it encouraged its members to actively participate in local congressional elections, for it was in the halls of the U.S. Congress that the necessity of political influence was, the NRA believed, most vital. After Clinton claimed victory in 1992, the NRA's relationships with both Bush and Clinton grew increasingly acrimonious throughout the remainder of the decade. The NRA resisted Clinton's efforts to pass the Brady bill as well as his attempts to register guns. Furthermore, the gun lobby denounced the entire Clinton crime bill for its cultural implications. The organization characterized the president's crime package as a "'midnight basketball, arts and crafts, dance, quality of life and self-esteem' program for criminals." The NRA advised gun-friendly congressional candidates to sell themselves as believers in "prisons, police and prosecutors" and to disassociate themselves from what they depicted as Clinton's criminal-friendly program.[28]

This was not just typical legislative criticism but actually a larger denunciation of Clinton's system of values. It was in the 1990s that the NRA began explicitly to associate gun rights with bourgeois values, a tactic that the organization came increasingly to rely on over the course of the next decade.

Beginning in 1992, the NRA, with Heston at the forefront, began to openly articulate cultural criticisms. That year, Tony Makris, a public relations executive for the Virginia-based Mercury Group, learned of the rapper Ice-T's forthcoming album *Cop Killer,* in which the controversial lyricist bragged about "dusting off" cops, sodomizing young women, and engaging in other unseemly activities. Makris alerted his two major clients, Heston and the NRA, about Time Warner's intention to distribute the album. Both responded by denouncing the corporation. NRA Vice President Wayne LaPierre issued a statement condemning Time Warner, which was carried as a news item on a local Los Angeles television station. Heston then held his own press conference in which he repeated LaPierre's disapproval. The publicity surrounding Heston's denunciation prompted Time Warner to change the title of the album; however, renaming it *Body Count* and including tiny black body bags in a promotional packet hardly placated Heston. Infuriated with the company, in which he held several hundred shares of stock, the actor demanded the floor at the annual shareholders meeting in Beverly Hills and read the full lyrics of one song to an audience of over two thousand investors. He claimed that, after he repeated "every vicious, vulgar dirty word they were selling, the room was death-still, a sea of shocked, frozen, blanched faces." Arguing that the company's position was a matter not of free speech but of corporate greed, Heston eventually forced the company to drop the rapper. He boasted that his shareholder activism was "the most significant victory in the public sector since the civil rights marches in the early sixties." He even conceded that single-handedly confronting an international corporation gave him a higher sense of accomplishment than his civil rights campaigns. "Then we were following Dr. King. This was just me and Time Warner," he wrote in his individualistic fashion.[29]

The confrontation with Time Warner energized Heston for a new political era in which he frequently debated cultural issues. He inserted himself into what was known as the culture war, the battle between traditional bourgeois values and increasingly relativist, or bohemian, ideals. In 1996, he spoke before the NRA annual meeting in Dallas, celebrating the freedom unique to America. He worried, however, that the country was losing touch with its roots by capitulating to political correctness, that is, speech codes regulating words deemed offensive. "If Americans believed in political correctness," he quipped, "we'd still be King George's boys—subjects enslaved to the British crown." This speech is significant because it was the first time that Heston named political correctness and condemned it, signifying that the Time Warner confrontation was not a one-time aberration. His willingness to discuss cultural issues signaled to the NRA board of directors that Heston could fill an even larger role in their organization.

Heston also campaigned extensively for conservative candidates, calling himself a "footsoldier" in the revolution that gave the Republicans control of Congress in 1994. For example, he taped a television commercial for the Republican George R. Nethercutt Jr., who was endorsed by the NRA, in a congressional race against the then Speaker of the House, the Democrat Thomas S. Foley of Washington. Foley lost Washington's Fifth District to Nethercutt, ending a thirty-year congressional career. Foley was not the only victim. A number of prominent Democratic incumbents lost, and Republicans generally won the races between newcomers. The NRA was one of the major forces behind the Republican victory, largely because of its major get-out-the-vote effort. Indeed, one national exit poll showed that 37 percent of voters in 1994 considered themselves supporters of the NRA. During election time, the NRA proved itself able to reunite and achieve its goal of voting in Republican candidates. Afterward, however, it fell into its old habits of internal bickering and outward public gaffes. Its internal weakness was illustrated immediately after the election when NRA representatives met with the new Speaker of the House, Newt Gingrich, about the assault weapons bill. According to one witness: "The NRA representatives said that their membership was getting restive, and that the congressional leaders should understand that if they don't do something the membership would 'get rid of us and then they'll get rid of you.'"[30]

The organization fared even worse on the public relations front because of its break with former President Bush, who was still a nominal member. Already strained in 1992, the NRA's relationship with Bush became more acidulous in 1995. Bush grew particularly disenchanted with the NRA because of its activities after antigovernment militants bombed the Federal Building in Oklahoma City earlier that year. The press had already accused the NRA of feeding such vigilante terrorism. The organization's leadership made matters worse with an NRA fund-raising letter in which LaPierre condemned agents of the U.S. Bureau of Alcohol, Tobacco, and Firearms (BATF). They wore "Nazi bucket helmets and black storm trooper uniforms," he charged, and were eager to "harass, intimidate, even murder law-abiding citizens." LaPierre listed examples of alleged BATF abuses and applauded the congressional hearing to which the agency was soon to be subjected. Bush found LaPierre's characterization of federal agents deeply offensive to his "own sense of decency and honor," especially in the wake of the Oklahoma tragedy. He resigned from the organization in a much-heralded statement that evoked the praise of President Clinton.[31] The break with Bush illustrated the organization's deteriorating relationship with the American mainstream as well as many of its more moderate members—in spite of its success in the 1994 midterm elections.

Heston, meanwhile, was determined to stay in the political arena. He established his own PAC in 1996, indicating his desire to campaign in a high-profile, systematic manner. Named ARENA PAC, the committee was set up to help his favorite conservative candidates—both Republican and Democrat—and to finance his travel on the hustings. By September, Heston had raised enough money for a twenty-two-state campaign tour for the 1996 election.[32] These activities indicated that Heston saw politics in his future. Wayne LaPierre was paying attention.

Even though his bellicosity sometimes led to public relations disasters, by the mid-1990s LaPierre realized that the NRA needed a leader who could permanently unite the membership and allow it to debate policy in a more effective manner. In order to recruit such a leader, LaPierre knew that he had to oust the firebrand Neal Knox. Knox had served on the board since the so-called Cincinnati Revolt and was one of the NRA's most valued operatives. However, Harlon Carter disapproved of Knox's Rasputin-like tactics and forced him to step aside in the early 1980s. A decade later, Knox managed to return to the board and win the first vice presidency. He then started his own Firearms Coalition in 1992 with the intent of pressuring NRA leaders not to compromise on gun legislation, and he was largely responsible for the divisiveness that continued to plague the NRA. Even though Knox and LaPierre were fellow hard-liners, the two fire-breathers were actually at odds. While Knox favored turning the NRA into a militia-type operation, LaPierre was a political animal. As a long-standing figure in the ILA and, at that point, the NRA's executive vice president, LaPierre recognized that Knox's tactics drove away members and undermined the NRA on Capitol Hill and among middle-class Americans. LaPierre devised a new political approach. He wanted to change the political culture to recast the terms of the gun debate. For such an endeavor, he needed a leader with a highly respected and firmly established public image. Therefore, he recruited Heston to run for the NRA's top leadership position. Despite his past mistakes and often hostile rhetoric, LaPierre's political acumen saved the NRA from a takeover by its lunatic fringe.

Heston began his ascendancy in the NRA's leadership at the organization's annual meeting in Seattle in 1997. NRA bylaws required Heston to hold a seat on the board before he could run for office and to win the first vice presidency before he could run for president. Heston easily acquired a board seat, a victory that allowed him to immediately contest Knox for the first vice presidency. The elections could not have turned out any better for LaPierre and his allies, for they made a clean sweep of the top officer positions. LaPierre and Marion Hammer retained their posts as executive vice president and president, respectively, while Kayne Robinson, another LaPierreite, unseated a Knox crony for the second vice presidency. The longtime national secretary, Edward (Jim) Land, supported LaPierre's plan as well. The final tallies of this election illustrated the divisions within the organization. Heston won by four votes and Robinson by only one. But, as the seventy-two-year-old Heston remarked: "A win's a win."[33]

Heston's assumption of the first vice presidency could not have been more fortuitous for either him or the NRA. The flailing organization des-

perately needed a strong and charismatic central figure to reunite and revitalize its membership and improve the organization's public reputation.
With Heston, the gun lobby gained an experienced politico who had already campaigned quite extensively for the NRA with his celebrity shootouts and promotions. Furthermore, his ARENA PAC had helped elect
conservative candidates friendly to the NRA agenda, and Heston had long
defended the cultural values crucial to LaPierre's vision. As a member of
the National Council on the Arts, Heston had resisted the "democratization" and racial separatism that the majority favored; as a former president
of the Screen Actors Guild, he led a caucus group to thwart the board's efforts to turn the Guild into a liberal partisan union; and, in a speech before
the Conservative Political Action Conference, he lambasted President
Clinton as the prime example of the moral decay in America.[34] Indeed,
Heston was already engaged in the culture war, and he now secured yet
another stage from which to wage it. Thus, the NRA and Heston helped
each other in achieving their mutually compatible goals.

The Heston team immediately set out to amass support for the actor's
forthcoming campaign for the NRA presidency and to quash the latent
influence of Neal Knox. Hammer and LaPierre both wrote articles for the
American Rifleman explaining their "Heston strategy" and how it was part
of an ambitious vision for the NRA, a crusade that would determine the
future of the organization. Raising money, recruiting members, electing
progun leaders, and educating "a pro-gun generation" were the top priorities, and Heston's presence was needed to "lead this march," LaPierre
claimed.[35] In the same issue of the magazine, Heston himself explained his
plans to carry out LaPierre's vision and detailed his experience promoting
gun rights. The articles worked to convince members that Heston was the
most qualified person to lead their organization out of the wilderness.

If some NRA members worried that recruiting a Hollywood actor
would make the organization appear frivolous, the photographs accompanying Heston's article would have ameliorated such concerns. The lead
picture portrayed a reflective Heston, conveying traditional solemnity and
enjoying the outdoors, with a musket in his hand and a cowboy hat on his
head. A group photograph of the NRA board of directors standing in front

of Capitol Hill assured readers that Heston was very much the "seasoned political activist" he appeared to be. The remaining photograph featured Heston alone, challenging the camera in steely-eyed determination, and exhibiting resolve with his trademark grimace.[36] With these photographs, the actor sustained his public image as a defender of traditional, conservative values.

Heston took the publicity circuit by storm to sell the NRA to the American public, presenting himself as the voice of reason and moderation. He appeared on radio programs and gave numerous interviews explaining his cause. In all these discussions, he chose his words carefully and took a moderate approach. For instance, he made no personal attacks on Knox but told one radio host that Knox "did indeed represent the—I prefer the term—extremist element" of the NRA. His reaction to the Brady bill, which had finally passed in 1995 (as the Brady Handgun Violence Prevention Act), also illustrated his moderate strategy. He was careful not to denounce the measure and merely stated: "The Brady bill in my opinion is irrelevant. It doesn't matter. The hassle it would take to repeal it isn't worth what you'd get out of it." According to Heston, local police forces ignored it, so "I don't care if they keep the Brady Act forever." Moreover, when one caller told Heston that he had once been an NRA member but then dropped his status because of some "disturbing" literature he had received in the mail, Heston diplomatically praised him. "I think—if I dare say this—you were right to resign," he admitted, but he went on to encourage the caller's return to the NRA fold. He promised that the "good guys" in office intended to reform the organization.[37] Just as he had done by taking a moderate stance at the Guild and with the Arts Group for the March on Washington, Heston hoped to unite the NRA by practicing restraint.

At the same time, Heston employed combative techniques against adversaries outside the organization. The actor immediately won the everlasting loyalty of the NRA membership by, in the words of NRA Secretary Land, "taking the national press to task" for the media's treatment of the gun lobby. On September 1, 1997, Heston delivered a speech to the National Press Club in Washington, DC, defending the integrity of the NRA. With tough rhetoric but a friendly tone, he minced no words about his purpose. He stated at the outset: "Today I want to talk about guns: why we have them, why the Bill of Rights guarantees that we have them, and why my right to have a gun is more important than your right to rail against it in print." Heston treated the members of the Press Club with little reverence, subjecting his audience to a "short refresher course in Constitutional history." He accused the media of launching "a crusade to undermine the right to keep and bear arms" in "an ill-contrived and totally naïve campaign against the Second Amendment." He explained that NRA members could not trust the media because, when covering gun control issues, the press obviously relied on the literature of gun control advocacy groups. He demanded that the press use the proper language regarding firearms or at least give the NRA equal time for rebuttals and advertising, if for no other reason than for the media's own protection. He warned that assaults against the Second Amendment would eventually lead to attacks on the First Amendment, which guaranteed free speech. Since the press "apparently can't comprehend that," Heston vowed that he and the NRA had a plan to protect those freedoms with or without the media's help. He promised that guns would once again hold "an honorable and proud place in our society."[38]

After the Press Club speech, Heston continued to impress NRA members with his adamant defense of the traditional values for which the organization stood. He feared that the liberal establishment had made gun owners ashamed to admit that they possessed firearms. Such shame was not limited to those who believed in the Second Amendment, however. Convinced that "Pentecostal Christians, pro-lifers, right-to workers, Promise Keepers, school voucher-ers," and other "non-fashionable" Americans suffered the same crisis of confidence, Heston remarked: "You have been assaulted . . . and robbed of the courage of your convictions. Your pride in who you are, and what you believe, has been ridiculed, ransacked and plundered . . . you and your country are less free." Heston admitted to his audience that he was "not really here to talk about the Second Amendment" as much as the culture war. He considered the two interdependent, however, because, in his mind, defending gun rights necessitated defending traditional values. The actor told conservatives to stand up for what they believed. "Don't run for cover when the cultural cannons roar," he warned.[39]

Heston's willingness to publicly confront other celebrities for their antigun views also impressed NRA members. For example, Barbara Streisand's starring role in NBC's television movie *The Long Island Incident* (Joseph Sargent, 1998) particularly vexed Heston. In the movie, Streisand played Carolyn McCarthy, a New Yorker who won a seat in Congress after a gunman killed her husband and five other passengers on a commuter train in 1993. Arguing that the film showed only one side of the story and put firearms in a bad light, the NRA purchased an advertisement in the *Los Angeles Times* protesting NBC's rendition of the heartbreaking, yet triumphant, story. Titling the ad "A Terrible Price to Pay for Ratings," the NRA accused Streisand of going "out of her way" to push the film's antigun politics with NBC. Indeed, Heston was so angry at what he considered irresponsible celebrity politicking that he labeled Streisand the "Hanoi Jane of the Second Amendment." He told one journalist that, even though the singer "is an iconic figure in pop music, she is not widely informed on the Constitution of the United States." He added somewhat pompously: "I really don't expect Miss Streisand will debate me because it would be unfair. She doesn't know about firearms. It would be like shooting fish in a barrel."[40] NRA members cheered on their future president, delighted by his willingness to get tough, especially with an entertainer of Streisand's stature.

The fact that Heston was one of the few professed conservatives in the liberal entertainment industry particularly impressed many NRA members. They believed that his message was even more powerful because he was a virtual novelty: a proud gun owner in Hollywood. To be sure, the NRA enjoyed more celebrity support than ever. Heston's celebrity shootouts brought several glamorous stars to the NRA, including the actresses Kim Catrell and Mira Sorvino and the supermodel Beverly Johnson.[41] Furthermore, the "I am the NRA" campaign featured such celebrities as the musician Charlie Daniels, the basketball star Karl Malone, and the actor Tom Selleck. However, these notables could not possibly compete with celebrities who favored gun control, in terms of both celebrity exposure and sheer numbers. Matt Damon, Diane Keaton, Paul Newman, Dennis Quaid, and Michelle Pfeiffer all lent their names to various gun control efforts.

The NRA executive board could not have been more pleased with the actor's apparent relish for his new role. LaPierre and Hammer continued to build Heston's presidential credentials in NRA literature and successfully forced Knox out of the organization. In the March 1998 issue of *American Guardian,* the NRA's legislative magazine, LaPierre himself interviewed Heston. The two officers discussed the upcoming year with little doubt that Heston would win and highlighted the progress that the NRA had made since Heston had taken office. "On behalf of our members, let me thank you for all you've done so far," LaPierre praised, in an obvious effort to campaign for Heston and to reconcile any lingering divisions. Indeed, Knox malcontents attempted to discredit Heston by building a Web site documenting the support the actor had lent Johnson for the 1968 Gun Control Act. These detractions did little to hurt Heston, however, since he had the support of the majority of the board. In fact, before the elections, the outgoing president, Marion Hammer, argued that "spiteful mean-spirited internal divisiveness" was weakening the organization. "It must stop," she implored.[42] Hammer's demand, however, was almost unnecessary. Heston won by a landslide, and any lingering divisions subsequently faded away. Knox's supporters gradually lost their seats on the board and eventually were forced out entirely. Heston's leadership was, thereafter, undisputed.

THE PRESS GENERALLY REACTED NEGATIVELY TO Heston's election to the NRA presidency at the 1998 annual meeting, but it undermined these condemnations by insistently drawing parallels between the actor and the prophet Moses. Heston gave twenty-nine interviews the day he assumed his new office, and almost every journalist referred to his iconic status as the biblical figure. For example, Margot Hornblower focused on Heston's long-standing image of hard-nosed masculinity. She tried to deconstruct that ideal, portraying the aging actor as a failing old man who romanticized the past and simplified the present. However, the layout of the article undercut Hornblower's argument by listing "Chuck Heston's Commandments" under a picture of the actor as Moses. LaPierre, for his part, relished such references, telling NRA members that, while their organization had been "demonized" by the media, "now Moses is here to set the record straight."[43]

In his inaugural address as NRA president, Heston presented a four-point agenda that focused on unifying the membership, entering the political mainstream, electing progun candidates, and educating future generations. Heston demanded membership unity by dramatically demanding personal accountability. He asked: "Have you come here to celebrate our freedom, or to divide this membership? Have you come here to show the world our unity, or to splinter it?" He did not intend for those to be rhetorical questions: "Because before we go any further, I want to know who's with me . . . and who's agin' me. Before I take one more step on this march into the next century though, I really need to know." He challenged the members out of their seats: "So I want those who stand with me—please, right now, rise from your chairs, take to your feet and show me, show the world—STAND WITH ME." While Heston still encouraged debate and dissent, he demanded: "After you've had your free speech . . . and the votes are counted, get together or get out of the way!" Achieving unity, Heston advised, was the most important goal for the organization to accomplish.[44]

Unity was the necessary precursor to Heston's second goal—asserting the NRA's "rightful place in the mainstream of American political debate." "Too many gun owners think we've wandered into some fringe of American life and left them behind," he lamented. He blamed this development on the cultural changes that he had witnessed since the 1960s: "I can tell you why they think that: Year after year of lie after lie by the press and the politicians who are hook-line-and-sinker stupid about lock-stock-and-barrel freedom!" Heston did not intend to compromise the NRA's principles and values in making the organization more mainstream. Instead, he planned to change the terms of the debate so that the mainstream would be more receptive to the NRA agenda. The first step in transforming a hostile culture, Heston believed, was reasserting NRA pride. The NRA could not change the terms of the debate if its energy was consumed by infighting. However, if they spoke "with one, proud, prudent voice," NRA members could effectively defend their traditions and recast the national discourse on guns to include "everything shooting used to be—a wholesome sport and an American tradition, proudly practiced in clubs and campuses and countrysides, a rite of passage treated with reverence and respect."[45]

Heston advised that his third goal, electing progun candidates, required a proudly unified membership willing to embark on the campaign trail and to fight the culture war if necessary. No office was too small for the NRA to target. City, state, and national offices all demanded the close eye of the lobby, Heston cautioned, especially since a gun control advocate occupied the White House. The NRA could not elect like-minded officials simply by walking into a polling booth, Heston warned. Electing progun candidates required a membership willing to discuss its agenda frankly and to fight for both the gun policies and the traditional cultural values for which the NRA stood. Heston's fourth goal, "to educate America's children," could be achieved with nothing less.[46] This four-point plan roused the NRA, and the culture war became an integral aspect of the organization's agenda.

Heston emboldened the NRA membership with his calls for prideful responsibility, yet his predilection for theatrical rhetoric weakened his message at times. While he often spoke in moderate, almost conversational tones, at points he sounded as if he were reprising the role of an epic movie with lines such as, "And believe me, your voice rumbles like thunder," or, "Economically we revel in the fat of the land. Yet spiritually we hunger."[47] One reason that such theatricality compromised Heston's message was that it allowed his critics to dismiss him as vacuous. Another was that his dramatics made it easier for the press to reduce his rhetoric to reversionary sound bites. Finally, his frequent references to "parting some waters" and driving chariots could mistakenly convey that he was living in a romanticized past and that perhaps the policies he favored were tainted by such romanticism. In reality, Heston was not compulsively wrapped up in memories of his film career. He certainly did not confuse his movie roles with reality or concoct stories to suit his purposes. However, he suspected that his audience could not escape the reliquary of epics past, and he acted accordingly. After all, he had enjoyed an exceptionally successful career with his epic roles, and he willingly continued such histrionic posturing for the NRA.

Heston's dramatics made for stirring speeches, and his methods perfectly complemented the NRA leadership. His presidency maintained the

NRA's traditional organization, which was similar to a parliamentary system. While the first vice president, Wayne LaPierre, worked as the chief executive of the lobby and assumed responsibility for its daily operation, he remained largely behind the scenes. As head administrator, he planned the NRA's direction in terms of policy and relied on Heston's personal charisma to sell the organization's goals. As ceremonial leader, Heston brought credibility, name recognition, and superior speaking ability to his office, contributions unmatched by any of his predecessors. Even if the NRA did not necessarily receive more favorable media attention during Heston's tenure, the organization garnered more press coverage and exposure because of this legendary actor with a flair for dramatic oration.

Heston unabashedly boasted of his success in carrying out his professed goal of healing the rifts plaguing the NRA. Moreover, the behavior of NRA members themselves indicated a strong sense of unity in the organization after he assumed the presidency. They reelected him to four more consecutive terms. The gun lobby actually changed its bylaws to accommodate the wishes of its members. Until Heston, no president was allowed to serve more than two terms, but his towering popularity allowed for a change in organizational tradition. Furthermore, audiences at NRA rallies reacted much more enthusiastically to Heston than to the other NRA officers, with women shrieking, "We love you!" on occasion. Throughout the course of his presidency, Heston even encountered fans who named their sons Charlton in his honor.[48]

Heston was also relatively successful in moving the NRA closer to the mainstream, thereby strengthening it. The success of two programs in particular enhanced the NRA's image. One was the "Eddie Eagle" gun safety program, designed to educate preschool and elementary school students about proper behavior when around firearms. Started in 1988, the program's basic premise revolved around a cartoon eagle who advised kids when they encountered guns: "Stop! Don't touch. Leave the area. Tell an adult." Over the years, the program gained in popularity and won the endorsement of hundreds of police departments nationwide, the National Sheriffs' Association, and even the media. When the Violence Policy Center (VPC) derided Eddie Eagle as "Joe Camel with Feathers," newspapers across the country defended the NRA. Journalists such as Stephen Chapman of the *Chicago Tribune* condemned the VPC for mistakenly assuming that all NRA efforts were conspiratorial in nature. "If the NRA came up with a cure for cancer, I'm sure the VPC would denounce it as a cynical effort to distract attention from gun deaths," he wrote. By 2002, Eddie Eagle had reached over 15 million children, and the program's focus on safety improved the NRA's public image.[49]

The NRA also earned accolades for its involvement with the Project Exile program, an undertaking first implemented in Richmond, Virginia, in February 1997 in response to exploding gun violence in the city. Project Exile had been crafted by the U.S. Attorney's Office in Richmond, but the NRA did provide initial funding for the program and, impressed with its results, adopted it as its own. The logic behind Project Exile was revealed in its name. That is, criminals caught in possession of a gun during the commission of a crime would face federal prosecution and a mandatory sentence of five to ten years in a federal prison—in other words, "exiled" from the community. Project Exile's success lay in its ability to deter criminals with the prospect of harsh punishment, an approach recommended in the NRA platform. The NRA usually favored local initiatives over federal involvement, but, when it came to crime control, the gun lobby made an exception. Mandatory sentences meant that criminals could not bargain with local judges and would be sent to faraway federal prisons, inconvenient for personal visitation. Project Exile's effectiveness also relied on its ability to keep the public informed of its goals and methods through a widespread advertising campaign. The program's success indicated that the methods of crime control advocated by the NRA were legitimate and, thus, improved the organization's public image.[50]

Over the course of the next year, both the NRA and its ideological rival, Handgun Control, praised the success of Project Exile. Indeed, between November 1997 and May 1998, homicide rates in Richmond dropped an astounding 65 percent from the same period the previous year. A number of criminals admitted that they no longer carried firearms, even when drug trafficking, because they did not want to be "exiled."[51] Sarah Brady, James Brady's wife and a vocal proponent of gun control since her husband's shooting, and Wayne LaPierre both congratulated the coordinators of Project Exile for curtailing violent assaults and creating an anticrime culture in Richmond. However, while Handgun Control continued to advocate gun control legislation, the NRA worked to expand Project Exile into a nationwide program and to build on it. The NRA believed that punishment should be the cornerstone of all crime control programs but that other measures, such as community building, could act as "carrots" in addition to the "sticks" of programs such as Project Exile.

Heston served as Project Exile's chief spokesperson, focusing first on gaining interest in the program at the local level and then on securing funds to implement it. When Heston was elected NRA president at the organization's annual meeting in Philadelphia in 1998, he challenged that city's mayor, Edward Rendell, to adopt Project Exile. Even though Rendell had previously sought gun control measures, he was willing to discuss the program with Heston. In fact, the NRA publicist Bill Powers says that Heston was "critical" in winning Rendell's cooperation because of the "celebrity and media attention he brought to the table." Powers testifies that Rendell was "very interested in meeting with Heston and making it a press event." Heston and Rendell agreed to work together to seek funding for a Project Exile in the "city of brotherly love." After Congress authorized $1.5 million to allow Philadelphia to serve as a test case for Exile, the NRA donated an additional $25,000. Furthermore, Heston held a fundraising event with city business executives, again using his celebrity status for Project Exile's gain.[52]

Then President Bill Clinton's and the NRA's competing philosophies on how best to prevent crime hampered efforts to nationalize Project Exile. Clinton favored more gun control measures, leading the NRA to attack both the president's policies and his character. Heston singled out Clinton in his attacks against the permissive liberal culture as early as his first presidential address to the NRA. "Mr. Clinton, sir," he bellowed, "America didn't trust you with our health care system, America didn't trust you with gays in the military, America doesn't trust you with our twenty-one-year-old daughters, and we sure Lord don't trust you with our guns!"[53] He even lent his support to the Republican movement against the president when the controversy surrounding Clinton's alleged affair with the White House intern Monica Lewinsky grew more feverish.

Heston's volatile relationship with Clinton further deteriorated in the spring of 1999 after two teenage gunmen killed a dozen fellow students, and then themselves, at Columbine High School in Littleton, Colorado. The NRA needed to be infinitely careful in the shooting's aftermath, especially because its annual meeting was to be held in nearby Denver the following week. Unfortunately, Heston committed an uncharacteristic gaffe the day after the shooting, announcing: "If there had been even one armed guard in the school, he could have saved a lot of lives and perhaps ended the whole thing instantly." What he didn't realize was that Columbine High School did, indeed, employ such protection. The guard had even exchanged gunfire with the attackers but still failed to prevent the tragedy. Such an obvious error did not bode well for the annual meeting, but the NRA shortened the affair from three days to one, observed a moment of silence for the victims, and reiterated the need to prosecute criminals. The NRA emerged from Denver relatively unscathed, despite the presence of protesters who gathered outside the meeting as well as several bomb threats to the hotel at which it was held.[54] However, the Columbine massacre did allow Clinton to accuse the NRA of fostering a gun culture that promoted violent behavior.

Furthermore, the tragedy prompted Clinton to propose a new gun control legislative package, which Heston opposed with a vengeance. Clinton's comprehensive legislation included raising the legal age for handgun possession from eighteen to twenty-one; holding parents liable for the criminal acts of their children; halting the importation of all high-capacity ammunition clips; limiting handgun purchases to one per month; and requiring gun safety locks, background checks at gun shows, and a three-day waiting period for all gun purchases. Heston found the proposed legislation maddening in light of the fact that Project Exile received federal support in only one U.S. city. He publicly questioned the need for more laws, accusing Clinton of not enforcing "the two thousand gun laws already on the books." "The problem is not the availability of arms," he continued, "but the government's poor record in prosecuting both juveniles and adults."[55] Heston grounded his opposition to Clinton's gun control package on the traditional argument that he and the NRA had long maintained: the need to enforce existing laws, not pass new ones.

Despite his previous efforts to present himself as a moderate, Heston did not hesitate in using fiery rhetoric against the president. He believed that he had the credibility and the statistics to substantiate his charges against the Clinton White House. In a House subcommittee meeting on criminal justice, Heston displayed his demagoguery when citing the findings of a study conducted by Syracuse University revealing that federal prosecutions of gun crimes dropped 44 percent during the Clinton administration. "Why does the President ask for more federal gun laws if he's not going to enforce the ones we have? Why does the President ask for more police if he's not going to prosecute their arrests?" he questioned. He continued his warning with characteristic drama: "This deadly charade is killing people and surely will kill more. When political hot air is turning into cold blood . . . when duplicitous spin becomes lethal . . . somebody's got to speak up." When Clinton continued to push his legislative package and gun control organizations enthusiastically rallied behind him, an increasingly frustrated Heston feared that more Americans would support the president. He appeared in an NRA ad forthrightly questioning the president's credibility: "Mr. Clinton, when what you say is wrong, it's a mistake. When you know it's wrong, that's a lie." Meanwhile, on ABC's Sunday morning news program *This Week,* LaPierre accused Clinton of being "willing to accept a certain level of killing to further his political agenda."[56]

The intemperate rhetoric of its leaders left the NRA again vulnerable to charges of extremism and certainly did not prompt Clinton to earmark funds for the NRA program. Nevertheless, Heston's testimony to Congress and publicizing of Project Exile did bear some fruit. In April 2000, the House of Representatives passed, 358–60, a bill allocating block grants totaling $100 million to fund Project Exile in communities across the country. The Senate, however, did not take up the bill. Meanwhile, Heston and the NRA continued to peddle Project Exile at the local level. Colorado and Virginia both received NRA donations to adopt it as a statewide program. By March 2000, the NRA had donated $3 million to various Project Exile efforts across the nation.[57] However, it was still struggling to achieve national funding for the program.

The NRA then set its sights on the upcoming presidential election, believing that a friend in the White House would result in victories for Project Exile and other gun-related legislation. During the 2000 national election campaign, the NRA endorsed the Republican candidate, Texas Governor George W. Bush, over Vice President Al Gore. Even though Bush kept his distance from the NRA, he was favored by the organization because of his progun record. Bush had signed a concealed-and-carry bill into law while governor of Texas and did not include any calls for gun control during his campaign. Furthermore, he had allocated $1.6 million in state funds to implement Texas Exile in 1999, and, during one presidential debate, he touted the merits of the program and indicated that he would initiate it at the federal level. As vice president to Clinton, whose popularity ratings were at record highs, and with a strong economy in his favor, Gore should have beat Bush by a strong margin. However, it was Gore's very affiliation with the Clinton White House and his calls for handgun licensing and registration that the NRA used to attack the Tennessee native. The NRA proudly declared political war on Gore and elected Heston to an unprecedented third term to lead the charge.[58]

The NRA amassed its resources to defeat Gore, utilizing three tactics: rhetoric, money, and Heston. The agenda of the NRA's 129th annual meeting in May 2000 was largely devoted to condemning the vice president. The NRA leadership accused Gore of trying to disarm the country and repeatedly called him a liar. Referring to the Million Mom March, held only a few days earlier in Washington, DC, in favor of gun control, LaPierre lashed out: "It wasn't a grass-roots rally but a Gore campaign rally, scripted and coached by the White House. It wasn't about safety. It was about Gore for president. But Mr. Gore, you're going to find out it's not smart to lie to mom." Representative J. C. Watts of Oklahoma recast Franklin D. Roosevelt's famous promise and told the crowd: "The Vice President has nothing to offer but fear itself." ILA Director James J. Baker prophesied that Gore would "slander" NRA members as "gun-toting, knuckle-dragging, bloodthirsty maniacs who stand in the way of a safer America. Will you remain silent?"[59] The

NRA barraged the public with this same rhetoric in a series of half-hour progun commercials, aimed especially at twelve key states, including Michigan, Missouri, and Pennsylvania, where congressional seats were on the line. The campaign worked to discredit Gore among NRA members and those voters sympathetic to the organization.

The NRA's aggressive tactics would have been impossible without substantial financing. The NRA pledged $15 million to fuel this massive political drive. It used part of this capital to communicate with its members through its traditional mailings and its Web site. It overhauled its Web site to include news reports as well as detailed information regarding every congressional district across the country. It also used some of the money for advertising. LaPierre admitted to a campaign budget of $1 million for television commercials alone. The NRA used the rest of its campaign funds to contribute record amounts of "soft-money donations" (money to party committees and not particular candidates) to Republican and Democratic committees and to the PACs of gun-friendly candidates. The NRA hoped that its well-financed campaign would divide the Democrats over the gun issue in what was the organization's most partisan campaign to date. It maintained good relations with about fifty conservative congressional Democrats, collectively known as the Blue Dog Coalition, but the gun lobby's general message was that the national Democratic Party had lost touch with rural, conservative values.[60] The NRA attempted to split the Democrats while delivering over 80 percent of its contributions to Republican candidates.

The NRA's biggest weapon in its election-year campaign was Heston himself, the celebrity officer who could be relied on to motivate voters at campaign rallies and through commercials. Heston puddle-jumped across the country as the star of NRA-sponsored events for local, state, and national candidates. He far surpassed his fellow NRA officers in drawing applauding crowds, and his flawless speeches motivated audiences to support NRA-endorsed candidates. Most of the NRA's commercials also featured Heston, who attacked Gore and the Democratic Party as a whole. In one such ad, Heston called the Clinton administration "the most antigun White House in history," warning that there would be only more gun control legislation with Gore at the helm. "From antigun mayors and marchers to gun-hating celebrities and politicians, they're almost all Democrats," he continued. "Tell me: why are so few Democrats willing to defend constitutional freedom?" Heston's heavy and personalized campaigning may have provided the extra push that Bush needed to win the election. The journalist John Judis noted that voters in swing states, such as West Virginia, found Bush appealing because of his opposition to gun control and environmental regulation. Bill Clinton said that his administration's advocacy of gun control measures had cost Gore "at least five states" where the NRA had "a decisive influence."[61]

After the 2000 election, the political climate generally became more favorable to the NRA agenda. One journalist observed that Congress "seems entirely cowed by the NRA's clout." The gun lobby had little reason to fear that Bush would initiate gun control legislation or that any gun control organization could rally enough support in Congress for such measures. In fact, the U.S. Fifth Circuit Court of Appeals dealt a setback to gun control activists, at least temporarily, with its ruling that gun ownership was an individual right, not one confined to the state militias. Furthermore, after the attacks on September 11, 2001, in which terrorists killed thousands of Americans by crashing hijacked planes into the World Trade Center towers and the Pentagon, individual gun sales rose dramatically. Apparently, many Americans concluded that terrorists could strike anytime, anywhere, and, therefore, they needed self-protection.[62] Nevertheless, some members of Congress pushed for more controls on gun shows and for ballistic fingerprinting, which would allow the government to establish a national database of the unique traces that a gun leaves on its bullets. This database would allow authorities to trace a bullet back to the person who originally bought the gun. However, neither of these proposals enjoyed enough support to advance in Congress.

Instead, Project Exile was the program that won out on Capitol Hill. It served as the basis for President Bush's $550 million Project Safe Neighborhoods initiative in May 2001. Bush noted the success of Project Exile in Philadelphia and Richmond in reducing gun-related crimes. However, an unacceptable rate of violence still plagued those cities as well as the nation at large, the president warned, and he expanded the scope of Project Exile. Project Safe Neighborhoods was designed to make Project Exile a national initiative, illegal gun ownership resulting in hard time for criminals across the country. The president's program also requires law enforcement officials at the local, state, and federal level to work together.[63] The initiation of Project Safe Neighborhoods can be considered a legislative victory for the NRA, an achievement largely attributable to Heston's efforts to win support for both Project Exile and the NRA itself.

A different political environment existed during the 2002 midterm elections, in which the NRA enjoyed even more credibility and influence than it had in 2000. In fact, congressional and gubernatorial hopefuls actually competed for NRA support in the fall elections. After Heston endorsed incumbent Democratic Governor Don Siegelman in his contest against the Republican challenger, Bob Riley, in Alabama, the disappointed state Republican Party chair sulked to the press, accusing Siegelman of engaging in "a gross manipulation" of the aging Heston and coercing him to sign a prewritten letter of endorsement. Those candidates previously affiliated with gun control groups tried to downplay this relationship. For example, in Missouri, the Republican senatorial candidate, Jim Talent, had already won the unqualified endorsement of the NRA, but the Democratic incumbent, Jean Carnahan, attempted to outflank the NRA anyway by hosting a skeet-shooting holiday in the state's rural and traditionally conservative Bootheel region. Carnahan's campaign staff published pictures of the candidate in camouflage, distributed "Hunters for Jean" bumper stickers, and bragged that she had won a shooting award in college. Meanwhile, Talent reassured Missouri voters of his outdoors credentials, citing his love of bass fishing. These shenanigans led one journalist to term the Missouri contest a "Bubba-rama." He wondered whether Talent's and Carnahan's attempts to capture the NRA vote would lead to similar struggles to win over the NASCAR, Demolition Derby, catfish noodling, and Skoal constituencies.[64] Over the course of his presidency, Heston transformed the NRA from a political pariah into a sought-after force in electoral politics.

Despite its electoral and legislative gains, few Hollywood luminaries grew to accept the NRA, and the entertainment industry's involvement in the gun control controversy produced a new level of celebrity activism. For example, the comedian and television talk show host Rosie O'Donnell grew more shrill in her denouncements of the NRA over the course of Heston's presidency. O'Donnell often used her talk show to express her preference for gun control, a sentiment that culminated in a televised confrontation between her and a guest, Tom Selleck, a popular actor and an NRA member. Selleck appeared on the show to publicize a movie, but he found that his host was more interested in his politics. Selleck had just filmed a commercial for the NRA and willingly discussed his attitudes about gun control and his reaction to the Columbine tragedy. However, he refused to debate specific gun bills or the NRA's stance on such legislation. O'Donnell pressured Selleck and complained: "You can't say 'I will not take responsibility for anything the NRA represents' if you're doing an ad for the NRA. You can't do that." Selleck objected: "I didn't come on your show to have a debate. I came on your show to plug a movie. . . . This is absurd." The tone of the conversation continued to deteriorate, and Selleck finally told O'Donnell not to talk about gun control until after he left. The incident made it clear that a new type of adversarial celebrity activism had developed by the late 1990s. Celebrities were feeling so comfortable discussing their politics that O'Donnell willingly berated guests who disagreed with her. This incident indicated that celebrities were willing to aggressively enter the political debate and make it personal. Other examples of this aggression include the director Spike Lee's remark in 1999 that he wanted to shoot Charlton Heston and the actor George Clooney's willingness in 2003 to make fun of Heston's recent announcement that he had Alzheimer's disease. When pressed about the comments, Clooney flippantly remarked: "I don't care. Charlton Heston is the head of the National Rifle Association. He deserves whatever anyone says about him."[65]

Nor did the press appear any more open to Heston's message at the end of his presidency than at the beginning. The media and the Hollywood community praised *Bowling for Columbine,* a 2002 film directed by Michael Moore denouncing America's gun culture and the NRA's contribution to it. Moore condemned the NRA's reverence for guns as responsible for crimes committed with firearms and was extremely insensitive in his handling of Heston, who very likely was suffering from early stages of Alzheimer's disease when he met with Moore. Moore ambushed Heston during what the actor believed would be a friendly meeting at his home. Heston walked out of the interview, but a recent hip replacement actually confined his stride to a shuffle. Moore let the camera linger on Heston's painful gait, then left a framed photograph of a gun victim on Heston's stoop, insinuating that Heston was responsible for her death. The film won the category of best documentary at the 2003 Academy Awards. Furthermore, the media was especially hard on the NRA after two deadly snipers terrorized the Washington, DC, area and killed over fifteen people. One editorial declared that Heston's trademark cry "from my cold, dead hands" was already a "stale harangue" and that, in light of the Beltway sniper, his exhortation had become "even harder to stomach."[66] As these examples indicate, even though Heston had demanded improved press coverage in 1997, most media outlets demonstrated little sympathy for the NRA.

Despite the obstinacy of Hollywood and the press, the NRA enjoyed large membership gains under Heston. The gun lobby boasted a membership of over 4 million at the end of his presidency, and, in 2002, the NRA teamed with NASCAR on a "Drive for Five" million members. The gun lobby received new endorsements from such celebrities as the country singer Reba McEntire and the retired football star Troy Aikman. Moreover, Rosie O'Donnell became less vocal on the gun control debate after it was revealed that one of her bodyguards had applied for a license to carry a concealed weapon. The revelation damaged her reputation as a voice for gun control because it appeared that she did not believe that such restrictions applied to her own celebrity lifestyle. A delighted NRA continued to make an example of O'Donnell's "hypocrisy" in its campaign literature. These developments indicated that the NRA could eventually earn widespread acceptance by the American mainstream.

THE NRA AND HESTON ENJOYED A symbiotic relationship during the actor's presidential tenure. Heston revived the NRA, and the organization grew markedly stronger because of his leadership. At the same time, the national forum to which Heston had access allowed him to become more politically active than ever. His establishment of ARENA PAC in 1996 had already indicated that he wanted to campaign for conservative candidates, and an NRA office allowed him to do so with striking success. Likewise, his victory over Time Warner suggested that he was prepared to go to battle in the culture war. Being president of a national organization guaranteed him a larger audience to which he could expound on cultural matters more frequently than perhaps he would have otherwise.

The NRA recruited Heston because of his reputation as a politically active and conservative moral leader. Indeed, his celebrity status strengthened the organization on a variety of levels. Furthermore, his presidency paved the way for more celebrities to inject themselves into the gun debate. However, those celebrities usually called for gun control, not gun rights. Heston retired from the NRA presidency in 2003, and other Hollywood luminaries were poised to dismantle his legacy. In subsequent years, it is possible that the NRA might lose influence because of the plethora of leftist celebrities who felt more comfortable entering into the political arena because Heston had done so first. But Heston hoped to win the culture war so that his ideas and traditions would endure, and it is in this contest that Heston fully blossomed as a visceral neoconservative.

CHAPTER EIGHT

CULTURAL CANNON

IN 1991, THE BERLIN WALL FELL, SYMBOLIZING THE END OF THE COLD War. Anticommunism had been the principle concern of the neoconservatives for half a century; now that the Soviet Union had been defeated, however, the neocons had no intention of fading from the public scene. In fact, they became increasingly prominent as they focused more specifically on American culture. Irving Kristol made his intentions clear in 1993. "So far from having ended, my cold war has increased in intensity, as sector after sector of American life has been ruthlessly corrupted by the liberal ethos," he warned. "Now that the other 'Cold War' is over, the real cold war has begun." Five years later, Charlton Heston made a similar declaration. "I have come to realize that a cultural war is raging across our land . . . storming our values, assaulting our freedoms, killing our self-confidence in who we are and what we believe, where we come from," he told the Free Congress Foundation at its twentieth anniversary gala.[1] Heston and Kristol, as well as a number of other neoconservatives, would become the chief spokespersons in the war over America's cultural values.

Heston and the rest of the neocons came to their conclusions from similar experiences. They had been defending bourgeois values as early as the 1960s when their standards were first challenged by the upheavals of the counterculture. Heston, however, offered a simplistic explanation for having come to this realization: after being a "point man" for the National Rifle Association (NRA), he described his suddenly becoming a "moving target for pundits who've called me everything from 'ridiculous' and 'duped' to a 'brain-injured, senile, crazy old man.'" These accusations allegedly led him to understand that "guns are not the only issue, and I am not the only target." "It is much, much bigger than that," he reasoned.[2] Such an account obscured Heston's longtime frustration with and activism against creeping liberalism. His refusal to accept film roles with an antimilitary bent, his concern over an inflated National Endowment for the Arts (NEA) bureaucracy, and his strong stance against Ed Asner's liberal allies at the Screen Actors Guild all indicated his early willingness to stand firm in the culture war. The notion of the politically savvy Heston being shocked by the negative press attention that he received on assuming office at the NRA was simply not plausible.

It was likely, however, that, with a high-profile leadership position at the NRA, Heston welcomed the opportunity to systematically articulate his beliefs. No longer having to rely on truncated press releases or superficial publicity pieces to air his complaints, he could now deliver full speeches to large audiences and converse with journalists over specific policy matters. And he did not talk just about guns. He considered gun rights to be only a small aspect of a larger debate and spoke considerably less about the right to bear arms than about the culture war in general. As the aging Heston's film career became limited to cameo roles, he spent far more time waging the culture war than acting. His autobiography *In the Arena* (1995) and subsequent book *To Be a Man: Letters to My Grandson* (1997) largely revolved around issues elevated by America's cultural divide. He devoted his book *The Courage to Be Free* (2000) solely to cultural issues and delivered numerous speeches in order to recruit "soldiers" to fight the war.

Heston addressed a multitude of topics when articulating his beliefs but consistently focused on three themes: the role of elites, the individual in the community, and the pursuit of happiness. At the heart of this discussion was what he called "a clash between the morally principled and the unprincipled."[3] Heston considered himself one of the principled and held steadfastly to his values when bashing elitism, explaining his model for a moral society, and focusing on the pursuit, not the guarantee, of happiness.

SCHOLARS AND POLITICAL PUNDITS disagreed over whether a culture war was really taking place in America. While some denied such a serious rift, the neocons did not. They unequivocally believed that a culture war was in progress. In fact, they accused those who opposed their paradigm of engaging in the very relativism that they believed to be so damaging. As Robert Bork asserted: "About the fact of rot and decadence there can be no dispute, except from those who deny that such terms have meaning, and who are, for that reason, major contributors to rot and decadence."[4]

Husband and wife Irving Kristol and Gertrude Himmelfarb wrote considerably on the subject of America's cultural schism—how it came about and its overall effect on society. According to Himmelfarb, the bohemian values that had been percolating quietly since the end of the nineteenth century exploded in the 1960s and eventuated a number of important movements. Racial, sexual, technological, demographic, political, economic, and psychological changes all reflected and affected the counterculture, fostering a revolution that rejected established institutions, traditional authorities, and conventional modes of thought and behavior. "Thus the counterculture, intended to liberate everyone from the stultifying influence of 'bourgeois values,' also liberated a good many people from those values—virtues, as they were once called—that had a stabilizing, socializing, and moralizing effect on society," Himmelfarb concluded. In other words, in attempting to loosen up American society, the counterculture had gone too far, severely damaging some of America's most honored standards. Kristol likened the process to a nervous breakdown: "Something important happened to us during that period—something which, even as we recover from it, will profoundly affect the rest of our lives. No one who has ever had a nervous breakdown is ever quite the same afterwards, no matter how pleased the doctor may be with his condition."[5]

While some Americans celebrated the bohemian ascent, others bemoaned its effects and its seeming relation to America's moral decline. According to Himmelfarb, Americans found themselves separated not by race or class or any of the other customary divisions. Instead, they were divided into two cultures marked by objective moral and cultural values on one side and relativist "anything goes" beliefs on the other. That cultural divide affected the public debate on a number of issues, including school choice, welfare, sex education, gay rights, affirmative action, and gun control. The degree to which individual liberty should be retained and what the building blocks of moral society should be were particularly at issue.[6] Only at its most extreme would she label the rift a *war*, but, even among the varying degrees of acquiescence and resistance, Himmelfarb believed that America was fragmented and polarized along moral and cultural divides. Although Himmelfarb was more elegant in presentation and more sophisticated in research, she and Heston reached similar conclusions.

Himmelfarb, Heston, and the rest of the neocons also advocated a similar solution—the politics of ideas—to overcome America's incipient moral depravity. Himmelfarb pointed out that politics, as "repositories, transmitors, even the creators of values," were reflective of and instrumental to cultural change.[7] Heston particularly took this notion to heart. As president of the NRA, he used his position to push for legislative and cultural change. He argued that gun legislation could promote a certain culture, one that promoted individual liberty but also punished harshly those who abused their freedoms. Furthermore, he encouraged members of the NRA to extol gun rights in cultural terms. The NRA increasingly promoted the upholding of the Second Amendment as reflecting a certain lifestyle—one that respected tradition, individuality, responsibility, and masculinity, among other virtues. In doing so, it purposely attempted to distinguish itself from the liberal America that coddled criminals, shirked responsibility, and elevated group rights over individual rights. The NRA paradigm made America look very polarized indeed.

Some scholars denied that society was so divided. For instance, the sociologist Alan Wolfe interviewed two hundred middle-class Americans and determined that, while a culture war was taking place, it was "one being fought primarily by intellectuals, *not by Americans themselves*." However, a number of problems beset Wolfe's study. His sample was too small to make such a definitive statement. Furthermore, Wolfe found that many middle-class Americans thought that they needed to be almost excessively tolerant, a belief that often led to ambivalence on issues such as feminism and the family. It is exactly this lack of conviction that the neocons mourned. Wolfe even admitted: "In our narcissistic preoccupation with ourselves, we are ignoring the important duty of transmitting to the next generation respect for virtues that will enable it to lead, not just self-fulfilling lives, but also meaningful ones." Neoconservatives ruefully agreed. But they did not agree with Wolfe's solution. Not wanting to push his virtues too forcefully, Wolfe offered the nonbinding "Ten Suggestions" as a replacement for the "Ten Commandments."[8]

Replacing the Ten Commandments was the last thing the neocons would have recommended, especially since they had consistently advocated the laws handed down by God to Moses as a good model for society. As early as the 1950s, the intellectual neocons drew from the Ten Commandments in their writings and would continue to do so throughout their careers. Kristol often tried to point to what he considered the absurdity of a liberal policy by juxtaposing it against rules that prohibited religious discourse in the public sphere. For example, he believed it outrageous that public school curriculums included "'sex education' that seems to encourage (or at least not discourage) teenage promiscuity" but that it was illegal for those same schools to "post the Ten Commandments in the classroom."[9] That Heston just happened to star as Moses in *The Ten Commandments* was no small coincidence and made his affinity with the neocons all the more compelling. Heston embraced his identification with Moses and Christianity even as late as 2000 with his dramatic video series *Charlton Heston Presents the Bible*. He enjoyed being associated with Moses not just because of the fame and fortune the role brought him but because of the religious standards and traditions that the prophet represented. The neocons believed that religious principles, especially those drawn from the Ten Commandments, needed to be defended from liberal hostility so that they could play a stronger role in the public sphere.

It was exactly Wolfe's type of complacency that the neocons detested, a complacency that, to them, was at the heart of the culture war. While Wolfe argued that the loss of distinction between right and wrong was not "necessarily a bad thing," the neoconservatives believed that excessive tolerance weakened America's moral fabric. Heston understood that Americans were preoccupied with the mundane details of raising families and making enough money to do so, and he lamented that middle America "should not have to go to war every morning for their values." Still, he considered reticence cowardly. He advised his audiences not to be "shamed into silence" but "to get some guts, stand on principle and lead [middle America] to victory in this cultural war."[10]

Like Wolfe, the political journalist David Brooks denied that a culture war split America. In a 2001 essay for the *Atlantic Monthly,* Brooks countered the notion that America was divided between two moral systems. He acknowledged that, indeed, the country was divided into an urban blue America and a rural red America, as indicated by the 2000 presidential election results: blue America voted for the Democrats, red America for the Republicans. However, Brooks did not consider these differences as polarizing as Heston did. He stated that the denizens of red America practiced "temperamental conservatism" by placing more value on being "agreeable, civil, and kind" than on winning a culture war against their neighbors. Instead, he argued, the real difference between red and blue America centered on "sensibility," or the "conception of the self." In red America, he found, there was enormous social pressure not to "put on airs," but, in blue America, status climbing was the norm. This difference, he contended, did not make for a fundamentally divided nation. Instead, he compared America to a high school cafeteria, the differences between the two sides being as important as those between the jocks and the nerds and the various other cliques.[11]

Again, Heston rejected such notions as temperamental conservatism and cafeteria-style culture. He believed that middle-class Americans could not vocalize their value systems because blue America ignored or intimidated them. Composed of elite urban professionals, blue America largely dominated the media, the nonprofit sector, and academe. Therefore, it exercised considerable cultural influence. Heston believed that the elites had twisted the grounds of debate so that anyone who opposed their policies was labeled as racist, sexist, or otherwise bigoted. Because of its control of America's institutions, Heston argued, blue America could ignore red America altogether or silence it by saddling its inhabitants with negative stereotypes.

Brooks admitted the power and inclinations of blue America in his book *Bobos in Paradise.* In this cultural study, he identified the new technocratic elite as the Bobo. The cultural combination of the 1960s bohemian and the 1980s yuppie, the Bobo merged artistic talent and capitalistic drive into one identity. Bobos did not represent highbrow snobbery like their WASPish bourgeois predecessors, who peaked culturally during the 1950s. Instead, they represented a "countercultural plutocracy" where humane principles, social peace, and organic living reigned supreme. Indeed, Bobos took pride in earning large salaries while performing jobs they loved in creative, communal environments. Because of their distinctive combination of values, they successfully absorbed both sides of the culture war, Brooks argued, extinguishing the old flames fueled by the excesses of 1960s radicalism and 1980s greed.[12]

Two problems plagued Brooks's attempt to lay the culture war to rest. First, Brooks contradicted his own thesis. The WASP elite of the immediate postwar era emphasized conspicuous consumption, moral objectivity, individualism, and freedom. A Bobo who valued "virtuous spending," moral relativism, community, and control indicated a dramatic shift to the left from the bourgeois order of the 1950s. The fact that the values of the country's elite shifted so dramatically in such a short amount of time left opportunity aplenty for dissatisfaction and dissent. Second, Brooks overlooked the significance of a new trend in American life that, indeed, challenged the Bobo: what the historian Bruce Schulman calls the "Southernization" of American life, a trend of which Heston and the NRA were an integral aspect. Not only did the Republican Party retake the South in the late 1960s, but evangelical Christianity, country music, and stock car racing swept the nation in the 1970s. In walked the "Bubba," a white social conservative who very likely owned a pickup truck, a gun, and a dog named Bud—otherwise known as a "redneck." Not that America's elites thought much about middle America, but, when they did, Brooks conceded, Bobos commonly assumed that those in "flyover country" were "racist and homophobic" and that, "when you see them at highway rest stops, they're often really fat and their clothes are too tight." The fundamentalist, rural redneck violated Bobo sensibility: hunting was an affront to its humane values, as were the rest of the Bubba's lifestyle patterns.

Clearly, the NRA was completely beyond the pale of Bobo respectability.[13] Therefore, Brooks dismissed the Bubba entirely. However, he underestimated the power of his Southern neighbor. Largely because of the efforts of the NRA, the Bubba constituted not a simple annoyance but a formidable challenge to the Bobo elite, and the struggle between the two constituted a culture war in progress.

One of the most significant consequences of the Bobo eclipse of the WASP was the change in the nature of America's elite. Whereas the bourgeois WASP had dominated the nation's cultural elite during the 1950s, the Bobo claimed that crown by the 1990s. In doing so, the Bobo established a preeminent set of values for the nation that contrasted with those personified by Heston. The actor pointedly based his discussion of the culture war on how to curtail the growing influence of the new elite.

Heston always prided himself on maintaining traditional standards of excellence: he arrived at work on time; he never called in sick; he consistently followed his mantra to do his best and keep his promises; he married his first sweetheart and remained a faithful husband; and he decided to "stand up and be counted" through active civic participation in the political arena. His choice of acting roles illustrated his admiration for the traditional exemplars of the standards he held dear. "I've played thirteen historical figures, three of them more than once, all either saints or presidents, geniuses or generals," he boasted. Heston performed numerous Shakespearean plays on stage. Additionally, he played such heroic characters as Cardinal Richelieu, Thomas Jefferson, Andrew Jackson, Moses, Michelangelo, and John the Baptist. Heston believed in heroes, and, when pressed for a sampling of his personal champions, he listed a virtual who's who of the Western canon. "Andrew Jackson. He was the first populist President. . . . He was also an extraordinary man. So was Jefferson, who I consider the only genius who has ever been in the White House," he explained. "[Laurence] Olivier, for the breadth of his talent. Shakespeare, Sir Thomas More, Michelangelo." Furthermore, Heston preferred to play characters, such as Ben-Hur, who were "conflicted heroes," suffering from moral and physical deficiencies. As the plot progressed, these characters overcame their flaws through newfound strength and eventually achieved moral and spiritual growth.[14]

Heston's reverence for traditional models of eminence was tested in the late 1960s when objective standards were challenged by the counterculture. Hippies, intellectuals, students, and other activists associated with the New Left often found the notion of excellence offensive because such a concept necessitated competition and, inevitably, some people and works fell short. Likewise, traditional thinking based on logic and reason fell into disrepute. Not only did such practical methods lack creativity and spontaneity, but they could also be destructive. Activists on the New Left, for instance, pointed out that the atomic bomb, capable of killing thousands of people, was a result of linear science. The counterculture rejected almost all middle-class norms. It discarded traditional Western religions in favor of Eastern mysticism. Casual sexual relationships, both homo- and heterosexual, were celebrated, while heterosexual monogamy was derisively deemed bourgeois. The nuclear family was considered a bore. The counterculture craved spontaneity and experimented with drugs, sex, and music to undergo new experiences. Despising the traditional virtues, artistic standards, and scholarly excellence that Heston so admired, the counterculture derided the actor as an "elitist." By the mid-1970s, the New Left counterculture effectively denigrated and discredited what was once regarded as normal and legitimate and glorified the abnormal and illegitimate.[15]

Heston fought to preserve standards of excellence over the course of two decades, but, in the meantime, the term *elitist* was inverted. For instance, during his attempt to establish the American Film Institute as a separate entity from the NEA in 1971, Heston was continually referred to by his opponents as an elitist. By 1978, he was exasperated with the term. In a House subcommittee meeting regarding a proposed White House conference on the arts, he exploded: "Every time you get into a discussion of the arts—when I was on the Council in the Arts, in testimonies of this kind—elitist comes up as a pejorative phrase and I'm getting bloody tired of it. As I said in my statement, art is nothing if not a search for the best." Finding "the best" necessitated establishing standards. Heston believed that the NEA could set those standards. By the mid-1990s, however, the concept of elitism reversed course. The 1960s countercultural idea that standards were inherently discriminatory had taken hold and had become the typical way of thinking in many sectors of American culture, including the National Council on the Arts. By the 1990s, Heston and other conservative critics had become those who complained about elitist norms. Heston pointedly declared: "Cultural war is fueled with one high octane vapor: elitism." That elitism, he elaborated, was based not on race or class but on "a point of view or certain social agenda" that emphasized antiestablishment views and narrow, politically correct interest groups.[16]

Concerns over the new elitism led the neocons to come to different conclusions about government funding of the arts. Most neocons agreed with Irving Kristol, who called the NEA a "mission impossible" and believed the government should discontinue its support of the organization. In a 1995 House committee hearing on appropriations for the NEA, the neoconservative allies Lynne Cheney, Edwin DeLattre, and William Bennett advocated that the government remove itself from the arts sector because of the elitism that Heston cited. For example, DeLattre recommended that the government discontinue the NEA because the funding served "a constituency within the arts rather than . . . the public." This self-appointed constituency, he complained, did not grant funds according to standards of excellence. Instead, it considered "federal funding as a virtual entitlement" and maintained a "preposterous and corrupting insistence that denying funds to any proposal in the arts amounts to censorship and abridgment of freedom of expression." Heston, however, testified in favor of continued funding. He believed that only a few of the NEA's many projects were controversial and that punishing the agency as a whole for those few projects by denying funding was unwarranted, especially as a withdrawal of funding would adversely affect any number of individual artists. He also felt strongly that the NEA actually boosted private support of the arts.[17] Although Heston frequently noted his dissatisfaction with the NEA, especially for its tendency to dilute artistic standards in favor of elitist political agendas, he continued to support the agency even as it became more controversial.

Heston accepted the fact that, because of the nature of its funding system, the NEA would never be able to control exactly what its grantees would later produce; however, a number of controversial projects in the 1980s and 1990s made the NEA a particularly easy mark for its foes. Art subsidized by the agency in its early years was sometimes attacked for its frivolity. For instance, in 1977, Ann Wilschulsky received a $6,025 grant for "Sculpting in Space," that is, flinging crepe paper out of an airplane. By the 1980s, other NEA grantees were questioned for their lack of decorum. In 1984, the NEA and the New York State Arts Council presented $204,930 and $73,370, respectively, to the Franklin Furnace of New York City. The Franklin Furnace then sponsored one show that included a feminist art exhibition entitled *The Second Coming*. Among other sexually explicit material, this exhibit included a photograph entitled *Jesus Sucks* in which a woman breastfed an infant. The year 1988 marked the high point of controversy for the NEA because of the notorious photographers Robert Mapplethorpe and Andres Serrano, both recipients of agency funding. Robert Mapplethorpe's *The Perfect Moment* included a self-portrait of the photographer with a bullwhip protruding from his rectum and a photograph of one man urinating into another man's mouth. Andres Serrano's famed *Piss Christ*—a photograph of Christ on a cross in a vat of the artist's own urine—also drew a media firestorm.[18]

As Congress deliberated over future funding for the NEA, Heston vocalized his support of the agency and used the controversies over Serrano and Mapplethorpe to call for the revival of the standards that the new elitists had discarded. However, the notorious exhibits resulted in a genuine crisis for the agency, and its future seemed shakier than ever. President George H. W. Bush organized a task force to consider what projects the NEA should fund. The task force rejected any sort of loyalty oath or obscenity pledges, as proposed by Senator Jesse Helms of North Carolina, but said that the agency should respect the American people as its financiers. Heston echoed this call for responsibility when he urged the NEA to remember that its money came from the "taxpayer's pocket."[19]

After Congress reauthorized the NEA, the agency's most prominent problem continued to center on standards, which reflected the evolving concept of elitism. The NEA staff increasingly concentrated on democratizing art after Heston's tenure had expired. For example, in a speech to the

National Press Club in December 2000, NEA Chair Bill Ivey called for an "American Cultural Bill of Rights" that would especially target "the chronically poor, the alienated young, the defeated midlifers, and the estranged elderly." Ivey called for art of the "highest aesthetic quality" and observed that improved artistic tastes were already on the rise. He noted: "Michael Graves designs dishware for Target Stores. Martha Stewart crafts designer elements for Kmart. Hard-hatted workers in the Endowment's office building order double lattes." To Heston, construction workers indulging in gourmet coffee hardly reflected improved artistic quality. Ivey's praise indicated that the NEA's standards had plummeted and that the Bobo elite had emerged victorious. Indeed, the neoconservative journalist George Will criticized Ivey's policy, terming it "the soft bigotry of low expectations." The complete democratization of art, he worried, would result in an unclassifiable form. Will argued: "The 'democratic' spirit . . . produces this exquisitely circular reasoning: Art is whatever an artist says it is, and an artist is anyone who produces art. So the word 'art' has become a classification that no longer classifies, there being nothing it excludes."[20] Heston deplored these relativist standards and attacked them as the product of a perverse elite.

It is this same type of corrupted elitism that, in Heston's mind, allowed art to fall prey to the political agendas of the so-called correct interest groups, as defined by the Bobo. One journalist described his visit to the Whitney Museum of American Art as a "P.C. Show" that divided the exhibits into categories of good and bad according to politics. The visitors were required to wear buttons reading, "I can't image ever wanting to be white," which set the tone of the exhibit. The show's "good art" included works featuring women, nonwhites, homosexuals, transvestites, gang members, people with AIDS, and gays in the military. "Bad art" included subjects and/or ideas that Heston celebrated. Americanism, straight white men, family, religion, hierarchies, lipstick (on women), and penises not attached to gay men were all considered expressions of the white-male dominance so detested by the artistic elite. Heston noticed the elitist effect on American films as well. As opposed to the "conflicted hero" that he had enjoyed playing, the "antihero" had risen to preeminence. The newly popular character was one who was devoid of strength and conviction and who failed to rehabilitate himself over the course of the movie. "Instead, our 'hero,'" Heston remarked, "either sinks deeper into his or her personal trash heap or calls it a draw with the villain (since right and wrong are situational) to either avoid judgmentalism or offer a sequel."[21] Whereas Heston's roles used to be considered elitist, at this point *elitist* had a different meaning.

Heston believed in one standard of truth, just like the nineteenth-century poet John Keats, who instructs: "'Beauty is truth, truth beauty,'— that is all / Ye know on earth, and all ye need to know." Conservative intellectuals repeatedly issued pleas to return to this once-dominant way of thinking and argued that "truth, beauty, and excellence" were not necessarily restrictive, as the new elites charged. Lynne Cheney contended that the standard-bearers of the humanities had the potential to transcend racial, class, and gender issues. Noting that the United States had become more inclusionary over the last forty years, Cheney argued that the humanities played an important role in this evolution.[22] However, elitist revisionists believed the opposite to be true: the humanities and scholarship in general were corrupt and assisted in the subjugation of minorities. The old academic mantras were not a source of liberation. Revisionists encouraged replacing those standards with a new way of thinking.

Heston maintained little respect for revisionists, calling them "the storm troops that lead the assault in the cultural war." He considered revisionist theory detrimental, largely because revisionists considered staple works and figures of academe to be tainted by white-male bias. Heston's pertinent question captures the frustration felt by many: "How did we get . . . to the point where the ethical foundations of Western civilization are now in question?" Various academic fields, including English and women's studies, indeed, tried to dismantle those foundations. At one Modern Language Association (MLA) annual convention, Sara Suleri of Yale and Steven Wartofsky of Loyola University mocked the very existence of Western studies. Wartofsky even predicted that the MLA could successfully displace "white male Eur-Americans' texts" at the next year's meeting. Likewise, because political, economic, and military history by necessity emphasized men and did not have women as their focus, some feminists wanted to minimize those topics. At the very least, feminists encouraged highlighting the relatively small contributions performed by women in those areas. Revisionists felt such a move to be necessary in part because they believed it impossible for students to draw inspiration from historical figures who differed from their race, ethnicity, or gender.[23]

Heston believed it foolhardy to dilute political and military topics with the everyday lives of men and women. Indeed, he frequently hailed the founding fathers, even if they were "just a bunch of wise, old, dead, white guys."[24] He was furious that being white had fallen into disrepute, blaming "guilt-driven class division" established by the new elitists. He frankly confessed to subscribing to the position that not "all men are the same": "Some are better than others." However, such greatness ought not, he contended, cause discouragement. It should, rather, be an inspiration. Likewise, the conservative feminist Christina Hoff Sommers argued that the radical feminists who dominated women's studies programs played "an undignified game of one-upsmanship" by altering the standards of "greatness" in order to include more women in the historical narrative.

Since revisionists believed that white-male "heroes" were embarrassments to the narrative, the new elitists denigrated the pursuit of truth in general. Revisionists questioned the systematic thinking that supported traditional academic study. Feminists especially contributed to this critique and based a new approach on Peggy McIntosh's ideas regarding vertical and lateral thinking. Carol Gilligan and other radical feminists upheld McIntosh's claims that white men engaged in vertical thinking while women and minorities utilized the lateral strategy. Vertical thinkers, they believed, were logical, competitive, exact, and focused. Horizontal thinkers, conversely, tended to be more relationship oriented, spiritual, and inclusive and, therefore, superior. Gilligan and McIntosh recommended rebuilding the system of academic thought to downgrade vertical thinkers and the topics, such as economics or politics, on which they focused.[25]

Gilligan's and McIntosh's hostility to the so-called vertical way of thinking went well beyond the scope of subject matter in schools to the traditional standards of grading utilized in the public education system.

Liberal elites eschewed competition, merit, and individualism, favoring instead cooperation and community. For instance, such educational methods as grade reports, spelling bees, and verbal debates were marked as damaging because they singled out individuals and set them up for humiliation. Heston believed discouraging individual achievement to be more detrimental than potential embarrassment. The public school system would have to accommodate itself to the less talented students. As Heston said: "That system is now in shambles, often with more bureaucrats than teachers, designed to drag a kid through with a dumbed-down program he cannot fail (lest his self-esteem be damaged)." Other critics focused on the potential politicization of such a horizontal system. Sommers pointed out that students would not be encouraged to think individually because they were expected to parrot the ideology of their instructors, a "reconceptualized" subject matter that she considered "unscholarly, intolerant of dissent, and full of gimmicks." Lynne Cheney pointed out a consequence of these trends that was even more troubling: a moral vacuum. Telling Americans that there's no truth except the belief that there is no truth "is full of arrogance and has moral consequences," she argued. Such relativism would not allow for a standard of fairness or acknowledge pain. Cheney believed that doubting the reality in which they lived caused Americans to lose their compassion when confronted by very real situations.[26]

Sexual behavior was one area where morality had been trivialized. Sexual activity had once been characterized as sinful if practiced too frequently or nonmonogamously. Bobos, however, regarded sex as a way to achieve higher moral understandings, believing that, as long as it was practiced safely, there was no sin involved. It was exactly this tendency to "encourage moral behavior through the back door," as Brooks put it, that conservatives believed diluted the moral standards of the nation. By emphasizing safe sex instead of moral principles, virtue took a backseat. In fact, religion itself no longer preached the same morality. The mainline churches redefined their theology in secular, humanist terms, accommodating modern lifestyles and views. Even with this dilution, many Americans did not adhere to any one religion. Instead, Brooks noted that they practiced "flexidoxy," an individually tailored religion in which one picks and chooses the orthodoxies one wants to follow while also attempting to maintain individual freedom. These so-called flexidoxists resisted submitting to any formal commandments but still hoped to bring out the spiritual implications of everyday life, thus paving the way for Wolfe's "Ten Suggestions."[27]

Brooks and Wolfe presented cafeteria-style morality as a reasonable way for Americans to live together, but more conservative critics bemoaned the consequences of such a lack of structure and spiritual guidance. Himmelfarb acknowledged that so-called moral statistics, like crime, welfare, and out-of-wedlock births, had improved over the course of the 1990s but noted numerous "causes of concern" that remained. If the rate of births to unmarried women had decreased, the ratio relative to all births had only leveled off; if older girls were less sexually active, girls under fifteen were more so; if divorce had declined, cohabitation had become more common.[28] These statistics indicated that, even if, as Brooks contended, Bobos offered some stability, a social pathology still haunted Americans.

Heston painted a picture of the world in which elitists, devoid of principles and values, were leading Americans into an abyss of evanescence, dysfunction, relativism, and conformity. First, he believed: "The ideal world being portrayed is one in which the masses have merged into a broad, lower/middle class that is economically prosperous (to a specific and limited degree) and lives for the pleasure of the moment." Second, he argued that aberrant behavior received a full hearing on television and was increasingly regarded as the norm. Third, he asserted: "What is 'right' is based upon opinion, not principle or fact." Fourth, everyone was stereotyped, classified by a "moniker" established by the elitists. The hero in this world, Heston remarked, "despises guns in the hands of the unwashed masses, loves all animals more than his fellow man, hates meat, wants to save the rain forest, considers homosexual relationships more enlightened than heterosexual ones, and sniffs at the inherent evil of all corporate enterprise."[29] Indeed, the vulgar behavior popularized by music videos, reality television, and violent movies indicated that authority, standards, and personal responsibility all had declined.

Heston unabashedly cast issues in matters of right and wrong, black and white. He unequivocally called Nazis and Communists *bad guys* and bemoaned the moral relativism that dissuaded some from making such judgments. Likewise, he defended the "evangelical Christian" in numerous speeches, and, as an author and a narrator, he pleaded for moral convictions. As the narrator of the audiobook version of William Bennett's *Death of Outrage,* a diatribe on the scandals of President Clinton, he repeated: "Moral judgments—need to be made." In fact, he firmly promised that a definite set of standards would actually make its adherents more free because they would not be confused by the ever-changing principles of moral relativism. "To remain viable as a free, moral nation," he commanded, "we must always seek the truth, simply because it is the truth." One by one, people across America needed "to abandon the look-alike, act-alike, think-alike, dress-alike, talk-alike media society" and reassert their individuality.[30]

In true Heston fashion, the method of combating the new elite that he suggested relied foremost on the individual, and he presented himself as a model of virtue and moral conviction. He offered his "Ten Covenants of Courage" to encourage others "to live by example and live loud":

1. Find ways to influence government in all its forms.

2. Be willing to disobey.

3. Take absolute and resolute pride in your own values.

4. Defend America as the peerless ideal—period.

5. Fiercely preserve all the rights outlined in the Bill of Rights.

6. Find the way to your loudest possible voice, and speak.

7. Embrace change.

8. Find myriad avenues to pass on your convictions.

9. Accept that sacrifice is just part of the deal.

10. Commit to the daily process of private prayer.[31]

By labeling these principles "covenants"—binding agreements to do or keep from doing a specified thing—Heston differentiated his list from

Wolfe's discretionary "suggestions." Even if Heston's covenants were not an adequate solution to the culture war, they were very much grounded in his standard political mechanisms of individualism. With them, he intended to quash the new elitism.

HESTON'S TEN COVENANTS OF COURAGE rested on his famous brand of individualism, but they also called for strong civic engagement in the community. Heston was no stranger to public involvement. A number of sociologists noted, however, that most Americans had lost touch with civic society and its responsibilities. Robert Putnam's *Bowling Alone* called attention to America's declining political and civic participation, a phenomenon that, he believed, weakened democracy and left Americans feeling abandoned, like bowlers without leagues. Likewise, the authors of *Habits of the Heart* characterized contemporary society as one that "enables the individual to think of commitments—from marriage and work to politics and religious involvement—as enhancements of the sense of individual well-being rather than as moral imperatives." As the importance of the individual heightened and outside involvements simply became methods of self-fulfillment, Americans abandoned their social relationships only to "be suspended in glorious, but terrifying isolation."[32] Heston never slipped into the hyperindividualism that these sociologists described. He maintained a constant involvement in the mediating structures encouraged by the neoconservatives. However, the inability of many Americans to simultaneously fulfill their individual needs and work for the greater good became a major source of concern in modern America, one that touched the film industry.

Heston illustrated the tension between the individual and the community in the director Oliver Stone's football movie *Any Given Sunday* (1999). Most of the characters in the film struggled with containing their own individualistic tendencies for the sake of their team, and Heston's presence in the movie exemplified how the needs of both the self and the community could be fulfilled. The story's basic theme is whether the integrity of professional football can remain intact as the media and the free agency system force the sport to modernize. Stone brought this struggle to life with the Miami Sharks, a team in transition between an old-school coach, Tony D'Amato (Al Pacino), and a business-oriented young owner, Christina Pagniacci (Cameron Diaz). Free agent players clamoring for generous contracts and media attention complicate the power struggle between D'Amato and Pagniacci. Stone then presents a deeper dilemma: how best to be a man, as an individual or a team player. Pagniacci, as a woman in a man's world, also struggles with that issue. In her quest to be the son her father always wanted, she attempts to out-testosterone everyone by becoming the most ruthlessly individualistic of them all.

In the movie's opening scene, the Shark's star quarterback and consummate team player, Cap Rooney (Dennis Quaid), is injured and replaced by the team's rising new star, Willie Beamen (Jamie Foxx). Beamen's contempt for tradition and teamwork is evident from the beginning. He has not studied his playbook and, ignoring D'Amato, changes the plays in the huddle to emphasize television-friendly long passes. Even though Rooney warns the rebel that the team will not respond to his type of "leadership," Beamen flippantly calls the injured quarterback an "old man." Beamen goes on to star in his own music video, scoff at the veteran players on a television sports program, and "diss" his own defensive squad at a team party. After the Sharks, many of whom are troubled by their own individualistic impulses, begin to rebel against Beamen, D'Amato invites the quarterback to his home to determine an effective leadership strategy. Beamen emphasizes individualism, while D'Amato insists on teamwork.

It is during this intense confrontation between Beamen and D'Amato that Stone uses Heston's public persona for the first time. D'Amato lectures Beamen that "this game has to be more than about winning" and reminds the maverick, "You're part of something here," citing football legends Vince Lombardi and Johnny Unitis as examples. Meanwhile, scenes from the chariot race in Heston's *Ben-Hur* explode on D'Amato's big-screen television. This sequence grows in intensity as Stone splices the race onto the movie screen itself, dramatizing Beamen's brand of individualism. As Stone later explained, in the chariot race "every man is an individual, not a team," and, indeed, Beamen boasts that he leads "by doing" and that "winning is the only thing I respect."[33] When D'Amato attempts to stress the merits of teamwork, Beamen scoffs at such old-fashioned ideas. For added emphasis, Stone splices the scene of Ben-Hur oaring in the slave galleys, suggesting teamwork to be the equivalent of slavery, or, at the very least, thankless menial labor. Ignoring D'Amato's warnings that his ego will work against him, Beamen announces that he plans to play his best, but merely for the purpose of increasing his value as a free agent.

Although Heston is portrayed as an excessive individualist in the first half of the movie, Stone understood that the iconic actor represented morality and respect for authority as well. Thus, he reappears later in the movie, in the role of the commissioner of the football league, as a "powerful moral presence" who also symbolizes the need for community.[34] Stone illustrates the necessity of civic society by portraying the deleterious effects of Beamen's and Pagniacci's lack of loyalty. The Sharks nearly miss the playoffs when Beamen's offensive line refuses to block for him, and the young quarterback suffers a severe pummeling as a consequence. Coach D'Amato's rousing address before the next game emphasizes community. "Either we heal as a team or we die as individuals," the coach thunders, curing Beamen of his hyperindividualism. Likewise, when the Football Commission learns of Pagniacci's plan to violate her contract by firing D'Amato and moving the team to Los Angeles, Heston pays her a visit and emphasizes the need for loyalty and respect. Concerned that "rules have been broken," he summons Pagniacci to a hearing regarding her actions. After their encounter, Heston remarks pityingly: "I honestly believe that woman would eat her young." Following an embarrassing episode with D'Amato over his coaching decisions, Pagniacci finally admits she is "out of control." She pledges to reconnect with her team and with the city of Miami. Although Heston had only a few lines in the movie, his presence is a powerful one that represents the necessity of balance between the individual and the community.

Any Given Sunday illustrated the tension that Heston believed marked the culture war: on the one hand, the excessive control of the "nanny state"; on the other, the extreme individualism indicative of multiculturalism and identity politics. Although the nanny state and multiculturalism were based on the same group mentality, they had two very different results.

Nanny state was a derisive term for government control of "dangerous" products or actions and was embraced by the Bobo elite. Tobacco, guns, pornography, and speech had all been legislated to restrict their use. Heston aggressively attacked the concept of a nanny state, believing that it led people into conformity. He advised: "Forget the contemporary model of 'big brother takes care of us' that the cultural reformers hope we'll buy."[35] The actor particularly warned against legislating guns and free speech, but he also addressed a number of other related subjects.

As someone deeply committed to a standard of morality but also fiercely devoted to free speech, Heston undertook considerable soul-searching on the question of regulating pornography. He disapproved of lascivious films, but he also pointed out that not everyone could agree on a definition of obscenity, noting that he welcomed freedom in the arts and that "the naked body is not of itself obscene." Despite his disapproval of the so-called smut industry and of the blatant sexuality in films in general, he consistently insisted that it was the public who needed to pressure the film industry to self-regulate, not the government. As the president of the Screen Actors Guild, he supported the Motion Picture Association of America ratings code, commenting: "Certainly this kind of self-regulation is infinitely preferable to government censorship, which has proven before now to be a lethally double-edged sword." Likewise, in a 1986 interview, he eschewed censorship and suggested: "Just as producers have the right to make bad films, citizens have the right to boycott."[36] This issue split the neoconservatives. Whereas Irving Kristol joined with conservative fundamentalists and some radical feminists to argue for government control of such material, most neocons shared Heston's position.

Heston also rejected the proposal to censor violent content in film, even though he believed that violence on the screen was directly related to aggressive, violent, and criminal behavior. Ironically, the media had long advocated gun control but also glorified the increasingly violent movies that Hollywood produced. Indeed, some of Hollywood's most liberal political activists starred in "shoot-'em-up" films during the 1990s. For example, Quentin Tarantino's brutal *Pulp Fiction* (1994) starred the liberal activists John Travolta and Samuel L. Jackson as sympathetic criminals.

Likewise, Ridley Scott's *Thelma & Louise* (1991), in which two women cavort about on a shooting spree, starred Susan Sarandon, one of Hollywood's most vocal leftists. Heston recently condemned such artistry, proclaiming: "For too long the so-called 'media experts' have been trying to convince us that violence on television and in movies is unrelated to crime statistics. They've been wrong and while we've intuitively known it as a nation of viewers, the statistics now confirm the bloody reality."[37] Even while acknowledging the direct link between violent films and criminal behavior, Heston called for public pressure, not government interference, to rein in the film industry.

Heston's work for the right to bear arms, despite his apprehension about violence in the media, stemmed from his reverence for the individual and his concern for the community. Although Heston deeply respected such authority figures as police officers and military personnel, he believed it naive to expect complete protection from them. Understanding its limits, he appreciated the community enough not to completely depend on it for safety. According to Heston, those who called for gun control did not respect the community but, instead, wanted to have someone other than themselves to blame in case of an assault. Furthermore, he simply did not believe that the government should have so much control that its forces were the only ones legally sanctioned to carry guns. He explained: "There is no such thing as a free nation where police and military are allowed the force of arms but individual citizens are not. That's a 'big brother knows best' theater of the absurd that has never boded well for the peasant class, the working class, or even for reporters."[38]

Heston drew a distinction between rural and urban values to illustrate the tension between the individual and the community and to explain the necessity of gun rights. He argued that rural communities were based on individual initiative and self-determination but that friendly relations with neighbors fostered a sense of mutual trust. A close-knit community naturally discouraged crime, but, in case of a trespasser, the country folk were able to take care of themselves. Heston believed that the rural individual enjoyed a large degree of safety while urban dwellers were more susceptible to danger, especially as they relinquished their gun rights.

By not knowing their neighbors, there was little sense of trust in their communities and, Heston believed, "a climate of fear." Furthermore, city residents traded their guns for police protection or personal security systems. These "mega-metropoli create," Heston argued, "compressed, distrustful little sub-societies that are willing to sacrifice privacy and surrender individual rights so they can be collectively protected by 'the system'—a complex, expensive, self-perpetuating bureaucracy with a manifesto that is generally self-defeating and pointlessly unenforceable."[39] According to Heston's argument, more guns would make people feel more secure, foster community interaction, and result in more trust between Americans.

Furthermore, Heston believed that the more acceptable that gun control became, the more other types of regulation would become unobjectionable as well. By associating free speech and gun rights, he attempted to put his opponents on the defensive. This linkage was not just a political ploy. Heston consistently defended free speech, even that of his opponents. Even though he disagreed vehemently with Jane Fonda's politics, particularly her anti-Vietnam and no-nukes protests, he publicly denounced the California State Senate's refusal to confirm Jane Fonda's appointment to the California Arts Council in 1979. Heston also defended Elia Kazan's right to receive the Lifetime Achievement Award from the American Film Institute (AFI). Some wanted to deny him the award for testifying to the House Un-American Activities Committee in 1952 against eight colleagues who had once belonged to the Communist Party. Heston condemned the idea of revoking the award, calling the proposal "an embarrassment to the AFI and to Hollywood." Likewise, he also defended the politics of the ultraliberal Vanessa Redgrave. "Politically, Vanessa and I could hardly be further apart. I'm a conservative; her radical beliefs make Jane Fonda sound like Herbert Hoover," he remarked. "Vanessa is openly blacklisted because of her anti-Zionist convictions. The film and theater communities should be ashamed of that." Indeed, Heston felt himself to be a victim of political correctness, a trend that he called a "plague upon the land, as devastating as the locusts God loosed on the Egyptians."[40]

Heston increasingly resisted "the social charade called 'political correctness,'" which also illustrated the tensions between the community and the individual. Political correctness, Heston warned, was another indication of the influence of the nanny state, in which the elite dictated what was acceptable to say. The actor confessed that his own friends urged him not to speak his mind about controversial issues, but he responded with his familiar quip: "If Americans believed in political correctness, we'd still be King George's boys." Heston was especially appalled that a public official was forced to apologize and then resign for using the word *niggardly*, which means "scanty" or "stingy," when discussing budgetary matters. Worst of all, he charged, the former champions of free thought, America's universities, were no longer protecting "the raw material of unfettered ideas." Indeed, speech codes originated on America's campuses, and funding for research often depended on politically correct projects. Heston believed that a "New McCarthyism" had taken hold, and he informed students on various campuses that they had been "conformed and silenced." He encouraged individual disobedience in the face of "social protocol" and "cultural correctness," much as he had done with Time Warner in his protest against Ice-T. However, Heston also encouraged group reprisal. "When an 8-year-old boy pecks a girl on the cheek on the playground and gets hauled into court for sexual harassment . . . march on that school and block its doorways," he advised.[41]

Political correctness also revealed the shift toward multiculturalism. The civil rights movement inspired other struggles for equality, including by the early 1970s the Chicano, women's, and gay rights movements. As these groups became more power oriented, the call for multiculturalism and the appreciation of many cultures became more fervent, as did the trend for minorities to construct political identities according to their respective groups. Heston believed multiculturalism to be at the root of political correctness because the credo began to shift from the tolerance of to the acceptance and celebration of everything different. Those who dared criticize another culture risked being branded a racist or some other intolerant breed. Those who celebrated being white were vilified. After Heston told a reporter, "We have to get back to the values and perceptions of those wise old dead white guys who invented the country," he was branded "with the familiar P.C. epithets."[42]

Furthermore, multiculturalism called for bonding as groups, but, in Heston's mind, the concept resulted in an emphasis on difference. "Stage One in cultural war 'division,'" Heston explained, "requires the introduction of dissension and hate between classes or racial groups." He inaccurately blamed 1960s revolutionaries for introducing categories of race and class. Those divisions had already been institutionalized by white society. However, he correctly lamented that, once the 1964 Civil Rights Act and the 1965 Voting Rights Act had been passed, some minorities grew more separatist in nature. And that trend continued into the twenty-first century. Some minorities began to characterize themselves with even more restrictive terms—for example, *Hispanic transvestite*—not only setting themselves apart from the original group, but also encouraging a mentality of victimization if the original group did not show respect for the new. The offshoots felt ostracized and alone after this ceaseless splintering because they surmised that only the people within their specific group could be capable of understanding their emotions. Thus, Heston believed that identity politics actually resulted in alienating individuals. Moreover, he warned: "We find ourselves sinking into a rogue culture that's shredding the fabric of the nation." These groups challenged the concept of one nation, he charged, and, if America succumbed to the notion of separatism, "then we're nothing, we're Albania, Bosnia, Zaire!"[43] He opposed the trend in general but particularly the extent to which it was taken by women and African Americans.

Heston believed in the equality of women but was never particularly attuned to their needs or sympathetic to the women's rights movement, especially as it grew more radical in the mid-1970s. As much as he loved and doted on his wife, Lydia, he seemed unable to comprehend the lifestyle pressures that contributed to her health problems in the 1970s. Likewise, he often grew exasperated with what he considered the "unprofessional" practices of his female costars. The film critic Bruce Crowther noted: "With the passage of time Heston's attitude toward his female co-stars was gradually to harden into general disapproval if not downright animosity." Heston's experience with his *El Cid* costar, Sophia Loren, was particularly illustrative of this attitude. He often vented in his journal about Loren's tardiness, lack of preparation, and refusal to wear aging makeup. He could not understand why she would be insecure about her appearance or her accent. Nor did he understand the habits of most of his female costars. He even complained to one journalist: "By and large, actresses are a different breed of cat. . . . It appalls and disgusts me, the amateur way most of them treat film-making. The rule of thumb for most of these broads is to be twenty minutes late in the morning and ten minutes late after lunch." Heston later apologized for his impatience and lack of sympathy, admitting that actresses generally have longer hair, makeup, and wardrobe calls. "There's not a lot you can do about it, except wait. This I did," he conceded, "but with a certain amount of Scots dour, for which I'm sorry."[44]

Although he could be insensitive to the needs of women, Heston was generally supportive of the legal achievements of the women's movement, especially in terms of employment. In an interview in 1986, he approvingly noted that women had many more options in Hollywood than they had when he had first arrived there. In the 1950s, the only jobs available to women, besides acting, had been as script clerks, hairdressers, and body makeup artists. He also applauded the increasing presence of women in politics. He endorsed the neoconservative Jean Kirkpatrick as the best vice presidential nominee for the 1988 Republican ticket. In general, he believed women in America to be "in great shape" because they enjoyed an unprecedented variety of opportunities. "Women can do whatever they want to do," he believed.[45]

However, Heston also noted that "women are realizing maybe they don't want to do it," showing his ambivalence about the cultural changes brought about by the increasingly radical feminist movement. He noted that some women preferred to suspend their career plans temporarily in order to raise families. He believed that women should be admired, and not feel ashamed, for making such a choice. Indeed, his wife had elected to be a stay-at-home mom. For their part, radical feminists considered Heston an archaic fool. Not only did many, such as Marilyn French, believe that there was a full-scale "war against women" being waged, but the general assumption in many women's studies textbooks was that a husband and a family were a suicide trap for newly empowered women. According to this scholarship, those women who said they wanted to be married were merely dupes of the patriarchal order.[46]

Heston opposed many of the social and cultural changes heralded by the radical feminists, believing that their ideas tore at the fabric of community. He was particularly disturbed by the claims of some feminists that men and women were not just equal but exactly alike, a proposition that he called a "ridiculous canard." He continued: "Gloria Steinem is out of her skull if she imagines she can, by shouting, convince any reasonable person that they are the same." The actor particularly did not welcome women wearing more masculine attire. He called the mod look of the late 1960s "a homosexual conspiracy to make women look terrible": "Boots . . . chains for belts . . . stubby thick shoes . . . long pants . . . short pants . . . men's suits . . . men's shirts . . . men's bathing suits for heaven's sake! And who designs all these ridiculous things! It is impossible to look ridiculous and sexy at the same time."[47] Heston also considered a strong father figure a necessity in the household, while some feminists saw men as entirely expendable. Heston noted that the radical feminists' narrow view of what was best for women did not result in unity but, instead, actually splintered the women's movement and alienated it from the American mainstream.

Heston also believed that the civil rights agenda had become too radical and that African American leaders had lost touch with the larger community. Heston's experience with the civil rights movement and his work with Martin Luther King Jr. gave him a vested interest in the evolution of the black struggle for equality. By the late 1960s and the 1970s, however, the leading black organizations focused on expanding affirmative action, winning reparations, and celebrating the unique culture of African Americans. As someone who marched for equality and a color-blind society, Heston found the new agenda particularly disturbing. For him, affirmative action violated the very Civil Rights Act for which he had demonstrated. He remembered when, during the heyday of the civil rights movement, singling out a certain race was anathema. "I stood in the Senate Gallery as our senators debated the Civil Rights Act in 1964," he reminisced. "Hubert Humphrey, God rest his soul, stood on the floor of the Senate, held the bill over his head, and swore to eat it page by page if anyone could find in it any mention of specific preference." Heston believed that as soon as integration and equality of opportunity had become a reality, some segments of the movement turned their backs on those values. They opted, instead, for equality of outcome and racial separatism. "The doors of opportunity" opened to minorities, he remarked, but "not all blacks chose to walk through them."[48]

While his criticisms were certainly legitimate, Heston sometimes overreached on the subject of civil rights. He had made an important contribution to the civil rights cause when he organized the March on Washington's Arts Group. However, that involvement was a flimsy base on which to construct a public image as a defender of civil rights. Heston frequently reminded audiences of his connection to the civil rights movement and used that experience to lend legitimacy to the goals of the NRA. "Supporting equal rights of blacks wasn't popular in 1963, supporting the rights of gun ownership isn't popular now," he often said. "Yet it's what I believe is right." He also frequently linked himself with King, commenting that they both fought for "personal freedom."[49] However, he rarely acknowledged the intricacies of the movement with which he had been involved. The movement itself was fractured, with several black leaders disappointed by the modest demands of the March on Washington, goals that Heston considered most acceptable. Moreover, King himself evolved toward a more radical position by 1967 when he began to attack economic inequality and to criticize the Vietnam War. Heston's experience with the civil rights movement was important, but the actor had, in reality, participated in only two civil rights projects. That was hardly enough experience for him legitimately to claim that he and King maintained the relationship, or the philosophical affinity, that he led his later audiences to believe.

Furthermore, when he used King to condemn aspects of black culture, Heston overstepped his authority. For instance, he criticized black rappers for their controversial lyrics, black athletes for "thrusting a bump-'n-grind in the end zone," and black singers for "grabbing their groins." Not only did white performers and athletes participate in this type of behavior, but Heston's faith that King would have been able to put an end to such displays was a bit misguided. King "would ascend the steps of the Lincoln Memorial a second time, summon together the legions of today's timid black leaders and tight-lipped press members and he would put a permanent end to it," Heston pronounced.[50] The civil rights movement did not produce the results that Heston had hoped for, and he was obviously frustrated with its cultural implications. He was particularly disturbed by the segregation that multiculturalism demanded and its effect on the overall community.

Heston believed that multiculturalism, identity politics, and the nanny state were destroying America's moral fabric. Political correctness and the nanny state resulted in overbearing control, and multiculturalism resulted in balkanization and disorder. These outcomes violated Heston's sense of the balance to be desired between the individual and the community.

AS HESTON FREQUENTLY REPEATED: "The Founding Fathers, in their prescient wisdom, promised us life and liberty, but not happiness . . . only the chance to pursue it." And his political philosophy ultimately rested on this belief. Such a belief in opportunity marked another crucial juncture in the culture war, for it was the cornerstone of Heston's position against an overbearing government. As he explained: "If even an omnipotent God will not guarantee us happiness, surely we're foolish to count on government to do it."[51] Heston often spoke out against what he considered to be an obsessive seeking of entitlements. Allowing the government to provide a wider array of services was, he believed, detrimental to both the individual and the community. On one hand, expecting government assistance chipped away at the sense of responsibility that Heston believed so important to individual integrity. On the other, winning these entitlements often required political organizing by so-called power groups who competed against each other for recognition—a contest that Heston believed tore at the fabric of the community.

Heston was impressed with Franklin D. Roosevelt's New Deal programs, and the actor preferred their limited scope to the welfare state that had emerged by the late 1960s. He complained that, after the death of John F. Kennedy, the Democrats actively sought this welfare state. He considered a welfare system acceptable if it prompted individual initiative, as did the NEA. However, he also lamented that some artists considered the arts program an entitlement, and he believed that all government programs had the potential to be exploited by rights-mongering recipients. Regarding the NEA in particular, he predicted: "Somewhere in the busy pipeline of public funding is sure to be a demand from a disabled lesbian on welfare that the Metropolitan Opera stage her rap version of *Carmen* as translated into Ebonics." In more general terms, Heston believed: "If you subsidize someone, he will accept that subsidy, and guaranteed incomes unfortunately mean that most people won't do anything."[52]

For this reason, Heston publicly criticized a wide array of entitlements. He opposed services for illegal immigrants, taking issue with one reporter who, Heston noticed, wrote "eloquently" about their "sorry plight" in a story about immigrant families. However, the reporter "seldom conceded that many of them are in fact illegal." "Does that word no longer have any meaning in our decaying culture?" he demanded. Heston believed it absurd that illegal trespassers should be afforded special services and suggested that they would be "better off legally deported back to a culture they can at least understand."[53] Likewise, he protested affirmative action and subsidized housing, calling federal housing projects "an invitation to failure." Nor did he consider safety an entitlement. He believed that Americans should ultimately rely on armed self-defense rather than police protection.

Foremost, Heston considered liberal solutions to societal ills to be counterproductive because they hindered individual initiative. Indeed, he turned the liberal quest for self-esteem and happiness on its head, arguing that the entitlement approach was actually damaging to the psyche. To him, it was demoralizing for people to depend on government handouts, and he drew from neoconservative scholarship to support his claims. He endorsed a study by Charles Murray, a sociologist who received grant money through his connection to Irving Kristol, to study the impact of welfare on recipients. In his *Losing Ground*, Murray used empirical data to show how the welfare system rewarded single mothers but not married couples, thus promoting the disintegration of the family. He also demonstrated how the then-current welfare system sapped the work ethic by making it more lucrative to be unemployed than to work at a low-paying job. Heston believed the unintended consequences of the welfare system to be detrimental: "In particular, the damage done to the black family by welfare programs, and the damage done to the black psyche—the sense of self-worth—by affirmative action, outweigh the possible benefits." The "self-esteem movement" would fail, he believed, if its adherents continued to rely on entitlements. The way to achieve confidence and happiness was, he argued, through a sense of self-reliance. That quest personally drove Heston as an actor, a citizen activist, and a hunter. "That instinctive sense of self-destiny and self-reliance, more than anything else, is still at the core of why I hunt," he explained.[54] Self-reliance constituted the base of Heston's political philosophy as well, and he believed it the best guarantor of happiness.

ELECTORAL POLITICS INDICATED THAT the tide was shifting in favor of the Bubba, a shift that was in some part due to Heston's intense campaigning. When Heston assumed the presidency of the NRA, the blue America Bobo clearly had the advantage in the culture war, especially with the Democrat Bill Clinton as president of the United States. However, after the Republican George W. Bush won the presidency in 2000 and the GOP swept the 2002 midterm elections, the Bobo hegemony was no longer assured. By 2004, the Republicans had set the terms of the debate with their emphasis on moral values during Bush's reelection campaign. Democrats scrambled to insist that they, too, had moral values but, by accepting the Republican vernacular, looked unoriginal and, apparently, unconvincing. Bush won a second term, and Republicans increased their majority in Congress.

A number of other indicators reflected the increasing cultural power of the Bubba as well. The September 11 terrorist attacks evoked renewed patriotism and militarism, two qualities that had been largely out of style. The bravery exhibited by the fire and police departments of New York City and Washington, DC, after the attacks on the World Trade Center and the Pentagon elicited praise for such traditional values as rugged masculinity and virility. Peggy Noonan, a former speechwriter in the Reagan administration who admitted to formerly shunning chivalry, hailed the man's man: "men who charge up the stairs in a hundred pounds of gear and tell everyone else where to go to be safe." Furthermore, David Brooks recanted his glorification of secular tolerance. In a recent essay, he admitted that, by viewing all faiths as valid approaches to God, secularists patronized religion by letting some invalid forms off too easily. "This approach is no longer acceptable," he wrote. "One has to try to separate right from wrong."[55] Religion seemed to be a crucial element in the GOP's 2004 victory, as Republicans successfully drew former Democratic stalwarts, such as Catholics and African Americans, to the party with their emphasis on moral issues, such as faith-based government programs, abortion policy, and gay marriage.

The neoconservative contribution to the ascendancy of conservatism was monumental. With their constant assaults on the liberal ethos, the neoconservatives made the liberal agenda more controversial than ever. Heston's neoconservative voice was just one among many. However, he was also one of the most famous and most vocal of the neoconservatives and, with his earthy vernacular, was arguably one of the most accessible. He was able to parlay his NRA presidency into a wide forum for his cultural critiques—criticisms that resembled those of the rest of the neocons but also bore his particular imprint and style. With his emphasis on the elite, the individual in society, and the pursuit of happiness, Heston effectively helped throw the liberals on the defensive. His long history of activism prepared him for his participation in the culture war, and he embraced his role in order to live up to his own Eighth Covenant: "Find myriad avenues to pass on your convictions. There's no way for your values to outlive you if you don't."

CONCLUSION

HESTON RETIRED FROM PUBLIC LIFE IN APRIL 2003 AFTER SERVING OUT his fifth term as president of the National Rifle Association (NRA). The actor would likely have preferred to stay in the arena. Unfortunately, failing health forced him to step aside. In August 2002, he had announced that he had been diagnosed with early symptoms of Alzheimer's disease. He had never missed work as a result of illness, but, in a taped speech revealing his diagnosis to the public, he admitted: "I am neither giving up nor giving in, but it's a fight I must someday call a draw."[1] Despite his withdrawal from films and politics, Heston's legacy of morality, responsibility, and conservative masculinity will endure. A number of his films showcasing those values continue to be viewed by audiences worldwide. *The Ten Commandments* remains a staple of Easter weekend television programming, and an animated version of *Ben-Hur*, which Heston narrates, was released in March 2003. Heston's legacy will also be sustained by the NRA. Because of his leadership, the NRA is stronger than ever. Not only does it have more money and more members, but it is also uncharacteristically unified, making it well prepared to handle future challenges effectively. Above all, Heston's legacy will persevere because of his aggressive work in the culture war. He attempted to reinstate pride in those Americans who had grown ashamed of their values in an increasingly relativistic society.

Heston's public career illustrated three important aspects of postwar politics. First is the emergence of the neoconservatives. This influential group revealed the variable nature of the national political parties. The neoconservatives' beliefs remained constant, but their political loyalties did not. Anticommunism, equality of opportunity, individual responsibility, and community involvement all constituted their basic philosophy, as did a suspicion of government activism. In the 1950s and 1960s, the Democratic agenda corresponded to their beliefs; after the 1970s, it did not. Consequently, Heston and the rest of the neocons came to increasingly trust the Republican Party, especially regarding matters of foreign policy. The neocons went on to exercise considerable influence on the GOP by contributing new ideas and bringing new personalities to the party. Their support carried legitimacy because they were former Democrats, and it garnered publicity because they were well-known. Furthermore, the fact that Heston and scholars like Irving Kristol and Norman Podhoretz followed similar political trajectories shows that neoconservatism should be understood not simply as an intellectual movement but as one composed of everyday Americans operating from a visceral standpoint.

Heston's activism also portrayed the importance of cultural values to the political landscape, an importance in large part due to the neoconservatives themselves. Although some historians have attributed the rise of conservatism primarily to economic alienation and racist white backlash, Heston illustrated another reason Americans left the Democrats: ideology and culture.[2] Heston believed in equality and marched for civil rights to prove it. Furthermore, he was economically secure. Obviously, he was not personally threatened by the Democrats' identification with civil rights and a liberal economic program. He simply disagreed with the philosophical principles—including group rights, permissive moral values, and a leftist foreign policy—from which the party was working. He represented numerous other Americans who left the Democrats, not because they were racially or economically insecure, but because they disagreed with the ideology driving the party and resisted the influence of that ideology on American culture. They blamed the Democrats for allowing a new elite to dominate society, one that shifted America to the left in terms of cultural norms. The new elite's emphasis on community control and group rights especially disturbed Heston. When he attempted to criticize the policies—for example, those on gun control and affirmative action—stemming from those values, the new elite labeled him as reactionary. A frustrated Heston retaliated, but he could not systematically fight the culture war until assuming office at the NRA. There, he had the large audiences and press coverage to thoroughly expound his beliefs. He argued for expanding individual freedoms, but he also wanted to reassert a basic moral framework within which everyone would work. Indeed, individual freedoms and conservative values are back in the political lexicon, but for how long and to what degree is anyone's guess.

Heston's activism also illustrated the increasing permeability between celebrity and politics. Moguls dominated the Hollywood political scene between the 1930s and the 1950s, and celebrities were merely trotted out during national election cycles. By the 1960s, however, celebrities assumed a new prominence in politics. LBJ increasingly used them to sell his policies, like the Gun Control Act of 1968, and to participate in cultural endeavors, like the National Endowment for the Arts (NEA). Celebrities also entered grassroots campaigns, including civil rights marches and both pro– and anti–Vietnam War rallies. Furthermore, the ever-proliferating special interest groups increasingly recruited them to bring publicity to their causes. Celebrities grew more prominent on the campaign trail and in their advocacy of certain policies. Heston himself combined partisan campaigning with special interest activism to achieve considerable results. He helped establish and ensure the longevity of the NEA, led the fight to return the Screen Actors Guild to its core principles and affected federal labor policy while doing so, and helped the NRA achieve both organizational and legislative success. As celebrity activists became more commonplace, so, too, did celebrity politicians. Ronald Reagan broke the ballot box barrier, inspiring a number of celebrities to pursue a variety of offices, particularly in California. Sonny Bono represented the state in the U.S. Congress, Clint Eastwood served as mayor of Carmel, and Arnold Schwarzenegger won the governorship in 2003. As celebrities grew more engaged in the political scene, they also became more combative and willing to publicly disagree with other stars. Heston battled Ed Asner and Paul Newman; twenty years later Rosie O'Donnell ambushed Tom Selleck on her own show; and in fall 2005 Warren Beatty lambasted Schwarzenegger for his lack of leadership as governor. It was not uncommon to see celebrities airing their political differences and even personally attacking one another by the turn of the century.

The consequences of celebrities in politics are still being debated. On one hand, celebrities have the potential to reinvigorate American politics by introducing new ideas and by bringing new blood to a profession dominated by career politicians. Besides, being financially secure and less beholden to political interests, they can afford to challenge conventional wisdom and adopt unpopular stances. Schwarzenegger made particular use of these possibilities. In his quest for the governorship, he made a campaign promise never to be corrupted by political contributions. "I'm already rich," he reminded audiences. Once elected, Schwarzenegger used his superstar status to try to bring business to his state. He appeared on billboards in nearly a dozen cities with the message: "Arnold Says: 'California Wants Your Business.'" Furthermore, he used his massive popularity in Japan to strengthen economic ties between California and the Asian powerhouse. However, scholars also point to the potential negatives of celebrity activism. Richard Schickel argues that celebrities "subvert rationalism in politics" because, in their use of the media, they simplify ideological complexities and foster a false sense of intimacy to connect with audiences. Likewise, Darrell M. West and John Orman argue that, in conjunction with the media, celebrities have dumbed down and sensationalized politics and bear some responsibility for the exploding costs of campaigns. West and Orman admit to the benefits that celebrities can bring to the political process. However, they believe that the negative consequences outweigh the positive: "In short, celebrity politics accentuates many of the elements in our society that drain substance out of the political process and substitutes trivial and nonsubstantive forces of entertainment."[3] While the consequences of celebrity activism and celebrity politicians may be seen in either positive or negative terms, actors and other entertainers have claimed a permanent and high-profile place for themselves in American politics.

Heston frequently amused fans with an anecdote that also reflects his success as a public figure. He had arrived in Rome six weeks before William Wyler began shooting *Ben-Hur* in order to train for the stunts he needed to perform in the physically demanding movie, working with the legendary stunt coordinator Yakima Canutt at least two hours a day learning to handle a chariot with a team of four horses. Over the course of his training, he grew more confident in his driving abilities but was still plagued with doubt about winning the actual race. He told Canutt: "Y'know, Yak, I feel pretty comfortable running this team now, but we're all alone here. We start shooting this sucker in ten days. I'm not so sure I can cut it with seven other teams out there." Canutt paused and solemnly looked Heston in the eye. "Chuck, you just make sure you stay in the chariot. I guarantee yuh gonna win the damn race," he replied.[4] Heston repeated this story to delighted audiences across the country, always enjoying the effect it had on the crowds. He won that chariot race. He also won the race of life. Not only did he boast a closely knit family and an accomplished film career, but he also emerged as the most influential celebrity activist of his time.

NOTES

The following abbreviations have been employed throughout the notes:

AAPCF	Actors and Actresses, Politics—Clippings File
AMPAS	Academy of Motion Picture Arts and Sciences, Beverly Hills, CA
CHCF	Charlton Heston—Clippings File
CHSC	Charlton Heston Special Collection
GBPL	George H. W. Bush Presidential Library, College Station, TX
JHSC	Jack Hirschberg Special Collection
LBJL	Lyndon Baines Johnson Presidential Library, Austin, TX
MHL	Margaret Herrick Library
NEAL	National Endowment for the Arts Library, Washington, DC
NRA Archives	National Rifle Association Archives, National Rifle Association Archives Headquarters, Fairfax, VA
Papers of LBJ	Papers of Lyndon B. Johnson, President, 1963–1969
RRPL	Ronald Reagan Presidential Library, Simi Valley, CA
SAG Archives	Screen Actors Guild Archives, Beverly Hills, CA
UCLA Film and Television Archive	Film and Television Archive, Powell Library, University of California, Los Angeles
WHORM	White House Office of Records Management
Wyler Papers	William Wyler Papers (Collection 53), Young Research Library, Special Collections, University of California, Los Angeles

It should also be noted that, many times, items in clipping files do not include page numbers.

INTRODUCTION

1. Irving Kristol, *Neoconservatism: The Autobiography of an Idea* (New York: Free Press, 1995), x.

2. Charlton Heston in *News Conference, Charlton Heston Supports Richard Nixon* (1972), UCLA Film and Television Archive.

3. Kristol in Michael S. Joyce, "The Common Man's Uncommon Intellectual," in *The Neoconservative Imagination: Essays in Honor of Irving Kristol*, ed. Christopher DeMuth and William Kristol (Washington, DC: AEI Press, 1995), 63–72, 66.

4. See Charlton Heston, *The Courage to Be Free* (Kansas City, KS: Saudade, 2000).

5. See Charlton Heston, *The Actor's Life: Journals, 1956–1976*, ed. Hollis Alpert (New York: Dutton, 1976).

6. "Publicity Schedule & Summary," "Charlton Heston—the Actor's Life" (file), CHSC, MHL, AMPAS.

1. SUPERSTAR

1. Heston, *Journals*, xii.

2. "Kaminsky Interview" (1975), CHSC, MHL, AMPAS.

Heston was born John Charles Carter. His great grandfather on his mother's side was named James Charlton. Although it is not clear when, Heston began using his great-grandfather's last name as his first name. After his parents divorced, his mother married Chet Heston, and Heston took his new stepfather's last name. Thus, John Charles Carter became Charlton Heston.

3. Charlton Heston in *The Start of Something Big* (Steve Allen, host), n.d. (ca. 1985–86), UCLA Film and Television Archive. Holly Heston in *Charlton Heston: For All Seasons* (Wombat Productions, 2000), Film Archive, AMPAS. *Fame, Fortune, and Romance* (Robin Leach, host), n.d. (ca. 1986–87), UCLA Film and Television Archive. Charlton Heston, *In the Arena: An Autobiography* (New York: Simon & Schuster, 1995), 33.

4. Heston, *Arena*, 33–35. Charlton Heston in Pete Hammill, "Larger Than Life," *Saturday Evening Post*, June 3, 1965, 87–90, 90.

5. Charlton Heston in Dotson Reader, "Charlton Heston Talks about Acting, Politics, and Himself," *Parade Magazine*, March 9, 1986, CHCF, MHL, AMPAS. Heston, *Arena*, 39, 44. Of course, self-responsibility is not really a Calvinist notion.

6. Heston, *Arena*, 42.

7. Ibid., 48. Lydia Heston in Marilyn Funt, "Lydia Heston: Cold-Water Flat . . . to Coldwater Canyon," *Los Angeles Times,* May 7, 1980, V2–3, V2.

8. Heston, *Arena,* 53.

9. Ibid., 73. Ruth Waterbury, "Charlton Loves Lydia," *Photoplay,* June 1953, CHCF, MHL, AMPAS.

10. Charlton Heston and Jean-Pierre Isbouts, *Charlton Heston's Hollywood: Fifty Years in American Film* (New York: GT, 1998), 25.

11. Kirk Douglas, *The Ragman's Son: An Autobiography* (New York: Simon & Schuster, 1998), 142–46, 269. Charlton Heston in *Studio System* (Chris Rodley, 1994), Academic Support Center Media Library, University of Missouri, Columbia. For more information on the studio system, see Douglas Gomery, *The Hollywood Studio System* (New York: St. Martin's, 1986).

12. Hal Wallis and Charles Higham, *Starmaker: The Autobiography of Hal Wallis* (New York: Macmillan, 1980), 118. Heston and Isbouts, *Heston's Hollywood,* 33.

13. "Charlton Heston—Notes for Sidney Skolsky" (file), n.d., JHSC, MHL, AMPAS. "Quickies," *Paramount News,* May 29, 1950, CHCF, MHL, AMPAS.

14. Steven Cohan, *Masked Men: Masculinity and the Movies in the Fifties* (Bloomington: Indiana University Press, 1997), 165–67. See also Gaylyn Studlar, *This Mad Masquerade: Stardom and Masculinity in the Jazz Age* (New York: Columbia University Press, 1996).

15. Charles L. Ponce de Leon, *Self-Exposure: Human-Interest Journalism and the Emergence of Celebrity in America, 1890–1940* (Chapel Hill: University of North Carolina Press, 2002), 4–5.

16. Heston, *Arena,* 100, 116. *Hollywood Guess Stars,* n.d., UCLA Film and Television Archive. *What's My Line,* October 28, 1956, UCLA Film and Television Archive. Aline Mosby, "Charlton Heston, New Film Find, Refuses Name Change," n.d., "Clippings" (file), CHSC, MHL, AMPAS.

17. "Kaminsky Interview." Heston and Isbouts, *Heston's Hollywood,* 38. Cecil B. DeMille, *The Autobiography of Cecil B. DeMille,* ed. Donald Hayne (Englewood Cliffs, NJ: Prentice-Hall, 1959), 405. Heston, *Journals,* xvi. Ronald Davis, "Charlton Heston Oral History" (Southern Methodist University Oral History Program, no. 464), 35, CHSC, MHL, AMPAS.

18. "Kaminsky Interview." Charles Higham, *Cecil B. DeMille* (New York: Scribner's, 1973), 83–89.

19. Interview with DeMille via Shirley Thomas, "NBC Program," April 14, 1959, "Ten Commandments—Publicity" (file), CHSC, MHL, AMPAS.

20. "The New Pictures: Ten Commandments," *Time,* November 12, 1956, 120–24, 122. Higham, *DeMille,* 304.

21. George M. Marsden, *Religion and American Culture* (New York: Harcourt Brace, 1990), 213–17.

22. Cohan, *Masked Men,* 122–24. Charlton Heston, *Charlton Heston Newsletter,* March 20, 1957, CHSC, MHL, AMPAS.

23. Cohan, *Masked Men,* 135. "Ten Commandments—Miscellaneous" (file), CHSC, MHL, AMPAS.

24. John Archer and Barbara Lloyd, *Sex and Gender,* 2nd ed. (Cambridge: Cambridge University Press, 2002), 17.

25. See Cohan, *Masked Men.* See also Barbara Ehrenreich, *The Hearts of Men: American Dreams and the Flight from Commitment* (Garden City, NY: Anchor/Doubleday, 1983). It was later discovered that Kinsey's study was skewed to exaggerate the incidence of homosexuality. See James H. Jones, *Alfred Kinsey: A Public/Private Life* (New York: Norton, 1997).

26. Cohan, *Masked Men,* 5–27.

27. David Riesman, *The Lonely Crowd: A Study of the Changing American Character* (New Haven, CT: Yale University Press, 1950).

28. Cohan, *Masked Men,* 148–55, 157–58. Charlton Heston, *Charlton Heston Newsletter,* July 1957, CHSC, MHL, AMPAS.

29. Charlton Heston in Vernon Scott, "Big Role Veteran: Charlton Heston Lacks Epic," *Hollywood Citizen-News,* March 38, 1959, 2, CHCF, MHL, AMPAS. Charlton Heston in Sheila Graham, "Heston Just Can't Escape Dark Ages," *Hollywood Citizen-News,* April 21, 1965, CHCF, MHL, AMPAS. Charlton Heston in Lowell E. Ruddings, "Heston Prefers Costume Films," *Hollywood Citizen-News,* March 22, 1961, CHCF, MHL, AMPAS.

30. Bruce Crowther, *Charlton Heston: An Epic Presence* (London: Columbus, 1986), 86. Hammill, "Larger Than Life," 88.

31. Charlton Heston, speech before the Bureau of Jewish Education, January 30, 1955, "Ten Commandments—Publicity" (file), CHSC, MHL, AMPAS. DeMille, *Autobiography,* 415. Heston, *Arena,* 132.

32. Brian Lowry, "Prime-Time TV Rankings; ABC's 16th Straight Win Has a Biblical Feature," *Los Angeles Times,* April 19, 2000, F11. Derek Elley, *The Epic Film: Myth and History* (London: Routledge & Kegan Paul, 1984), 35.

33. All quotations (ca. 1956) taken from undated, unpaginated clippings in "Ten Commandments—Clippings" (file), CHSC, MHL, AMPAS.

34. Heston and Isbouts, *Heston's Hollywood,* 97. Wyler had already won Academy Awards for such films as *The Little Foxes* (1941) and *Roman Holiday* (1953). Ibid., 98–99. Lew Wallace, a Civil War general in the Union army, wrote Judah Ben-Hur's fictional story. Wallace first began the work while living in Indiana after

the war and completed it eight years later in New Mexico while serving as the territorial governor. Harper Brothers bought Wallace's manuscript in 1880, and, by the end of the decade, half a million copies were in print, eventually returning greater royalties than any novel had ever earned. In fact, *Ben-Hur: A Tale of the Christ* is reported to have sold more copies than any other book besides the Bible, and, by 1904, it had been translated into every language. See *The Story of the Making of Ben-Hur: A Tale of the Christ* (New York: Random House, 1959), "Ben-Hur—Publicity" (file), CHSC, MHL, AMPAS. See also file 6, box 20, Wyler Papers.

35. Steven Cohan and Ina Rae Hark, eds., *Screening the Male: Exploring Masculinities in Hollywood Cinema* (London: Routledge, 1993), 11, 230. Yvonne Tasker argues that the notion of macho includes fighting ability, self-confidence, and a degree of arrogance. See Yvonne Tasker, *Spectacular Bodies: Gender, Genre, and the Action Cinema* (London: Comedia, 1993), 21.

36. The construction figures alone indicate the arena's enormity: 1 million pounds of plaster, 40,000 cubic feet of lumber, 250 miles of metal tubing, and 40,000 tons of white sand transported from Mediterranean beaches. Charlton Heston, *Charlton Heston Newsletter,* August 15, 1958, CHSC, MHL, AMPAS. *The Story of the Making of Ben-Hur.* File 3, box 22, and file 6, box 20, Wyler Papers. See also Jan Herman, *A Talent for Trouble: The Life of Hollywood's Most Acclaimed Director, William Wyler* (New York: Putnam's, 1995), 393–411.

37. Charlton Heston in "Dialogue on Film: Charlton Heston," American Film Institute Series of Seminars with Master Filmmakers, 1980, UCLA Film and Television Archive. Herman, *Talent for Trouble,* 406–7. File 2, box 22, Wyler Papers.

38. For more analysis of Judah Ben-Hur, see, e.g., Crowther, *Epic Presence,* 61. Heston, *Journals,* 48.

39. Crowther, *Epic Presence,* 60. Elley, *The Epic Film,* 130. "Script" (i.e., *Ben-Hur*), file 1, box 19, Wyler Papers.

40. Pete Martin, "I Call on Ben-Hur," *Saturday Evening Post,* August 20, 1960, 20–21 et seq., 21. James Powers, "S'Ben Swell—S'Do It Again," *Variety,* December 11, 1959, CHCF, MHL, AMPAS.

41. Charlton Heston, *Charlton Heston Newsletter,* August 14, 1958, CHSC, MHL, AMPAS.

42. Charlton Heston in Martin, "I Call on Ben-Hur," 42. Charlton Heston in Jim Clements, "Grey Lady Down: Down in the Depths with Charlton Heston," *Marquee,* January/February 1978, CHCF, MHL, AMPAS. Transcript, *This Is Your Life,* thirtieth anniversary special, November 26, 1981, CHSC, MHL, AMPAS.

43. For Vidal's claims, see Gore Vidal, "Writing 'Ben-Hur': On Love in the Time of Chariots," *Los Angeles Times,* June 17, 1996, F3. For Heston's denials, see

Davis, "Charlton Heston Oral History," 53, CHSC, MHL, AMPAS. See also "Love and Chariots II: Heston Responds to Vidal," *Los Angeles Times,* June 24, 1996, F4. For Van Slyke's comments on Heston's appeal to both sexes, see Helen Van Slyke, "From 'Moses' to 'Midway,' Charlton Heston Is Larger Than Life," *Saturday Evening Post,* January/February 1976, CHCF, MHL, AMPAS.

44. Martin, "I Call on Ben-Hur," 40. Clements, "Grey Lady Down."

45. On Kirk Douglas's sexual conquests, see his autobiography, *The Ragman's Son,* which leaves little to the imagination. In fact, his sexual prowess seems to be the focus of the book. Waterbury, "Charlton Loves Lydia." Beverly Ott, "Their Marriage Is a Lifetime Honeymoon," *Photoplay,* April 1954, CHCF, MHL, AMPAS. Hooton, *Arena,* 116. Hammill, "Larger Than Life," 89.

46. Waterbury, "Charlton Loves Lydia." Naomi Englesman, "The Billing for the Youngest Heston," *Parents Magazine,* August 1956, 40, 91–94, 40. Heston, *Journals,* 77.

47. Bill Davidson, "The House That Ben-Hur Built," *Look,* May 24, 1960, 56j–56n. See also Jim Liston, "At Home with Charlton Heston," *American Home,* May 1962, 14–16, 60–61. Funt, "Lydia Heston," V2.

48. Charlton Heston, *Charlton Heston Newsletter,* October 17, 1961, CHSC, MHL, AMPAS.

49. Heston, *Journals,* 139–40.

50. Charlton Heston, *Charlton Heston Newsletter,* July 18, 1963, CHSC, MHL, AMPAS. Heston, *Arena,* 220.

51. Crowther, *Epic Presence,* 68.

52. Funt, "Lydia Heston," V3. Heston, *Journals,* 407.

53. Heston, *Journals,* 482. Bob Baker, "Full-Time Photographer: Lydia Heston Shoots as Charlton Acts," *Los Angeles Times,* May 5, 1970, 6, CHCF, MHL, AMPAS.

54. Bill Powers, interview with the author, Alexandria, VA, May 29, 2002.

55. "Charlton Heston Retrospective—the USA Film Festival's Great Screen Artist Tribute" (flyer), CHSC, MHL, AMPAS. (The retrospective was held at Southern Methodist University's Bob Hope Theater on November 3–4, 1978.) Heston and Isbouts, *Heston's Hollywood,* 189. For a more detailed study of Heston's films, see Crowther's *Epic Presence.*

56. Richard Schickel, *Intimate Strangers: The Culture of Celebrity in America* (Chicago: Dee, 2000), 132.

57. Jeffry Richards, "Heroes, Misfits, and Megalomaniacs," *Sunday Telegraph,* December 10, 1997, 17. Carla Hall, "Fire Power: Conservative Actor Charlton Heston Has a Long History of Activism; Now, the Screen Icon Hopes to Help Lead the NRA to a Better Place," *Los Angeles Times,* May 21, 1997, E1. On John Wayne, an actor of similar qualities, see Garry Wills, *John Wayne's America: The Politics of Celebrity* (New York: Simon & Schuster, 1997).

58. Michael Druxman, *Charlton Heston: A Pyramid Illustrated History of the Movies* (New York: Pyramid, 1976), 11.

59. "Nader, Limbaugh Are Best Spokespeople," *O'Dwyer's PR Services Report,* July 1996, 20. This poll conducted by Porter/Novelli also includes Oprah Winfrey, Michael Jordan, Billy Graham, Robert Redford, Rush Limbaugh, and Ralph Nader as the country's most trusted celebrities.

2. COLD WAR LIBERAL

1. Ronald Brownstein, *The Power and the Glitter: The Hollywood-Washington Connection* (New York: Pantheon, 1990), 28. Mayer served as production chief of MGM until 1951.

2. Ibid., 27–41.

3. Ibid., 45–65.

4. On Stalin, who had starved, slain, or exiled over 5 million peasants in his attempt to collectivize farming, see William O'Neill, *A Better World: The Great Schism: Stalinism and the American Intellectuals* (New York: Simon & Schuster, 1982). Brownstein, *Power and Glitter,* 65–99, 93. The Alliance was especially upset with FDR's decision—based on the 1890 Sherman Antitrust Act—to forbid studios from owning theaters.

5. Ronald Reagan with Richard G. Hubler, *Where's the Rest of Me?* (New York: Karz-Segil, 1965), 169. The Hollywood Ten were Alvah Bessie, Herbert Biberman, Lester Cole, Edward Dmytryk, Ring Lardner Jr., John Lawson, Albert Maltz, Samuel Ornitz, Adrian Scott, and Dalton Trumbo.

6. Lauren Bacall, *By Myself* (New York: Knopf, 1979), 159. Brownstein, *Power and Glitter,* 118.

7. Ibid., 204, 199.

8. Lydia Heston in Marilyn Funt, *Are You Anybody? Conversations with Wives of Celebrities* (New York: Dial, 1979), 201. Kristol, *Neoconservatism,* 11–13.

9. Charlton Heston, "Other Faces, Other Faiths," n.d. (ca. 1955–56), "Writings" (file), CHSC, MHL, AMPAS.

10. Norman Podhoretz, *Breaking Ranks: A Political Memoir* (New York: Harper & Row, 1979), 124.

11. "El Cid—Clippings" (file), CHSC, MHL, AMPAS. Jack Holland, "Charlton Heston Speaks Out," n.d. (ca. 1967–68), "Articles" (file), CHSC, MHL, AMPAS. Charlton Heston, interview with Jean Belmont, ca. 1960–61, CHSC, MHL, AMPAS. Robert Bork, "Culture and Kristol," in DeMuth and Kristol, eds., *Neoconservative Imagination,* 134–46, 144.

12. Mark Gerson, *The Neoconservative Vision: From the Cold War to the Cul-*

ture Wars (Lanham, MD: Madison, 1996), 9–10, 279. See also Michael Novak, ed., *Democracy and Mediating Structures: A Theological Inquiry* (Washington, DC: American Enterprise Institute for Public Policy Research, 1980).

13. Heston, interview with Belmont. Rod Nordell, "Charlton Heston: A Profile in Books," *Christian Science Monitor,* March 31, 1960, CHCF, MHL, AMPAS. Gerson, *Neoconservative Vision,* 281.

14. Charlton Heston, *Charlton Heston Newsletter,* August 30, 1960, CHSC, MHL, AMPAS. Podhoretz, *Breaking Ranks,* 47.

15. Heston, interview with Belmont. Charlton Heston, *Charlton Heston Newsletter,* February 1, 1961, CHSC, MHL, AMPAS. Kristol, *Neoconservatism,* 176.

16. Hook in Gerson, *Neoconservative Vision,* 31. Irving Kristol, "On 'Negative Liberalism'" (1954), in DeMuth and Kristol, eds., *Neoconservative Imagination,* 177.

17. Irving Kristol, "'Civil Liberties,' 1952—a Study in Confusion" (1952), in DeMuth and Kristol, eds., *Neoconservative Imagination,* 177.

18. Kristol, *Neoconservatism,* xi. Irving Kristol, "An Odd Lot" (1960), in DeMuth and Kristol, eds., *Neoconservative Imagination,* 194.

19. See Alan Wolfe, *America's Impasse: The Rise and Fall of the Politics of Growth* (New York: Pantheon, 1981); and Donald Bruce Johnson and Kirk H. Porter, eds., *National Party Platforms, 1840–1972* (Urbana: University of Illinois Press, 1973), 435, 466–67.

20. See Nicol Rae, *The Decline and Fall of the Liberal Republicans from 1952 to the Present* (New York: Oxford University Press, 1989).

21. For more discussion of LBJ's strategies, see Bruce Schulman, *Lyndon B. Johnson and American Liberalism: A Brief Biography with Documents* (Boston: Bedford/St. Martin's, 1995), 47. For McCarthy's downfall, see David M. Oshinsky, *A Conspiracy So Immense: The World of Joe McCarthy* (New York: Free Press; London: Collier Macmillan, 1983).

22. Charlton Heston in Hedda Hopper, "No Restin' for Heston," *Chicago Sunday Tribune,* n.d. (ca. 1952–53), CHCF, MHL, AMPAS.

23. Charlton Heston in Jeff Rovin, *The Films of Charlton Heston* (Secaucus, NJ: Citadell, 1977), 22–23.

24. "Edison Memorial Proposed by Actor," *Los Angeles Times,* February 10, 1955, CHCF, MHL, AMPAS.

25. Charlton Heston, "Taped Interview, August 16, 1955," "Charlton Heston" (file), JHSC, MHL, AMPAS. Kristol in Gerson, *Neoconservative Vision,* 281.

26. Ad for Stevenson, ca. 1956, AAPCF, MHL, AMPAS. Charlton Heston, interview with the author, April 25, 2002, Reno, NV.

27. Lee Belser, "Some Stars Plan Boycott," *Los Angeles Mirror News,* September 16, 1959, AAPCF, MHL, AMPAS. Podhoretz, *Breaking Ranks,* 91.

28. Podhoretz, *Breaking Ranks,* 95.

29. Heston, *Arena,* 260.

30. Heston, *Journals,* 97. Brownstein, *Power and Glitter,* 137.

31. Herbert Parmet, *JFK: The Presidency of John F. Kennedy* (New York: Dial, 1983), 19 ("Kennedy's campaign never faltered for lack of money"). C. Wright Mills, *Power Elite* (New York: Oxford University Press, 1956), 75. The Rat Pack included Frank Sinatra, Dean Martin, Sammy Davis Jr., and Peter Lawford (who, incidentally, married a Kennedy). Brownstein, *Power and Glitter,* 167.

32. Robert Collins, "Growth Liberalism in the Sixties: Great Societies at Home and Grand Designs Abroad," in *The Sixties: From Memory to History,* ed. David Farber (Chapel Hill: University of North Carolina Press, 1994), 15. Stephen Ambrose, *Rise to Globalism: American Foreign Policy since 1938,* 6th ed. (New York: Penguin, 1991). For a more detailed description of Kennedy's campaign strategies regarding African Americans, see Parmet, *JFK,* 54–55. See also John Hope Franklin and Alfred A. Moss Jr., *From Slavery to Freedom: A History of African-Americans* (New York: Knopf, 1994), 498–99.

33. Press release, n.d., "Writings" (file), CHSC, MHL, AMPAS.

34. Inaugural address, January 20, 1961, in John F. Kennedy, *Public Papers of the Presidents of the United States* (Washington, DC: U.S. Government Printing Office, 1961), 1961:1–3. Collins, "Growth Liberalism," 19. Ambrose, *Rise to Globalism,* 140. Heston, *Journals,* 157.

35. Podhoretz, *Breaking Ranks,* 70. Heston, *Journals,* 119.

36. "Charlton Heston Joins Integrationist Marchers," *Los Angeles Times,* May 28, 1961, CHCF, MHL, AMPAS. Clara Luper, *Behold the Walls* (Oklahoma City: Jim Wire, 1979), 134–36. Heston, *Arena,* 261. See also Jimmie Lewis Franklin, *Journey toward Hope: A History of Blacks in Oklahoma* (Norman: University of Oklahoma Press, 1982).

37. Parmet, *JFK,* 249–58. Kennedy, *Public Papers,* 1963:468–71.

38. Henry Hampton and Steve Fayer, with Sarah Flynn, comps., *Voices of Freedom: An Oral History of the Civil Rights Movement from the 1950s through the 1980s* (New York: Bantam, 1990), 165–66. The Big Six were John Lewis, A. Philip Randolph, Martin Luther King Jr., Whitney Young, Roy Wilkins, and James Farmer. The use of civil disobedience and primarily black participants had been the focus of the march in its early stages.

39. Heston, *Journals,* 177.

40. Committee meeting notes, press release, and lists of participants, "Hollywood March on Washington" (file), CHSC, MHL, AMPAS. Heston, *Journals,* 178. Herbert S. Parmet, *Nixon and His America* (Boston: Little, Brown, 1990), 486.

41. Heston and Isbouts, *Heston's Hollywood,* 122. Sidney Poitier, *The Measure of*

a Man: A Spiritual Autobiography (San Francisco: HarperCollins, 2000), 86. Melvin Patrick Ely, *The Adventures of Amos 'n' Andy: A Social History of an American Phenomenon* (New York: Free Press, 1991), 213–18.

42. "Top Film Group Plans to Join Rights March," n.d., "Hollywood March on Washington" (file), CHSC, MHL, AMPAS. "Brando Group Denies 'Rabble Rousing' Cry," *Los Angeles Times*, August 24, 1963, "Hollywood March on Washington" (file), CHSC, MHL, AMPAS. Heston, *Journals*, 178.

43. Charlton Heston in Don Alpert, "Heston Willing to Be a Face in the Crowd," *Los Angeles Times*, December 5, 1965, CHCF, MHL, AMPAS. Heston, *Journals*, 178.

44. Heston, *Journals*, 177.

45. Ibid.

46. Mike Mosettig, "March Tramples on D.C. Boxoffice; Showfolk in Demonstration," *Variety*, August 29, 1963, AAPCF, MHL, AMPAS. Sue Clark, "Stars Plan Performers' Boycott," *Los Angeles Times*, August 29, 1963, AAPCF, MHL, AMPAS. Hampton and Fayer, comps., *Voices of Freedom*, 169.

47. Brownstein, *Power and Glitter*, 170. Heston, *Journals*, 179, 221.

48. Podhoretz, *Breaking Ranks*, 71, 118–29.

49. Parmet, *JFK*, 102.

50. "Berlin Film Festival" (file), CHSC, MHL, AMPAS; and "FDR Scripts" nos. 4 and 5 (files), CHSC, MHL, AMPAS. Besides representing the United States, Heston's duties also included filing a report along with submitting copies of materials and photographs.

51. Heston, *Journals*, 184.

52. Parmet, *JFK*, 352. Kristol in Gerson, *Neoconservative Vision*, 126.

53. Mary Brennan, *Turning Right in the Sixties: The Conservative Capture of the GOP* (Chapel Hill: University of North Carolina Press, 1995), 86. Heston, *Arena*, 353.

54. George Nash, *The Conservative Intellectual Movement in America since 1945* (New York: Basic, 1976), 218. Donald J. Senese, "'Whistlin' Dixie': Republican Gains in the South," *New Guard* 47 (January 1965): 16–18, 16.

55. Brownstein, *Power and Glitter*, 179–92.

56. Garry Wills, *Reagan's America: Innocents at Home* (1987; reprint, New York: Penguin, 2000), 342–48.

57. Memo from Bess Abell to Lyndon Johnson and Jack Valenti, November 23, 1963, EX AR 11/23/63, box 1, "AR ARTS 12/20/64–11/5/65" (file), LBJL. White House Daily Diary Cards for Gregory Peck, Kirk Douglas, and Lew Wasserman, LBJL.

58. Kennedy, *Public Papers*, 1961:614, 673–74. Lyndon B. Johnson, *Public Papers of the Presidents of the United States* (Washington, D.C.: U.S. Government Printing Office, 1965), 1965:117–18. "The Administrative History of the Department of State, Volume I, Chapters 10–13," 47, box 4, "Chapter 12" (file), LBJL.

59. "Administrative History," 50. Charlton Heston, *Charlton Heston Newsletter*, May 1, 1965, CHSC, MHL, AMPAS. Roger Bower, "Heston 'Takes' Nigeria: Hollywood and Politico Offset to 'Ugly American,'" *Variety Weekend*, April 21, 1965, CHCF, MHL, AMPAS. Heston, *Journals*, 254. "Heston Tours Down Under for Department of State," *Hollywood Reporter*, June 24, 1966, CHCF, MHL, AMPAS. Charlton Heston, *Charlton Heston Newsletter*, August 18, 1966, CHSC, MHL, AMPAS. Papers of LBJ, EX LE/AR, box 28, "LE/AR" (file), LBJL.

60. Heston, *Journals*, 253.

61. "Is There Time?" (advertisement), *Variety*, October 27, 1964, 5, AAPCF, MHL, AMPAS. See also "Film Stars Rally against Proposition 14," *Los Angeles Herald Examiner*, September 10, 1964, AAPCF, MHL, AMPAS; and Harold Hefferman, "Actors in Politics Say, 'I've Had It,'" *Hollywood Citizen-News*, November 3, 1964, AAPCF, MHL, AMPAS.

62. Art Sidenbaum, "Make Way for the New Performing Art—Politics," *Los Angeles Times*, November 14, 1965, Calendar Section, AAPCF, MHL, AMPAS. Robert Vaughan in Hal Humphrey, "Actors Take Active Role in Politics," *Los Angeles Times*, November 14, 1966, AAPCF, MHL, AMPAS.

63. Podhoretz, *Breaking Ranks*, 239.

3. UNION LEADER

1. Charlton Heston in "Heston's Rx for Ailing Hollywood," July 20, 1969, Charles Champlin Special Collection, "57, Articles-Bio (Heston)" (file), MHL, AMPAS.

2. Murray Ross, *Stars and Strikes: Unionization of Hollywood* (New York: Columbia University Press, 1941), 6, 28–37. The major studios at the time included MGM, Warner Bros., Paramount, 20th Century Fox, and RKO.

3. Ibid., 41, 44.

4. David F. Prindle, *The Politics of Glamour: Ideology and Democracy in the Screen Actors Guild* (Madison: University of Wisconsin Press, 1988), 22–24.

5. Gerald Horne, *Class Struggle in Hollywood, 1930–50: Moguls, Mobsters, Stars, Reds, and Trade Unionists* (Austin: University of Texas Press, 2001), 39. "SAG History," http://www.sag.org/history/index.html.

6. Frank "Junior" Coghlan, http://www.sag.org/history/founders_flat.html. Fay Wray, Ginger Rogers, and Maureen O'Sullivan, http://www.sag.org/history/founders_flat2.html.

7. Binnie Barnes, Frank "Buddy" Ebsen, and Milton Berle, http://www.sag.org/history/founders_flat.html. Jack Haley took over the role of the Tin Man from Ebsen.

8. Reagan, *Rest of Me?* 130. Ross, *Stars and Strikes*, 108. Dorothy Granger, Frank

"Junior" Coghlan, Don Defore, and Douglas Fairbanks, http://www.sag.org/history/founders_flat.html. Dickie Moore, http://www.sag.org/history/founders_flat2.html.

9. Prindle, *Politics of Glamour,* 22.

10. Paul Conkin, *The New Deal* (Wheeling, IL: Davidson, 1992), 33. Ross, *Stars and Strikes,* 104–5.

11. Mary Brian and Ann Doran, http://www.sag.org/history/founders_flat. html. Gloria Stuart, http://www.sag.org/history/founders_flat2.html. Ivy Brown, "Building the Guild" (printout in author's files; originally but no longer available through the SAG Web site).

12. Ross, *Stars and Strikes,* 161, 172.

13. Jack Dales, *Pragmatic Leadership: Ronald Reagan as President of the Screen Actors Guild* (an interview with Dales conducted by Mitch Tuchman), California State Archives, California State Oral Histories, OH R-34 (1981), 2, Oral History Program, Young Research Library, Special Collections, University of California, Los Angeles. Montgomery served several one-year terms as president of the Screen Actors Guild: from 1935 to 1938 and then again from 1946 to 1947. Murphy served two terms from 1944 to 1946. Brownstein, *Power and Glitter,* 89–90.

14. Brownstein, *Power and Glitter,* 22–23.

15. Dales, *Pragmatic Leadership,* 43–44.

16. Ibid., 8. Prindle, *Politics of Glamour,* 194.

17. Reagan, *Rest of Me?* 127. Mike Nielsen and Gene Mailes, *Hollywood's Other Blacklist: Union Struggles in the Studio System* (London: British Film Institute, 1995), 4–5, 15–17. Horne, *Class Struggle in Hollywood,* 97–111.

Horne carefully documents the friendships between various studio executives and mobsters, including the one between Bioff and Joseph Schneck, the head of production and then board chair of Fox. Schneck entertained Bioff in his home, purchased twenty-five hundred shares of various stocks for him, and lent him $95,000 to buy a sprawling ranch in southern California. Schneck defended these gifts as being given out of fear. Ibid., 120–21. But it was the rumors surrounding Schneck and Browne that prompted the investigative reporter Westbrook Pegler to meticulously dig into Bioff and Browne's alleged criminal origins, and the Guild supported his efforts. When Pegler discovered that Bioff still needed to serve six months for pandering, the Illinois police took over the probe. The authorities found evidence of extortion and indicted Browne and Bioff in 1941.

The craft locals organized painters, scenic artists, hairdressers, makeup artists, laborers, costumers, draftspersons, plumbers, engineers, boilermakers, blacksmiths, machinists, linoleum workers, sheet metal workers, and culinary workers, among others.

18. Nielsen and Mailes, *Hollywood's Other Blacklist,* 67, 71, 86. While the num-

ber of strikes averaged around 2,300 per year between 1935 and 1940, no fewer than 4,956 broke out in 1944, a statistic compounded by the fact that the average duration of strikes doubled that year as well. Ibid., 71–72.

19. Sorrell issued the CSU's strike against the studios on October 5, 1944, a work stoppage that included the participation of seven thousand workers. Starting with MGM, the CSU wanted the studios to recognize its set decorators and ignored the WLB when it ordered a cooling-off period. IA leaders retaliated by directing IA locals to perform the work of the strikers and also convinced projectionists to start picketing if the producers capitulated to the demands of the CSU. Nielsen and Mailes, *Hollywood's Other Blacklist,* 100.

The CSU blacklist eventually included Rosalind Russell, Robert Montgomery, John Wayne, Leo Carrillo, Humphrey Bogart, and Susan Hayward, among others. Horne, *Class Struggle in Hollywood,* 162.

The Guild negotiated with the CSU so that stars need not physically cross the picket lines to keep working, and they thus encountered little harm. Despite this compromise, the Guild never lent its support to the CSU.

20. Horne, *Class Struggle in Hollywood,* viii, 173. Nielsen and Mailes, *Hollywood's Other Blacklist,* 86.

21. Horne, *Class Struggle in Hollywood,* 209. See also Prindle, *Politics of Glamour,* 209; and Nielsen and Mailes, *Hollywood's Other Blacklist,* 151–58. Reagan carried a gun for the next seven months. Ronald Reagan, *An American Life* (New York: Simon & Schuster, 1990), 108. Reagan, *Rest of Me?* 156–57.

22. Reagan, *An American Life,* 114.

23. Steven Vaughn, *Ronald Reagan in Hollywood: Movies and Politics* (Cambridge: Cambridge University Press, 1994), 144, 147. Prindle, *Politics of Glamour,* 52–54.

24. Vaughn, *Reagan in Hollywood,* 156. Dales, *Pragmatic Leadership,* 21–22.

25. Prindle, *Politics of Glamour,* 94–95.

26. Harry Bernstein, "Heston Tells of Need for Actors Guild," *Los Angeles Times,* August 14, 1966, CHCF, MHL, AMPAS. John Dales, "Memo," *Screen Actor,* September/October 1970, 1, SAG Archives. Dales, *Pragmatic Leadership,* 35.

27. Prindle, *Politics of Glamour,* 83.

28. Dales, *Pragmatic Leadership,* 36. Charlton Heston, interview with the author, April 25, 2002, Reno, NV. Heston, *Arena,* 237. Reagan, *Rest of Me?* 282. Laraine Day, http://www.sag.org/history/founders_flat.html. Prindle, *Politics of Glamour,* 87.

29. "Reagan's World View," *Albuquerque Journal,* January 14, 1989, reprinted in *Reagan as President: Contemporary Views of the Man, His Politics, and His Policies,* ed. Paul Boyer (Chicago: Dee, 1990), 280–81. Lydia Heston, interview with Jean Belmont, n.d. (ca. 1961), "Interview Transcripts" (file), CHSC, MHL, AMPAS.

30. Martin E. P. Seligman, *Learned Optimism* (New York: Knopf, 1990), 79–82, 113.

31. Ibid., 187–88.

32. Charlton Heston, "Text of Address by SAG President," *Screen Actor,* January/February 1967, 7–9, SAG Archives. Jack Dales, "Notes," *Screen Actor,* July/August 1967, 3, SAG Archives.

33. Charlton Heston, "Speech to Annual SAG Meeting," Hollywood Palladium, November 12, 1967, "Charlton Heston—SAG" (file), CHSC, MHL, AMPAS. Bryant apparently was an actor looking for work and appealing to the Guild for help. Letter from Charlton Heston to Paul Bryant, March 7, 1969, SAG Archives.

34. "Statement of Charlton Heston as Third Vice-President, SAG, Before the Subcommittee on the Impact of Imports and Exports on American Employment House Committee on Education and Labor," December 2, 1961, "Screen Actors Guild" (file), CHSC, MHL, AMPAS. Heston, *Journals,* 142.

35. Heston, "Statement as Third Vice-President."

36. "Minutes of Board," January 29, 1968, SAG Archives.

37. Letter from Charlton Heston to George Moscone, March 10, 1968, SAG Archives. "Guilds and Unions Win Fight against Unfair Tax on Films," *Screen Actor,* September/October 1968, 2, SAG Archives.

38. Buck Harris, "Unions and Guilds Seek Runaway Production Cure," *Screen Actor,* April/May 1968, 1–3, SAG Archives.

39. "Minutes of Board," January 29, 1968, SAG Archives. Heston, *Arena,* 412. Heston in "Heston's Rx for Ailing Hollywood."

40. "Experimental Contract Changes Seek to Boost Film Production," *Screen Actor,* March/April 1970, 1–2, 14, SAG Archives. "Notes," *Screen Actor,* May/June 1970, 1, SAG Archives. "Actors as Union Men" (guest column for Victor Reisel), July 1970, "Screen Actors Guild" (file), CHSC, MHL, AMPAS.

41. Charlton Heston, "Speech to Annual SAG Meeting," Hollywood Palladium, November 22, 1970, "Charlton Heston—SAG" (file), CHSC, MHL, AMPAS. "Reagan, Tunney Ask Film Industry Aid," *Los Angeles Herald Examiner,* December 1, 1970, SAG Archives. John Dales, "Reagan Urges Nixon to Support Tax Incentive Plan," *Screen Actor,* March/April 1971, 4, SAG Archives. John Dales, "Memo," *Screen Actor,* January 1972, 13, SAG Archives. John Dales, "Memo," *Screen Actor,* October 1971, 3, SAG Archives.

42. Heston, "Speech to Annual SAG Meeting," November 22, 1970.

43. "SAG Memo," n.d., SAG Archives. Heston, "Speech to Annual SAG Meeting," November 22, 1970.

44. Charlton Heston in Jeane Beaty, "TV Shirking Its Creative Responsibilities—Heston," *Los Angeles Times,* April 12, 1967, Calendar Section, CHCF, MHL,

AMPAS. "Text of Address by SAG President," *Screen Actor,* January/February 1967, 7, SAG Archives.

45. The rating "PG-13" was added in 1984, and CARA struggled to find an adequate rating for movies that had adult themes but should not be considered pornographic, as X insinuated. It finally settled on "NC-17" in 1990. David Prindle, *Risky Business: The Political Economy of Hollywood* (Boulder, CO: Westview, 1993), 156–59. Charlton Heston, untitled speech, December 9, 1969, "Screen Actors Guild" (file), CHSC, MHL, AMPAS.

Although the Hays guidelines have been characterized as "rather prissy," some historians argue that the struggles between the artists and the censors throughout the 1930s and 1940s may have produced a more creative, quality product. After all, that time period is considered the golden age of Hollywood, and self-restraint can often be rewarding. See Prindle, *Risky Business,* 156–59.

46. Vaughn, *Reagan in Hollywood,* 176–77.

47. Murray Schumach, "Stars Join Drive against Bigotry," *New York Times,* July 15, 1963, CHSC, MHL, AMPAS.

48. "Talent Feels Producers Anti-Negro, but Latter Put Blame on Bankers," *Variety,* July 16, 1963, CHSC, MHL, AMPAS. Heston, *Arena,* 437.

49. "Reader Letters," *Screen Actor,* September/October 1970, 21, SAG Archives. "Discussion from the Floor," *Screen Actor,* January/February 1969, 11, SAG Archives. Gerson, *Neoconservative Vision,* 86.

50. Dales, *Pragmatic Leadership,* 43.

51. Paul Ehrman, "Too Much Courtesy?" *Screen Actor,* January/February 1971, 27, SAG Archives. "Discussion from the Floor." Heston, *Journals,* 215.

52. Prindle, *Politics of Glamour,* 96.

53. Ibid., 101. Heston, *Journals,* 371.

54. Prindle, *Politics of Glamour,* 97.

55. Kristol, *Neoconservatism,* 359.

4. ARTS PATRON

1. Memo from George Stevens to Jack Valenti, January 27, 1964, Papers of LBJ, Peck file, LBJL. The Headliners Club of Austin was established in 1954 by Charles Green, the editor of the *Austin American-Statesman,* to foster camaraderie between those who make headlines and the journalists who write them. For the Peck remark, see fax from Gregory Peck to Jack Valenti, January 31, 1964, Papers of LBJ, Peck file, LBJL. Letter from Gregory Peck to Jack Valenti, February 19, 1964, Papers of LBJ, Peck file, LBJL.

2. Lyndon Johnson, "The Great Society," in William Chafe and Harvard Sit-

koff, eds., *A History of Our Time: Readings on Postwar America* (New York: Oxford University Press, 1983), 149–52. Livingston Biddle, *Our Government and the Arts: A Perspective from the Inside* (New York: ACA, 1988), 75–77.

3. Doris Kearns Goodwin, *Lyndon Johnson and the American Dream* (New York: Harper & Row, 1976), 210–50.

4. "NEA History" (file), NEAL.

5. Joseph Wesley Zeigler, *Arts in Crisis: The National Endowment for the Arts versus America* (Pennington, NJ: A Cappella, 1994), 3.

6. Ibid., 5.

7. Ibid.

8. Barbara Leaming, *Orson Welles: A Biography* (New York: Viking, 1985), 133–36.

9. Dick Netzer, *The Subsidized Muse: Public Support for the Arts in the United States* (Cambridge: Cambridge University Press, 1978), 57.

10. David Smith, "Covered Wagons of Culture: The Roots and Early History of the National Endowment for the Arts" (Ph.D. diss., University of Missouri, Columbia, 2000), 33.

11. Charlton Heston, testimony before the Special Subcommittee on Labor of the Committee on Education and Labor, U.S. House of Representatives, and the Special Subcommittee on Arts and Humanities of the Committee on Labor and Public Welfare, U.S. Senate, 89th Cong., 1st sess., February 23 and March 3, 1965, 72. Charlton Heston, testimony before the Subcommittee on Communication and Power of the Committee on Interstate and Foreign Commerce, U.S. House of Representatives, 91st Cong., 1st sess., November 18, 19, 20, 21, and 24 and December 9, 10, 11, and 12, 1969, 141. Charlton Heston, testimony before the Select Subcommittee on Education of the Committee on Education and Labor, U.S. House of Representatives, 93rd Cong., 1st sess., March 16, 1973.

12. Netzer, *Subsidized Muse*, 16.

13. Smith, "Covered Wagons," 97, 107.

14. "Statement by the President upon Establishing the Advisory Council on the Arts," June 12, 1963, in Kennedy, *Public Papers*, 1963:473–75.

15. Smith, "Covered Wagons," 198, 203.

16. Charlton Heston, testimony before the Special Subcommittee on Labor of the Committee on Education and Labor, U.S. House of Representatives, and the Special Subcommittee on Arts and Humanities of the Committee on Labor and Public Welfare, U.S. Senate, 89th Cong., 1st sess., February 23 and March 3, 1965, 73, 74.

17. Eric F. Goldman, "The White House and the Intellectuals: The Inside Story of LBJ's Festival of the Arts and the Artists and Writers Who Participated," *Harper's Magazine,* January 1969, 31–45, 31. Press release, June 14, 1965, Papers of LBJ,

White House Social File, Liz Carpenter's Subject File, box 16, "White House Festival of the Arts" (file), LBJL. "Tentative Scenario, White House Festival of the Arts, June 14, 1965," Papers of LBJ, White House Social File, Social Entertainment, box 54, "Festival of Arts" (file [2 of 2]). Also "Scenario" and "Tentative Guest List," Papers of LBJ, White House Social Files, Bess Abell, White House Social Office, box 11, "White House Festival of the Arts" (files), LBJL.

18. Letter from Robert Lowell to Lyndon Johnson, May 30, 1965, Papers of LBJ, "AR/MC, November 23, 1963–June 4, 1965" (file), LBJL. Memo from Jack Valenti to Lyndon Johnson, June 8, 1965, Papers of LBJ, "AR/MC, June 5–12, 1965" (file), LBJL. Goldman, "White House and Intellectuals," 36–37.

19. Letter from John Hersey to Eric Goldman, July 26, 1965, Papers of LBJ, "AR/MC 6/15/65–6/12/65" (file), box 2, Gen AR, LBJL. Goldman, "White House and Intellectuals," 44.

20. Memo from B. Diamonstein to Eric Goldman, May 11, 1966, Papers of LBJ, "AR/MC 6/13/65" (file), LBJL. Jack Valenti, "Valenti Oral History, Chapter 5," 32–34, LBJL. "Arts and the Man—and the State," *Newsweek*, June 28, 1965, 22–24, 23. Heston, *Journals*, 228.

21. Telegram from Kirk Douglas to Lyndon Johnson, October 1, 1965, Papers of LBJ, EX LE/AR, box 28, "LE/AR" (file), LBJL. Valenti, "Oral History," 35.

22. Netzer, *Subsidized Muse*, 62.

23. Smith, "Covered Wagons," 257–87. See also memo from NEA Chair Roger Stevens to Lyndon Johnson, May 20, 1966, Papers of LBJ, EX FG 11-9/A, box 123, "FG 11–12 National Council on the Arts" (file), LBJL. Roger Stevens, "Stevens Oral History, Chapter 4," 18, LBJL.

24. Smith, "Covered Wagons," 190. Heston and Isbouts, *Heston's Hollywood*, 164.

25. Heston, *Journals*, 260, 272.

26. Minutes of the Eighth Meeting of the National Council on the Arts, May 12–14, 1967, 32, NEAL. Heston, *Journals*, 272.

27. Biddle, *Government and the Arts*, 204.

28. Smith, "Covered Wagons," 352–62. Zeigler, *Arts in Crisis*, 26.

29. Melvin Small, *The Presidency of Richard Nixon* (Lawrence: University Press of Kansas, 1999), 220. Smith, "Covered Wagons," 364–67.

30. Minutes of the Fourteenth Meeting of the National Council on the Arts, January 27–28, 1969, 22, NEAL. Michael Straight, *Nancy Hanks: An Intimate Portrait* (Durham, NC: Duke University Press, 1988), 202.

31. Minutes of the Twelfth Meeting of the National Council on the Arts, June 14, 1968, 5, NEAL. Minutes of the Fourteenth Meeting of the National Council on the Arts, January 27–28, 1969, section tab 8, n.p., NEAL.

32. Heston, *Journals,* 368. Minutes of the Twenty-second Meeting of the National Council on the Arts, September 10–12, 1971, 14–15, 24, NEAL.

33. Minutes of the Twenty-second Meeting of the National Council on the Arts, September 10–12, 1971, 14–15. See also "Three Grants Totaling $55,000 Are Awarded Street Theater," *Ossining, NY, Citizen Register,* July 19, 1972, Vertical File, NEAL.

34. Heston, *Journals,* 368. Charlton Heston, testimony before the Subcommittee on Select Education of the Committee on Education and Labor, U.S. House of Representatives, and the Subcommittee on Education, Arts, and Humanities of the Committee on Human Resources, U.S. Senate, 95th Cong., 1st and 2nd sess., January 3, 1978, 360.

35. Heston, *Journals,* 371.

36. Norman Podhoretz, *Making It* (New York: Random House, 1967). Podhoretz, *Breaking Ranks,* 268, 320.

37. Kristol, *Neoconservatism,* 340.

38. Schulman, *LBJ and American Liberalism,* 101.

39. Kristol, *Neoconservatism,* 29.

40. Irving Kristol, "On Corporate Capitalism in America," *Public Interest* 41 (fall 1975): 124–41.

41. Dee Rutger, "Bridging the . . . Culture Gap," *Los Angeles Herald Dispatch,* February 12, 1972, Vertical File, "Expansion Arts" (file), NEAL.

42. Podhoretz, *Breaking Ranks,* 169.

43. Straight, *Nancy Hanks,* 210. Joel Dreyfuss, "Theater Also Stars Audience," *New York Post,* April 13, 1972, Vertical File, "Expansion Arts" (file), NEAL. Heston, *Arena,* 569. Irving Kristol, "The Tragedy of Multiculturalism," *Wall Street Journal,* July 31, 1991, A10.

44. Nathan Glazer, *The Limits of Social Policy* (London: Harvard University Press, 1988), 1–2.

45. Daniel Patrick Moynihan, *The Negro Family: A Case for National Action* (Washington, DC: U.S. Department of Labor, Office of Policy Planning and Research, 1965). Irving Kristol in Robert Glasgow, "The Suburbanized World: 'Countries That Become More Equal Don't Necessarily Become Happier'; a Conversation with Irving Kristol and about Irresponsible Intellectuals, the Loss of Provincial Values, the Volatility of Urban Life, and the Prospects for Change," *Psychology Today* 7, no. 9 (February 1974): 71, 73–76, 78, 80 (quote).

46. Biddle, *Government and the Arts,* 181. Minutes of the Seventeenth Meeting of the National Council on the Arts, January 23–26, 1970, 17, NEAL. Heston, *Journals,* 257. Stanford Research Institute, *Organization and Location of the American Film Institute,* February 1967 (prepared for the Committee on Form, the National

Council on the Arts, the National Endowment for the Arts, and the National Foundation for the Arts and Humanities), 3–10, NEAL. Letter from Lyndon B. Johnson to Gregory Peck, May 24, 1967, EX/AR, LBJL.

47. Straight, *Nancy Hanks*, 229.

48. Minutes of the Seventeenth Meeting of the National Council on the Arts, January 23–26, 1970, 34, NEAL.

49. Chloe Aaron, "A Special Report to the Chairman on Public Media" (December 31, 1970), 17–20, presented at the twentieth meeting of the National Council on the Arts, February 12–14, 1971, NEAL.

50. Straight, *Nancy Hanks*, 231–32.

51. Heston, *Journals*, 373.

52. Ibid., 403.

53. Ibid., 387. Straight, *Nancy Hanks*, 233.

54. Heston, *Journals*, 402.

55. Ibid., 12.

56. Jack Valenti, transcript, *This Is Your Life*, thirtieth anniversary special, November 26, 1981, CHSC, MHL, AMPAS. Charlton Heston, testimony before the Special Subcommittee on Arts and Humanities of the Committee on Labor and Public Welfare, U.S. Senate, 93rd Cong., 2nd sess., December 11, 1974, 39–50.

57. See, e.g., "Heston Responds to Film Institute Story," *New York Times*, February 16, 1975, Vertical File, "AFI" (file), NEAL. Straight, *Nancy Hanks*, 236.

58. Heston, *Journals*, 455, 405.

59. John Frohnmayer, *Leaving Town Alive: Confessions of an Arts Warrior* (Boston: Houghton Mifflin, 1993), 48.

5. DEMOCRAT FOR REPUBLICANS

1. Heston, *Journals*, 295.

2. Allen Matusow, *The Unraveling of America: A History of Liberalism in the 1960s* (New York: Harper & Row, 1984), 395.

3. Under the guidance of the Communist Ho Chi Minh, colonial Indochina declared its independence from France in 1945, just as the Cold War was developing between the United States and the Soviet Union. American containment theorists worried that, if Vietnam was allowed to achieve independence through Communist insurgency, such a victory would inspire Communist revolutions throughout the Third World. In 1950, the Truman administration armed and funded the French forces fighting to maintain domination of the colony. After France retreated in 1954, President Eisenhower maintained an American presence in South Vietnam, building an anti-Communist client state there, sending Amer-

ican military "advisers" to train the South Vietnamese army, and installing Ngo Din Diem as the country's president. Kennedy later augmented this support when he doubled the number of military advisers stationed in the region. In November 1963, sixteen thousand advisers were stationed in Vietnam. See Ambrose, *Rise to Globalism,* 102–235. See also Schulman, *LBJ and American Liberalism,* 131–34.

4. Schulman, *LBJ and American Liberalism,* 135, 138. Matusow, *Unraveling of America,* 160.

5. Ambrose, *Rise to Globalism,* 211.

6. Charlton Heston, *Charlton Heston Newsletter,* March 30, 1966, CHSC, MHL, AMPAS.

7. Ibid.

8. Heston, *Journals,* 244. Memo from George Thomas to Charlton Heston, "Actors Life" (file), CHSC, MHL, AMPAS. Heston and Isbouts, *Heston's Hollywood,* 159.

9. Charlton Heston, *Charlton Heston Newsletter,* March 30, 1966, CHSC, MHL, AMPAS. *News of the Day,* vol. 38, no. 295, excerpt from an MGM U.S. savings bond trailer, July 7, 1967, UCLA Film and Television Archive.

10. Jerry Bigel, "Showfolk Plan July 4 TV Special to Explain U.S. Goals in Vietnam," *Variety,* May 10, 1967, AAPCF, MHL, AMPAS.

11. The review could not perform at bases but staged shows at the towns closest by. Leticia Kent, "It's Not Just 'Fonda and Company,'" *New York Times,* March 21, 1971, AAPCF, MHL, AMPAS. Brownstein, *Power and Glitter,* 253–60.

12. Podhoretz, *Breaking Ranks,* 218.

13. A group of activists, both black and white, traveled to the Democratic national convention in the hopes of unseating Mississippi's all-white delegation, only to be rebuffed by the president. King agreed to LBJ's offer of honorary seats for the MFDP, but the delegates considered this deal a sellout. To Carmichael, the MFDP's failure proved that the Democrats and King could not be trusted. In Selma, Carmichael resented King's decision to back down from police on Pettis Bridge. See Hampton and Fayer, comps., *Voices of Freedom,* 177–209.

14. Matusow, *Unraveling of America,* 352–60. Hampton and Fayer, comps., *Voices of Freedom,* 343.

15. On June 4, 1965, in a speech at Howard University, LBJ promised federal action to promote equality as fact and result in employment, education, and social life. However, politics demanded that the president retreat from this position, and he ultimately presented the War on Poverty as not focused solely on race. For the most part, LBJ vetoed any suggestion of a guaranteed income, but this is exactly the direction in which the Democrats were headed. As Gareth Davies puts it: "In a war which sought to tap the buoyant optimism and idealism of the American

people, the guaranteed income, far from representing the triumph of liberalism, would have been considered the ultimate admission of its defeat." Gareth Davies, *From Opportunity to Entitlement: The Transformation and Decline of Great Society Liberalism* (Lawrence: University Press of Kansas, 1996), 53. Likewise, Whitney Young Jr. called for a "Marshall Plan for the American Negro." Ibid., 57.

16. Ibid., 98. Matusow, *Unraveling of America,* 198.

17. Irving Kristol, "Skepticism, Meliorism, and *The Public Interest,*" *Public Interest* 81 (fall 1985): 31–41, 33–34.

18. Podhoretz, *Breaking Ranks,* 287.

19. Kristol, "On Corporate Capitalism in America," 134.

20. Inspired by the Southern civil rights struggle, the students instigated their own direct action programs with their Economic Research and Action Project (ERAP) in 1963, where they lived among poor citizens in Northern cities and sought to organize them politically. The following year, SDS workers joined SNCC in the Mississippi Freedom Summer. Most ERAP projects folded after one summer, and the Mississippi venture resulted in considerable tension between black and white volunteers, but the spirit did not die. When those project volunteers returned to their respective campuses, they surprised Hayden when they proved themselves a radical force. Tom Hayden et al./Students for a Democratic Society, "The Port Huron Statement," in Chafe and Sitkoff, eds., *History of Our Time,* 345–50, 348. Matusow, *Unraveling of America,* 309. Godfrey Hodgson, *America in Our Time* (Garden City, NY: Doubleday, 1976), 283–323.

21. Matusow, *Unraveling of America,* 277.

22. Noam Chomsky, "The Responsibility of Intellectuals," *New York Review of Books,* February 23, 1967, 16–26, 16, 26. Matusow, *Unraveling of America,* 385–87. Lewis Chester, Godfrey Hodgson, and Bruce Page, *An American Melodrama: The Presidential Campaign of 1968* (New York: Viking, 1969), 88. Herbert S. Parmet, *Democrats: The Years after FDR* (New York: Macmillan, 1976), 263.

23. Heston, *Journals,* 291. Matusow, *Unraveling of America,* 395.

24. Hodgson, *America in Our Time,* 363. Heston, *Journals,* 295.

25. Memo from George Reedy to the President, June 5, 1968, "JL3/Kennedy, Robert" (file), LBJL. "Address to the Nation Following the Attack on Senator Kennedy," June 5, 1968, in Johnson, *Public Papers,* 1968:691.

26. "Administrative History, Department of Justice, Vol. II, Pt. 1 Criminal Division, Narrative History [1 of 2]," 1–2, LBJL.

27. Memo from B. Marvel to Fred Panzer, December 20, 1967, Subj: Possible Republican Issues to be Stressed in the Next Session of the 90th Congress, "11/15/67–12/20/67, Judicial-Legal Matters (ExJl 3 11/15/67)" (file), LBJL. Memo

from Fred Panzer to the President, February 27, 1968, Subj: Advance Gallup for Wednesday, February 28, 1968, "12/21/67–2/29/68, Judicial-Legal Matters (ExJl 3 11/15/67)" (file), LBJL.

28. Memo from Larry Levinson to Joseph Califano, June 14, 1968, Subj: Materials on Gun Control for Briefing, box 27, "JL3, 6/1/68–6/19/68, Judicial-Legal Matters (ExJl 3/11/67)" (file), LBJL. "Letter to the President of the Senate and to the Speaker of the House Urging Passage of an Effective Gun Control Law," June 6, 1968, in Johnson, *Public Papers,* 1968:694.

29. "Firearms Stats June 1968," Personal Papers of Ramsey Clark, LBJL.

30. Memo from Liz to the President, June 11, 1968, "LE/JL3, JL3, CM/Firearms, FG999" (file), LBJL. Memo from Joseph Califano to the President, June 20, 1968, "SP LE/JL3 UT1-1" (file), LBJL.

31. Letter from Dick McKay to Joseph Califano, June 18, 1968, Legislative Background, Gun Control 1968, "Public Concern-1968" (file), box 1, LBJL.

32. Charlton Heston, interview with the author, April 25, 2002, Reno, NV. Heston, *Journals,* 296.

33. "Statement by the President upon Signing the Omnibus Crime Control and Safe Streets Act of 1968," June 16, 1968, in Johnson, *Public Papers,* 1968:725.

34. Press release, June 24, 1968, Personal Papers of Ramsey Clark, "PP of R. Clark: Gun Control, Emergency CTE for 1968" (file), box 95, LBJL.

35. Heston, *Journals,* 296. "Remarks upon Signing the Gun Control Act of 1968," October 22, 1968, in Johnson, *Public Papers,* 1968:1059.

36. Andrew M. Greeley, *Building Coalitions: American Politics in the 1970s* (New York: New Viewpoints, 1974), 10, 15.

37. Chester, Hodgson, and Page, *American Melodrama,* 387.

38. Ibid., 507–784. Matusow, *Unraveling of America,* 423. Seymour Martin Lipset and Earl Raab, "The Election and the National Mood," *Commentary,* January 1971, 43–50, 49. Lou Harris, "Public Favors Gun Control," *Los Angeles Times,* 1968, AAPCF, MHL, AMPAS.

39. Chester, Hodgson, and Page, *American Melodrama,* 516.

40. Ibid., 400.

41. Heston, *Journals,* 326–28.

42. Chester, Hodgson, and Page, *American Melodrama,* 540–44. Podhoretz, *Breaking Ranks,* 292.

43. Some evident problems included the overwhelming control of the party leaders, the unreasonably early selection of delegates, the unrestrained use of majority rule, the holding of secret and enclosed meetings, and the underrepresentation of minorities. Indeed, delegate selection was so early that 33 percent of the

delegates had been selected before 1968—before LBJ had withdrawn and other candidates had entered the race. McGovern's report also revealed various loopholes that left major decisions to the discretion of elected or appointed party officials. Some examples included the Unit Rule, in which delegates were bound to vote for the preference of the majority, even if they personally favored someone else, and proxy voting, in which one person was authorized to speak for an entire state. Since Humphrey was LBJ's vice president, these rules had made him the favorite. See Democratic Party National Committee, Commission on Party Structure and Delegate Selection, *Mandate for Reform* (Washington, DC, April 1970), 10–11, 22–30; and Robert Sam Anson, *McGovern: A Biography* (New York: Holt, Rinehart & Winston, 1972), 204. In February 1971, McGovern instituted four broad requirements for the party: (1) the adoption of explicit, written rules; (2) new procedural rules and safeguards; (3) methods to seek a broad base of party support; and (4) a revamped delegate selection process. More specifically, proxy voting and the Unit Rule were stricken from the by-laws, while affirmative action became official policy. Ronald Radosh, *Divided They Fell: The Demise of the Democratic Party, 1964–1996* (New York: Free Press, 1996), 134.

44. Radosh, *Divided They Fell*, 176–78.

45. Brownstein, *Power and Glitter*, 237, 244–45.

46. Davies, *From Opportunity to Entitlement*, 212. Hodgson, *America in Our Time*, 426. Lipset and Raab, "Election and National Mood," 43.

47. These had been particularly vexing issues for those who opposed the war. Parmet, *Nixon*, 592.

48. Kristol, *Neoconservatism*, x. Heston, *Journals*, 388. Podhoretz, *Breaking Ranks*, 342.

49. *News Conference, Charlton Heston Supports Richard Nixon.*

50. Heston, *Journals*, 394–95, 401.

51. Ibid., 396.

52. Hodgson, *America in Our Time*, 367.

53. Lisa McGirr, *Suburban Warriors: The Origins of the New American Right* (Princeton, NJ: Princeton University Press, 2001), 226.

54. Samuel Huntington termed this notion *categorical representation*. Political leaders within the party were encouraged to act in their own self-interest and not for the party at large, and the Democrats became more divided and fractious as new liberals told people to emphasize their differences, not their similarities. Furthermore, the McGovern reforms weakened the central leadership of the party, thus making it more difficult for an elder statesman to rise up and unite the party. "One might have thought," Huntington writes, "that the proper role of the political party was to transcend or, failing that, to blur, or failing that, at least to obfus-

cate the lines between groups, not to institutionalize them." Samuel Huntington, "The Visions of the Democratic Party," *Public Interest* 79 (spring 1975): 63–78, 67.

55. Radosh, *Divided They Fell,* 200.

56. Gregory L. Schneider, *Cadres for Conservatism: Young Americans for Freedom and the Rise of the Contemporary Right* (New York: New York University Press, 1999), 145. See also William Rusher, *The Rise of the Right* (New York: Morrow, 1984), 153, 237.

57. Gerson, *Neoconservative Vision,* 109.

58. Kristol, *Neoconservatism,* 31. Heston in Rovin, *Films of Heston,* 22–23. Irving Kristol, "Utopianism, Ancient and Modern," *Imprimus* 2, no. 4 (April 1973): 1–6.

59. Heston in Rovin, *Films of Heston,* 22–23. Kristol, *Neoconservatism,* 146.

60. Matusow, *Unraveling of America,* 306.

61. Irving Kristol, "Thoughts on Reading about a Summer-Camp Cabin Covered with Garbage," *New York Times Magazine,* November 17, 1974, 38, 126 (quote), 128, 130–31, 135, 137, 146.

62. Gerson, *Neoconservative Vision,* 131. Irving Kristol, "Pornography, Obscenity, and the Case for Censorship," *New York Times Magazine,* March 28, 1971, 24 (quote), 112–14, 116. Podhoretz, *Breaking Ranks,* 303.

63. Craig W. Anderson, *Science Fiction Films of the Seventies* (Jefferson, NC: McFarland, 1985), 2–7.

64. Delighted with the success of *Planet of the Apes,* Fox went on to make four sequels: *Beneath the Planet of the Apes* (Ted Post, 1970), *Escape from the Planet of the Apes* (Don Taylor, 1971), *Conquest of the Planet of the Apes* (J. Lee Thompson, 1972), and *Battle for the Planet of the Apes* (J. Lee Thompson, 1973). Heston did not star in any of these sequels, but he did agree to a brief appearance in *Beneath the Planet of the Apes.* The series achieved cult status, and, in 2001, Tim Burton directed a modified remake of the film in which Heston made a cameo appearance as a dying elder ape.

65. John Bell, "The Omega Man: A Modern Allegory of Love and Plague," *Journal of Orgonomy* 14, no. 1 (May 1980): 74–85, 85.

66. Heston, *Journals,* 449, 489. Heston did not mention the titles of these movies, so it is not evident whether they were ever made.

67. Gerson, *Neoconservative Vision,* 270.

68. Heston in Rovin, *Films of Heston,* 22–23.

69. Prindle, *Politics of Glamour,* 111.

70. Ibid., 115–16.

71. Heston, *Journals,* 449. Prindle, *Politics of Glamour,* 113.

72. Irving Kristol, *Reflections of a Neoconservative: Looking Backward, Looking Ahead* (New York: Basic, 1983), xv.

6. REPUBLICAN IDEOLOGUE

1. Heston and Isbouts, *Heston's Hollywood*, 156–57.

2. Heston, *Arena*, 470. Heston made the transition to action pictures relatively easily. He noted: "You didn't have to work much; each of us did maybe two or three weeks of shooting, the rest was special effects, and you walked away with a lot of money." Heston and Isbouts, *Heston's Hollywood*, 179–80.

3. Steven Gillon, *The Democrats' Dilemma: Walter F. Mondale and the Liberal Legacy* (New York: Columbia University Press, 1992), 188–89. For example, Carter directed a major shift in U.S. relations with Central America when he delivered foreign aid to left-wing rebels and repudiated traditional rightist allies. Ambrose, *Rise to Globalism*, 293–314.

4. Robert M. Collins, *More: The Politics of Economic Growth in Postwar America* (New York: Oxford University Press, 2000), 110–20. Indeed, Nixon brought four more years of war, increased dissension within the United States, and a secret bombing campaign in Cambodia. Ambrose, *Rise to Globalism*, 240.

5. Gareth Davies, "The Great Society after Johnson: The Case of Bilingual Education," *Journal of American History* 88, no. 4 (March 2002): 1405–29, 1407.

6. Heston, *Journals*, 393.

7. McGirr, *Suburban Warriors*, 219–22.

8. Jerome Himmelstein, *To the Right: The Transformation of American Conservatism* (Berkeley and Los Angeles: University of California Press, 1990), 139–45.

9. Commercials, Anheuser-Bush Corporate Spots, with Charlton Heston, n.d., UCLA Film and Television Archive.

10. Bruce Schulman, *The Seventies: The Great Shift in American Culture, Society, and Politics* (New York: Free Press, 2001), 205–17.

11. Other organizations allied with CAGI in the fight against Proposition 15 as well, including the California Wildlife Federation, Gun Owners of California, the California Rifle and Pistol Association, the Citizens Committee for the Right to Keep and Bear Arms, and the Southern California Arms Collector Association. For money raised, see Edward F. Leddy, *Magnum Force Lobby: The National Rifle Association Fights Gun Control* (Lanham, MD: University Press of America, 1987), 119. "Proposition 15 Campaign in Full Swing," *American Rifleman*, October 1982, 58. Roy Rogers in Aric Press and Ron LaBrecque, "California's Gun Battle," *Newsweek*, November 1, 1982, 98.

12. Laffer and Wanniski argued that high marginal rates, or those tax rates that applied to the last dollar of income, most discouraged extra effort and enterprise. Collins, *More*, 182–83. Sidney Blumenthal, *The Rise of the Counter-Establishment:*

From Conservative Ideology to Political Power (New York: Times Books, 1986), 153. Jude Wanniski, "The Mundell-Laffer Hypothesis—a New View of the World Economy," *Public Interest* 39 (spring 1975): 31–52. Jude Wanniski, *The Way the World Works: How Economies Fail—and Succeed* (New York: Basic, 1978).

13. WHORM Subject File—Federal Government—Organizations, box 82, "000192" (file), RRPL. Program Flyer, "The Beginning of a Great New Beginning," "1981 Presidential Inaugural Gala" (file), CHSC, MHL, AMPAS. Blumenthal, *Rise of the Counter-Establishment*, 142, 159, 221.

14. Zeigler, *Arts in Crisis*, 46.

15. Biddle, *Government and the Arts*, 501–3. Heston, *Arena*, 529.

16. Letter from Jack Burgess, Special Assistant to the President, Office of Public Liaison, to Charlton Heston, October 5, 1981, WHORM Subject File—Ag, 042112 (file), RRPL. "White House Fellowships" (file), CHSC, MHL, AMPAS. Allan Parachini, "For Top-Secret Narration, Call Charlton Heston," *Los Angeles Times*, November 9, 1989, CHCF, MHL, AMPAS. *Fame, Fortune, and Romance.*

17. "French Culture Minister Hands Olive Branch to Visiting Charlton Heston," *Variety*, September 22, 1982, CHCF, MHL, AMPAS. For Beirut details, see Army Archer, "Just for Variety," *Variety*, January 11, 1984, CHCF, MHL, AMPAS. For Ethiopia, see WHORM Subject File—Public Relations, 277860, RRPL. White House Press Release, n.d., WHORM Subject File—Public Relations, 277860, RRPL.

18. Letter from Mrs. Alfred E. Meyer to Ronald Reagan, March 25, 1982, WHORM Alpha File—Heston, RRPL. "Charlton Heston—Miscellaneous" (file), CHSC, MHL, AMPAS. Letter from Phil Gramm to Ronald Reagan, November 14, 1988, WHORM Alpha File—Heston, RRPL. Letter from George Bush to Charlton Heston, February 21, 1986, Vice Presidential Records, WHORM Alpha File—Heston, GBPL.

19. Paul Dileski, "Celebrity Spotlight: Outspoken Heston Pursues Passion, Political Pet Causes," *Hollywood Reporter*, April 13, 1987, CHCF, MHL, AMPAS. Charlton Heston, interview with the author, April 25, 2002, Reno, NV.

20. John Judis, *The Paradox of American Democracy: Elites, Special Interests, and the Betrayal of Public Trust* (New York: Pantheon, 2000), 132. The offices of many special interest groups are located on K Street in Washington.

21. Ambrose, *Rise to Globalism*, 315. Schulman, *Seventies*, 226.

22. "Heston on the Freeze #1 and #2," Californians for a Strong America, October 16, 1982, Political Spots, UCLA Film and Television Archive. Transcript, *700 Club*, n.d. (ca. 1982), CHSC, MHL, AMPAS. "The Nuclear Arms Freeze: Proceedings of a Roundtable Discussion, February 14, 1983," "The Strom Thurmond Insti-

tute" (file), CHSC, MHL, AMPAS. "Newman, Heston Debate Nuclear Freeze on TV," *Los Angeles Herald Examiner,* October 31, 1982, AAPCF, MHL, AMPAS.

23. The ASC's original name was the Mid-America Research Library, and its initial function constituted screening applicants for fifteen hundred employers who worried about communism. In 1972, the ASC shifted its focus to international security and nuclear strategy, lobbying for a hard line against communism and the Strategic Arms Limitation Treaty.

24. Bill Paul, "Actor Heston's Fiery Telephone Pitch Enlists Support to Save Vietnam POWs," *Wall Street Journal,* December 27, 1984, CHCF, MHL, AMPAS.

25. "October 18, 1983 News Release: Charlton Heston Dramatizes Need for Renewable Energy: Actor Donates Methanol-Powered Automobile to Solar Lobby Effort," "Solar Lobby" (file), CHSC, MHL, AMPAS.

26. "U.S. Space Foundation Environmental Impact Project Script," Heston/Steinem, 1987, "Miscellaneous" (file), CHSC, MHL, AMPAS. "National Arbor Day Foundation Scripts," Heston/Denver, 1990 and 1991, "Miscellaneous" (file), CHSC, MHL, AMPAS. "Forests Are Us," Ad, "Clippings" (file), CHSC, MHL, AMPAS. Scripts for Anheuser-Bush, "Miscellaneous" (file), CHSC, MHL, AMPAS.

27. Brownstein, *Power and Glitter,* 292.

28. Ibid., 294.

29. Ibid., 302–12.

30. One event included songs and readings by Jackson Browne, Kris Kristofferson, Woody Harrelson, and Elizabeth Perkins. See Kevin Allman, "Into the Night: El Salvador's Tenth Year of Civil War Marked by Speeches, Songs in L.A.," *Los Angeles Times,* March 6, 1990, E3.

31. Charlton Heston in Jack Slater, "Arts Task Force: Heston's New Role," *Los Angeles Times,* August 26, 1981, CHCF, MHL, AMPAS.

32. Will Tusher, "GOP's Favorite Son Isn't Necessarily SAG's," *Variety,* July 17, 1980, AAPCF, MHL, AMPAS.

33. Letter from Kim Fellner to Ken Orsatti and the Executive Committee, November 12, 1981, SAG Archives.

34. Michael Schaller, *Reckoning with Reagan: America and Its President in the 1980s* (New York: Oxford University Press, 1992), 44.

35. Letter from Kim Fellner to Ken Orsatti and the Executive Committee, November 12, 1981, SAG Archives.

36. Schulman, *Seventies,* 233. Prindle, *Politics of Glamour,* 138.

37. Letter from Isabel Boniface to Kim Fellner, November 23, 1981, "Reagan Award Controversy" (file), SAG Archives. Prindle, *Politics of Glamour,* 142.

38. "Heston Denounces Denial of SAG Nod to Reagan," *Variety,* December 21,

1981, CHCF, MHL, AMPAS. Letter from Charlton Heston to Dean Santoro, January 13, 1982, SAG Archives.

39. Brownstein, *Power and Glitter*, 291. Letter from Charlton Heston to Ronald Reagan, January 13, 1982, WHORM Subject File—Public Relations, 057082, RRPL.

40. Prindle, *Politics of Glamour*, 146. "Hollywood's Divided Unions," *Business Week*, July 5, 1982, 89. David Robb, "Battle of the SAG Presidents," *Hollywood Reporter*, February 12, 1982, AAPCF, MHL, AMPAS. For the "stooge" comment, see Lennie LaGuire and Nicole Szulc, "Lou Grant Calls Ben-Hur a Stooge," *Los Angeles Herald Examiner*, May 18, 1982, AAPCF, MHL, AMPAS.

41. Ambrose, *Rise to Globalism*, 328.

42. "Get Down, Moses . . . ," *Los Angeles Herald Examiner*, February 17, 1982, CHCF, MHL, AMPAS.

43. Letter from Charlton Heston to Ed Asner, February 11, 1982, SAG Archives. Mark Starr and Ron LaBrecque, "Asner the Activist," *Newsweek*, March 8, 1983, 23.

44. Transcript, "Charlton Heston Discusses the SAG," *The Phil Donahue Show*, March 9, 1982, "Heston" (file), SAG Archives. Mark Starr with Ron LaBrecque, Martin Kasindorf, and Janet Huck, "Ed Asner's Star Wars," *Newsweek*, March 22, 1982, 90.

45. David Robb, "SAG Board Dissenter Dubbins Quits in Wake of Recent Actions," *Hollywood Reporter*, March 24, 1982, "AWAG" (file), SAG Archives. Prindle, *Politics of Glamour*, 158.

46. "Heston Rejects SAG Board Seat," *Variety*, January 27, 1982, CHCF, MHL, AMPAS.

47. "Heston Sues to Stop Merger Balloting," *Los Angeles Herald Examiner*, April 29, 1982, CHCF, MHL, AMPAS. "AWAG" (file), SAG Archives.

48. Starr, "Ed Asner's Star Wars," 90. "Hollywood's Divided Unions," 89. "1982 Asner/Heston Press; AWAG" (file), SAG Archives.

49. "AWAG Letter to SAG Membership," November 1983, "AWAG" (file), SAG Archives. "AWAG Blasts SAG Board Vote for Rent-Control Initiative," *Variety*, October 6, 1983, "AWAG" (file), SAG Archives.

50. AWAG Flyer, 1984, "AWAG" (file), SAG Archives. SAG Flyer, "Actors: Do Not Be Deceived," "AWAG" (file), SAG Archives. Prindle, *Politics of Glamour*, 154.

51. Minutes to Special Meeting between the Executive Committee and AWAG, April 25, 1984, SAG Archives. Letter from Ken Orsatti to Morgan Paull (After the Meeting), May 1, 1984, SAG Archives. Prindle, *Politics of Glamour*, 154. Charlton Heston in Laura Anne Ingraham, "A Conservative in Hollywood," *Heritage Foundation Policy Review*, spring 1986, 18–28, 21.

52. Prindle, *Politics of Glamour,* 171–75.

53. Ibid., 176. "Heston Spots for Conservative Causes," America Is Watching, May 29, 1986, UCLA Film and Television Archive.

54. Allen Halperin, Advertisement for *Variety,* written August 7, 1986, published December 11, 1986, SAG Archives. Robert Sam Anson, "Chapter One: Political Fund-Raisers Strike a Rich Vein in Tinseltown," *Los Angeles Examiner,* May 27, 1984, AAPCF, MHL, AMPAS. Charlton Heston in "Labor's Love Lost: An Interview with Charlton Heston," *California Business,* July 1987, CHCF, MHL, AMPAS.

55. Charlton Heston in David Robb, "Heston Defends Right of Speech in SAG Missive," *Variety,* December 17, 1986, CHCF, MHL, AMPAS. David Robb, "Letter Campaign Backs Heston's Right to Speak," *Variety,* December 29, 1986, AAPCF, MHL, AMPAS. Richard Dreyfuss in "Dreyfuss Adds Two Cents to Heston Dispute," *Variety,* January 7, 1987, AAPCF, MHL, AMPAS.

56. See *Communications Workers of America, et al. v. Beck, et al.,* 487 U.S. 735 (1988). Letter from Charlton Heston to Ken Orsatti, September 17, 1988, SAG Archives.

57. Letter from Charlton Heston to Elizabeth Dole, March 13, 1990, WHORM Subject File—General, FG021, 123055, GBPL.

58. Letter from Charlton Heston to Actors' Equity Association of America, August 14, 1990, Bush Presidential Records, WHORM Subject Files—General, CO 001-07, GBPL.

59. Letter from Charlton Heston to Elizabeth Dole, August 27, 1990, Bush Presidential Records, WHORM Subject Files—General, CO 001-07, GBPL. David Robb, "Bush Inks Order Curbing Unions, Praises Heston," *Hollywood Reporter,* April 14, 1992, CHCF, MHL, AMPAS.

60. Letter from George H. W. Bush to Charlton Heston, January 3, 1990, Bush Presidential Records, WHORM Subject Files—General, 107767 PR010, GBPL. Department of State, Heroes/Rewards Campaign against Terrorism, 1990, "Miscellaneous" (file), CHSC, MHL, AMPAS. Transcript, "War and Dissent," *The Phil Donahue Show,* February 13, 1991, UCLA Film and Television Archive. "Get Out the Vote/Air Force One Special," September 27, 1990, Bush Presidential Records, WHORM Subject File—General, 184226SS PR010, GBPL. Letter from Charlton Heston to George Bush, May 3, 1990, Bush Presidential Records, WHORM Subject File—General, C0091: 138987, GBPL. Letter from George Bush to Charlton Heston, May 17, 1990, Bush Presidential Records, WHORM Subject File—General, C0091: 900519, GBPL.

61. George Bush Presidential Message for the Annual Meeting and Dinner of the Washington Institute for Policy Studies, March 21, 1991, WHORM Subject File—General, ME002 Case #: 229509, GBPL.

7. GUN GURU

1. Edward (Jim) Land (national secretary, NRA), interview with the author, May 29, 2002, Fairfax, VA.

2. James B. Trefethen and James E. Serven, eds., *Americans and Their Guns: The National Rifle Association Story through Nearly a Century of Service to the Nation* (Harrisburg, PA: Stackpole, 1967), 10–13.

3. Ibid., 10, 34.

4. Mark A. Keefe IV, "NRA . . . Celebrating 125 Years of Service to America," *American Rifleman,* January 1996, 40–45, 42. Trefethen and Serven, eds., *Americans and Their Guns,* 209, 251.

5. Keefe, "Celebrating 125 Years," 41, 44 (Truman quote).

6. "Federal Firearms Law," *American Rifleman,* September 1933, box 26-5, NRA Archives.

7. "How to Secure the Help of Your Congressmen and Senators," *American Rifleman,* September 1933, box 26-5, NRA Archives.

8. Trefethen and Serven, eds., *Americans and Their Guns,* 292. "How to Secure the Help of Your Congressmen and Senators."

9. Trefethen and Serven, eds., *Americans and Their Guns,* 292–94.

10. Ibid., 295.

11. Ibid., 300.

12. Keefe, "Celebrating 125 Years," 44. Osha Gray Davidson calls Carter's group *hard-liners* and his opponents the *old guard.* However, these labels are inaccurate since Carter followed the NRA platform that had been established in 1933 and updated in 1957. Actually, Carter was more of a traditionalist than the rest, and he wanted more resources to carry out the NRA's legislative agenda. I scrapped Davidson's labels in favor of *politicos* and *sportsmen,* respectively, indicating where each wanted NRA money to be most heavily directed. Osha Gray Davidson, *Under Fire: The NRA and the Battle for Gun Control* (New York: Holt, 1993), 34–35.

13. Davidson, *Under Fire,* 31–41.

14. Leddy, *Magnum Force Lobby,* 35.

15. Charlton Heston, interview with the author, April 25, 2002, Reno, NV. Davidson, *Under Fire,* 47.

16. In fact, the campaign was so successful that it is now reprinted in college textbooks as a model. Davidson, *Under Fire,* 47.

17. Letter from ILA Executive Director J. Warren Cassidy to NRA Members, September 19, 1983, box 26-4, NRA Archives. One story told of a police officer who owned a gun shop. The officer maintained a dealer's license but believed that

he did not have to log his personal collection as part of his shop's inventory. When he sold some guns from his private collection, he was charged with six felonies. According to the NRA pamphlet publicizing this "horror story," the prosecution "agreed that a dealer's personal collection did not have to be logged in the shop's inventory." Nevertheless: "The police officer was still convicted as the judge offered a strict and narrow interpretation of the Gun Control Act." Letter from ILA Director of Governmental Affairs Wayne LaPierre to NRA Members, July 15, 1985, box 26-5, NRA Archives.

18. The bullets were originally designed for police use, allowing them shoot through car doors at criminals. However, the bullets were so powerful that they could actually go through the other side of the car and had a tendency to ricochet. Since these bullets had a high risk of injuring innocent bystanders, they were deemed too dangerous for police work. Thus, manufacturers were no longer interested in producing them. Davidson, *Under Fire*, 88.

19. Ibid., 99–105.

20. Edward Land, interview with the author, May 29, 2002, Fairfax, VA.

21. Davidson, *Under Fire*, 196. "NRA-ILA Firearms Glossary," 1995, available through NRA-ILA, Fairfax, VA.

22. Davidson, *Under Fire*, 212.

23. "Heston Keynote Speaker at St. Louis Banquet," *American Rifleman*, July 1989, 49.

24. Edward Land, interview with the author, May 29, 2002, Fairfax, VA. Charlton Heston, "Commercials," National Rifle Association, 1989, UCLA Film and Television Archive.

25. Charlton Heston, "Guns and Moses," *The McLaughlin Group*, December 11, 1989, UCLA Film and Television Archive.

26. Davidson, *Under Fire*, 262, 272–73.

27. Beau Bridges and Charlton Heston, "Guns: Open Season or Cease Fire?" *Elle*, February 1993, 58, 60.

28. Letter from NRA-ILA Office of the Executive Director to Candidate, n.d., part of briefing book "The Clinton Crime Bill: A Guide for Congressional Candidates," box 26-30, NRA Archives.

29. Charlton Heston, "Remarks before the Conservative Political Action Conference 'Conservative Challenge for a New Millennium,'" January 1999, Washington, DC, reprinted in Heston, *Courage to Be Free*, 209–19. Heston, *Arena*, 566.

30. Mark Johnson, "Heston Becomes NRA's Top Gun," *Tampa Tribune*, September 10, 1997, 3. Clyde Wilcox, *The Latest American Revolution? The '94 Elections and Their Implications for Governance* (New York: St. Martin's, 1995), 15. Elizabeth Drew, *Showdown: The Struggle between the Gingrich Congress and the Clinton White House*

(New York: Simon & Schuster, 1996), 100–101. With this midterm victory, Republicans controlled the House 230–204 (with one Independent) and the Senate 53–47. The Democrats had controlled the House since 1952, the longest period of single-party control in U.S. history. See Wilcox, *Latest American Revolution?* 1.

31. Press release and letter from Wayne LaPierre to George Bush, May 10, 1995, box 26-23, NRA Archives. "George Bush Takes Tardy Parting Shot at NRA," *Newsday,* May 12, 1995, A42.

32. Peter Stone, "Counting on Their Connections," *National Journal* 28, no. 27 (July 6, 1996): 1486. Peter Stone, "Along the Campaign Trail," *National Journal* 28, no. 36 (September 7, 1996): 1911.

33. Katharine Q. Seelye, "Close Votes in NRA Elections Quash Hope for Internal Unity," *New York Times,* May 6, 1997, A18.

34. Charlton Heston, "Be Yourselves, O Americans," remarks before the Conservative Political Action Conference, January 25, 1997, Washington, DC, reprinted in Heston, *Courage to Be Free,* 170–74.

35. Wayne LaPierre, "Standing Guard," *American Rifleman,* September 1997, 7.

36. Charlton Heston, "My Crusade to Save the Second Amendment," *American Rifleman,* September 1997, 30–34.

37. Charlton Heston on *The Larry Elder Show in Los Angeles,* May 9, 1997, KABC-AM Radio, http://vikingphoenix.com/news/stn/1997/pirn9713.htm.

38. Edward Land, interview with the author, May 29, 2002, Fairfax, VA. Charlton Heston, "The Second Amendment: America's First Freedom," remarks before the National Press Club, September 1, 1997, Washington, DC, reprinted in Heston, *Courage to Be Free,* 175–82.

39. Charlton Heston, "Armed with Pride," remarks before the Conservative Political Action Conference, January 27, 1998, Alexandria, VA, reprinted in Heston, *Courage to Be Free,* 182–90.

40. "A Terrible Price to Pay for Ratings" (NRA advertisement), *Los Angeles Times,* n.d., AAPCF, MHL, AMPAS. "The Hanoi Jane of the Second Amendment," *Hollywood Reporter,* n.d., AAPCF, MHL, AMPAS. "Firepower and Brimstone," *People,* June 22, 1998, 17, CHCF, MHL, AMPAS.

41. Various NRA members, interviews with the author, April 26–27, 2002, NRA annual meeting, Reno, NV. "Charlton Heston Celebrity Shoot," 1995, box 30-2, NRA Archives.

42. Marion Hammer, "President's Column: United We Stand, Divided We Fall," *American Guardian,* June 1998, 8–9, 8.

43. Margot Hornblower, "Have Gun, Will Travel: But Can Heston's Celebrity and Rhetoric Revive the NRA?" *Time,* July 6, 1998, 43–46.

44. Charlton Heston, "Remarks before the 127th Annual Meeting of the Mem-

bers of the National Rifle Association," May 22, 1998, Philadelphia, reprinted in Heston, *Courage to Be Free,* 190–92.

45. Ibid.

46. Ibid.

47. Ibid. Charlton Heston, "With Firmness in the Right," remarks before the Christian Coalition, September 19, 1998, Washington, DC, reprinted in Heston, *Courage to Be Free,* 196–201.

48. Charlton Heston, interview with the author, April 25, 2002, Reno, NV.

49. Stephen Chapman in "NRA Wins Rare Media Support in Attack on 'Eddie Eagle,'" *O'Dwyer's PR Services Report,* January 30, 1998, Features, 14. NRA Press Release, "National Sheriffs' Association Endorses Eddie Eagle Gunsafe Program," March 11, 2002, NRA Archives.

50. U.S. Attorney's Office for the Eastern District of Virginia, "Project Exile," July 15, 1998, 5, available through the NRA's Institute for Legislative Action, Fairfax, VA. Criminals learned the message "an illegal gun gets you five years in prison" through fifteen billboards scattered throughout the city, a fully painted city bus, television commercials, fifteen thousand small flyers, and print advertising. A telephone number accepting anonymous tips was established to field citizen reports of illegal guns. Ibid., 11, 13.

51. Ibid., 2.

52. Bill Powers, telephone interview with the author, March 29, 2004. While the Philadelphia program was modeled specifically on Project Exile, city leaders, targeting at-risk young people and gang-related crime, decided to name it Operation Cease Fire. Meki Cox, "Philly to Prosecute Gun Criminals Federally under New Program," Associated Press, January 25, 1999.

53. Heston, "Remarks Before the 127th Annual Meeting," 190–92. In a 2002 interview with Matt Lauer on the *Today* show, Heston later admitted regretting making such an ugly statement about the president of the United States.

54. "Charlton Heston's Tablets of Stone," *Economist,* May 1, 1999. Katharine Q. Seelye and James Brooke, "Terror in Littleton: The Gun Lobby," *New York Times,* May 2, 1999, sec. 1, p. 28.

55. Charlton Heston in Jim Abrams, "Heston: Gun Laws Not the Answer," Associated Press, May 3, 1999.

56. Charlton Heston, testimony before the Subcommittee on Criminal Justice, Drug Policy, and Human Resources of the Government Reform Committee, U.S. House of Representatives, 106th Cong., 1st sess., November 4, 1999. Charlton Heston and Wayne LaPierre in Andrew Peyton Thomas, "Hair-Trigger Politics," *Weekly Standard,* March 27, 2000, 20.

57. "Gun Control, 1999–2000 Legislative Chronology" (2002), in *Congress and the Nation, 1998–2001* (Washington, DC: CQ, 2002), vol. 10, retrieved March 30,

2004, from CQ Electronic Library, CQ Public Affairs Collection, catn97-97-6354-325772. Carla Crowder, "Meeting Keeps Colorado in Gun Control Spotlight, Heston Brady Are Invited for Kickoff of Project Exile," *Denver Rocky Mountain News*, March 2, 2000, 4A.

58. Ken Herman, "Bush Targets Illegal Gun Use; 'Texas Exile' Program to Hire Eight," *Austin American-Statesman*, September 12, 1999, A1. James Dao, "NRA Leaders Cast Gore as Archenemy," *New York Times*, May 21, 2000, sec. 1, p. 28.

59. Wayne LaPierre, J. C. Watts, and James J. Baker in Dao, "NRA Leaders Cast Gore as Archenemy," 28.

60. James Dao, "The 2000 Campaign: The Ad Campaign," *New York Times*, October 10, 2000, A18.

61. John B. Judis, "Two More Years," *American Prospect*, December 4, 2000, 10. Bill McAllister, "Clinton Pins Gore Loss on NRA," *Denver Post*, December 20, 2000, A6.

62. Peter Stone, "Lethal Weapons," *American Prospect*, May 7, 2001, 46. The rise in gun sales was anywhere from 9 to nearly 22 percent during the period September–November 2001 and included a "steady stream of serious-minded first-time buyers." Law enforcement officials and gun industry insiders attributed the September 11 attacks as the primary reason for the increase. Al Baker, "A Nation Challenged: Personal Security; Steep Rise in Gun Sales Reflects Post-Attack Fears," *New York Times*, December 16, 2001, 1A.

63. "Remarks by the President on Project Safe Neighborhoods," www.whitehouse.gov/news/releases/2001/05/print/20010514-1.html.

64. Phillip Rawls, "Heston Aide Says GOP Shouldn't Be Surprised by Endorsement," *Tuscaloosa News*, September 23, 2002. Kevin Horrigan, "Carnahan vs. Talent: It's Not a Campaign, It's a Bubba-Rama," *St. Louis Post Dispatch*, September 29, 2002, B3.

65. David Bander, "Rosie O'Donnell and Tom Selleck Slug It Out over Gun Control," Associated Press, May 20, 1999. For Lee, see Rod Patterson, "Ha Ha, What a Joker Spike Lee Turned Out to Be When He Said Charlton Heston Should Be Shot," *Oregonian*, May 29, 1999, Living, D2. For Clooney, see *Melbourne Sunday Herald Examiner*, January 26, 2003, CUE, 96.

66. "The NRA's Cold, Dead Agenda," *New York Daily News*, October 24, 2002, Editorial Section, 40.

8. CULTURAL CANNON

1. Heston, "Armed with Pride," 183.
2. Ibid.
3. Heston, *Courage to Be Free*, 15.
4. Bork, "Culture and Kristol," 134.

5. Gertrude Himmelfarb, *One Nation, Two Cultures* (New York: Knopf/Random House, 1999), 18. DeMuth and Kristol, eds., *Neoconservative Imagination*, 187. For other scholars who make similar assertions regarding the culture war, see Edwin DeLattre, *Character in Cops: Ethics in Policing* (Washington, DC: AEI Press, 2002). See also William J. Bennett, *Why We Fight: Moral Clarity and the War on Terrorism* (New York: Doubleday, 2002).

6. Himmelfarb, *One Nation, Two Cultures*, x.

7. Ibid., 62.

8. Alan Wolfe, *One Nation, After All: What Middle-Class Americans Really Think about God, Country, Family, and Racism* (New York: Viking, 1998), 126–291.

9. Kristol, *Neoconservatism*, 359.

10. Heston, "Armed with Pride," 187–88.

11. David Brooks, "One Nation, Slightly Divisible," *Atlantic Monthly*, December 2001, 53–65, 63–64.

12. David Brooks, *Bobos in Paradise: The New Upper Class and How They Got There* (New York: Simon & Schuster, 2000).

13. Brooks, "One Nation," 53. Brooks, *Bobos in Paradise*, 47.

14. Heston and Isbouts, *Heston's Hollywood*, 49. Ingraham, "Conservative in Hollywood," 18. Heston, *Courage to Be Free*, 96.

15. Himmelfarb, *One Nation, Two Cultures*, 28.

16. Charlton Heston, testimony before the Subcommittee on Select Education of the Committee on Education and Labor, U.S. House of Representatives, and the Subcommittee on Education, Arts, and Humanities of the Committee on Human Resources, U.S. Senate, 95th Cong., 1st and 2nd sess., January 3, 1978, 370. Heston, *Courage to Be Free*, 20.

17. DeLattre and Heston in Lynne Cheney, Edwin DeLattre, William Bennett, and Charlton Heston, testimony before Subcommittees of the Committee on Appropriations, U.S. House of Representatives, 104th Cong., 1st sess., January 24, 1995, 951. Lynne Cheney had been the director of the National Endowment for the Humanities, William Bennett had been the U.S. secretary of education under Ronald Reagan, and Edwin DeLattre was a professor of ethics at Boston University.

18. See Zeigler, *Arts in Crisis*, 69–73. "Sculptors in Space," in "The National Endowment for the Arts: Misusing the Taxpayers' Money," *Backgrounder* (newsletter of the Heritage Foundation), no. 803, January 18, 1981, Vertical File, "Heritage Foundation" (file), NEAL.

19. In 1989 and again in 1991, Jesse Helms had proposed an amendment requiring grantees to promise not to produce "obscene" art. According to Helms, the obscene included, but was not limited to, depictions of sadomasochism, homoeroticism, the exploitation of children, or individuals engaged in sex acts.

Helms would also have prohibited the denigration of religions or particular people, groups, or classes of citizens on the basis of race, creed, sex, handicap, age, or national origin. Zeigler, *Arts in Crisis*, 79, 126. Peter J. Ognibene, "Charlton Heston Talks Candidly about the NEA and Its Impact," *Horizon*, September 1985, special insert, "The Art of Patronage," 15.

20. Bill Ivey, "An American Cultural Bill of Rights," remarks before the National Press Club, Washington, DC, December 18, 2000. George Will, "'Art' Unburdened by Excellence," *Washington Post*, January 25, 2001, A19.

21. John Leo, *Two Steps Ahead of the Thought Police* (New Brunswick, NJ: Transaction, 1998), 17–18. Heston, *Courage to Be Free*, 96–97.

22. John Keats, "Ode on a Grecian Urn," in *Lyric Poems* (Toronto: Dover, 1991), 36–37, 37. Lynne V. Cheney, *Telling the Truth: Why Our Culture and Our Country Have Stopped Making Sense—and What We Can Do about It* (New York: Simon & Schuster, 1995), 14–15.

23. Heston, *Courage to Be Free*, 54. Heston, *Arena*, 569. Christine Stolba, "Lying in a Room of One's Own: How Women's Studies Textbooks Miseducate Students" (Arlington, VA: Independent Women's Forum, 2002), 15. Leo, *Thought Police*, 29.

24. Charlton Heston, "Remarks before the 125th Annual Meeting of Members of the National Rifle Association," March 30, 1996, Dallas, Texas, reprinted in Heston, *Courage to Be Free*, 164–70.

25. See Laura Lein and Peggy McIntosh, "Putting Research to Work: Applied Research on Women" (Wellesley, MA: Wellesley College, Center for Research on Women, 1982). See also Carol Gilligan, *In a Different Voice: Psychological Theory and Women's Development* (Cambridge, MA: Harvard University Press, 1982).

26. Charlton Heston, *To Be a Man: Letters to My Grandson* (New York: Simon & Schuster, 1997), 95. Christina Hoff Sommers, *Who Stole Feminism? How Women Have Betrayed Women* (New York: Simon & Schuster, 1994), 90. Cheney, *Telling the Truth*, 203.

27. Brooks, *Bobos in Paradise*, 191, 216–17, 224. Himmelfarb, *One Nation, Two Cultures*, 98.

28. Himmelfarb, *One Nation, Two Cultures*, 23.

29. Heston, *Courage to Be Free*, 26–29.

30. William J. Bennett, *The Death of Outrage: Bill Clinton and the Assault on American Ideals* (New York: Free Press, 1998), 123. The audiobook version of *The Death of Outrage*, which Heston narrated, was released by Simon & Schuster in 1998. Heston, *Courage to Be Free*, 39.

31. Heston, *Courage to Be Free*, 149–59.

32. See Robert D. Putnam, *Bowling Alone: The Collapse and Revival of American Community* (New York: Simon & Schuster, 2000). Robert N. Bellah et al.,

Habits of the Heart: Individualism and Commitment in American Life (Berkeley and Los Angeles: University of California Press, 1985), 6, 47.

33. Oliver Stone in Richard Mowe, "Maybe Mellow but Never Yellow," *Glasgow Herald,* March 27, 2000, 28.

34. "Moral presence" reference in Warner Bros. publicity and production packet for *Any Given Sunday: Life Is a Contact Sport,* copyright 1999, Any Given Sunday—Production File, MHL, AMPAS.

35. Heston, *Courage to Be Free,* 50.

36. Charlton Heston, speech before congressional committee, n.d., "Charlton Heston—SAG" (file), CHSC, MHL, AMPAS. Ingraham, "Conservative in Hollywood," 18.

37. Heston, *Courage to Be Free,* 97.

38. Ibid., 68.

39. Ibid., 39, 43.

40. Les Keyer, *Hollywood in the Seventies* (San Diego: Barnes, 1981). Patrick Goldstein, "Kazan Finds Honor," *Chicago Sun-Times,* January 26, 1999, 25. Heston, *Arena,* 537. Heston, *Letters to My Grandson,* 97.

41. Heston, *Arena,* 574–75. Charlton Heston, "Remarks before the Conservative Political Action Conference," January 1999.

42. Heston, *Courage to Be Free,* 9.

43. Ibid., 128. Heston, *Letters to My Grandson,* 94, 106.

44. Crowther, *Epic Presence,* 29, 73. Heston and Isbouts, *Heston's Hollywood,* 131.

45. Ingraham, "Conservative in Hollywood," 18.

46. Stolba, "Lying in a Room of One's Own," 20–23.

47. Jill Powell, "Chuck Heston Interview," n.d. (probably ca. 1971–72), "Charlton Heston—Articles" (file), CHSC, MHL, AMPAS. Charlton Heston in Dorothy Manners, "A New Heston Looks at Outdated Girls," *Los Angeles Herald Examiner,* September 17, 1967, CHCF, MHL, AMPAS.

48. Heston, *Courage to Be Free,* 83.

49. Ibid., 16, 79.

50. Ibid., 89.

51. Heston, *Letters to My Grandson,* 90.

52. Heston, *Courage to Be Free,* 97. Charlton Heston in Kristine McKenna, "Old Warrior, Back in the Arena," *Los Angeles Times,* September 16, 1995, CHCF, MHL, AMPAS.

53. Charlton Heston, letter to the Editor, *New York Times,* October 13, 1996, sec. IV, p. 12.

54. Peter Steinfels, *The Neoconservatives: The Men Who Are Changing Ameri-*

ca's Politics (New York: Simon & Schuster, 1979), 294. Heston in Ingraham, "Conservative in Hollywood," 18. Heston, *Courage to Be Free,* 116.

55. Peggy Noonan in Patricia Leigh Brown, "Heavy Lifting Required: The Return of Manly Men," *New York Times,* October 28, 2001, sec. 4, p. 5. David Brooks, "Kicking the Secularist Habit," *Atlantic Monthly,* March 2003, 26–28, 28.

CONCLUSION

1. Charlton Heston, "Alzheimer's Disease Statement," August 9, 2002, http://www.online-shrine.com/heston/alzheimers_text.html.

2. For an example of a historian who emphasizes economic and racist reasons, see Dan T. Carter, *From George Wallace to Newt Gingrich: Race in the Conservative Counterrevolution, 1963–1994* (Baton Rouge: Louisiana State Press, 1996), xiv, 23.

3. Kimberly Edds, "States Make It Their Business to Lure Away Other States' Business," *Washington Post,* October 17, 2004, 2A. Schickel, *Intimate Strangers,* xi–xii, 19. Darrell M. West and John Orman, *Celebrity Politics* (Upper Saddle River, NJ: Prentice-Hall, 2003), 113.

4. Heston, *Arena,* 186.

SELECT BIBLIOGRAPHY

ARCHIVES AND SPECIAL COLLECTIONS

George H. W. Bush Presidential Library, College Station, TX

Papers of George H. W. Bush.

Margaret Herrick Library, Academy of Motion Picture Arts and Sciences, Beverly Hills, CA

Charles Champlin Special Collection.
Charlton Heston—Clippings File.
Charlton Heston Special Collection.
Jack Hirschberg Special Collection.

Lyndon Baines Johnson Presidential Library, Austin, TX

Administrative History, Department of State.
Administrative History, Department of Justice.
Charlton Heston File.
Papers of Lyndon B. Johnson.
Gregory Peck File.
Oral History Collection, Roger Stevens.
Oral History Collection, Jack Valenti.
White House Diary Cards.

National Endowment for the Arts Library, Washington, DC

Minutes of NEA Council Meetings.
Vertical File.

National Rifle Association, Fairfax, VA

American Guardian, renamed *America's First Freedom.*
American Rifleman.
Archives.

Powell Library, University of California, Los Angeles

Film and Television Archive.

Ronald Reagan Presidential Library, Simi Valley, CA

Papers of Ronald Wilson Reagan.

Screen Actors Guild Archives, Beverly Hills, CA

Memos, letters, and speeches regarding Charlton Heston.
Memos, letters, fliers, and pamphlets regarding Actors Working for an Actors
    Guild.
Screen Actor, 1960–85.

Young Research Library, Special Collections, University of California, Los Angeles

Oral History Program.
William Wyler Papers.

INTERVIEWS

Heston, Charlton. Interview with the author. April 25, 2002, Reno, NV.
Land, Jim E. (National Rifle Association national secretary). Interview with the
    author. May 29, 2002, Fairfax, VA.
Members of the National Rifle Association. Interviews with the author. April 26–
    27, 2002, National Rifle Association annual meeting, Reno, NV.
Powers, Bill (Mercury Group). Interview with the author. May 29, 2002, Alexan-
    dria, VA.
———. Telephone interview with the author. March 29, 2004.

CONGRESSIONAL TESTIMONY

Cheney, Lynne, Edwin DeLattre, William Bennett, and Charlton Heston. Testimony before Subcommittees of the Committee on Appropriations, U.S. House of Representatives. 104th Cong., 1st sess., January 24, 1995.

Heston, Charlton. Testimony before the Special Subcommittee on Labor of the Committee on Education and Labor, U.S. House of Representatives, and the Special Subcommittee on Arts and Humanities of the Committee on Labor and Public Welfare, U.S. Senate. 89th Cong., 1st sess., February 23 and March 3, 1965. Re H.R. Res. 334, H.R. Res. 3617, and similar bills establishing national arts and humanities foundations.

———. Testimony before the Subcommittee on Communication and Power of the Committee on Interstate and Foreign Commerce, U.S. House of Representatives. 91st Cong., 1st sess., November 18, 19, 20, 21, and 24 and December 9, 10, 11, and 12, 1969. Re H.R. Res. 420 ("To Amend the Communications Act of 1934 so as to Prohibit the Granting of Authority to Broadcast Pay Television Programs") and related bills.

———. Testimony before the Select Subcommittee on Education of the Committee on Education and Labor, U.S. House of Representatives. 93rd Cong., 1st sess., March 16, 1973. Re H.R. Res. 3926 and H.R. Res. 4288, bills to extend the National Foundation on the Arts and the Humanities Act.

———. Testimony before the Special Subcommittee on Arts and Humanities of the Committee on Labor and Public Welfare, U.S. Senate. 93rd Cong., 2nd sess., December 11, 1974. Re H.R. Res. 17504.

———. Testimony before the Subcommittee on Select Education of the Committee on Education and Labor, U.S. House of Representatives, and the Subcommittee on Education, Arts, and Humanities of the Committee on Human Resources, U.S. Senate. 95th Cong., 1st and 2nd sess., January 3, 1978. Re J. Res. 600 to authorize the president to call a White House conference on the arts.

———. Testimony before the Subcommittee on Criminal Justice, Drug Policy, and Human Resources of the Government Reform Committee, U.S. House of Representatives, 106th Cong., 1st sess., November 4, 1999. Re Project Exile.

FILMS

Any Given Sunday. Directed by Oliver Stone. Warner Brothers, 1999.
The Battle of Midway. Directed by Jack Smight. Universal Pictures, 1976.
Ben-Hur. Directed by William Wyler. Metro-Goldwyn-Mayer, 1959.

El Cid. Directed by Anthony Mann. Dear Film/Allied Artists, 1961.
The Omega Man. Directed by Boris Sagal. Warner Brothers, 1971.
Planet of the Apes. Directed by Franklin J. Schaffner. 20th Century Fox, 1968.
Soylent Green. Directed by Richard Fleischer. Metro-Goldwyn-Mayer, 1973.
Studio System. Directed and produced by Chris Rodley. American Cinema 2, 1994.
     Academic Support Center Media Library, University of Missouri, Columbia.
The Ten Commandments. Directed by Cecil B. DeMille. Paramount, 1956.

INTERNET SOURCES

"The Founding Members." http://www.sag.com/fundmembers.html.
Heston, Charlton. "Larry Elder Show in Los Angeles." KABC-AM Radio, May 9,
     1997. http://vikingphoenix.com/news/stn/1997/pirn9713.htm.
———. "Alzheimer's Disease Statement." August 9, 2002. http://www.online-
     shrine.com/heston/alzheimers_text.html (accessed February 11, 2006).
Rawls, Phillip. "Heston Aide Says GOP Shouldn't Be Surprised by Endorsement."
     Tuscaloosa News, September 23, 2002.

ARTICLES

Andolina, Molly W., and Clyde Wilcox. "Public Opinion: The Paradoxes of Clin-
     ton's Popularity." In *The Clinton Scandal and the Future of American Govern-
     ment,* ed. Mark J. Rozell and Clyde Wilcox, 171–94. Washington, DC:
     Georgetown University Press, 2000.
Bell, John. "The Omega Man: A Modern Allegory of Love and Plague." *Journal of
     Orgonomy* 14, no. 1 (May 1980): 74–85.
Bridges, Beau, and Charlton Heston. "Guns: Open Season or Cease Fire?" *Elle,*
     February 1993, 58, 60.
Chomsky, Noam. "The Responsibility of Intellectuals." *New York Review of Books,*
     February 23, 1967, 16–26.
Collins, Robert. "Growth Liberalism in the Sixties: Great Societies at Home and
     Grand Designs Abroad." In *The Sixties: From Memory to History,* ed. David
     Farber, 11–44. Chapel Hill: University of North Carolina Press, 1994.
Davidson, Bill. "The House That Ben-Hur Built." *Look,* May 24, 1960, 56j–56n.
The Economist, "Charlton Heston's Tablets of Stone," May 1, 1999, 30.
Englesman, Naomi. "The Billing for the Youngest Heston." *Parents Magazine,* Au-
     gust 1956, 40, 91–94.
Goldman, Eric F. "The White House and the Intellectuals: The Inside Story of

LBJ's Festival of the Arts and the Artists and Writers Who Participated." *Harper's Magazine,* January 1969, 31–45.

Horrigan, Kevin. "Carnahan vs. Talent: It's Not a Campaign, It's a Bubba-Rama." *St. Louis Post Dispatch,* September 29, 2002, B3.

Huntington, Samuel. "The Visions of the Democratic Party." *Public Interest* 79 (spring 1975): 63–78.

Ingraham, Laura Anne. "A Conservative in Hollywood." *Heritage Foundation Policy Review,* spring 1986, 18–28.

Ivey, Bill. "An American Cultural Bill of Rights." Remarks before the National Press Club, Washington, DC, December 18, 2000.

Lee, Richard. "AFI Confidential." *Washingtonian,* October 1976, 268–76.

Lein, Laura, and Peggy McIntosh. "Putting Research to Work: Applied Research on Women." Wellesley, MA: Wellesley College, Center for Research on Women, 1982.

Liston, Jim. "At Home with Charlton Heston." *American Home,* May 1962, 14–16, 60–61.

Martin, Pete. "I Call on Ben-Hur." *Saturday Evening Post,* August 20, 1960, 20–21 et seq.

McAllister, Bill. "Clinton Pins Gore Loss on NRA." *Denver Post,* December 20, 2000, A6.

Mowe, Richard. "Maybe Mellow but Never Yellow." *Glasgow Herald,* March 27, 2000, 28.

Ognibene, Peter J. "Charlton Heston Talks Candidly about the NEA and Its Impact." *Horizon,* September 1985, special insert, "The Art of Patronage," 15.

Stolba, Christine. "Lying in a Room of One's Own: How Women's Studies Textbooks Miseducate Students." Arlington, VA: Independent Women's Forum, 2002.

Will, George. "'Art' Unburdened by Excellence." *Washington Post,* January 25, 2001, A19.

BOOKS

Ambrose, Stephen. *Rise to Globalism: American Foreign Policy since 1938.* 6th ed. New York: Penguin, 1991.

Bacall, Lauren. *By Myself.* New York: Knopf, 1979.

Biddle, Livingston. *Our Government and the Arts: A Perspective from the Inside.* New York: ACA, 1988.

Brennan, Mary. *Turning Right in the Sixties: The Conservative Capture of the GOP.* Chapel Hill: University of North Carolina Press, 1995.

Brooks, David. *Bobos in Paradise: The New Upper Class and How They Got There.* New York: Simon & Schuster, 2000.

Brownstein, Ronald. *The Power and the Glitter: The Hollywood-Washington Connection*. New York: Pantheon, 1990.

Blumenthal, Sidney. *The Rise of the Counter-Establishment: From Conservative Ideology to Political Power*. New York: Times Books, 1986.

Chester, Lewis, Godfrey Hodgson, and Bruce Page. *An American Melodrama: The Presidential Campaign of 1968*. New York: Viking, 1969.

Cohan, Steven. *Masked Men: Masculinity and the Movies in the Fifties*. Bloomington: Indiana University Press, 1997.

Crowther, Bruce. *Charlton Heston: An Epic Presence*. London: Columbus, 1986.

Davidson, Osha Gray. *Under Fire: The NRA and the Battle for Gun Control*. New York: Holt, 1993.

DeMille, Cecil B. *The Autobiography of Cecil B. DeMille*. Edited by Donald Hayne. Englewood Cliffs, NJ: Prentice-Hall, 1959.

Democratic Party National Committee. Commission on Party Structure and Delegate Selection. *Mandate for Reform*. Washington, D.C., April 1970.

DeMuth, Christopher, and William Kristol, eds. *The Neoconservative Imagination: Essays in Honor of Irving Kristol*. Washington, DC: AEI Press, 1995.

Douglas, Kirk. *The Ragman's Son: An Autobiography*. New York: Simon & Schuster, 1998.

Druxman, Michael. *Charlton Heston: A Pyramid Illustrated History of the Movies*. New York: Pyramid, 1976.

Elley, Derek. *The Epic Film: Myth and History*. London: Routledge & Kegan Paul, 1984.

Frohnmayer, John. *Leaving Town Alive: Confessions of an Arts Warrior*. Boston: Houghton Mifflin, 1993.

Funt, Marilyn. *Are You Anybody? Conversations with Wives of Celebrities*. New York: Dial, 1979.

Gerson, Mark. *The Neoconservative Vision: From the Cold War to the Culture Wars*. Lanham, MD: Madison, 1996.

Greeley, Andrew M. *Building Coalitions: American Politics in the 1970s*. New York: New Viewpoints, 1974.

Heston, Charlton. *The Actor's Life: Journals, 1956–1976*. Edited by Hollis Alpert. New York: Dutton, 1976.

———. *In the Arena: An Autobiography*. New York: Simon & Schuster, 1995.

———. *To Be a Man: Letters to My Grandson*. New York: Simon & Schuster, 1997.

———. *The Courage to Be Free*. Kansas City, KS: Saudade, 2000.

Higham, Charles. *Cecil B. DeMille*. New York: Scribner's, 1973.

Himmelfarb, Gertrude. *One Nation, Two Cultures*. New York: Knopf/Random House, 1999.

Himmelstein, Jerome. *To the Right: The Transformation of American Conservatism.* Berkeley and Los Angeles: University of California Press, 1990.

Horne, Gerald. *Class Struggle in Hollywood, 1930–50: Moguls, Mobsters, Stars, Reds, and Trade Unionists.* Austin: University of Texas Press, 2001.

Johnson, Lyndon B. *Public Papers of the Presidents of the United States: Lyndon B. Johnson.* Washington, DC: U.S. Government Printing Office, 1963–69.

Kennedy, John F. *Public Papers of the Presidents of the United States.* Washington, DC: U.S. Government Printing Office, 1961–63.

Kristol, Irving. *Neoconservatism: The Autobiography of an Idea.* New York: Free Press, 1995.

———. *Reflections of a Neoconservative: Looking Backward, Looking Ahead.* New York: Basic, 1983.

Leddy, Edward F. *Magnum Force Lobby: The National Rifle Association Fights Gun Control.* Lanham, MD: University Press of America, 1987.

Leo, John. *Two Steps Ahead of the Thought Police.* New Brunswick, NJ: Transaction, 1998.

Matusow, Allen. *The Unraveling of America: A History of Liberalism in the 1960s.* New York: Harper & Row, 1984.

Nash, George. *The Conservative Intellectual Movement in America since 1945.* New York: Basic, 1976.

Netzer, Dick. *The Subsidized Muse: Public Support for the Arts in the United States.* Cambridge: Cambridge University Press, 1978.

Nielsen, Mike, and Gene Mailes. *Hollywood's Other Blacklist: Union Struggles in the Studio System.* London: British Film Institute, 1995.

Novak, Michael, ed. *Democracy and Mediating Structures: A Theological Inquiry.* Washington, DC: American Enterprise Institute for Public Policy Research, 1980.

Parmet, Herbert S. *JFK: The Presidency of John F. Kennedy.* New York: Dial, 1983.

Podhoretz, Norman. *Breaking Ranks: A Political Memoir.* New York: Harper & Row, 1979.

Poitier, Sidney. *The Measure of a Man: A Spiritual Autobiography.* San Francisco: HarperCollins, 2000.

Reagan, Ronald, with Richard G. Hubler. *Where's the Rest of Me?* New York: Karz-Segil, 1965.

Rovin, Jeff. *The Films of Charlton Heston.* Secaucus, NJ: Citadell, 1997.

Rusher, William. *The Rise of the Right.* New York: Morrow, 1984.

Schneider, Gregory L. *Cadres for Conservatism: Young Americans for Freedom and the Rise of the Contemporary Right.* New York: New York University Press, 1999.

Schulman, Bruce. *The Seventies: The Great Shift in American Culture, Society, and Politics.* New York: Free Press, 2001.

Sommers, Christina Hoff. *Who Stole Feminism? How Women Have Betrayed Women.* New York: Simon & Schuster, 1994.

Straight, Michael. *Nancy Hanks: An Intimate Portrait.* Durham, NC: Duke University Press, 1988.

Trefethen, James B., and James E. Serven, eds. *Americans and Their Guns: The National Rifle Association Story through Nearly a Century of Service to the Nation.* Harrisburg, PA: Stackpole, 1967.

Vaughn, Steven. *Ronald Reagan in Hollywood: Movies and Politics.* Cambridge: Cambridge University Press, 1994.

Wallis, Hal, and Charles Higham. *Starmaker: The Autobiography of Hal Wallis.* New York: Macmillan, 1980.

Wills, Garry. *John Wayne's America: The Politics of Celebrity.* New York: Simon & Schuster, 1997.

Wolfe, Alan. *One Nation, After All: What Middle-Class Americans Really Think about God, Country, Family, and Racism.* New York: Viking, 1998.

Zeigler, Joseph Wesley. *Arts in Crisis: The National Endowment for the Arts versus America.* Pennington, NJ: A Cappella, 1994.

DISSERTATION

Smith, David. "Covered Wagons of Culture: The Roots and Early History of the National Endowment for the Arts." Ph.D. diss., University of Missouri, Columbia, 2000.

INDEX